Iran and French Orientalism

Iran and French Orientalism

Persia in the Literary Culture of Nineteenth-Century France

Julia Caterina Hartley

I.B. TAURIS
LONDON • NEW YORK • OXFORD • NEW DELHI • SYDNEY

I.B. TAURIS
Bloomsbury Publishing Plc, 50 Bedford Square, London, WC1B 3DP, UK
Bloomsbury Publishing Inc, 1385 Broadway, New York, NY 10018, USA
Bloomsbury Publishing Ireland, 29 Earlsfort Terrace, Dublin 2, D02 AY28, Ireland

BLOOMSBURY, I.B. TAURIS and the I.B. Tauris logo
are trademarks of Bloomsbury Publishing Plc

First published in Great Britain 2024
This paperback edition published in 2025

Copyright © Julia Caterina Hartley, 2024

Julia Caterina Hartley has asserted her rights under the Copyright, Designs
and Patents Act, 1988, to be identified as Author of this work.

For legal purposes the Acknowledgements on pp. xi–xii constitute
an extension of this copyright page.

Cover design: Holly Capper
Cover image: 'Turquoise Hunt' by Reza Derakshani

All rights reserved. No part of this publication may be: i) reproduced or transmitted in any form, electronic or mechanical, including photocopying, recording or by means of any information storage or retrieval system without prior permission in writing from the publishers; or ii) used or reproduced in any way for the training, development or operation of artificial intelligence (AI) technologies, including generative AI technologies. The rights holders expressly reserve this publication from the text and data mining exception as per Article 4(3) of the Digital Single Market Directive (EU) 2019/790.

Bloomsbury Publishing Inc does not have any control over, or responsibility for, any third-party websites referred to or in this book. All internet addresses given in this book were correct at the time of going to press. The author and publisher regret any inconvenience caused if addresses have changed or sites have ceased to exist, but can accept no responsibility for any such changes.

A catalogue record for this book is available from the British Library.

Library of Congress Cataloging-in-Publication Data
Names: Hartley, Julia Caterina, author.
Title: Iran and French orientalism : Persia in the literary culture of
nineteenth-century France / Julia Hartley.
Description: London ; New York : I.B. Tauris, 2023. |
Includes bibliographical references and index.
Identifiers: LCCN 2023020500 (print) | LCCN 2023020501 (ebook) |
ISBN 9780755645596 (hardback) | ISBN 9780755645633 (paperback) | ISBN
9780755645602 (pdf) | ISBN 9780755645619 (epub) | ISBN 9780755645626
Subjects: LCSH: French literature–19th century–History and criticism. |
Iran–In literature. | Orientalism in literature. | Persian literature–
Appreciation–France. | LCGFT: Literary criticism.
Classification: LCC PQ283 .H37 2023 (print) | LCC PQ283 (ebook) |
DDC 840.9/007–dc23/eng/20230727
LC record available at https://lccn.loc.gov/2023020500
LC ebook record available at https://lccn.loc.gov/2023020501

ISBN: HB: 978-0-7556-4559-6
PB: 978-0-7556-4563-3
ePDF: 978-0-7556-4560-2
eBook: 978-0-7556-4561-9

Typeset by Newgen KnowledgeWorks Pvt. Ltd., Chennai, India

For product safety related questions contact productsafety@bloomsbury.com.

To find out more about our authors and books visit www.bloomsbury.com
and sign up for our newsletters.

– for Ali

Contents

List of Figures	ix
Acknowledgements	xi
A Note on Terminology	xiii
Transliteration	xv
Introduction	1
Iran in nineteenth-century France: Competing narratives	1
Iran and Orientalism	4
Beyond the paradigm of difference	6
The politics of genre	9
1 Poetry	17
Translation and poetic innovation	17
From Paris to 'Persia' and back again (Hugo, Théophile Gautier, Noailles)	21
Persian poems made in France (Renaud, Lahor/Cazalis)	35
Intertextuality and universalism: The case of 'Les Roses de Saadi' (Desbordes-Valmore)	50
Conclusion	54
2 History and historical fiction	57
Rewriting human history	57
'Nos parents, les Aryas' (Gobineau, Renan, Michelet)	61
The Persian Alexander: Hybridity and queer (anti-)imperialism (Judith Gautier)	78
Ancient history? Iran as a mirror to French feminism (Jane Dieulafoy)	88
Conclusion	101
3 Travel-writing	105
'Tout chemin ne conduit pas en Perse'	105
Defining the Persians	110
Among women: Scenes from the harem	114
Understanding Shi'ism	129
'Esfahān, nesf-e jahān'	136
Remembering 'the great of the earth'	142

	Plagued by the West	149
	Books versus reality	156
	Conclusion	168
4	Performing arts	171
	Orientalism and the stage	171
	A tale of two *Péris*: Iran, the imaginary Orient, and ballet (Théophile Gautier, Paul Dukas)	176
	Of poets, prophets and kings: French opera's love affair with Iranian men (*Lalla-Roukh, Le Mage* and *Thamara*)	189
	A puppet play about Omar Khayyām (Maurice Bouchor)	205
	Rebuilding Susa: Jane Dieulafoy and Camille Saint-Saëns's *Parysatis* (1902)	214
	Conclusion	222

Conclusion 225

Notes 233
Bibliography 265
Index 275

Figures

1.1 Three Sa'di quotations in Hugo's hand. 22
 Source: Fonds Victor Hugo. II *Orientales* manuscript folio 3r.
1.2 Armand Renaud: 'In the name of God, the Most Gracious, the Most Merciful'. 38
 Source: Armand Renaud's *Les Nuits persanes* (Paris: Lemerre, 1870): 13.
3.1 Street scene by Eugène Flandin showing two women in outdoor clothing. 115
 Source: Eugène Flandin, 'Bazar et entrée de mosquée, Casbin', *Voyage en Perse. Perse moderne: Planches* (Paris: Baudry, 1851).
3.2 Vista of Esfahan's Naqsh-e Jahan Square by Eugène Flandin. 137
 Source: Eugène Flandin, 'Meidan-i-Chah ou Place Royale, Ispahan', *Voyage en Perse. Perse moderne: Planches* (Paris: Baudry, 1851).
3.3 Vista of Persepolis by Eugène Flandin. 143
 Source: Eugène Flandin, 'Vue des ruines de Persépolis', in *Voyage en Perse. Perse moderne: Planches* (Paris: Baudry, 1851).
3.4 Inauguration of the Susa finds, showing Jane Dieulafoy (leaning over the display case) and Ernest Renan (foreground, bottom right). 155
 Source: 'Inauguration des collections Dieulafoy, au Louvre, par M. Le Président de la République', *L'Univers Illustré* (16 June 1888): 376.
4.1 Natalia Trouhanova as 'La Péri' in Dukas's *La Péri*, design by Léon Bakst (1911). 185
 Source: Bibliothèque nationale de France, département Bibliothèque-musée de l'opéra, AID-931 (1, 144–212). 'Programme officiel des Ballets russes, Théâtre du Châtelet, juin 1911' [deuxième spectacle 13 et 15–17 juin 1911]: 181.
4.2 Nijinsky as 'Iskender' in Dukas's *La Péri*, design by Léon Bakst (1911). 186
 Source: Bibliothèque nationale de France, département Bibliothèque-musée de l'opéra, AID-931 (1, 144–212). 'Programme officiel des Ballets russes, Théâtre du Châtelet, juin 1911' [deuxième spectacle 13 et 15–17 juin 1911]: 145.
4.3 Trouhanova and Bekefi in *La Péri*, costumes and set by René Piot (1912). 187
 Source: *Comœdia illustré* (24 May 1912): 1.

4.4	René Piot's set for *La Péri* in a later production of the ballet. *Source*: *Comœdia illustré* (1 July 1921): 494.	188
4.5a	Charles Bianchini's costume design for a female 'slave' (*Le Mage*, 1891). *Source*: 'Le Mage: soixante-sept maquettes de costume' (1891), BNF, département Bibliothèque-musée de l'opéra, D216-46 [ark:/12148/btv1b8455869r], folio 56.	198
4.5b	'Ziba Khanoum', illustration from Jane Dieulafoy's travelogue. *Source*: Jane Dieulafoy, *La Perse, la Chaldée, et la Susiane* (Paris: Hachette, 1887), 271.	199
4.6	The marionettes of the Petit-Théâtre de la Galerie Vivienne. *Source*: Recueil. Petit théâtre des marionnettes de Maurice Bouchor (1888–1926). Bibliothèque nationale de France, département Arts du spectacle, 8-RO-13530 (3).	207
4.7a	Photograph of Dieulafoy's production of *Parysatis* (1902), with orchestra. *Source*: Historic postcard, author's own collection.	216
4.7b	Photograph of Dieulafoy's production of *Parysatis* (1902), with audience members. *Source*: Historic postcard, author's own collection.	216

Acknowledgements

This book is first and foremost the product of one person's faith in my abilities: Ali Rafiee, who never doubted for a second that I could learn Persian, familiarize myself with authors, genres of writing, and critical theories that I had never worked on before, and produce a major contribution to these fields. Each time I stopped and asked myself if the enterprise was mad, Ali calmly dismissed my doubts. As well as being the person who first encouraged me to work on Iran and Orientalism, Ali also remained an attentive sounding board throughout the project, patiently listening to me read out the many drafts of the following chapters and sharing his reactions. Without him, this book would not exist.

On a material level, I was able to undertake ambitious research into, what was for me, uncharted territory thanks to the generous support of the Leverhulme Trust. It is no understatement to say that my three years as a Leverhulme Early Career Fellow at the University of Warwick were transformational, not only in terms of affording me the time and financial resources to research and write this book, but also in allowing me to offer a research-led undergraduate course, the syllabus of which included several of the texts studied here. I improved both as a teacher and as a researcher as a result of this experience. I am grateful to my two mentors James Hodkinson and Margaux Whiskin for their support during the fellowship, all the more so given that it coincided with the Covid-19 pandemic.

Prior to my Leverhulme Fellowship, I also received support from the Queen's College, Oxford, where as a Laming Fellow I enjoyed being part of a wonderful community of Modern Languages scholars, and SOAS, where a generous Kamran Djam Scholarship covered my fees for an MA in Iranian Studies.

Thanks are owed to Sahba Shayani, my unparalleled teacher of Persian language and literature, whom I first met when I audited his Intermediate Persian classes at the University of Oxford's (then) Oriental Institute. Sahba, along with Richard Williams who was then a Leverhulme Early Career Fellow, also offered advice and encouragement when I first began formulating the project and working on my Leverhulme application.

At these early stages, I also greatly benefited from the insights of Jennifer Yee. I am particularly grateful to Jennifer for pointing me in the direction of Judith Gautier's *Iskender*, one of the most rewarding works to be analysed here. The collaborative work I did with Jennifer and Wanrug Suwanwattana on a conference and later an edited volume, *French Decadence in a Global Context: Exoticism and Colonialism*, also significantly enhanced my appreciation of the political dimensions of French *fin de siècle* literature.

I am grateful to my fellow Jane Dieulafoy scholars, namely Margot Irvine who sent me copies of the texts by Dieulafoy that I could not access during the pandemic, and

Heidi Brevik-Zender and Rachel Mesch, who shared their manuscripts with me ahead of publication.

The process of writing this book benefited from the insights and support of two brilliant groups of scholars. The online meetings of the international European Networks of Orientalism network, which I have the pleasure of co-convening with Alexander Bubb, were a dynamic forum for sharing insights and advice on our work in progress. The London-based writing group of early career researchers initiated by Jessica Stacey gave me a sense of routine and of community. I am particularly grateful to Sarah Arens and Sophie Stevens for maintaining that sense of connection even when the pandemic interrupted our in-person meetings.

The manuscript was significantly enhanced by the detailed feedback that I received from the anonymous readers at I.B. Tauris. I am grateful for their time and for their thoughtful engagement with my work. Peter Asimov also provided valuable comments on Chapter 4, and Ziad Elmarsafy on sections of Chapter 2.

I am grateful, finally, to my editor Rory Gormley for his cordiality and efficiency throughout the process of preparing this book for publication and to Reza Derakshani for his kind permission to feature his beautiful painting 'Turquoise Hunt' on the cover.

– Glasgow, March 2023

A Note on Terminology

This is a book about the representation of a place that has historically been known by two names. A clarification is therefore in order.

'Iran' is the native name of a region that has at its heartland the modern nation of Iran, though its borders have extended further at different points of history. Indeed, Iran's borders were still being renegotiated during the period covered by this book, when the Russian Empire annexed such historically Iranian cities as Samarkand.

In this book I use the term 'Persian' to refer to the Persian language (also known as Farsi) and, by extension, to literature written in that language. The adjective 'Persian' is also used to refer to the ancient empire founded by Cyrus the Great, which had its centre in the province of Pars or Fars, known in Greek as 'Persis', which would later lead to Iran becoming known as 'Persia' in the West. On occasion, the adjective Persian is also used for set phrases in English, such as 'Persian gardens' and 'Persian miniatures'.

The authors discussed here predominantly refer to Iran as Persia ('la Perse') and to Iranians as Persians ('les Persans'). In order to remain close to the original texts, I therefore use these terms whenever I am translating or paraphrasing primary sources. In the same manner, I also use the terms Orient and Orientals ('les Orientaux') when these are used in my sources. Although most of the authors studied in this book speak of 'Persia', there are, however, exceptions to this rule. Judith Gautier, for example, used the term 'Iran' because this was the name used in her source text, Ferdowsi's epic poem the *Shāhnāmeh* (*Book of Kings*). Indeed, calling Iran by its native name could serve to signal an author's erudition. As early as 1789, William Jones spoke of 'one of the most celebrated and most beautiful countries in the world [...] which Europeans improperly call *Persia*, the name of a single province being applied to the whole Empire of *Iràn*, as it is correctly denominated by the present natives of it, and by all the learned *Muselmans*, who reside in these *British* territories' (emphases in the original).[1] Travel-writers might also find themselves adopting the local name as a result of hearing it spoken around them. Marthe Bibesco, for instance, switches from 'le roi d'Iran' when quoting an Iranian host to 'le roi de Perse' a few sentences later, when narrating in her own voice. I, too, will on occasion switch between the two names in order to mark a distinction between two perspectives: my own voice as a critic, who knows Iran by its own name, and the voices of the authors under study.

I have chosen to use the name Iran because it is important to remember that Europe's fantasies surrounding 'Persia' are based on a real place, which has always been known by its native population as Iran. One of the central claims of this book is that it was Iran's rich cultural heritage, as made manifest by its literature, art and architecture, religious and imperial history, and cultural customs that motivated the attention of French writers and inspired the variety of creative engagements that are examined here. Iran is a real place with its own unique history and culture. As such, it deserves to be known by its own name.

Transliteration

Transliteration follows the *Iranian Studies* journal transliteration scheme.

Consonants

ب	b	ج	j	د	d	س	s	ع	'	ل	l
پ	p	چ	ch	ذ	z	ش	sh	غ	gh	م	m
ت	t	ح	h	ر	r	ص	s	ف	f	ن	n
ث	s	خ	kh	ز	z	ض	z	ق	q	و	v
				ژ	zh	ط	t	ک	k	ه	h
						ظ	z	گ	g	ی	y
										ء	ʼ

Vowels and diphthongs

a (dast) دست	ā (kār) کار	ay (hay) حَی	āy (āy) آی
e (gereft) گرفت	i (did) دید	ey (pey) پی	ow (rowshan) روشن
o (shod) شد	u (bud) بود	uy (guy) گوی	oy (khoy) خوی

Introduction

Iran in nineteenth-century France: Competing narratives

'Les Persans sont les Italiens de l'Asie'

[The Persians are the Italians of Asia]

Victor Hugo[1]

'On a dit d'eux que c'étaient les Français de l'Orient.'

[It has been said that they are the French of the Orient.]

Eugène Flandin[2]

When I tell people that I work on Iran in French literature, one text springs to everyone's mind: Montesquieu's famous epistolary novel *Lettres persanes* [*Persian Letters*] (1721). Indeed, representations of 'Persia' and diplomatic relations with Iran in early modern France have been the subject of several important studies.[3] But this book argues that it was in the nineteenth century that French writing on Iran peaked and was at its most multifaceted. Between 1830 and 1900, Persianists such as Jules Mohl worked indefatigably to make Persian literature available in French translation, introducing the French public to a rich literary corpus that had developed independently from the Western canon.[4] Poets from across generations and literary movements would find in these translations a spur for experimentation and innovation, from Victor Hugo's rallying cry for a transcultural Romantic movement to the Parnassian poets' formal imitations of Persian ghazals and quatrains. New world histories, archaeological excavations and the racialist myth of the Aryan race reframed France's vision of the Persian Achaemenid Empire. France had traditionally defined its cultural heritage as Greco-Roman, which made the Persians historical enemies. Indeed, Edward Said goes so far as to identify Æschylus's play *The Persians* as the earliest example of what he calls Orientalism.[5] But following the Oriental Renaissance of the nineteenth century, the ancient Persians became viewed as a great civilization in their own right, and even as the ancestors of modern Europeans.[6] The nineteenth century also saw an increased European diplomatic presence in Iran and improved transport links between Eastern Europe and Tehran. These developments, which were in large part the result of the Western powers' imperial ambitions in Asia, meant that more Europeans were travelling to Iran than ever before. Many of these travellers, whose motivations were alternatively diplomatic, touristic and scientific, published travelogues, offering readers at home tantalizing glimpses of everyday life in modern Iran. And by the end of the century, there was a small but increasingly established Iranian diplomatic presence in Paris, which left its trace in works such as Judith Gautier's *Iskender: Histoire persane*, a novel dedicated to a certain Mohsen Khan, 'in homage to a faithful friendship'.[7] These multiple layers of cultural transfer, from French imitations of Persian poetry to new knowledge regarding the folklore and religions of Iran, to museum exhibits, theories of race and encounters with 'real-life' Iranians, seeped into the French performing arts. Iran was staged in a number of formats and venues, from the modest marionette play to the grand pomp of the opera. By the end of the century, Iranian history and culture had become so entrenched in French cultural life that one journalist went so far as to observe 'nous sommes mieux renseignés sur la Perse au temps des Achéménides que sur des époques et des pays beaucoup plus rapprochés de nous' [we are better informed about Achaemenid Persia than we are about historical periods and countries that are much closer to us].[8] And yet, this breadth and diversity has up until now been largely ignored by scholarship.[9]

Nineteenth-century French engagements with Iranian culture have been obfuscated by a tendency either to lump together the entire Middle East as one monolithic Orient or to focus on France's colonial empire, which does not include Iran.[10] This book asks: what if instead of viewing Orientalism as a "one size fits all" category, we consider the treatment of one specific Oriental language and culture at a particular time and in a particular place?[11] In other words, how does the picture change if instead of asking how did the West create the Orient? we ask how was Iran perceived by nineteenth-century French authors? What were these authors' sources? And what does their instrumentalization of these sources tell us about their conceptions of cultural difference? This specificity allows us to gain in both nuance and accuracy. Indeed, as I will show, Iran had its own place in French literary culture, one that differed to that of Turkey or the Arab world. Moreover, Iran's representation evolved over time: nineteenth-century French narratives surrounding Iran were influenced in large part by Persian literature and the Aryan myth, factors that had not yet come into play during the Enlightenment. Finally, different authors approached Iran in different ways based on their own personal history and motivations. This is most evident in travelwriting, where we find authors who travelled to the same places around the same time (and in the case of Claude Anet and Marthe Bibesco in each other's company), and yet recount entirely different experiences. This book therefore makes two important contributions to our understanding of nineteenth-century French literary culture: first, it reveals the distinctions, nuances and historical changes that are erased if we rely too heavily on vague categories such as 'Orientalism' or 'exoticism'. Secondly, it extends the remit of a recent turn 'Towards a Postcolonial Nineteenth Century' by taking the discussion beyond France's colonial empire.[12]

In writing this book I have identified five distinct, though interrelated, narratives surrounding Iran in nineteenth-century French culture, narratives that are brought to the fore in different literary genres.[13] The first narrative is based on medieval Persian literature. The newly translated ghazals of Hāfez, quatrains of Khayyām, mystical poetry of 'Attār and epics of Ferdowsi and Nezāmi all had something new to offer

French readers, both formally and thematically. Across all these works, there breathed a different relationship with religion, one where God was described through the language of intimacy as the poet's beloved. Many therefore pictured 'Persia' as a delicate and refined place, where sentiments are elevated, gardens flower all year round and God is loving. While this image of Iran was extremely idealized, it would be inaccurate to call it a Western invention, since it was derived from Iranian cultural products. Persian poetry also left its imprint on some of nineteenth-century France's most original poetry, making it not only a source of fantasy, but also a model for imitation. The French reception of Persian poetry will be the focus of Chapter 1, where we shall see that French poets of different generations, ideologies and genders, all found in Persian poetry a gateway to better self-expression. Beyond the poetic reception of Persian literature, I also examine historical novels, ballets and plays inspired by works such as Ferdowsi's *Shāhnāmeh*, as well as references to Persian literature in travel-writing.

The second and third image of Iran are two faces of the same coin, since they both centre on the Persian Achaemenid Empire. Ever since the Renaissance, Ancient Greece and Rome had been perceived as the world's first two great civilizations, and much of French culture – up until Victor Hugo and the advent of Romanticism — had been based on emulating these classical models. Greek authors tended to portray the Persians as decadent, effeminate and despotic, in opposition to Greek virility and philosophical enlightenment, although the Persians could command respect as worthy adversaries. Over the course of the nineteenth century, however, a new narrative emerged, presenting the ancient Persians not as rivals, but as long-lost cousins: fellow members of the 'Aryan' family. A key facet of these positive treatments of ancient Iran as Europe's noble ancestor is their focus on Zoroastrianism. Deeply idealized by authors such as Jules Michelet, the Zoroastrian religion became viewed as evidence that modern Iranians were only Muslim on the surface: forced to convert to Islam following the seventh-century Arab invasion, they had in reality remained loyal to their ancestral faith. This made them more appealing to French writers than other Middle Eastern peoples whose faith in Islam could not be questioned. Chapters 2 and 4 explore how these two conflicting narratives (Iran as ancient adversary and Iran as ancestor) were negotiated by different writers and in different genres (history, the historical novel, opera). In Chapter 3, I also show that visits to the sites of the ancient Persian capitals of Susa and Persepolis led writers to re-examine their preconceptions about the ancient Persians and ultimately challenge the idea that this civilization was inferior to Greek civilization.

While the first three narratives centre on Iran's past (medieval poetry and ancient history), the fourth centres on the present, that is the modern state under Qajar rule. Contemporary Iran aroused curiosity as a modern Muslim nation which had a strong sense of its individual cultural identity and which was independent from Western rule, though British and Russian diplomatic influence was increasingly encroaching on its agency. In such accounts, we find both an ethnographic interest in local customs, in particular gender segregation and religious practices, and a geopolitical interest in Iran's relationship with its neighbours. Modern Iran is the subject of one single genre in this book: travel-writing, though as we shall see, the case of Marthe Bibesco's *Les Huit paradis* (1908) demonstrates that even travelogues could intertwine descriptions of the 'real' geographic location with an idealized vision based on Persian literature.

The fifth and final image of Iran differs from the first four, which were all based on specific aspects of Iranian history and culture, since it is instead based on generalization: Iran is subsumed into the wider category of the Islamic Orient. This narrative can be recognized by its reliance on a set of clichés, most famously described by Edward Said, which portray the Muslim world as sensual, primal and barbaric, inspiring in equal measure desire and fear. This Orient was a screen on to which European writers could project their most colourful fantasies, as made clear by Victor Hugo, who refers to the poems of *Les Orientales* as a series of 'rêveries'.[14] The performing arts in particular show a predilection for this Orient of the Western popular imagination, which was associated with Antoine Galland's translation of the *Mille et Une Nuits* [*Thousand and One Nights*, better known in English under the title of *Arabian Nights*]. We can recognize the fairy-tale charm of the *Mille et une nuits* in the 1843 ballet *La Péri* (about a fairy from Iranian folklore) and the 1862 opera *Lallah-Roukh* (a love story between an Indian princess and an Iranian prince), as well as the archetypal character of the despotic and sexual Oriental king in the operas *Thamara* (1891) and *Parysatis* (1902), whose model is Scheherazade's husband King Shahryar. These examples remind us that not all writers were equally invested in Iranian culture and that works about Iran were often best sold to the public for their association with the familiar Orient of French fantasy, rather than on the basis of Iran's individual history and culture. But this does not mean either that there is a clear-cut differentiation between, on the one hand, works that meaningfully engage with Iranian culture and, on the other hand, works that perpetuate the clichés described by Said. The reality is far more complicated. Indeed, this book considers several texts that elevated Iranian culture while reinforcing negative stereotypes about the Orient. Overall, Iran emerges as a different Orient: more refined, more sympathetic and culturally closer to Europe. Iran is 'Oriental', but it is also superior to its Oriental neighbours. We encounter this trope in a variety of texts, from Ernest Renan's use of Iran as the exception that confirms the general rule that the Islamic world is culturally and intellectually inferior to Europe, to Flandin and Dieulafoy's categorical pronouncements on the moral superiority of Iranians over Turks and Arabs. Rather than invalidating Edward Said's account of 'Orientalism', the case of Iran in nineteenth-century French literature invites us to re-evaluate it, bringing to light new questions, paradoxes and modalities of cross-cultural representation.

Iran and Orientalism

> In a sense the limitations of Orientalism are, as I said earlier, the limitations that follow upon disregarding, essentializing, denuding the humanity of another culture, people, or geographical region.
>
> Edward Said[15]

Edward Said's *Orientalism* (1978) is the book that fathered the academic field of Postcolonial Studies, but what is often forgotten is that Said's key case studies are all taken from late-eighteenth- and nineteenth-century French and English writing.[16]

Indeed, the present book studies several of the authors cited by Said, namely, Victor Hugo, Théophile Gautier, Arthur de Gobineau and Ernest Renan. Said offers three different definitions for his title word 'Orientalism'. First, '[a]nyone who teaches, writes about or researches the Orient [...] either in its specific or general aspects, is an Orientalist and what he or she does is Orientalism'.[17] Secondly, 'Orientalism is a style of thought based upon an ontological and epistemological distinction made between "the Orient" and (most of the time) "the Occident"'.[18] And thirdly, Orientalism is 'the corporate institution for dealing with the Orient – dealing with it by making statements about it, authorizing views of it, describing it, by teaching it, settling it, ruling over it: in short, Orientalism as a Western style for dominating, restructuring, and having authority over the Orient'.[19] The second definition is the one that has gained the most currency in critical discourse. When we use 'Orientalist' as an adjective to describe a text or work of art, we mean that it dehumanizes (or 'others') the Middle East with the aim of proclaiming Western cultural superiority. I too will be using the adjective 'Orientalist' in Said's sense of the word as a shorthand for a set of negative stereotypes that include Islamophobic sentiment, an eroticizing and/or dehumanizing gaze on Iranians, and the assumption of Western cultural supremacy. The first and third definitions, however, are less useful to me since the former can be referred to by its disciplinary name (Oriental Studies, not Orientalism) and the latter is synonymous with imperialism in all its forms (cultural, financial and colonial). I therefore find it more clear in the latter case to speak of imperialism. Said, of course, is intentionally ascribing three different meanings to one same word in order to blur the distinction between the academic study of Oriental languages, the ideological dehumanization of the Muslim world and imperialism.[20] But while this drives home Said's argument about the political nature of all forms of institutional knowledge, it is not conducive to the level of nuance that I wish to achieve here.

A further issue with Said's triple definition, and the book *Orientalism* as a whole, is that it presents a major tension in that the term 'Orient' is alternatively used by Said to refer to a real place and to an imaginary construction. One of the earliest and to this day most cogently argued discussions of this limitation is that of James Clifford, who observes that Said never makes more than a passing reference to 'the "brute reality" of the "cultures and nations whose location is in the East [...]"', and thus 'Orientalist inauthenticity is not answered by any authenticity'.[21] This approach offers Said some advantages in that it avoids the problem of speaking of a unified or historically consistent 'Oriental culture'. Yet, by basing its analysis solely on Western sources, *Orientalism* presents us with an intellectual blind spot, since it discusses the politics of representation without studying that which is being represented. An important dimension of my study is therefore its inclusion of Iranian sources, in particular, Persian literature as mediated through translation, into the remit of the discussion. Iran's rich cultural heritage is not an imaginary construction but a fact, one that inspired the wide range of intellectual and creative responses covered in this book.

A third point of contention for critically engaged readers of *Orientalism* is the categorical way in which the book insists that *all* nineteenth-century authors who described the Middle East were guilty of Orientalism: whether this was done deliberately or not, their writing promoted an imperialist ideology.[22] While it is certainly true that for some authors, such as Ernest Renan, the ultimate goal was to proclaim the superiority of Western civilization, this was far from the rule. The majority of the authors studied here did not write about Iran in order to state its inherent inferiority to France or to promote the *mission civilisatrice*. The reasons behind their curiosity were far more personal and idiosyncratic, ranging from Hugo's advancement of the Romantic cause to Dieulafoy's interest in powerful women from history. Moreover, Iranian cultural artefacts, from Achaemenid art and Safavid architecture to Persian poetry, were subject to great admiration among these writers, an admiration that could lead them to question the aesthetics that they had previously taken for granted.[23] In the cultural arena at least, Europe's superiority was far from a given. Indeed, the most common observation made by French travellers who visited Naqsh-e Jahan Square in Esfahan (Figure 3.2) was how far Shah Abbas's vision surpassed that of his European contemporaries. Processes of comparison were not all predicated, as Said suggests, on a hierarchical ranking of Occident over Orient. On the contrary, cultural comparison was often a way to find parallels and common ground, and thus to undermine any 'ontological and epistemological distinction' between France and Iran. Whether authors opted for a universalist emphasis on the commonalities of all human experience outweighing local cultural practices, or whether they homed in on specific parallels between Iranian and French culture, one thing is clear: Said's paradigm of difference tells us only one part of the story.

Beyond the paradigm of difference

J'identifiais ma vie avec celle des grands de la terre.

[I identified my life with that of the great of the earth.]

Jane Dieulafoy[24]

Al-Ghazali m'étonna: j'y retrouvais une partie de ma pensée; sa vie, quand je vins à la connaître, ressemblait à la mienne.

[Al-Ghazali surprised me: I found there a part of my own thinking; his life, once I came to know it, resembled mine.]

Jean Lahor (Henri Cazalis)[25]

Et qu'importe si la victime adorable eut le flanc déchiré par la dent du sanglier, le cimeterre du Kalife ou la lance du centurion?

[And what does it matter if the adorable victim had his side torn by the tusk of a boar, the scimitar of the Caliph or the lance of a centurion?]

Marthe Bibesco[26]

Edward Said defines Orientalism as a hierarchical opposition that serves to elevate one part of humanity over another. The Orient is the Other in opposition to which the West defined itself, relying on binaries such as civilized versus barbaric, enlightened versus backward, rational versus sensual, masculine versus feminine. This book demonstrates that identification and familiarization played just as significant a role in French writers' apprehension of Iran as othering or – to use a more ambivalent term – exoticism did. Indeed, as Charles Forsdick has persuasively argued, although in contemporary critical discourse the term exoticism 'has almost universally pejorative overtones and is restricted by its coupling to colonial discourse', the close analysis of texts such as, in Forsdick's case, Victor Segalen's *Essai sur l'exotisme* or, in my case, the works by Dieulafoy, Cazalis and Bibesco cited above, brings to light 'the potential reflexivity or reciprocity within exoticism'.[27] By making exoticism a feature of colonial discourse and relying on the paradigm of difference as the sole frame for his analysis, Said's *Orientalism* provides us with a rather narrow understanding of cross-cultural representation. French writers' encounter with Iran was much more multifaceted than this, since it typically involved a negotiation between what made Iran familiar and what made it foreign.[28] Far from being monolithic, French accounts of Iran feature ambivalences, nuances and even contradictions. In order to do justice to this complex landscape, one must be prepared to transcend the dualism of the Orient/Occident binary. To this end, I have found it useful to complement Said's focus on difference with two works that offer a more flexible understanding of cross-cultural encounters: Anil Bhatti and Dorothee Kimmich's *Similarity: A Paradigm for Culture Theory* (2017) and Tzvetan Todorov's *Nous et les autres: la diversité humaine dans la pensée française* (1989).

In their co-authored introduction, Bhatti and Kimmich define similarity as a double-edged term, denoting both commonalities and differences: to be similar is not to be *the same*.[29] Although similarity is admittedly a vague concept, it has the advantage of offering a levelling perspective that escapes hierarchical oppositions. Bhatti and Kimmich acknowledge that the risk of overemphasizing similarity is that of cultural assimilation; however, at its best, similarity allows one to depart from the notions of cultural exceptionalism on which nationalist ideologies and notions of Western cultural superiority are often based. Here, they give the example of Jack Goodie's *Renaissances*, a book that challenges the myth of the Renaissance being an inherently European phenomenon by studying it through a global lens.[30] Bhatti and Kimmich's main aim is to offer a more generous perspective from which to approach today's globalized world and the culturally diverse milieux it has generated. But the paradigm of similarity in fact predates globalization and can already be found in nineteenth-century texts. As this section's epigraphs illustrate, the authors studied in this book did not only apprehend Iranians in terms of their differences, but also their commonalities, going so far as to suggest that they identified with their perspective. Whether they were speaking of Achaemenid monarchs (Dieulafoy), the great Islamic theologian Al-Ghazali (Cazalis) or the ritualized mourning of contemporary Iranian Shi'i women (Bibesco), these authors were not seeking to dehumanize the people they spoke of, but to empathize with them. Of course, one might argue that these European authors were merely projecting their own feelings on to Iranians (past and present) and that the term 'empathy' is therefore an overstatement. Indeed, this was a charge levelled at Dieulafoy by their own contemporaries, who noted that nobody could possibly imagine how the ancient Persians lived, thought and felt.[31] Yet, whatever the limitations of French writers' desire to identify with Iranians may be – and this is an issue that I shall revisit, in particular in the section 'Among Women' in Chapter 3 – the fact remains that these writers viewed Iranians as alter egos because they saw them as people. Contrary to Said's argument, then, being from 'the Orient' did not necessarily make a person less relatable or, to put it more strongly, less human. Today's critical discourse is highly sceptical of universalism, since the concept has historically been associated with Eurocentrism. Yet to reject universalism wholesale is just as dangerous as to adopt it unquestioningly. No critic has made this point more eloquently than Todorov whose intellectual history *Nous et les autres: La réflexion française sur la diversité humaine* (1989) foreshadows Bhatti and Kimmich's argument that commonality and difference are equally important parameters in apprehending cultural others.

The Bulgarian–French literary theorist Tzvetan Todorov has come under criticism from postcolonial theorists for his Eurocentric vision of literary criticism and his writing's silence on the lived experiences of race.[32] This might make him a surprising critic to read alongside Said, Bhatti and Kimmich. Yet, while it is important to acknowledge Todorov's limitations, these do not invalidate his analysis of white male eighteenth- and nineteenth-century French philosophers and writers, which is the subject of *Nous et les autres*. In this book, Todorov describes two views of cultural diversity that have been competing in French thought ever since the Enlightenment: universalism and cultural relativism. Todorov's most original contribution is his twin critique of both ideologies, which leads him to conclude that when taken to the extreme, universalism and relativism will both lead to the same negative outcome. Universalism, Todorov argues, is all too often synonymous with ethnocentrism. 'Universal ideals' have historically been used to justify the enforcement of cultural assimilation. The ideology of the French *mission civilisatrice*, for example, rests upon the assumption that the entire world would benefit from adopting a French way of life. Yet, it is equally true that if left unchecked, cultural relativism will also lead to the assumption that not all humans are equal: if one argues that democracy is a Western value, one both condones totalitarianism in the rest of the world and assumes that not all humans are deserving of the same freedoms. The only ethical path therefore is to combine both ideologies: to accept that many of our values are culturally relative and at the same time acknowledging that there is a universal dimension to the human condition. This allows us to admit that human rights transcend culture.[33]

Todorov's and Bhatti and Kimmich's contributions show us that the human experience of cultural difference is complex and multi-layered, and that universalism and relativism can coexist. This more nuanced perspective on human diversity will allow us to account for those works that escape the dualism described by Said. While some authors turn the Occident/Orient binary to their advantage, others test it and erode it, combining the familiar with the exotic. The poets Marceline Desbordes-Valmore and Armand Renaud wove together the French and the Persian lyric, finding the universal within the specific and highlighting the commonalities between French and Persian traditions. Marthe Bibesco's travel-writing and Jane Dieulafoy's historical novels oscillate between othering and identifying with Iranians, depending on the theme at hand and the author's evolving knowledge and opinions. Finally, the sense of distance created by cultural difference meant that nineteenth-century authors would also use Iranian characters (both fictional and historical) as mouthpieces to express the feelings and political views that they dared not speak in their own voice, just as Montesquieu had done before them by writing 'in the voice' of Iranian travellers Uzbek and Rica. The question of who is speaking *to* whom and *for* whom is central to the close readings conducted by Said in *Orientalism*. But it is also essential to a field which from the outside seems far less political: genre theory.

The politics of genre

> It is because genres exist as institutions that they function as 'horizons of expectation' for readers, and as 'models of writing' for authors.
> Tzvetan Todorov[34]

This extract from Todorov's 'The Origin of Genres' alludes to the double dimension of genre, which is defined not only on a textual level through certain identifiable norms that the author chooses to follow, but which also exists beyond the text, through readers' expectations for the genre. This dual dimension was revisited in more dynamic and fluid terms by Thomas Pavel in 2003. Pavel argues that on a textual level, different genres and sub-genres work towards different goals, which has a direct consequence on the techniques employed by authors.[35] In other words, the 'norms' that we associate with a specific genre exist not because they are 'obligatory', but because they have proven 'effective'. Norms were developed as artistic solutions to the representational problems associated with each genre and then repeated by later authors who saw that these norms achieved the desired impact on readers. Pavel thus puts the focus on a writer's artistic goals and their audience's response as determining factors in the development of genres. But he also notes that there are cases in which there is no qualitative difference between texts from different genres: 'The difference between fiction and nonfiction is, in a sense, invisible, as the biography of *Marlot* by Wolfgang Hildersheim irrefutably proves. *Marlot* is calculated to be read as a scrupulous documentary biography […], but is in fact a work of fiction. Its fictionality is an extratextual feature, as it were, a spiritual property […], a cultural function […].'[36] Extrapolating from Todorov and Pavel, we can therefore say that genre plays a decisive role in literary representation of cultural difference in two ways: first, in terms of the stylistic strategies that it favours and, secondly, in terms of the expectations with which readers will come to a text.

I have chosen to analyse the treatment of Iran across a range of different genres and sub-genres, because I believe, like Todorov and Pavel, that each genre approaches the subject with its own set of formal conventions and reader expectations. Working across genres, rather than focusing on any single one, allows us to reformulate the question how was Iran perceived by nineteenth-century French authors? in more technical and, therefore, specific terms. The question now becomes: how was Iran *written*? In other words, how did different types of writing shape different visions of Iran? Form and content do not lead separate lives: they inform one another. Different genre conventions will lead to the favouring of certain themes. Travel-writing, for example, privileges the detailed description of architecture, geography and everyday life in contemporary Iran because it is a genre predicated on personal observation; its value lies in its truth claims, not in its formal elegance or feats of imagination. In turn, lyric poetry, which is the most stylistically codified of all genres, will privilege the world of classical Persian poetry because this sister genre offers opportunities for the kind of formal imitation and intertextual dialogue on which poets have historically thrived. On a more granular level, the stylistic conventions associated with different genres will have a direct impact on the text's treatment of cultural difference. The style and structure of a work of literature play just as great a part in communicating a certain idea of Iran as the author's choice of subject matter and statements do. In order to illustrate this point, I shall briefly contrast two works about the same subject matter, but written in different genres.

Gobineau's pseudoscientific *Essai sur l'inégalité des races humaines* [*Essay on the Inequality of the Human Races*] and Dieulafoy's historical novel *Parysatis* both describe the imperial might of the Achaemenids and the inevitable decline of their power. Gobineau, who is writing a grand narrative – his subject is how race has been made manifest throughout the entirety of human history – offers a broad-brushstroke account that goes from the rise of the Achaemenid dynasty under Cyrus the Great to the consolidation of their power under Darius I, to their fall. Dieulafoy, who is writing a character-driven work, focuses on a ten-year period, the early reign of Artaxerxes II. This was a time when the Persian Empire was still mighty, though beginning to face serious threats (a civil war and incursions from Greece), and Dieulafoy dramatizes these political events as conflicts between the members of the royal household. In Gobineau's text, the ancient Persians are referred to by the pseudoscientific narrator as specimens of the 'Aryan' race. This style of writing does not invite readers to see the ancient Persians as human beings with agency or psychological depth. Indeed, Gobineau's Persians have just about as much personality as a diagram, and that is because they only exist in the text as demonstrations of the author's racist principles. The titular anti-heroine of *Parysatis*, in contrast, is presented with a great level of psychological depth. Using a combination of narratorial exposition, dialogue and *discours indirect libre*, Dieulafoy draws on all the tools of the nineteenth-century novel to paint a Machiavellian and fearless woman, one who will stop at nothing to protect the Persian Empire and rise to the top of its chain of command, and yet whose gender acts as a constant barrier to her ambitions. We relate to the Achaemenid queen because we see her as a person, with both admirable qualities and terrible flaws. She is not an Oriental Other, nor is she an illustration of obtuse laws of race or ethnicity: she is a person who dared to act against the rules of her society – a universal theme if ever there was one. The sharp contrast between the portrayal of the Achaemenid dynasty in the *Essai* and *Parysatis* shows us that cultural difference is not only a matter of opinion, but also of style. Certainly, Gobineau and Dieulafoy each had their own views on ancient Iran, views that were informed by such factors as their experiences, knowledge of history and conceptions of race and culture. But these views were better served, and indeed consolidated, by the genres that they wrote in. Dieulafoy did not need to tell her readers that the Achaemenids were people: this was shown through the characters' thoughts and feelings. And Gobineau's central theory that all is predetermined by race was communicated not only through his statements, but through his decision to retell world history with a (pseudo-)scientific detachment that saw human individuals not as agents, but as manifestations of natural laws. Gobineau and Dieulafoy remained within the conventions of their genre because these conventions were effective in reaching the desired impact on readers. But there were also authors whose goals required the breaking of genre conventions. In order to tell history 'from the inside', Michelet crafted his own unique historiography, which as we shall see is deeply personal and highly fictionalized. In turn, Judith Gautier's novel *Iskender: Histoire persane* blended the European genres of the historical novel and the fairy tale, in order to better imitate another genre altogether: the medieval Persian epic. These innovations should not surprise us since, as Todorov notes, transgression has always been an important part of how writers engage with genre.[37]

As previously noted, genre also has a paratextual (or, to use Pavel's term, extratextual) dimension. This dimension is associated with the author's intentions and the reader's expectations, but is not identifiable within the text itself. Pavel's example of the fictional biography *Marlot* reminds us that there are cases in which genre distinctions are 'invisible'. Indeed, read in isolation, certain passages from Dieulafoy's *Parysatis* are interchangeable with passages from Michelet's chapter 'La Perse': a first-person omniscient narrator describes the lives of ancient Iranians, covering everything from the way they prayed to what they ate. Both authors achieve this by combining a limited set of historical sources with flights of the imagination. And yet, one text bears the label of 'history' and the other of 'fiction'. The fact that the former is written by a man and the latter by a woman is no coincidence.[38] Todorov's observation that genres 'function as institutions' is key here, since institutions have historically excluded minorities. This raises a question that is left undiscussed by both Todorov and Pavel: that of access. Not everyone could choose what genre they wrote in, since access to certain genres was contingent on a certain level of education and social status, factors that privileged men. This meant that the genres most accessible to women writers were those considered least authoritative; in other words: those associated with amateurism. Dieulafoy's first publications were articles in the travel-writing journal *Le Tour du Monde*: travel-writing was a journalistic, personal and not 'serious' form of writing, especially in comparison to scholarly publications such as those of their husband Marcel.[39] Dieulafoy's travel-writing was consecrated six years after its first publication, when it was published as a bound volume, an upgrade that notably only took place *after* Dieulafoy had been awarded the Legion of Honour, that most masculine of awards. As a popular travel-writer and a successful archaeologist, the door was finally open for Dieulafoy to publish many more books and even experiment with new genres. But even after they had been published, the women writers studied in this book, from Marceline Desbordes-Valmore to Anna de Noailles, all suffered to different degrees from the same critical response: a general tendency from their contemporaries to emphasize the 'feminine' qualities of their work, such as sensitivity, honesty and vulnerability. This strategy was used by critics and reviewers to avoid commenting on the technical merits of these works, thereby reinforcing the notion that women writers were inherently amateurish. Genre is thus doubly political, both in terms of the conventions that will affect how an author presents Iran and in terms of the hierarchy of genres, which informs the wider reading public of what types of writing and what authors are most authoritative. It is therefore no accident that among the works analysed in this book it is those written by women authors, who are by definition at the margins of the literary establishment, that are the most nuanced in terms of their treatment of Iran and the most experimental in their use of genre. This illustrates the intimate connection between the politics of genre and the politics of representation, a connection that is alluded to by Edward Said, though never fully explored.

In the introduction to *Orientalism*, Said eloquently argues that authority is not 'mysterious or natural', but constructed.[40] This leads him to outline his two 'methodological devices for studying authority', which are

> *strategic location*, which is a way of describing the author's position in a text with regard to the Oriental material he writes about, and *strategic formation*, which is a way of analyzing the relationship between texts and the way in which groups of texts, types of texts, even textual genres, acquire mass, density, and referential power among themselves and thereafter in the culture at large.[41]

Said only refers to genre in his definition of 'strategic formation', but in fact both facets of the West's textual authority over the Orient are by-products of genre. Indeed, if 'strategic formation' refers to how a text relates to other texts in its genre and how it is met by the reader's horizon of expectation, in other words, the extratextual dimension of genre referred to by Todorov and Pavel, then 'strategic location' is clearly situated within the text, since Said uses the term to refer to certain stylistic conventions. These stylistic conventions, which Said borrows from Anwar Abdel Malek, present 'the Orient and Orientals' as objects of study; in other words, as passive and devoid of both agency and subjectivity.[42] The Western author's 'location' vis-à-vis what he is describing is one of distance and detachment, maintaining a clear-cut separation between himself – and with Said it is always a 'him' – and his object of study. This 'absence of sympathy covered by professional knowledge' is what allows 'the modern Orientalist' to appear objective, when in fact he is seeking to dehumanize the Orient.[43] The author's strategic location at a remove from the object of study is recognizable in several of the texts studied here. A particularly rich example of it can be found in Pierre Loti's description of Shi'i ritual mourning, in which the author portrays himself as a horrified witness to barbaric customs.[44] But strategic location is to a large degree contingent on an author's choice of genre. The essay and the travelogue are two genres in which the author is identified as the narrator, expresses personal observations and draws conclusions, and is usually the only voice in the text. These are therefore far more likely to maintain the 'Western subject versus Oriental object' binary than a lyric poem or a novel with an Iranian protagonist. And indeed, although Said names texts from a wide array of genres, from Disraeli's novel *Tancred* to Goethe's collection of poems the *West-östlicher divan* and Æschylus's play *The Persians*, his key case studies are all taken from two genres: travel-writing and the academic survey.[45] Moreover, the authors of these texts are all politicians, established academics and canonical authors: members of the 'boys club' of textual authority who had little reason to question existing hierarchies. Had Said devoted as much attention to poetry and fiction as he did to essays and travel-writing, and had he considered the contributions of women as well as that of men, he would not have been able to craft such a unified narrative. Said was right to note that authority is constructed and that one should dissect it through the close analysis of style. But in order to afford the question of textual authority the depth and complexity that it warrants, we must account for genre and gender. A key contribution of this book will therefore be its exploration of how the hierarchies of gender, genre and Orientalism intersect and how these intersections give rise to different modalities of cross-cultural representation.[46]

The book's first chapter analyses the place of Iran in nineteenth-century French poetry. My overarching question is: what was the impact of the newfound availability of Persian poetry in translation on French poetry? The chapter's sections (each of them chronological) explore different threads of this poetic reception. In 'From Paris to Persia and Back Again' I analyse the function of 'Persia' as an imaginary space in the poetry of Victor Hugo, Théophile Gautier and Anna de Noailles. What did Persia symbolize for these authors? What qualities did its association with the Persian poetic canon offer that were not available in a loosely defined 'Orient'? In the section 'Persian Poems Made in France', I compare two poets who prided themselves on their formal and thematic imitations of Persian poetry and theology: Armand Renaud and Henri Cazalis (pseudonym: Jean Lahor). I ask what we should make of cultural transfers of this kind: are these pastiches that do nothing more than exaggerate the otherness of the Orient? Or should we appreciate these poems as intertextual experiments that cross cultural boundaries? I end the chapter with a reading of Marceline Desbordes-Valmore's poem 'Les Roses de Saadi', a piece which recast the medieval Persian author's reflections on the powers and limitations of poetic language in the modern French poet's own terms, thereby emphasizing the universality rather than the cultural specificity of Persian poetry.

Chapter 2 analyses the treatment of Iran in two genres that were concerned with recovering the past: history and historical fiction. Nineteenth-century France saw a surge in interest in ancient Iran as a result of the rediscovery of the languages of ancient Asia and the subsequent new translations and essays on ancient religions and cultures. These developments conspired to challenge the prevalent Eurocentric view that the only great civilizations of the past were ancient Greece and Rome. The chapter asks: how did French authors tackle the difference of ancient Iran, which was both cultural and temporal? And how did historiography and historical fiction differ in this regard? The chapter's first section 'Nos parents les Aryas' [our parents the Aryans] explores the rise of the Aryan myth and how it changed the narrative surrounding ancient Iran. The section analyses three authors, who had very different agendas, yet whose works all played a great part in giving currency to the racist binary of the so-called 'Aryan' and 'Semitic' races. They are the racial theorist Arthur de Gobineau, the philologist Ernest Renan and the historian Jules Michelet. The chapter's second section focuses on one work: Judith Gautier's *Iskender: Histoire persane*, a historical novel that retells Alexander of Macedon's conquest of the Achaemenid Empire through the lens of Ferdowsi's *Shāhnāmeh*. The section explores the many layers of Gautier's engagement with her source text, as well as the queer dimension that she injects into the narrative through the story of an intimate friendship between Alexander and an Iranian warrior. The chapter's final section explores three works of historical fiction by Jane Dieulafoy which are all centred on powerful female characters. How was ancient Iran instrumentalized by Dieulafoy to reflect on the present moment? And how are we to interpret Dieulafoy's strategic location with regard to their subject matter? Are these works suggesting an equivalence between the author and these historical characters or do they serve to assert Dieulafoy's dominance over them as an expert on ancient Iran?

Chapter 3 analyses and compares eight travelogues recounting journeys across Iran. It explores how travelling to Iran differed from reading about Iran. Or did it? Edward Said's emphasis on the mediated nature of Western perceptions of the Orient has brought under question the extent to which travellers were able to form new opinions about the places that they visited or whether they simply rehashed pre-existing stereotypes. This chapter shows that travellers' experiences of Iran were in fact extremely personal and varied depending on their gender, education and social status. I explore both the continuities and the divergences that come to light when studying travelogues about Iran written by a range of different authors. Due to the wealth of material to select from, this is the longest chapter in the book. It covers six different aspects of French travel-writing on Iran. Its first section 'Defining the Persians' explores what made the Persians 'Persian' according to French travel-writers. The second section moves from Iranians in general to Iranian women in particular, focusing on the travelogues of Jane Dieulafoy and Marthe Bibesco, the only two authors to be granted regular access to the *andaruni* (Persian for harem). Did being 'Among Women' create a greater sense of proximity? Or did Iranian women remain first and foremost cultural others? Gender segregation in Qajar Iran was motivated by religious customs and the chapter's third section turns to travel-writers' wider impressions of Shi'i Islam. I compare in particular Eugène Flandin, Jane Dieulafoy, Pierre Loti and Marthe Bibesco's descriptions of the mourning rituals of the month of Muharram, as well as of the religious seminary of Esfahan. The two sections that follow turn from descriptions of customs to descriptions of places. The architecture of the city of Esfahan gives rise to a particularly rich array of cultural and aesthetic comparisons. Do comparisons of this kind serve, as Said claims, to assert Western cultural superiority or is the process of analogy in fact equalizing, as is suggested by Bhatti and Kimmich? We then travel south, and back in time, to the ancient ruins of the cities of Persepolis and Susa. How did standing among the earthly remains of the Achaemenid Empire compare to reading about it in Plutarch? Did the experience change how these writers made sense of the past? Iran's ancient heritage was also subject to its exploitation by the French state, which appropriated finds from ancient Susa with Marcel and Jane Dieulafoy acting as its agents. The chapter's penultimate section 'Plagued by the West' considers how French travellers addressed – or in some cases avoided addressing – the realities of Europe's political and financial interventionism in Iran. This was a phenomenon that would have been invisible to those authors for whom Iran existed only in an idealized past, but that would have been obvious to any observant traveller. The comparison between the literary ideal of Iran and Iran as geographical reality is the subject of the chapter's final section, which analyses the role of intertextuality in Iranian travelogues. But instead of analysing travel-writers' citations from fellow Western authors, as Said does in *Orientalism*, I study references to Middle Eastern literature, namely, Galland's translation of the *Mille et Une Nuits* [*Thousand and One Nights*] and Persian poetry. What was the function of such citations in the context of travel-writing? And what did writers have to say about the difference between experiencing Iran in literature and in reality?

The book's final chapter is devoted to the performing arts and the multilayered nature of their engagement with Iranian culture. I begin by comparing two ballets entitled *La Péri*, which both centre on the female mythological creature of the same name (in Persian *pari*). Théophile Gautier and Burgmüller's ballet (1843) completely amalgamates Iran with the Islamic Orient of the French imagination. Paul Dukas's *La Péri* (aborted production 1911, première 1912), in contrast, draws heavily on the literary and visual culture of Iran. The section asks why it is that these two ballets took such different approaches to the figure of the *pari* and also explores the interpretative relationship between the text of the ballet libretto and the visual and aural elements of the production. The chapter's second section is devoted to opera and covers three works: Michel Carré, Hippolyte Lucas and Félicien David's wildly successful *opéra comique Lalla-Roukh* (1862), and two more austere grand operas: Jean Richepin and Jules Massenet's *Le Mage* (1891) and Louis Gallet and Louis-Albert Bourgault-Ducoudray's *Thamara* (1891). These three operas each have different historical settings, yet they all centre on a story of forbidden love between an Iranian man and a non-Iranian woman. What is particularly interesting is that none of these women are European. These three operas therefore eschew the binary typically favoured by Orientalist operas of the European male hero and the exotic and dangerous female native, presenting us instead with an East/East relationship and more ambivalent characters. This complexity, I argue, speaks to Iran's wider ambivalence in the French imagination, as both alter ego and exotic other. The chapter's third section takes us from the pomp of the opera to the small-scale Petit-Théâtre de la Galerie Vivienne to analyse Maurice Bouchor's play for marionettes *Le Songe de Khèyam* (1892). What were the implications of replacing human actors with these small mechanical figures? And how did this influence the play's dramatization of Khayyām's quatrains? The chapter ends with another experimental production, but takes us from the intimacy of the marionette theatre to the grand open air venue of the Arènes de Béziers, a setting that dwarfed even the Paris operas. Jane Dieulafoy's collaboration in 1902 on a stage version of their novel *Parysatis* with Camille Saint-Saëns and Southern industrialist-turned-producer Fernand Castelbon des Beauxhostes would lead to a life-sized re-creation of the Achaemenid court at Susa, complete with hundreds of extras and horse-drawn chariots. I will be particularly interested in what changed for Dieulafoy in the transition from novelist to theatre producer and librettist and how this put under pressure the alignment of their political, artistic and scientific agenda.

1

Poetry

Translation and poetic innovation

Si les précieux volumes des Orientaux qui se trouvent dans les inestimables bibliothèques de Paris, de Leyde, d'Oxford, de Vienne, & de Madrid, étoient publiés avec l'avantage ordinaire des notes & explications: si les langues Orientales étoient enseignées dans nos universités, [...] un nouveau champ seroit ouvert à nos contemplations; nous pénétrerions plus avant dans l'histoire du cœur humain; notre ésprit seroit pourvû d'un nouvel assortiment d'images & de comparaisons; en conséquence en on verroit paroitre plusieurs excéllentes compositions sur lesquelles les critiques futurs auroient à s'exércer, & que les poëtes à venir pourroient imiter.[1]

[If the precious Oriental volumes kept in the fine libraries of Paris, Leyden, Oxford, Vienna, and Madrid were published with the ordinary advantage of notes and explanations: if Oriental languages were taught at our universities, [...] a new field would be open to our contemplation; we would penetrate further into the history of the human heart; our mind would be furnished with a new assortment of images and comparisons; and in consequence we would see several excellent compositions being published, which would give the critics of the future something to contend with and the poets of tomorrow something to imitate.]

These are the words of Sir William Jones, the first author to publish French translations of Hāfez. His 'Traité sur la poesie Orientale' (1770), which would form the basis for his later essay: 'On the Poetry of the Eastern Nations' (1772), is an introduction to Arabic, Persian and Turkish literature aimed at European readers. Despite this wide scope, the essay focuses predominantly on Persian poetry, for which Jones declares his preference,[2] a preference that would come to be shared by the French poets studied in this chapter. In the passage above, Jones asserts that Oriental poetry's lack of popularity abroad is not for lack of quality, but due to practical obstacles.[3] His belief that greater familiarity with the Persian, Turkish and Arabic canons will provide a step towards a greater understanding of 'the human heart' is essentially universalist, since it makes a case for the shared humanity of European readers and Asian poets. Yet, at the same time, the poetry described by Jones also manifests important cultural differences: it comes with an 'assortment of images and comparisons' that has no equivalent in European poetry. And this is precisely what makes it exciting. Poets such as Hāfez are an antidote to the stultification of European literature because they are universal enough to be intelligible, yet culturally different enough to be 'new'. Jones's case in favour of literary cross-pollination thus follows the same logic as that outlined in the work of Todorov and of Bhatti and Kimmich: balancing difference with commonalities.[4]

Jones's ambition for new translations to function as catalysts for poetic innovation was prophetic, as was his foregrounding of Persian poetry among all other Oriental literatures. A century later, the French poet Armand Renaud would echo Jones's sentiment that among all Oriental literatures (under which he lists Arabic, Persian, Turkish and Sanskrit literature): 'c'est la forme persane qui, en poésie surtout, est la plus originale et la plus complète' [it is the Persian form which, in poetry especially, is the most original and well-rounded].[5] The elite status held by Persian poetry transcended the antagonism between the different poetic schools of the French nineteenth century. The names of Hāfez and Saʿdi were enlisted by Victor Hugo as founts of inspiration for the Romantic movement, whose mission, much like Jones's, was to counteract the derivativeness of Classicism. Yet, Persian poetry was equally invoked by Théophile Gautier in order to distance himself from the Romantic movement and defend his vision of Art for Art's sake. This vision, in turn, inspired the Parnassian and Symbolist movements, which remained equally invested in the Persian poetic canon. Persian poetry was also used by the women poets Marceline Desbordes-Valmore and Anna de Noailles to carve a space for themselves outside of these male-dominated schools. What makes the French poetic reception of Persian literature therefore so fascinating is its continuous repurposing of one same canon as an inexhaustible source of creative independence. Across generations, politics and aesthetics, French poets valued the Persian canon as a literary world that was free from the grip of tradition – the 'tradition' in question continuously redefined according to the individual poet's position, in a sequence of redefinitions that long outlived Jones. There was arguably also a causal link between Jones's prophecy and the popularity of Persian poetry in France: his essays and translations were touchstones for nineteenth-century scholars and translators, who idealized him as a pioneer in the study of Persian poetry in Europe. The Bibliothèque Royale in Paris, a key resource for the writers of the time including Victor Hugo, held a copy of Jones's 'Traité sur la poesie Orientale'. And, moreover, his friend Ernest Fouinet referred Hugo to Jones's work in their correspondence over *Les Orientales*.[6] It is therefore not inconceivable that Hugo's passionate defence of Oriental Studies in *Les Orientales* (1829), which heralded French poetry's eastward turn, was inspired by the passage quoted above. But it would take a fiery young Victor Hugo for Jones's defence of Oriental literature to enter the 'mainstream' of French literary debates, earning Hugo the title of 'le prédicateur de l'Orient' [the preacher of the Orient].[7]

Hugo's collection of poems *Les Orientales*, which is the chronological starting point for this book's field of inquiry, marks a turning point for French interest in Iran in three important ways. First, it announces the beginning of a widespread enthusiasm for all things Oriental and explicitly aligns this enthusiasm with a literary agenda: Romanticism, defined in opposition to Classicism. Secondly, it places an emphasis on the study of languages as a point of entry into foreign cultures. Last but not least, it announces the French literary scene's favouring of Persian over all other Asian languages and literatures. Indeed, although Hugo's preface enthuses about 'the Orient' in general, the only Oriental authors that he cites in his collection's numerous epigraphs are Ḥāfeẓ and Saʿdi. One cannot underestimate the influence that Hugo held over contemporary and subsequent French poets, whether they embraced it or resisted it. In the words of Charles Baudelaire: 'Jamais royauté ne fut plus naturelle, plus acclamée par la reconnaissance, plus confirmée par l'impuissance de la rébellion' [Never was royalty more natural, more acclaimed by gratitude, more confirmed by the impossibility of resistance].[8] It is therefore safe to say that Hugo's *Orientales* set the tone for the rest of the century. But what exactly was this tone?

The preface of Hugo's collection is highly defensive: the author ventriloquizes 'la critique' [literary critics], whom he portrays as being horrified by these poems: 'Ne voyez-vous pas […] que le sujet chevauche hors des *limites de l'art*?' [Do you not see that the subject matter goes beyond the *limits of art*?] To which Hugo responds: 'qu'il ne savait pas en quoi étaient faites les *limites de l'art*, que de géographie précise du monde intellectuel, il n'en connaissait point' [that he did not know of what the *limits of art* were made, that he knew of no precise geography of the intellectual world].[9] This geographical metaphor makes a general statement about the creative independence of the poet, but the choice of imagery also foreshadows the real issue at hand, which is the collection's imaginary journey to the Orient, regarded by the ventriloquized critic as a journey beyond the realms of good taste. Hugo goes on to make an ambitious and original claim, which is that he hopes that his collection's place in his oeuvre will be similar to that of a mosque in an Andalusian medieval town.[10] The mosque not only functions as an analogy for the bright colours and formal variety that characterize Hugo's poems, but it is also a metonymy: it belongs to the Islamic world and so too, it is implied, does this collection. Hugo's mosque is depicted as the polar opposite of the edifice of French Classicism which is metaphorized, aptly enough, as a neoclassical building: 'des oves et des volutes, un bouquet de bronze pour les corniches, un nuage de marbre avec des têtes d'anges pour les voûtes, une flamme de pierre pour les frises, et puis des oves et des volutes!'[11] [Ovums and volutes, a bronze bouquet for the cornices, a cloud of marble with cherub heads for the ceiling, stone flame for the friezes, and yet more ovums and volutes!] Like Jones before him, Hugo characterizes the current state of literature as derivative and repetitive. Fortunately, the tide is changing: 'Les études orientales n'ont jamais été poussées si avant. Au siècle de Louis XIV on était helléniste, maintenant on est orientaliste. Il y a un pas de fait.'[12] [Oriental Studies have never been more advanced. In the century of Louis XIV one was a Hellenist, now one is an Orientalist. That is some progress.] Thanks to the exciting new research being undertaken by Orientalists, the nations of Asia are no longer merely apprehended through their visual and material culture, but through their literature. Hugo would have been thinking in particular of Jules Mohl, the long-time president of the Société Asiatique and the French translator of the Persian epic poem the *Shāhnāmeh*, whose salon he frequented, and of Ernest Fouinet, the friend who personally selected, translated and commented verses from Persian and Arabic poetry for Hugo.[13] These, then, were the iconoclasts whose work challenged the French neo-Classicists' narrow and nationalistic definitions of 'good taste'.

Les Orientales caused a sensation. The collection broke the rules of versification that had solidified over the course of the seventeenth and eighteenth centuries. The themes tackled in its poems were explicitly violent and erotic. Its stylistic texture, finally, was made of foreign words, bright clashing colours and naive similes, which at the time were all considered markers of bad taste.[14] In Maxime Du Camp's words, it was a veritable 'artistic crusade'.[15] Based on the posturing of the collection's preface, readers assumed that Hugo's innovations – or, depending on one's perspective, indiscretions – were the result of his study of Oriental literature. One editor, Emmanuel J. Chételat, was so offended by this that he published a pamphlet entitled *Les Occidentales ou Lettres critiques sur les Orientales de M. Victor Hugo* (1829) in which he warned the public against the dangers of reading this collection. The pamphlet bears the ominous epigraph 'Delenda Est Carthago' conjuring a sense of a historical and inevitable enmity between the Middle East and the West by referring back to the destruction of ancient Carthage in modern-day Tunisia by the ancient Romans. According to Chételat,

> C'est [...] un intérêt sérieux pour la France que le maintien de sa gloire littéraire, et elle doit être assez fière de ses propres grandeurs pour repousser avec dédain toutes les influences étrangères sur son génie comme sur sa puissance. Or, voici venir de l'Orient, c'est-à-dire de la Barbarie, des inspirations nouvelles faites pour altérer la pureté de notre belle littérature.[16]
>
> [It is [...] in France's serious interest to protect her literary glory, and she must be proud enough of her own greatness to scornfully repel foreign influences upon her genius just as upon her might. And yet, here come from the Orient, that is to say from barbarians, new inspirations made to alter the purity of our beautiful literature.]

French poetry had to be a national project following certain set conventions and, in Chételat's eyes, Hugo had betrayed this project by allowing his writing to become corrupted by 'foreign influences'. If we read through the pages of the pamphlet, what emerges, however, is that more than the collection's formal innovations, what seems to incur most ire are those poems in which Hugo presented the people of the Orient in a sympathetic light.[17] Maintaining the oppositional binary of Orientalism (as defined by Said) is thus just as important a concern to this critic as maintaining the set conventions of French poetry. Although Chételat's views are diametrically opposed to those expressed by William Jones in 1770, they do arise from the same assumption: the availability of Oriental poetry in translation must surely result in European literary traditions being challenged and a greater emphasis being placed on the commonalities of human experience. But to what degree was this actually true?

In this chapter I will be exploring this question by examining the reception of Persian poetry in the works of six different poets: Victor Hugo, Théophile Gautier, Marceline Desbordes-Valmore, Armand Renaud, Henri Cazalis (under the pseudonym Jean Lahor) and Anna de Noailles. These authors each bring their own style and creative ideology to bear on their Persian sources, yet they also fall into recognizable trends. The first is to portray the Persian literary sphere as an idealized space defined in opposition to Paris, where the lyric I can find and redefine themselves. The second is to attempt to write 'in the style of' Persian poetry. When done successfully, this results in an original blending of poetic forms. However, imitation could also be used as a pretence, to bolster a rather superficial form of self-exoticization. Finally, French poets could on rare occasions draw inspiration from the Persian canon without calling attention to the fact that they were doing so. This process is more akin to forms of intertextuality that we typically encounter among French or, more broadly, European authors: the Persian author is not drawn on as an exotic specimen, but as a fellow poet, which belies a universalist understanding of poetry.

Lyric poetry is a genre that allows for many different forms of intertextual engagement, ranging from citation to formal imitation to the borrowing of a particular image or metaphor. For this reason, I am limiting the scope of this chapter to poets who cite Persian poetry and/or write poems inspired by Persian poetry. This excludes poems that merely refer to Iran as a setting, such as Leconte de Lisle's famous pantoum 'Les Roses d'Ispahan'. The overall structure of this chapter is thematic rather than chronological: that being said, the order in which I discuss the poets within each section is chronological, since I am interested in exploring the poetic genealogies that connect them to each other, as well as to the Persian canon. Moreover, although I have grouped these poets into three categories for the sake of argument, in some cases I do identify parallels that go beyond this categorization. This is most true of Marceline Desbordes-Valmore and Armand Renaud, who both – though each in their own way – predicate the relationship between their oeuvre and Persian poetry according to the paradigm of similarity, as defined by Bhatti and Kimmich.

From Paris to 'Persia' and back again (Hugo, Théophile Gautier, Noailles)

The poems of *Les Orientales* will come as somewhat of a disappointment to anyone who believed in the promise of Hugo's preface. While the collection does challenge Eurocentrism in so far as it includes many poems spoken in the voice of Oriental characters, these characters act and speak in clichés: sequestered women, scenes of jealousy, brutal acts of violence and, for relief, exotic landscapes. Hugo, when writing these poems, does not seem to have been overly concerned with the emerging knowledge on Oriental literature that he so praises in the preface. The collection has two rather different thematic centres: current affairs, specifically the French news coverage of the Greek War of Independence, and the timeless Orient of Western fantasy, as represented in particular through painting.[18] This choice of focus is all the more surprising if we examine the manuscript of the collection preserved at the Bibliothèque Nationale de France, which includes letters from Hugo's friend Fouinet, who painstakingly selected, translated and explicated verses by Ferdowsi, 'Attār, Rumi and Hāfez for Hugo's benefit.[19] Moroever, the poet and moralist Sa'di also features prominently on the manuscript's cover page, which Hugo has annotated with three quotations from the *Golestān* (see Figure 1.1). As has been noted by Pierre Larcher,

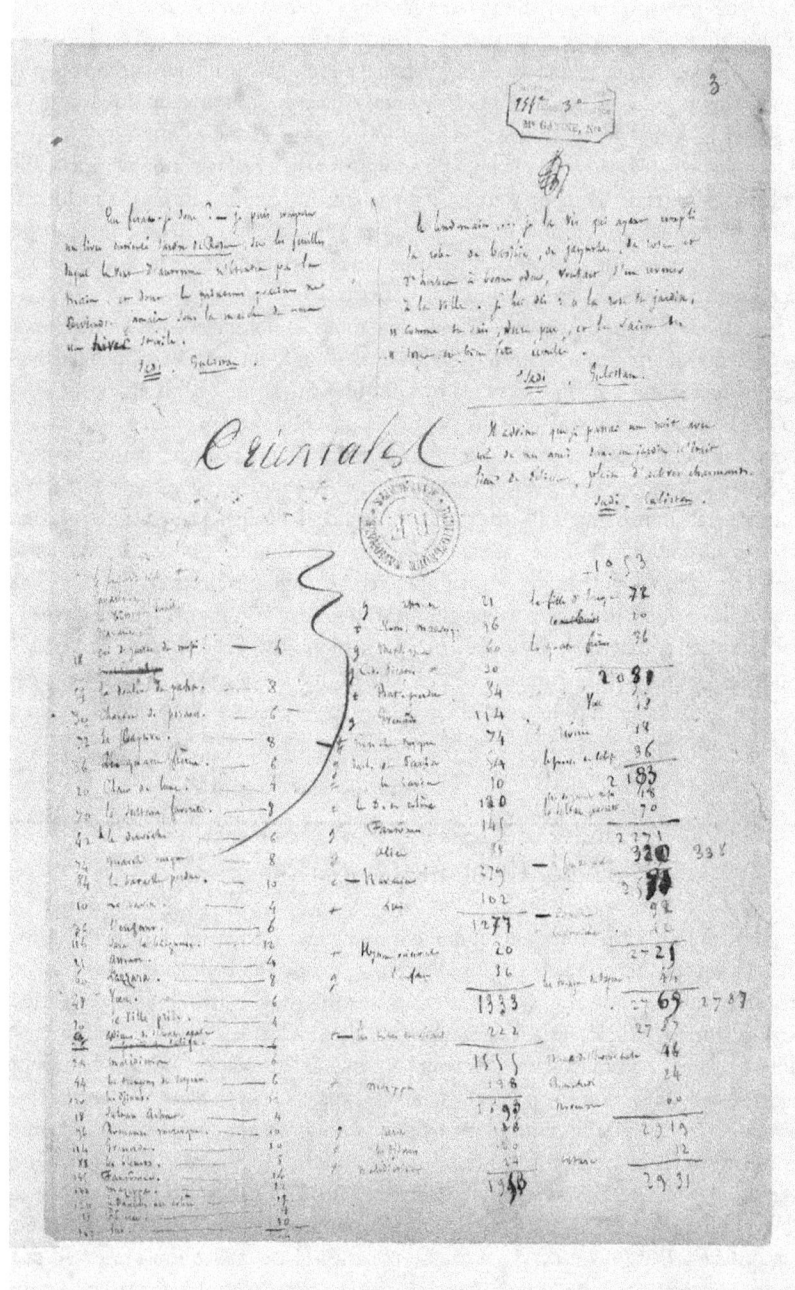

Figure 1.1 Three Sa'di quotations in Hugo's hand.

Source: Fonds Victor Hugo. II *Orientales* manuscript folio 3r.

the paradox of *Les Orientales* is that despite having Fouinet's selection available to him, Hugo does not seem to have engaged with it in the poems.[20] This, however, is partly explained by the fact that many of the poems in the collection predate Fouinet and Hugo's correspondence.

The peripheral position of Saʿdi on the upper margin of Hugo's cover page is a fitting metaphor for the wider position of Persian poetry in *Les Orientales*. Indeed, although Persian poetry is foregrounded in Hugo's paratext, in particular, through the use of epigraphs from Ḥāfez and Saʿdi and endnotes introducing the reader to Persian poetry (the latter plagiarized from Fouinet),[21] there are only two pieces in the collection that seem to respond to the 'foreign influences' so decried by Chételat. The first, entitled 'Le Derviche', imitates the genre conventions of Saʿdi's *hekāyat* (moral tales) by staging a dialogue between a dervish and a monarch, in which the former ultimately proves the wisest.[22] But whereas Saʿdi's tales are parables, Hugo gives his poem a historically and culturally specific setting by identifying the ruler in the poem's story as Ali Pasha, the Albanian governor of the Ottoman Empire's Western territories, who had attempted to secede from the Sublime Porte and died shortly after in 1822. We find a similar amalgamation in the second poem with an identifiable Persian lyric influence. The poem is entitled 'Sultan Achmet', which is the Turkish form of the name Ahmad, and is part of a cluster of poems set in Andalusia. Achmet, the speaker of the poem, addresses a Christian woman named 'Juana la Grenadine' [Juana of Granada], which suggests that the poem is set against the historical backdrop of the late fifteenth century when the Christians of Iberia fought to expel local Muslims (known as Moors) and counteract incursions from the Ottoman Turks. Such a setting serves to enhance the tenor of Achmet's declaration of love: the Muslim character declares that he is prepared to convert to Christianity to win over Juana. Religious conversion as an act of love is a common theme in Persian Sufi literature: it is found for instance in ʿAttār's influential poem *The Conference of the Birds* as well as in one of the translations of Ḥāfez that Fouinet sent to Hugo.[23] Hugo's verses 'Je donnerais sans retour / Mon royaume pour Médine / Médine pour ton amour' [I would give / My kingdom for Medina / Medina for your love] also echo Ḥāfez's famous 'Shirazi Turk' ghazal (Ghazal °3),[24] which had been popularized in Europe by several English renditions, beginning with Jones's.[25] However, the fact that even Hugo's most Persian poem is set in Andalusia illustrates the degree to which his Orient is an amalgamation of signifiers of the Islamic world, one that makes little to no differentiation between medieval Persian poetry, Spanish history and recent events in Greece. While Persian poetry did provide a sense of 'local colour' through the collection's epigraphs and also inspired the subject matter and rhetorical flourishes of 'Le Derviche' and 'Sultan Achmet', it otherwise left no trace on Hugo's style, versification, or imaginary geography. As such, Chételat's fear of 'foreign influences' seems to have been unjustified.

Les Orientales shocked and delighted audiences with its exoticism and defiance of the norms of French versification. But these existed independently of Hugo's putative Oriental sources. Rather than an influence of Oriental poetry (Persian or otherwise) on Hugo's writing, it is more accurate to speak of a strategic alliance: by celebrating Saʿdi and Ḥāfez, Hugo made his readers aware that there existed a whole universe beyond the type of poetry to which they were accustomed. That Hugo's writing and

Persian poetry had little in common did not matter: what mattered was that they both symbolized a rebellion against French Classicism. As well as disassociating Hugo from the French poets who came before him, the collection's Persian epigraphs could also enhance his material by setting the tone with concision. This is the case of the collection's concluding poem 'Novembre', which is introduced by an epigraph from Saʿdi's *Golestān*: 'Je lui dis: La rose du jardin, comme tu sais, dure peu; et la saison des roses est bien vite écoulée.' [I said to him: The garden rose, as you know, does not last; and the season of the roses is soon over.] Saʿdi's broader reflection on the ephemerality of all human experiences, which in the original passage he goes on to contrast with the endurance of his poetry,[26] introduces Hugo's far more specific reflection on the ephemerality of his collection's exotic fantasies, and imbues it with a feeling of nostalgia. The poem itself lists the myriad characters and landscapes that vanish when confronted with the crushing reality of Paris in November, as seen through the poet's window:

> 7 Devant le sombre hiver de Paris qui bourdonne,
> Ton soleil d'orient s'éclipse, et t'abandonne,
> 9 Ton beau rêve d'Asie avorte, et tu ne vois
> Sous tes yeux que la rue au bruit accoutumée,
> Brouillard à ta fenêtre, et longs flots de fumée
> Qui baignent en fuyant l'angle noirci des toits.[27]

> [7 Before the sombre winter of the buzzing city of Paris
> Your Oriental sun is eclipsed, and abandons you,
> 9 Your beautiful dream of Asia aborts, and all you see
> Beneath your eyes is the noisy street,
> The fog pressing at the window, and the wisps of smoke
> 12 Which blacken the roof corners as they float away.]

But while the body of the poem presents the collection's imaginary Orient – an amalgamate that includes Ottoman Turkey, Egypt, India and Persia – as unsustainable, the presence of the epigraph points the reader towards another Orient, one that can withstand the onslaught of the Parisian winter: the world of Persian literature. Saʿdi's words, accessed in translation, continue to be enjoyed by Hugo and his readers even after the imaginary geography of *Les Orientales* has disintegrated. Indeed, the words grow in relevance as the poem unfolds: after mourning the loss of his Oriental visions, Hugo's lyric I expresses the far more profound nostalgia felt towards memories of childhood and first love: 'Frais papillons dont l'aile, en fuyant rajeunie, / Sous le doigt qui la fixe est si vite ternie, / Essaim doré qui n'a qu'un jour dans tous nos jours.'[28] [Fresh butterflies whose wing, youthful when it flees, / Quickly tarnishes when fixed under our finger, / A golden swarm which only has one day among all of our days.] By comparing these memories to butterflies that live only for a day, the poem points back, in a circular fashion, to its epigraph, which had also used a natural image to describe the ephemerality of all things. The Saʿdi quotation thus enhances Hugo's poem not only through its metonymic association with the external and culturally specific

Orient of Persian literature (as opposed to the collection's personal, imaginary and all-encompassing Orient), but also because it foreshadows the poem's ultimate theme, which is the lyric I's confrontation not with the limits posed by space, but the limits posed by the passage of time.

Read alone, the poem 'Novembre' presents a binary opposition between two spaces: Paris (or the real world) and the Orient of the imagination, a patchwork fantasy redolent of Orientalism as defined by Edward Said. But if we take into account the Sa'di epigraph, the relationship becomes triangular. Persian poetry connects and complicates the two terms of the binary: on the one hand, it is a clearly defined body of literature that exists in reality and thus cannot be reduced to Western fantasy; on the other hand, reading Persian poetry is often a spur for the fantasy of the Western reader, who apprehends it by drawing upon a vast reservoir of pre-existing images of the Orient. Hugo's epigraph also acts as a bridge between Paris and the Orient by virtue of its universal theme. The passage of time and the end of youth are things that are experienced by all humans, everywhere. The example of 'Novembre' therefore shows us that even though Hugo's writing was not significantly influenced by Persian poetry, the very presence of Persian poetry within the pages of his collection, even in the form of extracts relegated to the paratext, serves to complicate the simple oppositions of East and West, and of imagination and reality.

The triangular relationship formed by real places, imaginary places and Persian literature, which is implicit in Hugo's collection, would become an explicit theme in the work of two poets who sought to acknowledge the legacy of *Les Orientales* while also demarcating themselves from it: Théophile Gautier and Anna de Noailles. Whereas Hugo's 'rêve d'Orient' was an amalgamate, the Oriental day dreams of Gautier's 'Préface' (1852) and the Persian poems of Noailles's collection *Les Éblouissements* (1907) all stem from one source: the literature and arts of Iran. This firmly delineated focus was the result of the availability of Persian poetry in translation, the publication of illustrated travelogues and the presence of Iranian art in museums and private collections, all of which dramatically increased over the course of the second half of the nineteenth century. Through these sources, Gautier and Noailles were able to give substance to their daydreams by anchoring them in a material reality – to use Noailles's own words 'je sais qu'on le voit, qu'il existe' [I know that one can see it, that it exists.] Read in succession, these three poets thus mark an evolution from a time when the names of Sa'di and Ḥāfez were beginning to be foregrounded within the broader category of all things 'Oriental', to an era when things 'Persian' had emerged as a category of their own and the names of Iranian authors and cities had become familiar to French readers. Yet, it is also a testament to the enduring influence of *Les Orientales* that in spite of this wider cultural shift, Gautier and Noailles nonetheless continued to pay homage to Hugo's collection when writing poems about Persian poetry.

Published in the wake of the coup d'état that invested Napoleon III with absolute powers, the preface to Théophile Gautier's collection *Émaux et Camées* (1852) takes the form of a sonnet, in which the poet describes himself withdrawing from the political turmoil of his day and following the example of Goethe, who wrote the *West-östlicher Divan* during the Napoleonic invasion of Germany.[29]

PRÉFACE

Pendant les guerres de l'Empire,
Goëthe, au bruit du canon brutal,
Fit *Le Divan occidental*,
Fraîche oasis où l'art respire.

Pour Nisami quittant Shakspeare,
Il se parfuma de çantal,
Et sur un mètre oriental
Nota le chant qu'Hudhud soupire.

Comme Goëthe sur son divan
À Weymar s'isolait des choses
Et d'Hafiz effeuillait les roses,

Sans prendre garde à l'ouragan
Qui fouettait mes vitres fermées,
Moi, j'ai fait *Émaux et Camées*.[30]

[PREFACE

During the wars of the Empire,
Goethe, at the sound of the brutal canon,
Made the Western Divan,
A fresh oasis where art alone breathes.

Leaving Shakespeare for Nezāmi,
He perfumed himself with sandalwood,
And on an oriental metre
Noted down the song of the sighing Hudhud.

Like Goethe, who on his divan
In Weimar isolated himself from things
And plucked the roses of Hāfez,

Ignoring the hurricane
That lashed at my closed window (*vitres*),
I made *Émaux et Camées*.]

The poem's portrayal of the poet sitting behind a window and its references to Oriental poetry suggest that Gautier had in mind his former mentor's poem 'Novembre'. Yet, in contrast to Hugo's concluding poem, in which we found a composite Orient that combined different regions and historical eras, in Gautier's 'Préface', the Orient means only one thing: medieval Persian literature. In the space of only fourteen lines, we find references to four different authors. The poem names the poets Nezāmi, whose *Eskandar Nāmeh* (*Book of Alexander*) had been partially published in French translation in 1829, and Hāfez, but it also makes indirect allusions to two further poets. In the second stanza, Gautier refers to the 'Hudhud' (hoopoe), who is the lead character of ʿAttār's mystical epic poem *The Conference of the Birds*. Since the first French translation of *The Conference of the Birds* was only published in 1863, Gautier could only have learned about this work through his personal acquaintance with Persianists.[31] The reference to the hoopoe would therefore have signalled what was then a 'cutting edge' familiarity with the Persian literary canon. Finally, the poem's reference to 'plucking roses' is most likely in reference to the *Golestān*. Gautier's use of the verb *effeuiller*, which in nineteenth-century French can mean either to pluck a plant or to leaf through a book (as in *feuilleter* in modern French), indeed replicates the original pun in Saʿdi's text, in which the author instructs his friend to take a leaf (*vargh*) out of his book, since unlike the rose, it will outlast the seasons. This is in fact the same passage from which the epigraph of Hugo's 'Novembre' is taken. By only referring to the passage indirectly through a play on words, Gautier simultaneously situates himself in the wake of *Les Orientales* and also differentiates his approach from that of Hugo.

Where Gautier most explicitly sets himself apart from Hugo is in his treatment of the relationship between poetry and the outside world. In 'Novembre', the sight of Paris outside the window overpowers and 'aborts' the poet's imaginary journey to the Orient, but in 'Préface' the poet resists the outside world by focusing his attention on composing poetry. That this is a deliberate choice to exercise the poet's agency is conveyed by Gautier's image of the storm beating on the window, which significantly ups the ante on the mist silently pressing against Hugo's window. The poet's agency is further highlighted through the verbs *quitter* and *s'isoler*, which describe his choice to withdraw, and the verb *faire*, used in the parallel 'Goethe […] Fit le *Divan occidental*' / 'Moi, j'ai fait *Émaux et Camées*', which shows the poet crafting his own alternative space. The alternative world offered by poetry, in particular, Goethe's *West-östlicher Divan*, which is metaphorized as a *locus amoenus* ('Fraîche oasis où l'art respire'), is portrayed as the very opposite of the turmoil of the Napoleonic wars and of the Second Republic. While Europe is characterized by violence and noise ('bruit'), Persian poetry is associated with tranquillity and music ('le chant'). The opposition between the world of poetry and that of politics is thus bolstered by poetry's association with Persia, which creates a geographic distancing between the two contexts. Moreover, it also implies that European poetry was no longer able to provide a refuge. This is most strongly suggested in the fifth line, in which Goethe's creative process is defined as that of abandoning a European author (Shakespeare) in favour of a Persian author (Nezāmi). This is a particularly loaded image, both in light of Gautier's literary career and in the context of the Persian poetic canon.

Gautier had entered the world of letters as an ardent supporter of Victor Hugo, who had famously proclaimed Shakespeare as a role model for the French Romantic movement.[32] Gautier even participated in the riot that broke out on the opening night of Hugo's play *Hernani*, where the Romantic supporters of a Shakespearian vision of theatre and the supporters of French Classical drama came to actual blows. 'Leaving Shakespeare for Nezāmi' is thus an indirect way of saying 'Leaving Hugo for Goethe'. On an ideological level, the verse is a declaration of independence from the Romantic movement's commitment to a literature that is both anti-Classical and political. On a personal level, it is a declaration of independence from Gautier's mentor, Hugo. The fact that Persian poetry remained a touchstone for Gautier, even when he was declaring a break from the author of *Les Orientales*, shows us that the Persian canon was no longer the preserve of the Romantics. What is striking about the choice of Nezāmi, however, is that it also goes against the commonly held view that Persian poetry for Gautier is a safe haven from the realities of life and in particular the horrors of war.[33] Epic poems such as Nezāmi's *Eskandar Nāmeh* in fact describe military conquests: 'Eskandar' is the Persian name for Alexander of Macedon – more on him in Chapter 2. By turning to Nezāmi specifically, the poet is therefore trading a contemporary 'guerre de l'Empire' for a historical 'guerre de l'Empire'. This, on Gautier's part, is clearly a deliberate choice. The lyric poets Hāfez and Rumi feature prominently in Goethe's collection and would therefore have been obvious references for describing the *Divan*'s aesthetics. By choosing instead to portray Goethe reading an epic poet in times of war, Gautier signals that there remains a connection between the private world of literary creation and the outside world of politics and, by extension, between medieval Persian literature and modern Europe. Indeed, Nezāmi plays the same role in the poem as the windowpane ('vitres'), which both separates the lyric I from what is happening outside, yet also connects him to it by allowing him to hear and observe.[34] Persian literature in 'Préface' is thus a form of escapism that allows its reader to ponder on his own life and times. By grounding his imaginary Orient in the act of reading, Gautier is thus able to admit to a relationship between the private world of the poet's imagination and the outside world. This, in turn, is what allows his day dream to live on in the face of a storm, in contrast to Hugo's fantasy, which breaks down for the very reason that it is incompatible with reality. Noailles's poems too present reading as the superior way to travel to the Orient, but they go even further: whereas Hugo travels through his imagination and Gautier through reading, Noailles's collection actually recounts a biographical journey to the Orient, specifically Istanbul (then Constantinople), in order to better dramatize how preferable reading Persian poetry is to travelling to the Orient 'in real life'.

The poem to which I have just alluded is Anna de Noailles's 'L'Occident', one of the most wry and original pieces in *Les Éblouissements* (1907). The collection, which Proust declared incomparable,[35] explores a female lyric I's dazzlement by various forms of beauty, from the spectacle of nature to the pleasures of reading Persian poetry. In 'L'Occident', Noailles lampoons French literature's fascination with the Orient through a tale of anticipation, disappointment and redirection. The poem opens on a day of departure, with the female lyric I overwhelmed with anticipation: 'ô voyage/ O divine aventure, appel des cieux lointains / Presser des soirs plus beaux, baiser d'autres matins' [o journey, / O divine adventure, calling from the distant skies / To press more beautiful evenings, to kiss other mornings].[36] As she sits on the train, the lyric I already imagines herself as a character from *Les Orientales*: 'Je suis […] / Une captive, ardente et languide sultane' [I am […] / A captive, a passionate and languid sultana], a vocabulary that consciously echoes the titles of Hugo's poems 'La Captive' and 'La Sultane favorite'. Once the train sets off, Noailles lists, through an anaphoric repetition of verbs in the infinitive, the pleasures to be experienced upon arrival, combining references to sight, touch, taste and smell with proper names: 'Eyoub', 'Koran', 'Yildiz', 'Buyukdéré'. This use of the infinitive is ambiguous since it collapses the distinction between anticipation and realization: are we reading a continuation of the lyric I's yearning for the destination or is this a description of what happens upon arrival? The increasingly specific references to places, activities and foods end up suggesting the latter: the lyric I has arrived in Istanbul and is as excited and enchanted as on the day of her departure. But this all comes to a screeching halt when, in an abrupt transition, the lyric I declares that she has not found any of the things that she was searching for. And now, her most ardent desire is for a new – or rather, old – destination: home. 'Partir, fuir, s'évader de ce lourd paradis / […] Et rentrer dans sa ville' [To leave, to flee, to escape this heavy paradise / […] And to return to one's city].[37]

'L'Occident' ends with a description of Paris, which utilizes the very same tropes that had been introduced in the description of Istanbul: anaphoric repetition of verbs in the infinitive, and the combination of references to the senses of sight, taste, smell and touch, with names of places.[38] We even find the metaphor of physical intimacy formerly employed to describe the day of departure: the lyric I wanted to 'presser des soirs plus beaux'; now it is Paris that she wants to 'Attirer dans ses bras, sur le cœur qui s'entr'ouvre' [To draw into one's arms, against one's half-open heart].[39] Crucially, these stylistic repetitions serve to express a contrast and not a similarity: whereas in Istanbul the lyric I bemoaned the absence of 'la volupté sans fin, sans bord' [Pleasure without end, without limit], in Paris she finds 'la volupté / Montant à tout instant de toute la cité' [the pleasure / Rising at every moment from the entire city].[40] This leads to the emphatic hemistich 'Repousser l'Orient' [to reject the Orient], which inverts the poem's central trope: the verb in the infinitive no longer expresses desire, but repulsion.[41] Instead of dreaming of the Orient, the lyric I tells her readers, one should celebrate the West and enjoy summers spent 'sur les routes françaises' [on French roads].[42] Given the savage wit with which Noailles pastiches the Orientalism of French poetry – and in particular of Hugo's *Orientales* – before finally declaring it vapid and praising Paris instead, it may come as a surprise to readers that her collection also contains effusive poems about imaginary journeys to Persia. What are we to make of this paradox?

Noailles's rejection of Istanbul and idealization of an Iran that she never visited seems the perfect illustration of Said's argument that the Orient of the imagination was 'a place preferable, for the European sensibility, to the real Orient'.[43] But there is more to Noailles's poem than this. First, 'L'Occident' is not so much a condemnation of Istanbul as a real place, as an exploration of the subjectivity of exoticism: the city struggles to live up to the lyric I's expectations because these are so absurdly high; Paris, in turn, is perceived as beautiful because it is approached with a defamiliarized gaze. Secondly, there is a biographical dimension to Noailles's celebration of France, which stems from her own identity as a cultural transplant: she was born in Paris to foreign parents (her mother was Greek and born in Istanbul, her father Romanian and born in Poland) and due to her 'meridional' appearance (dark eyes and jet black hair) she was frequently described as an Oriental woman.[44] 'L'Occident' is thus a vindication of Noailles's own French-ness, encapsulated by the poem's final word 'françaises', an adjective which has a homonymy with the noun *Française* (French woman). Noailles also implies that her origins do not prevent her from being Parisian through a subtle analogy between herself and the flora which have a pride of place in her description of Paris: both the 'vernis du Japon' [Japanese lacquer tree] and 'arbre de Judée' [tree of Judea] are placed in rhyming positions.[45] The author of the poem, like these plants, may have distant origins, but she has become part of the Parisian landscape. Noailles's mixed identity as a cultural transplant also provides a pertinent point of entry into her Persian poems.

Whereas in 'L'Occident' Noailles stakes a claim to French-ness and Parisian-ness, her Persian-themed poems are where she shores up her public perception as an exotic figure by situating herself alongside Saʿdi, Hāfez and Khayyām. If the world of Persian poetry was preferable to her mother's home city, it is partly because, as Said argues, it was a place visited only in the imagination. But Persian poetry played another important function: it allowed Noailles to make a statement about her aesthetics. Noailles's fantasy was grounded, like Gautier's, in an external reality: the literature and visual arts of Iran. Medieval Persian poetry resonated in particular with Noailles due to the similarities that she could identify between its dominant themes and those of her own writing: the imagery of the natural world, a subtle eroticism and the celebration of *ivresse* (drunkenness) as a state of mind. Noailles's Persia is therefore not so much an Other as an alter ego: it is the literary canon which – she suggests by association – best represents her own poetic identity. Gautier had moved in this direction by grounding his safe haven in Persian literature and using this to make a wider comment on the relationship between poetry and lived experience. But by presenting himself as a reader, he ultimately remained a detached spectator. Noailles's Persian poems, by contrast, when read in sequence, illustrate a process of assimilation, in which the lyric I goes from being a desiring spectator to an active participant.

The four Persian poems of *Les Éblouissements* are all written in quatrains, a formal allusion to the Persian *robāʿe*, which had become fashionable in fin de siècle France following the popularity of Edward Fitzgerald's *Rubaiyat of Omar Khayyam*.[46] By using quatrains as stanzas within longer poems rather than stand-alone poems (as is the case of the Persian *robāʿe*), Noailles however remains within the norms of French versification. In the poems 'Danseuse persane' [Persian dancer] and 'Paysage persan' [Persian landscape], which come early in the collection, Noailles's lyric I gazes longingly at Persian miniature art.[47] As she tells the 'Danseuse persane': 'J'étais faite aussi pour danser / Sur la tulipe et la jacinthe / Que vos pieds viennent caresser'.[48] [I too was made to dance / On the tulip and the hyacinth / That your feet come to caress.] In the final pair of Persian poems 'Le Jardin-qui-séduit-le-cœur' [The Garden-that-seduces-the-heart] and 'Rêverie persane' [Persian rêverie], which shall be my focus, Noailles's lyric I takes the plunge and imagines herself entering this idealized world.[49]

> Je l'ai lu dans un livre odorant, tendre et triste,
> Dont je sors pleine de langueur,
> Et maintenant je sais qu'on le voit, qu'il existe,
> Le Jardin-qui-séduit-le-cœur!
>
> Il s'étend vers Chirâz, au bas de la montagne
> Qui porte le nom de Sâdi.
> Mon âme, se peut-il que mon corps t'accompagne
> Et vole vers ce paradis?[50]

[I read it in a fragrant, tender, melancholy book,
Which I leave full of languor,
And now I know one can see it, it exists,
The Garden-that-seduces-the-heart!

It lies near Shiraz, at the foot of the mountain
Which bears the name of Sa'di.
My soul, might my body accompany you
And fly to this paradise?]

The two opening stanzas of 'Le Jardin-qui-séduit-le-cœur' refer to two types of travel: the imaginary journey of the 'soul' made possible by reading – specifically reading Sa'di, given that his book title *Golestān* means 'rose garden' – and physical travel. The lyric I's dream is for these two journeys to become one, so that she might experience in the flesh the world contained in her books: 'Ah! rencontrer Sâdi, Hafiz et l'astronome, [...] Les suivre, quand ils vont d'un pas noble et qui rêve' [Ah! to meet Sa'di, Hāfez and the astronomer, [...] To follow as they walk, their step noble and dreaming].⁵¹ The poem relies on the same trope that had been used in 'L'Occident', that is, the anaphoric repetition of verbs in the infinitive to express a desired destination. The difference here is that this desire will never be disappointed because it cannot be enacted. Not only can Noailles not travel back in time, but S'adi, Hāfez and Khayyām (the astronomer) were not even contemporaries. And yet, the poem insists that the place that it describes truly 'exists'. So what does the poet mean by this?

Noailles's Shiraz is best understood not as a city, but as an allegory for the poet's experience of reading. We might compare it for instance to Canto IV of Dante's *Inferno*, in which Dante, the first-person protagonist, walks behind Virgil, Homer, Lucan, Ovid and Horace, just as Noailles imagines herself walking behind Sa'di, Khayyām and Hāfez. These scenes serve to convey a literary lineage, by rendering literal the metaphor that the lyric I follows in the footsteps of other great writers, thereby implying that s/he is their worthy successor. Indeed, just as Dante strives to assert his worthiness to inherit and reinvent the classics, so too does Noailles strive to portray herself as a natural successor to the medieval Persian poets. This becomes all the more clear in the poem 'Rêverie persane', in which the literary journey to Persia is presented both as a journey to heaven and as a home coming:

O Mort, s'il faut qu'un jour ta flèche me transperce,
Si je dois m'endormir entre tes bras pesants,
Laisse-moi m'éveiller dans l'empire de Perse,
Radieuse, éblouie, et n'ayant que quinze ans.

Alors, je connaîtrai, moi qui rêvais tant d'elle,
Ispahan, feu d'azur, fruit d'or, charme des yeux!
Les jardins de Chirâz et la tombe immortelle
Où Sâdi refleurit en pétales joyeux.⁵²

[O Death, if your arrow must one day pierce me,
If I must fall asleep in your heavy arms,
Let me awake in the empire of Persia,
Radiant, dazzled, and only fifteen years old.

Then, I shall know, I who dreamed of her so long,
Esfahan, fire of blue, fruit of gold, charm of the eyes!
The gardens of Shiraz and the immortal tomb
Of Sadi, who flowers again in joyous petals.]

'Rêverie persane' combines, as Hugo's 'Novembre' had done, the desire for time-travel (returning to one's own youth) with that of geographical travel. But whereas the Orient of *Les Orientales* was a composite ranging from Spain to India, Noailles's paradise is grounded in the architecture, arts and crafts, miniature art and literature of Iran. Indeed, the opening stanza refers to the blue-and-gold tile-work adorning the city of Esfahan and the gardens of Shiraz, where the mausoleums of Sa'di and Hāfez are located. The shrine of Fatima in Qom also features prominently in the poem. Noailles never visited these places, but verbal descriptions and illustrations (including drawings, etchings and photographs) were available to her in the numerous travelogues published over the course of the nineteenth century, one of which was by her own cousin Marthe Bibesco (see Chapter 3). The lyric I's reverie is also, as it had been in 'Le Jardin', rooted in the Persian poetic canon: the image of Sa'di being born again through the flowers on his grave combines Sa'di's own wordplay that his *Golestān* (rose garden) will outlive the roses of the natural world with the conceit that roses rise from the dust of the dead, a recurring theme in the quatrains of Omar Khayyām. Finally, the poem also refers to Persian decorative objects, specifically carpets, enamelware and an illustrated box. Such examples of Iranian arts and crafts had become widely popular among the Parisian elite following the Paris World Fairs of 1878 and 1889, in which they were both exhibited and available for sale.[53] Noailles was thus constructing her daydream by drawing together a variety of sources available to her in Paris. This, of course, is a highly selective version of Iran: Noailles's Persian paradise does not include any of the elements that those who travelled to Iran criticized in their publications, such as rough roads, overcrowded caravanserais, architecture in disrepair, or self-flagellation rituals. But while this selective account is certainly skewed towards idealization, it is based on Iranian cultural artefacts. As such, it would be inexact to dismiss Noailles's image of Persia as pure fabrication; it is, rather, a case of appropriation and embellishment. Moreover, unlike Hugo's *Orientales*, where Persian epigraphs were used to introduce poems that referred to Ottoman rulers and Egyptian pyramids, Noailles takes particular care to make her fantasy unadulteratedly Persian, foregrounding the cultural specificity of Iran. We have therefore come a long way from the jumbled Orientalism of the first decades of the nineteenth century.

When read in sequence, Noailles's 'Le Jardin-qui-séduit-le-cœur' and 'Rêverie persane' present us with a grammatical evolution from a longing – and to a certain extent uncertain – infinitive to an assertive future tense. This serves to foreground the lyric I's rather different attitude in the two poems: whereas in the former it is she who spots and follows a set of Persian characters, in the latter, it is the Persian locals who approach the lyric I.

> Je verrai s'avancer, curieux, familiers,
> De beaux garçons persans en bonnets de fourrure,
> […]
> Ils me diront avec des gestes et des poses,
> Des accents étonnés et des regards d'enfants:
> "C'est vous, sœur de nos cœurs, vous, l'amante des roses
> Le souffle du matin et des soirs étouffants!"[54]

> [And I will see coming forward, curious, familiar,
> Handsome Persian boys in fur hats,
> […]
> They will say to me with gestures and poses
> Surprised voices and child-like gazes:
> "It's you, sister of our hearts, you, lover of roses
> Breath of the morning and of the oppressive evenings!]

The lyric I is an outsider to this world, and yet, it is as though she has been there before. She is instantly identified as a kindred spirit by the local boys who, depending on how we read the poem are either curious-looking or curious about her, or both. Their reference to her as a 'lover of roses' can equally be read in more than one way: the epithet emphasizes not only the speaker's delicate sensitivity, but it might also be a reference to her love of Persian literature, since the rose functions as a metonymy for works such as Sa'di's *Golestān*. The lyric I is a foreigner in this Persian paradise and yet, despite this, she belongs. This is brought across most vividly in the poem's seventh stanza, in which the Persian boys invite the speaker to pray alongside them, even though she does not share their religion: 'Vous direz chaque soir vos prières païennes / Dans la mosquée ardente où dort sainte Fatmé' [Every night you will say your pagan prayers / In the blazing mosque where Saint Fatemeh sleeps].[55] The poem, however, soon collapses the cultural distinction between the lyric I and her imaginary friends. Noailles relies here, as she had done in 'L'Occident', on a symbolically charged reference to flora:

> Je verrai scintiller, dans la nuit sans égale,
> Sur ce terrain d'amour aux rosiers si clément,
> La rose du Calife et celle du Bengale,
> Et mes tendres rosiers des soirs du lac Léman.

> [I will see gleaming, in the incomparable night,
> In this land of love that carries such clement rosebushes,
> The rose of the Calif and of Bengal,
> And my sweet rosebushes from the evenings on Lake Geneva.]

Whereas in Hugo's 'Novembre' childhood memories eventually displaced the Oriental daydream, here the two worlds are fully integrated, as Noailles uses the rose as a connecting point between the imagery of Persian poetry and the landscapes that she encountered during her childhood holidays in Switzerland.

The line between Persian art and Noailles's life is rapidly disappearing and indeed, by the end of the poem, Noailles's poetic persona has become so fully assimilated into this foreign yet familiar world that she now resembles a woman in a Persian miniature:

> Et pensive, j'aurai la paix douce et narquoise
> Des dames que l'on voit ouvrir un si bel œil
> Sur une vieille boîte en pâte de turquoise
> Qui parfume et verdit comme un divin tilleul…[56]

> [And pensive, I will have the sweet and knowing peace
> Of those ladies who open their beautiful eyes
> On an old box made of turquoise paste
> Which perfumes and turns green like a divine lime tree…]

The ending of 'Rêverie persane' acts as a beautifully circular *clin d'œil* to the collection's first Persian poem, 'Danseuse persane', in which becoming a character in a Persian miniature painting had been an unreachable goal. Noailles, moreover, not only compares herself to a picture on a box, but in turn compares this box to a lime tree. This further collapses the lines of demarcation between Persian art, the lyric I and the natural world, recalling the use of natural imagery in Persian poetry, in which plants are typically shorthands for parts of the beloved's appearance (tulip for cheek, narcissus for eye, cypress for stature, etc.). It also confirms that the Persia of Noailles's poems is not a geographic location, but a place that can only be accessed through the imagination, by immersing oneself in the art and poetry of Iran. Yet, it is precisely because Persia is not a lived experience that it is so rich in potentiality. *Éblouie* (dazzled) by a world that she has never visited except in her imagination, Noailles is able to describe herself in the same idealized manner that she describes Persia. Unmarred by the vicissitudes of everyday life and the literary institutions of her day, the art and literature of Iran provided Noailles with a context in which she could define her poetic identity on her own terms. This was the place where she could pronounce herself: 'Petite fille avec des âmes anciennes, / Amoureuse des dieux et du monde enflammé' [Young girl with old souls, / Lover of the gods and of the blazing world].[57]

Publishing their collections in 1829, 1852 and 1907, respectively, Hugo, Gautier and Noailles all instrumentalize Persian poetry to present their lyric I, and by extension themselves, in a certain light. Hugo's Persian epigraphs served to bolster the exotic allure of *Les Orientales* and helped him take a stand against French Classicism's nationalist vision of literature. Hugo is not so much interested in Iran specifically as he is invested in an Orient that could stand for everything that France was not. It was a world not just imagined as free, colourful and sensual, but also dangerous. As such, it followed many of the tropes described by Edward Said in *Orientalism*. *Les Orientales* ventriloquizes many different Oriental characters, but in the end, the lyric I admits that these are all just day dreams, condemned to disappear before the sight of a grey November day. In this context, Saʻdi and Hāfez provide something that is more durable: Oriental words of wisdom that live on, even when the French poet's imagination fails. Gautier and Noailles, in contrast, demonstrate the French literary scene's growing familiarity with Persian poetry in the second half of the nineteenth century. With both these poets, there is a sense that Persia is a class apart from the rest of the Orient. And, unlike Hugo's violent and restless Orient, Gautier and Noailles's idealized Persia provides peace and sanctuary. Persian literature is also far more intimately connected to these author's poetic identity than it was for Hugo. Persian poets such as Nezāmi allowed Gautier to distance himself from both the French Classicists and Romantics and to express a more flexible and indirect connection between poetry, fantasy and lived reality. The language and imagery of Persian poetry provided Noailles with an antecedent for her own exploration of the 'éblouissements' associated with the beauty of the natural world and female desire. This allowed her to situate herself in a noble lineage of delicate dreamers and wordsmiths. And yet, for all their differences, Noailles and Gautier remain heavily indebted to *Les Orientales*. Noailles plays with her authorial persona, making herself alternatively French, alternatively Oriental, in a manner not dissimilar to Hugo's use of multiple voices in *Les Orientales*. Her central theme of the imaginary voyage, though anchored on specific works of literature, is nonetheless a continuation of Hugo's Oriental day dreams. And Gautier may have claimed his poetic independence from Hugo, but in associating the Orient with a new style of poetry, he was repeating what his former mentor had done.

Persian literature offered all three poets an external point of reference from which to formulate their identity and position within French letters. None of them, however, took advantage of the innovative potential offered by Persian poetic forms, nor did they examine the different perspectives that Persian literature offered on such central themes as love and religion. One of the consequences of this is that their poems do not challenge the Occident/Orient binary: defined in opposition to France, Persia is the oasis that the poet visits to find reprieve from everyday life, before returning to Paris, their voice and style unchanged by their encounter with a different poetic culture. Contrary to Chételat's concerns about 'foreign influences', Hugo was mainly preoccupied with redefining French poetry within its own context: rather than imitating Oriental poetic traditions, he was questioning, breaking and remoulding France's existing traditions. Gautier, while seeking to extricate himself from the national context of the clash between Romantics and Classicists, was nonetheless defined by it. And although 'Préface' describes a turn towards Persian poetry, it does so through a poetic form that is quintessential of French Classicism: the sonnet. So too is Noailles's claim to Persian-ness expressed entirely through French alexandrines. So what happens when French poets take the next logical step and decide that in order to write about Persia, one must do so in a Persian style?

Persian poems made in France (Renaud, Lahor/Cazalis)

Among the titles published by the patron of the Parnassian movement Alphonse Lemerre, Armand Renaud's *Les Nuits persanes* (1870, re-issued 1895) and Henri Cazalis's

Les Quatrains d'Al-Ghazali (1896, re-issued 1907) are not the best remembered. This is because both collections are exercises in imitation that can only be appreciated if one has a basic familiarity with Persian poetry, something most French readers would today consider a rather big ask. The collections' limited endurance is however in itself telling, since it illustrates the degree to which Persian poetry was popular in fin de siècle Paris – enough for one same publisher's list to include two volumes of 'Persian poems made in France'. Renaud and Cazalis chose to imitate the two most classical genres of Persian lyric poetry, the ghazal and the quatrain (*robā'e*), respectively. They also engaged with the themes of earthly and divine love, which medieval Persian authors had famously explored from a Sufi perspective. At the same time, the collections were written in modern French and from a fin de siècle perspective of disillusionment and loss of religious faith. They are as much the product of the context in which they were written as they are of the Persian sources that inspired them. There was also a limit to the degree to which a nineteenth-century French poet could formally imitate medieval Persian poetry, since the two poetic traditions followed very different rules. Persian poetry has a strict prosody, which is based on a division between short and long syllables, which must be placed in a prescribed order.[58] French versification, in contrast, has no requirement in terms of shorter or longer syllables: its sole defining feature is rhyme, which can follow a number of different patterns.[59] Rhyme does not play such a prominent role in Persian poetry. A ghazal or a *robā'e* will use only one rhyme for an entire poem and, moreover, both forms include verses that do not need to rhyme at all: in a ghazal, after the opening rhyming couplet, only every second line is required to rhyme, the same goes for the *robā'e*, where the third line is not required to rhyme. At the time that Renaud and Cazalis were writing, French poetry was witnessing important innovations, such as the emergence of the prose poem and *vers libre*. Yet even in this context, it would have been unthinkable for a French poet to compose a verse poem in which only one single rhyme is used and, moreover, certain verses do not even rhyme at all. Conversely, it would be unthinkable for a Persian *robā'e* not to follow a strictly defined rhythmic pattern. These differences present an important challenge for anyone seeking to write across poetic cultures. Yet, the very difficulty of this enterprise is what makes Renaud and Cazalis's attempts all the more intriguing.

The preface of Armand Renaud's *Les Nuits persanes* opens with the words: 'Ce livre n'est fait pour parader devant aucune théorie littéraire.'[60] [This book is not made to be paraded before any literary theory.] Renaud is well aware of the fact that Persian poetry had been instrumentalized by his predecessors to serve their poetic manifestoes. He, by contrast, is interested in Persian poetry for its own sake. This is signalled by the academic tone of his preface, which even includes an *état présent* of French translations of Persian literature, something that one would typically encounter in a preface to a translation or indeed in an academic survey, such as Barbier de Meynard's *La Poésie en Perse*, rather than a French poetry collection.[61] In the collection's second edition, Renaud further added endnotes informing the reader of the specific Persian verses that had inspired his poems.[62] A similar strategy had been employed by Hugo in *Les Orientales*, which had included endnotes, as well as a preface and epigraphs. The difference is that Renaud's research informs his creative practice. As we shall see, all of the poems in *Les*

Nuits persanes borrow from the dominant forms, themes and imagery of the Persian poetic canon. In doing so, they showcase a range of approaches to poetic imitation. As well as demonstrating the author's erudition, Renaud's preface also serves to explain that the collection is organized teleologically according to subject matter, progressing from earthly love and other dissatisfactions encountered on earth (including war and intoxication) to divine love. This organization of individual lyric poems into an overarching narrative of spiritual development is something foreign to Persian poetry and is rather the product rather of nineteenth-century aesthetics, the most canonical example of this approach being Charles Baudelaire's sequencing of his poems in *Les Fleurs du Mal* (1857). Persian *divāns* are not organized thematically but alphabetically, with poems grouped according to the final letter of their rhyming verses. Moreover, the Persian ghazal as a form is characterized by fragmentation and ambivalence: its stanzas can shift between different speakers or situations, and when describing a beloved, the ghazal will typically use metaphorical terms which create an ambiguity as to whether the lyric I is speaking of a person, or God, or both in turn.[63] Persian lyric poetry is therefore structurally resistant to progress narratives, both in terms of the sequencing of the poems in a collection and, in the case of ghazals, in terms of the poems themselves. Although Renaud engages extensively with the themes of Persian poetry, the structure of his collection interprets these themes from a modern Western perspective. Renaud was an assiduous student of Persian poetry. But he was also a poet and as such, he sought ways to innovate upon this canon and to reformulate it in a manner that spoke to a nineteenth-century French audience. In doing so, he made it his own.

As we turn from Renaud's preface to the poems in the collection, we are met with another surprise: a page headed with the words 'Au nom de Dieu clément et miséricordieux' [In the name of God, the Most Gracious, the Most Merciful] (Figure 1.2), a French translation of the set phrase used by Muslims to invoke God. The words are followed by twelve verses penned by Renaud, which praise God for all of creation. By including this page, Renaud is overtly mimicking medieval Persian book culture, specifically the tradition of devoting the opening verses of any work to praising God.[64] Though certainly more concise, Renaud does accurately recreate the sentiment of gratitude that is typical of such introductions. Moreover, his choice to use the French word 'Dieu' rather than Allah is significant, since it establishes that while the collection will imitate Persian poetry, this will be done through the use of a familiar vocabulary.

The choice has political implications too: by using a familiar language to speak of God, the author places emphasis on Christianity and Islam's shared monotheism, rather than their differences.[65] Renaud wants his readers to get a taste of the religious character of Persian poetry without this being experienced as a source of otherness. Renaud's imitation, moreover, is respectful: it does not seek to exaggerate or parody Islamic texts. Indeed, if we return to the preface, there seems to have been a fear on Renaud's part that his collection might be judged as being too sympathetic towards Islam. Having enthused about Persian poetry for several pages, Renaud ends the preface by stating that he does not share the views represented in his collection. It is following these words of warning that the reader then encounters the words 'Au nom de Dieu clément et miséricordieux'. This warning may seem like a rather unnecessary precaution: would Renaud's readers really assume that enjoyment of Persian poetry

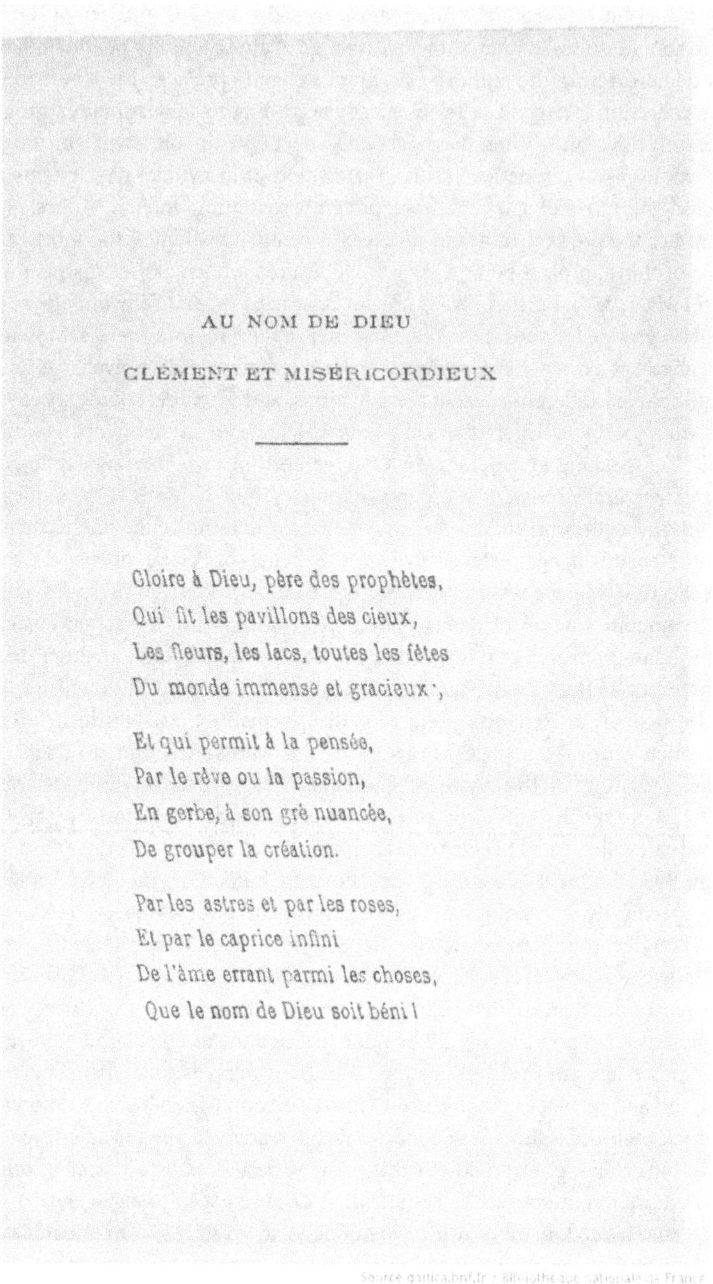

> AU NOM DE DIEU
>
> CLEMENT ET MISÉRICORDIEUX
>
> ---
>
> Gloire à Dieu, père des prophètes,
> Qui fit les pavillons des cieux,
> Les fleurs, les lacs, toutes les fêtes
> Du monde immense et gracieux ;
>
> Et qui permit à la pensée,
> Par le rêve ou la passion,
> En gerbe, à son gré nuancée,
> De grouper la création.
>
> Par les astres et par les roses,
> Et par le caprice infini
> De l'âme errant parmi les choses,
> Que le nom de Dieu soit béni !

Figure 1.2 Armand Renaud: 'In the name of God, the Most Gracious, the Most Merciful'.
Source: Armand Renaud's *Les Nuits persanes* (Paris: Lemerre, 1870): 13.

was tantamount to a conversion to Islam? After all, over fifty years had passed since the publication of Hugo's *Orientales*. It is likely that Renaud deemed the caveat necessary because of the way in which his collection fused French and Persian traditions into a coherent whole, something that had never been attempted before. The risk lay not in the Islamic underpinnings of Persian poetry, but in the familiarizing manner in which Renaud addressed these in his writing. *Les Nuits persanes* is not a pastiche, but a hybrid. It represents the coming together of the voices and concerns of two different worlds: medieval Iran and fin de siècle France.

The collection's most successful fusion of the two poetic traditions comes in the section entitled 'Gazals en N'. Renaud explains in a 'notice' that this portion of *Les Nuits persanes* is intended to read like a section in a Persian *divān*, in which poems are traditionally grouped by end-letter – hence the title 'Ghazals ending in N'.[66] Structurally, the poems are perfect ghazals: they all consist of couplets which have the opening two verses rhyming and then the rest of the poem rhyming every second line. They also end with a *takhalloz*, a Persian tradition in which the author reveals their name in the final couplet, as a way of signing off. And since Persian poets often had nicknames, for example Hāfez, which means 'the one who remembers', Renaud signs off with the chosen epithet 'Rêveur' (the Dreamer). The Persian ghazal has no set metre, and this is reflected by Renaud's use of several different metres in the section: the decasyllable, the octet and, rather more unusually, nine-syllable verses.[67] The choice to lay the poems out on the page as two-line stanzas was a bold one: even today, most European-language translators choose to render ghazal couplets as quatrains since these feel more natural to Western readers.[68] Moreover, as noted above, a verse poem half made up of verses that do not rhyme would have been considered a nonsense at the time that Renaud was writing, for, as Théodore de Banville argued one year after the publication of *Les Nuits persanes*, the single requirement of French verse is 'that it *always* end with a sound which *cannot exist* at the end of a verse unless it is repeated at the end of another or several other verses'.[69] Borrowing from translation theory, we can therefore describe Renaud's approach as foreignizing (as opposed to domesticating), since he does not seek to adapt the form to the conventions of the language in which he is writing.[70] But what about the content of these poems?

Renaud's first ghazal, 'Largesse', imitates a medieval Persian setting complete with a king and a vizier, characters typical of the world of Saʿdi's *Golestān*. But the poem is concerned with a contemporary issue: the devaluation of poetry as a consequence of the rise of the novel. Simply put: fiction sold more copies. Indeed, Renaud's own publisher, Alphonse Lemerre, had a monopoly on contemporary poetry precisely because no one else would touch it.[71] The status of poetry becomes the dominant theme of Renaud's ghazals, which soon drop their medieval Persian trappings. The section's concluding ghazal, 'Brouillard', best exemplifies how Renaud successfully adopted the poetic form favoured by Hāfez to reflect on the status of poetry in 1870 France:

BROUILLARD

L'inconnu troublait l'homme ancien;
Savoir tout ne paraît plus rien.

Autrefois s'étalaient les monstres;
Tout porte le masque du bien.

Plus de rêve triste; on préfère
Le joyeux et vide entretien.

Plus de misère! le génie
A les aumônes pour soutien.

D'avoir une émotion forte
La logique ôte le moyen.

O Rêveur, brise-moi ta lyre;
Le sphinx s'est fait plat comme un chien.[72]

[FOG

To the ancients the unknown was troubling;
Knowing it all now seems nothing.

Once upon a time there were monsters;
Now virtue can be worn like a mask.

No more melancholy dreams; it's
Vapid conversations people want.

No more misery! Genius
Can turn to charity for a living.

Having strong feelings is now
A thing of the past, thanks to logic.

O Dreamer, shatter your lyre;
The sphinx has turned as dull as a dog.]

The force of this ghazal comes from Renaud harnessing the form's two-line stanzas to express binary oppositions in a lapidary manner. The opposition is between the past, introduced in the first line with the adjective 'ancient' and described in the imperfect, and the present, described in the present indicative. This structure is however subverted in the final couplet, which contains the *takhalloz* and tells us that the poet might as well stop composing poetry, since the time of myth (embodied by the sphinx) has been replaced by the flatness of the time of banality (embodied by the dog). By breaking the alternation of imperfect and present with a final *passé composé*, Renaud communicates that this transformation is irrevocable. The vices that the ghazal denounces allow us to identify its intended target, which is the fin de siècle literary scene. The opening reference to a lack of mystery speaks to the replacement of religion with science in an increasingly secular age obsessed with progress, as perhaps most fantastically captured by Flaubert's satirical ekphrasis of an allegorical painting of Jesus driving a locomotive in *L'Éducation sentimentale* (1868). The rest of the poem continues in a similar vein, further condemning hypocrisy, superficiality and the commercialization of art. Although Renaud's ghazal is on occasion elliptic, its theme could not be more explicit: modern man lacks depth and seeks fulfilment in pecuniary gain; the loss of religion has made him lose sight of his inherent limitations; such a context is anathema to poetry. The poem invokes a lost golden age, but this age is never defined, although it has inklings of classical antiquity in its references to the lyre and the sphinx. The golden age could also be interpreted as that of Persian poetry, which is underpinned by religious faith and acknowledges both the transience of human life and the mystery of the divine. Another key feature of the Sufi perspective informing much of medieval Persian poetry is that it privileges love and passion over logic. This would tie in with Renaud's mourning of a time when being 'troubled' and experiencing 'strong emotions' was valued. For Gautier (and Goethe) Persian poetry had been a refuge from political unrest. For Renaud, it represents a prelapsarian literature, uncorrupted by the economic forces that governed the nineteenth-century French literary market.

Renaud's final 'Ghazal en N' also seems to make a broader statement about the poet's endeavour in *Les Nuits persanes*: having successfully written Persian ghazals in French, the poet concludes 'brise-moi ta lyre', suggesting that this kind of poetry has no place in the time in which he is living. And yet, the disillusioned condemnation of one's society is in no way contrary to Persian poetry. As well as the rich, sensuous and on occasion irreverent celebration of earthly love for which he is famous, Hāfez, the poet who brought the Persian ghazal to its apogee, also penned ghazals that commented bitterly on a political context that was unfavourable to poets. Ghazal n°169, translated by Dick Davis as 'I see no love in anyone', for example, describes the atmosphere in Shiraz after the political *coup* of 1353, which replaced King Abu Es'haq, who was a great patron of poets, with the religiously conservative warlord Mobarez al-din, who banned music and wine and was consequently nicknamed the Morals Officer (*mohtasebam eyb*). Far from being incompatible with artistic disillusionment, the Persian ghazal was already being used to comment on poetry's status in society. 'Brouillard' is therefore a poem that is both entirely consonant with the forms and themes of medieval Persian poetry *and* fully embedded in the literary context of 1870 France, which is the subject of its critique. In doing so, it reveals surprising commonalities between these two distinct poetic worlds.

Beyond Renaud's creation of French ghazals, *Les Nuit persanes* showcases a variety of other approaches to intertextuality. These range from a section entitled 'Gul et Bulbul' (the Rose and the Nightingale, both nouns are in Persian in reference to the phrase *gol o bolbol*), which is devoted to the common Persian literary theme of the nightingale's love for the rose, which was then gaining popularity in Europe – in English literature, it would inspire Oscar Wilde's 1888 short story 'The Nightingale and the Rose' – to a section entitled 'La Solitaire', in which Renaud takes the themes and images of the Persian love lyric, but inverts their perspective: instead of having a poet-lover address a silent beloved, Renaud has the beloved address the poet-lover.

In contrast to the rather sombre tone of some of the 'Ghazals en N' and the slightly derivative character of the section 'Gul et Bulbul', the poems in 'La Solitaire' playfully revisit the classic themes and tropes of Persian poetry and subvert them in a manner that one might call postmodern. Thus, in the poem 'Floraison', Renaud takes the common Persian metaphor of the lyric I being ensnared in his beloved's hair, but places it in the mouth of the beloved, which has the effect of presenting her in an active role: 'j'enchaînerai / De mes cheveux ce cœur farouche' [I will chain / This wild heart with my hair].[73] This switch in perspective may be tongue-in-cheek, but by questioning the gendered conventions of lyric poetry via a Persian context, Renaud is indirectly commenting on the gender politics of the French nineteenth century. Indeed, as late as 1870, French poetry remained a male field in which love poetry was typically written from a heterosexual male perspective, with women playing the role of idealized and silent muses.[74] In such a context the final two Renaud poems that I shall be discussing, 'Délire' and 'Floraison', are decisively provocative.

DÉLIRE

Le marchand de perles m'a dit:
Ton front veut-il une couronne?
Tout mon bazar qui resplendit,
Pour ta prunelle, je le donne.

Le marchand de roses reprit:
Laisse les perles chez l'orfèvre;
Tout mon royaume qui fleurit,
Je l'échange contre ta lèvre.

Le poète au rêve étoilé
Dit à son tour: vivante flamme,
De ton cœur donne-moi la clé,
Et dans mes chants je te proclame.

Mais que m'importe aucun trésor?
Je garde cœur, lèvre et prunelle
Pour quelqu'un n'ayant pas encor
Soupçonné ma plainte éternelle.

Perles, roses, vers, à mes yeux
Cela ne vaut pas un grain d'orge.
Du bien-aimé j'aimerais mieux
Que l'étrier broyât ma gorge.[75]

[RAPTURE

The pearl merchant said to me:
Would you like to wear a crown?

> I would give my sparkling bazaar,
> For your eyes.
>
> The rose merchant chimed in:
> Forget the jeweller's pearls;
> I would give my blooming kingdom,
> For your lips.
>
> The starry-eyed poet
> Said in turn: o living flame,
> Give me the key to your heart,
> And I shall sing your praises.
>
> But what do I care for their treasures?
> My heart, lips and eyes belong
> To someone who does not even
> Suspect my eternal plight.
>
> Pearls, roses, verses, to me
> Aren't worth a grain of wheat.
> I would much rather have
> My beloved's horse trample me to death.]

'Délire' centres on the trope made famous by Hāfez's 'Shirazi Turk' ghazal: exchanging material possessions for a part of the beloved's body. The difference here is that the lyric I is the one receiving the offers, rather than the one making them. By playing with the repetition of having three different men offer the lyric I everything they own, the poem implies that this has by now become a tired cliché. In narrative terms, the presence of three characters and the sense of escalation created by the offers becoming less and less material and more and more poetic leads the reader to anticipate that the speaker will accept the third – and presumably final – offer. What woman could resist being immortalized in verse? This, after all, is the central conceit of one of the French canon's most famous poems: Corneille's 'Stances à marquise' (1658). But the reader's expectation is subverted when the lyric I finds the poet's proposition just as unappealing as those of the merchants. This narrative twist serves to satirize the age-old tradition of self-important poets believing flattery will get them anywhere. At the same time, it also expresses a sentiment that is frequently encountered in Persian lyric poetry. The female speaker's rhetorical question 'Mais que m'importe aucun trésor?' is a line that could be lifted from Hāfez (see for instance Ghazal n°46). Moreover, the secrecy and masochism surrounding her affections (she would rather be trampled to death than be loved by someone else) are also typical attributes of the medieval Persian lover.[76] Ultimately, then, it is the female speaker who emerges as the poem's greatest lover, surpassing even the poet from the third stanza.

'Floraison' [In Bloom] is another poem that breaks gender norms, but does so in an even more provocative fashion in the context of nineteenth-century mores: it portrays a sexually satisfied woman who praises the joys of love with Hāfezian eloquence. The poem brings home the fact that the section 'La Solitaire' functions as a diptych with the section that precedes it in the volume, which is entitled 'Volupté' [Pleasure] and explores sexuality from a traditionally male perspective, suggesting for instance that a woman's most precious attribute is her virginity.[77] The final stanzas of 'Floraison', spoken by a female lyric I, directly respond to this type of sexism:

> Qu'on ne me parle plus du palais des rois,
> Du paradis aux fraîches ondes;
> Je peux boire la terre et le ciel au choix;
> L'amour m'a donné les deux mondes.
>
> Qu'on ne me parle plus de la Kaasbah,
> Où l'on baise la pierre noire.
> L'amour plus sûrement du ciel me tomba;
> A lui seul mon baiser veut croire.
>
> La rose blanche était le triste ornement
> De la vierge, aux langueurs en proie.
> Femme aimée, ôte-la; mets pour ton amant
> La rose rouge de la joie.[78]

> [Do not speak to me of the palaces of kings,
> Or of paradise and its fresh waters;
> I'll drink from earth and heaven as I please;
> Love has given me both worlds.
>
> Do not speak to me of the Ka'bah,
> Where one goes to kiss a black rock.
> Love far more certainly came from heaven;
> In love alone my kiss will believe.
>
> The white rose is the sad ornament
> Of the virgin, who lies languid and tormented.
> Woman in love, throw it away; and wear
> The red rose of joy.]

'Floraison' is Renaud's closest imitation of Hāfez's attitudes towards love in his *Ghazalyiat*. Within only two stanzas, we find the observation that requited love makes one greater than any king (Ghazal n°46); the statement that human love is both earthly and divine ('la terre et le ciel'), a recurring theme for Hāfez; and the provocative association of religious rite and eroticism (here kissing the Ka'bah and kissing one's beloved, an analogy made by Hāfez in Ghazal n°36, along with comparisons between the kiss of the beloved to the reviving breath of Christ, both in this ghazal and several others).[79] The key difference is that Renaud writes this poem from a female perspective.

In doing so he breaks the conventional portrayal of the lyric I as a male lover, which existed in both French and Persian poetry, as well as the more particular moral codes of nineteenth-century France, according to which sexual pleasure is an indecent thing for a woman to speak of – and perhaps even experience. Although Renaud would not have had the resources to be aware of this, it is also worth noting that this more flexible understanding of the gender and sexuality of the lyric I does in fact have a Persian antecedent: although this fact was hidden by translators, desire in Persian ghazals was often explicitly expressed towards male figures.[80] Moreover, there existed women poets in medieval Shiraz, most notably Jahan Malek Khatun, whose ghazals are now gaining a wider European readership through English translations and academic studies.[81]

Although the poems in 'Gazals en N' and 'La Solitaire' differ widely in versification, tone and perspective, they all find ways to engage with the medieval Persian lyric in a manner that resonates with contemporary concerns. This is because poetic imitation, for Renaud, does not amount to a narrowing down of scope or a distancing from his own context. On the contrary, it is through creative dialogue with medieval Persian sources that the fin de siècle poet was best able to comment on the status of poetry in his day. In doing so, Renaud sent his readers a subtle message: if it was possible for a genre of poetry belonging to a different time, place, language and religion to be relevant to a modern French audience, this was because there was already something within Persian poetry that could travel across time and place. The familiar can exist within the foreign. This creative approach eschews reductive Orientalist stereotypes and conjures instead a sense of similarity as defined by Bhatti and Kimmich: in other words, an interplay of differences and commonalities. Such a project would not have been possible were it not for the newfound availability of Persian literature in translation, a treasure trove of source material which Renaud could take in many different directions.

Armand Renaud's attempt to merge French and Persian poetic traditions was by far the most successful, but it was by no means the last. In 1896, the minor Parnassian poet Henri Cazalis published a collection entitled *Les Quatrains d'Al-Ghazali*, under the pseudonym Jean Lahor.[82] This collection too appeared with Alphonse Lemerre and was re-issued in a second edition that paired it with other pieces of 'Oriental' inspiration, specifically Cazalis's 'translations' of Khayyām and the Song of Songs,[83] just as Renaud's *Les Nuits persanes* were repackaged in 1895 alongside his *Idylles japonaises* and under the broader descriptor 'Orient'.[84] The parallels between the publishing histories of these two collections demonstrate how French imitations of Persian literature, for all their efforts to be anchored in a specific cultural context, continued to be marketed to readers under the wider category of things 'Oriental', in direct continuation of the exotic eclecticism that had defined Hugo's *Orientales*.

Henri Cazalis had shown an interest in Persian poetry in his previous collection *L'Illusion*, which had included a poem in honour of Hāfez. In *Les Quatrains d'Al-Ghazali*, he goes further, writing the entire collection in (he claims) the voice of the eleventh-century Iranian theologian Al-Ghazali, with whom he claims to have a great affinity:

Il a eu, *lui aussi,* la passion de la vérité; *lui aussi* à travers le monde, à travers toutes les écoles philosophiques, s'est mis à sa poursuite et ne l'a pas trouvée; *lui aussi* au sortir des religions, comme de ces écoles où il avait donc si longtemps et si vainement erré, il s'est contenté, pour vivre, de quelques lueurs çà et là entrevues, de quelques notions scientifiques et morales. […] Une phrase, rencontrée un jour, du philosophe Al-Ghazali m'étonna: *j'y retrouvais une partie de ma pensée; sa vie, quand je vins à la connaître, ressemblait à la mienne.* C'est ainsi que j'eus l'idée d'écrire ces quatrains sous son nom, *comme si j'étais un peu lui, ou qu'il eût été un peu moi.* (My emphasis.)⁸⁵

[*He too* had a passion for truth; *he too* pursued it, across the world, across all philosophical schools; *he too* leaving religions, as he did those schools in which he had thus erred in vain for such a long time, contented himself with a few glimmers glimpsed here and there, of a few scientific and moral notions. […] A sentence, encountered one day, by the philosopher Al-Ghazali surprised me: *I recognized within it a part of my own thought; his life, once I came to know it, resembled mine.* That is how I had the idea of writing these quatrains under his name, *as if I were a little him, or he were a little me.*] (My emphasis.)

The similarity between Cazalis and Al-Ghazali is emphasized not only through the use of verbs such as *ressembler* and *retrouver*, but also through the anaphoric repetition of *lui aussi* and the chiasmus in the final clause: Cazalis cannot decide whether it is he who resembles Al-Ghazali or Al-Ghazali who resembles him. The key parallel between the two authors is their existential angst, which Cazalis argues transcends the differences of history, geography and religion. Yet although the preface deploys the rhetoric of similarity, it also shrouds the collection in exoticism, referring to Cazalis's poems as 'parfums d'orient' [Oriental perfumes].⁸⁶ The exoticism of the collection is further emphasized by the author's choice to refer to God in his poems through the Arabic 'Allah', rather than the French 'Dieu', as was done by Renaud. Cazalis's sources, that is, Nicolas's translation of Khayyām's quatrains and the two available French translations of Al-Ghazali's treatise *al-Munqidh min al-Dalāl*, all translate the word God as 'Dieu'.⁸⁷ It is therefore clear that Cazalis deliberately chose to write 'Allah' in order to emphasize Al-Ghazali's religious and cultural difference from nineteenth-century French readers.

The collection consists entirely of quatrains, a formal choice that Cazalis justifies on the basis that Al-Ghazali and Khayyām were contemporaries and that the form therefore belongs to Al-Ghazali's cultural milieu.⁸⁸ Although it governs the logic of the entire collection, Cazalis's homage to the Persian quatrain does not go very far. As was noted earlier, the Persian *robā'e* follows an *aaba* rhyme structure. In contrast to Renaud's formal imitation of the ghazal, Cazali's quatrains all use French forms of versification (rhyming couplets, *rimes embrassées* and *rimes croisées*). The *robā'e*, moreover, is the only Persian poetic form to be strictly defined by its length: it is always formed of two couplets, in contrast to the ghazal, which is typically anywhere between five and seventeen couplets, and the *qasida* which is even longer. The required brevity of the *robā'e* gives it an axiomatic quality, which serves to showcase the poet's powers of synthesis. Indeed, the reason behind the popularity of Omar Khayyām, the author of Persian literature's most famous *Robāiyāt*, is his ability to pose existential questions within the space of only four lines. Cazalis, however, arranges his quatrains into clearly signposted sequences, which makes them read not as stand-alone poems but as stanzas within longer poems.[89] In other words, Cazalis signals the Persian *robā'e* without actually engaging in a formal imitation of it. His are not so much Persian quatrains, as French quatrains – in this regard, he follows the same process as Anna de Noailles.

The closest that Cazalis comes to emulating the *Robāiyāt* is in his quatrains that are not explicitly marked as belonging to a sequence and which emulate Khayyām's somewhat nihilistic emphasis on making the most of life on earth, since soon all that will be left of us is dust (in Persian *khāk*):

> Songes-tu, quand tes pieds marchent dans la poussière,
>   Qu'ils foulent bien souvent ce qui fut autrefois
> Les yeux clairs d'une amante où riait la lumière,
>   Et la bouche fleurie où tremblait une voix?[90]

> [Do you consider, that when your feet walk the earth,
>   They often step over what once was
> The bright eyes of a lover, in which the light played,
>   And the blossoming lips where trembled a voice?]

The same applies to the great kings of Persian legend whose mighty reign inevitably ends with death:

> La brique faite un jour peut-être avec la cendre
>   D'Omar, de Feridoun ou du grand Alexandre,
> Servit à rebâtir des palais aux vivants,
>   Dont la cendre à son tour est dispersée aux vents.[91]

> [The brick moulded perhaps from the same ash
>   As Omar, Fereydun or the great Alexander,
> Served to build the palaces of the living,
>   Whose ashes are now in turn blowing in the wind.]

Both these examples offer convincing pastiches of Khayyām. However, in paying tribute to Khayyām's nihilism and scepticism,[92] these quatrains are completely at odds with the views of Al-Ghazali, who as a devout Muslim believed in an afterlife. Cazalis's attempt to weld these two authors together is inherently flawed because their religious perspectives are incompatible. Just because two authors lived in Iran in the medieval period does not mean that their writing styles and ideas are interchangeable. And yet this is by no means the most egregious of the collection's misrepresentations.

Henri Cazalis's source text and, according to the preface, motivation for writing the collection is Al-Ghazali's spiritual autobiography, *al-Munqidh min al-Dalāl*. In this work, the theologian compares the various religious and philosophical schools that he studied during his lifetime, before concluding that truth can only be found within Islam. Cazalis takes inspiration from Al-Ghazalis's narrative of an epistemological search, but rewrites its outcome. The speaker of *Les Quatrains d'Al-Ghazali* doubts and ultimately renounces Islam in favour of a syncretism composed of non-monotheistic religions. The loss of faith experienced by Cazalis's fictional Al-Ghazali is dramatized in the section 'Le Doute', where we find verses such as 'J'avais la foi jadis et n'ai plus que le doute' [I once had faith, now all I have is doubt],[93] and a positing of science as an alternative to religion: 'La Science guérit des vanités humaines, / Et le repos par Elle est quelquefois rendu' [Science can cure human vanity, / And sometimes, She can put the mind at rest].[94] These views are a far cry from Al-Ghazali and the Islamic theologians who followed him, who were all driven by their faith in God and did not consider scientific inquiry to be incompatible with their religious faith, a notion that was in great part a nineteenth-century French fabrication, propounded by scholars such as Ernest Renan (see Chapter 2). At best, the quatrains in 'Le Doute' might be viewed as reminiscent of Khayyām, who was known for his scepticism and religious irreverence. But even Cazalis's enthusiasm for Khayyām fails to explain the reasoning behind the collection's final section ('La Pitié du renoncement'), in which the fictional Al-Ghazali turns to Buddhism: 'Bouddha, maître sublime, ô le plus saint des maîtres, / Fais-moi riche de ta sagesse et de tes dons' [Buddha, sublime master, o most saintly of all masters, / Bestow upon me your wisdom and your gifts].[95] We also seem to have migrated to India, since the poems in this final section refer to figures such as the 'rajah'.[96] How could Cazalis justify rewriting so completely the life and beliefs of the man who was the very *raison d'être* for his collection?

The collection's references to science, Buddhism and India all stem from Cazalis's own personal interests: he worked as a doctor and devoted his spare time to studying the religions of India. Thus, while the preface presents the collection as giving new voice to Al-Ghazali through the medium of poetry, the poems in fact show little interest in Al-Ghazali's religion and culture, focusing instead on Cazalis's favourite topic: Indian spirituality as an antidote to the disillusions of modern life. This Orientalist eclecticism may at first seem reminiscent of Hugo's *Orientales* – Islam or Buddhism, what does it matter, as long as the religion is exotic? But Cazalis's amalgamation of India and Iran also had academic underpinnings. By the fin de siècle, the racialist narrative of the 'Aryan' peoples (which will be analysed in Chapter 2) had become widely accepted and, concomitantly, scholars had become keen to explore the connections between the religions of India and the religions of Iran. Sylvestre de Sacy and Jules Mohl, in particular, had argued that Sufism, though Islamic by name, was in practice a form of Hinduism.[97] Cazalis's re-imagining of Al-Ghazali could therefore have been inspired by the academic argument that mystical Islam was itself syncretic.[98] Ultimately, though, I do not believe Cazalis was as interested in Al-Ghazali's writings as he was in borrowing the theologian's name. The phonetic proximity between Ghazali (pronounced with a French accent) and Cazalis would not have escaped the attention of a poet who had previously employed the Italian pseudonym 'Caselli'. The title *Les Quatrains d'Al-Ghazali* can thus be read as an elaborate pun on the name of Cazalis, who is ultimately acknowledged as the one speaking from behind the mask of the Islamic theologian. If we revisit the preface from this perspective, it yields a different meaning. The words 'comme si j'étais un peu lui, ou qu'il eût été un peu moi' are no longer an expression of intimacy, but a playful admission of guilt: Al-Ghazali is none other than Cazalis himself. It is however not entirely clear who was in on the joke: while Persian poetry gained in popularity, Islamic theology did not enjoy a wide non-academic readership. It is therefore unlikely that Cazalis's readers, unless they were personal friends, would have realized that the religious views expressed in the poems were not those of a medieval Islamic theologian, but of a contemporary French poet and physician.

Whereas the authors explored in the previous section characterized Persian poetry in terms of its distance from the French literary sphere, Renaud and Cazalis asserted its proximity, but did so in very different ways. Renaud demonstrated that the structures and themes of Persian poetry could be applied to contemporary French concerns. His approach to familiarization embodies the more nuanced and flexible understanding of similarity advocated by Bhatti and Kimmich. Renaud acknowledges and explores the formal and religious differences between French and Persian poetry, while also homing in on common features, such as the predicament of the poet in a society that has grown unresponsive to his art and the conventions of the love lyric. In doing so, Renaud was not afraid to question French lyric traditions, such as the gendered trope of the male poetic voice and female muse. Cazalis's operation is altogether different in both method and intention. His aim in asserting the profound similarities between himself and Al-Ghazali is not to familiarize readers with the Islamic theologian, but rather to exoticize himself as Al-Ghazali's modern alter ego. This also serves to invest his personal brand of religious syncretism with greater authority by identifying a respectable precursor for it. The problem, of course, is that there is nothing syncretic about Al-Ghazali's *Munqid*, since its entire purpose was to exalt Islam above all other faiths and philosophies. This leads to the greatest contradiction of all: poems that present the founding father of Islamic law, theology and philosophy as a non-Muslim. Neither Todorov's nor Bhatti and Kimmich's paradigms can be applied to Cazalis, for he does not, as he claims, find parallels between himself and Al-Ghazali. Rather, he rewrites Al-Ghazali's identity so that the mask may fit him.

The eccentric case of Cazalis seems an apt illustration of Edward Said's argument that Western depictions of the Orient are not so much 'inaccurate' as 'not even trying to be accurate'.[99] But there is also more at play here than in the naive exoticism with which Victor Hugo had declared allegiance to all things Oriental over half a century earlier. By the fin de siècle, it had become common practice among French scholars to elevate Iran above all other Middle Eastern nations by erasing its Islamic identity and emphasizing instead its 'Aryan' origins. Cazalis's choice to refer to Al-Ghazali not as an 'Islamic theologian' but as a 'Persian philosopher',[100] and to write poems in which he is sympathetic to the religions of India is therefore symptomatic of a wider tendency to make Iranian figures appear more sympathetic to Western audiences by divorcing them from their Islamic heritage. Persian in neither form nor content, Henri Cazalis's quatrains show us a version of Persian-ness that was marketable to readers as being Oriental without being 'too Muslim'. This erasure of Al-Ghazali's faith follows not the logic of similarity, but of assimilation. It ultimately suggests – ironically perhaps, for a work that had opened with such a strong emphasis on similarity – that 'Muslims and Europeans', to quote Ernest Renan, 'have nothing in common'.[101] *Les Quatrains d'Al-Ghazali*, therefore, stands in stark opposition to Renaud's *Nuits persanes*, a collection that foregrounds Islam as an essential part of medieval Persian culture without viewing it as ontologically other, for, as Renaud's poetic experiments show, differences and commonalities will feature in any encounter with another culture.

Intertextuality and universalism: The case of 'Les Roses de Saadi' (Desbordes-Valmore)

We have considered three poets for whom the world of Persian poetry marked an escape from their local literary contexts and two poets who sought to incorporate their own French fin de siècle context into poems borrowing from Persian versification and themes and, in Cazalis's case, the name of Iran's most influential theologian. Although their approaches differed, these poets were all drawn to the sense of innovation that was associated with looking outside of the Western canon, a sentiment that had been shared in the late eighteenth century by William Jones, when he made his case for greater efforts in translation. The final poem to be studied in this chapter is rather exceptional in that it closely engages with a Persian source text, but does not imitate Persian poetry formally and makes no reference to a Persian setting. Indeed, were it not for the title of Marceline Desbordes-Valmore's 'Les Roses de Saadi' (1860), readers would be hard-pushed to notice this poem has anything to do with Iran – unless, that is, they are intimately acquainted with the preface of the *Golestān*. By lifting Sa'di's meditations on human language from their original context and recasting his central metaphor through a modern secular perspective, Desbordes-Valmore removes any hint of cultural relativism and stresses instead the universalism of Persian poetry. Whereas Renaud's integration of Persian and French literature foregrounded elements of cultural difference, such as the Islamic faith, and was therefore illustrative of Bhatti and Kimmich's paradigm of similarity, Desbordes-Valmore's discarding of local markers in favour of those aspects of the *Golestān* that travelled easily across languages and cultural contexts is best understood in light of Todorov's study of the fraught relationship between universalism and relativism in modern French thought.

It is no coincidence that the author chosen by Desbordes-Valmore to make a case for the universality of Persian poetry is Sa'di. Sa'di's *Golestān* was the most translated, and thus most widely available, work of Persian literature in Europe at the time.[102] This was a consequence, first, of the book's cultural significance in the Muslim world, where it had enjoyed a great popularity for many centuries, but also of certain qualities within the work that made it eminently translatable. The majority of the *Golestān* is written in simple and clear prose, with short passages of verse inserted for stylistic effect. This made the text easier to understand and to translate for non-native speakers of Persian, since they did not have to contend with the ambiguities of lyric poetry, and, aside from the book's brief passages in verse, they were not presented with the challenges associated with rendering formal elements such as metre and rhyme. A further notable quality of Sa'di's work is his sense of humour and irreverence towards figures of authority. This made the *Golestān* far more accessible to non-Muslims than the mystical works of authors such as 'Attār or Rumi. Casimir Barbier de Meynard argued in his inaugural lecture as Chair of Persian at the Collège de France that of all Oriental poets, 'Saadi est peut-être le seul qui puisse être compris en Europe, le seul qui puisse y conserver en partie la popularité dont il jouit chez les lecteurs musulmans' [Saʿdi is perhaps the only one who could be understood in Europe, the only one who could maintain a part of the popularity that he enjoys among his Muslim readers].[103] Yet, for all his popularity and the immediacy of his writing, Saʿdi nonetheless remained strongly associated with the Persian, and more broadly Oriental, setting of his works. Translations of the *Golestān* appeared in volumes of 'Contes orientaux', which sought to capitalize on the success of Antoine Galland's *Mille et Une Nuits* [*Thousand and One Nights*].[104] Poets such as Victor Hugo and Anna de Noailles used Saʿdi's name to invoke an exotic world that modern French readers could only access through their imagination. Desbordes-Valmore's decision to dispel any sense of exoticism from her poem is therefore remarkable. What makes matters even more interesting is that she chose to apply this universalizing approach to what is arguably the most mystical passage of the *Golestān*. But before I go any further, let us take a look at the poem itself:

LES ROSES DE SAADI
J'ai voulu ce matin te rapporter des roses;
Mais j'en avais tant pris dans mes ceintures closes
Que les nœuds trop serrés n'ont pu les contenir.

Les nœuds ont éclaté. Les roses envolées
Dans le vent, à la mer s'en sont allées.
Elles ont suivi l'eau pour ne plus revenir;

La vague en a paru rouge et comme enflammée.
Ce soir, ma robe encore en est tout embaumée…
Respires-en sur moi l'odorant souvenir.[105]

[SAʿDI'S ROSES

This morning I wanted to bring you back some roses;
But I had gathered so many inside my closed belts
That the tightly fastened knots were not able to contain them.

The knots burst. The roses carried off
By the wind went away to sea.
They followed the water to no longer come back;

The wave seemed to turn red from them, almost ablaze.
This evening, my dress is still full of their perfume…
Breathe in from me their fragrant memory.]

As I have argued elsewhere, Desbordes-Valmore's poem is inspired by two passages from the preface to Saʿdi's *Golestān*, which she would likely have read in the 1834 translation by Sémelet.[106] In the first of these two passages, Saʿdi describes a sage in a state of spiritual ecstasy who is approached by a group of friends. The sage informs his friends that he was in a beautiful garden and had intended to bring roses back for them, but their perfume was so intoxicating that his robe slipped out of his hand and the roses were lost. Sa'di's story makes it clear to the reader that the 'beautiful garden' referred to by the sage is a metaphor for divine bliss. As a result, the sage's inability to carry the roses to his friends is clearly intelligible as a symbol for language's inability to carry, and thus transmit, spiritual experiences. Desbordes-Valmore, in contrast, embraces the brevity and ambiguity of lyric poetry and leaves the meaning of her roses open to interpretation. In doing so, she expands on Sa'di's symbolic comment on the insufficiency of human language to speak worthily of God, making the lost roses speak to language's broader inability to bridge the divide between self and other, and thus to truly convey one's subjective experiences, which is precisely how Desbordes-Valmore's poem has been interpreted by the critic and poet Yves Bonnefoy.[107] There is also an important difference in the story that Desbordes-Valmore tells with Sa'di's metaphor. Whereas in the *Golestān* the sage is immediately incapacitated by the perfume of the roses, thereby illustrating the broader claim that those who have experienced the divine cannot speak of it, Desbordes-Valmore's lyric I, by contrast, makes a valiant attempt to bring back the roses, even if the enterprise is doomed to failure. The fact that the lyric I persists until the skirts burst metaphorically suggests a pushing of language to the limits of its capacity. And though the poem for the most part describes a failure in so far as the roses are lost, Desbordes-Valmore's lyric I does manage to bring something back: the roses' perfume, which she is able to share with the poem's addressee, unlike Sa'di's sage who has nothing to offer his companions. Ultimately, then, the lyric I's enterprise was not to no avail.

'Les roses de Saadi' follows an optimistic movement, beginning with that which could not be brought back and ending on that which remains. The first two stanzas are framed by verbs with the prefix 're': *rapporter* and *revenir*. In the opening verse 'rapporter' outlines the lyric subject's intention. The poem then narrates the loss of the roses, ending on the verb 'revenir', which is given in the negative form and concludes the second stanza. The third stanza offers a solution to this problem through the poem's final word 'souvenir' (memory), which points back to 'revenir' with which it shares the infix *venir*, as well as its rhyming position. We learn that although the roses themselves, or, metaphorically, the experience itself, cannot be brought back, one may still share something of it. The sensuality of the adjective *odorant* (fragrant) in 'l'odorant souvenir', moreover, can be interpreted as an indication of the pleasure that can still be conveyed through language, and in particular poetry, despite its inability to exactly recreate an experience. In the absence of the roses, the sensuality of their perfume – in other words, of their description through language – is an entirely satisfactory experience in its own right.[108] The 'moi' of the final verse thus becomes pivotal in so far as it can be read as standing simultaneously for the physical body of the character who filled her dress with roses and for the voice of the poet, who through her artful manipulation of language has provided her reader with a literary experience as pleasurable as smelling roses.

Desbordes-Valmore's poem ultimately tells us that although poetic language is unable to bring back the past, it is nonetheless able to create something precious in its own right. The seeds of this solution to the problem of loss can be traced back to the *Golestān* itself. As previously mentioned, there are two references to collecting roses in Saʻdi's preface. After the story of the sage who could not communicate his mystic visions to his companions, Saʻdi tells another story, about a friend who began collecting roses and herbs in the skirts of his robe in order to take them back to the city. Noting that the rose is ephemeral, Saʻdi chastizes his friend (this is the line used by Hugo as the epigraph to 'Novembre') and suggests instead that he 'take a leaf out of my *Golestān*, / A rose lives five, six days at the most / But this *Golestān* will never fade'.[109] Having previously used the image of the rose to describe the insufficiency of human language and by extension poetry, Saʻdi now uses the same image to make the opposite point. The rose is no longer a source of analogy but of contrast, used to describe the longevity, and therefore superiority, of Saʻdi's roses (i.e. the pages of the *Golestān*) over the ephemeral roses of the natural world. The inventiveness of Desbordes-Valmore's poem lies in the fact that its nine verses reconcile Saʻdi's two conflicting parables. Acknowledging both the limitations of language and the longevity of literature, 'Les roses de Saadi' tells us that although poetry cannot completely preserve an original experience, it is nonetheless valuable both as a memory of an experience and as a source of pleasure in its own right. The idea that Desbordes-Valmore's poetry lives on through time, just as Saʻdi announces that his *Golestān* will do, is also carried across by the imperative mode in the verse's final line ('Respires-en'), which can be read as an authorial address to the reader. If the poet can still speak to readers after her death, this means that her written words are not destined to fade like roses, but to live on like Saʻdi's *Golestān*.

Desbordes-Valmore offers a subtle rewriting of Saʻdi, which hinges on one of the *Golestān*'s most universal images and themes, which are removed from the religious context in which they had originally been formulated. The ephemerality of all things, the pleasures and limits of the written word, and the attempt to use language to bridge the gaps that both time and subjectivity create between individuals, are neither French nor Iranian concerns: they are those of all humankind, and in particular of poets. There is no tension between difference and commonality in Desbordes-Valmore's poem because all markers of cultural difference have been removed. What is lost in the process is the historically and geographically situated dimension of the *Golestān*. Yet, Desbordes-Valmore does not seek to mould Saʻdi's imagery after her own cultural context either: aside from the fact that it is written in modern French, the poem bears no markers of Desbordes-Valmore's own context. Her approach to universalizing Saʻdi, therefore, cannot be defined as one of assimilation, in the manner that Henri Cazalis's had been in *Les Quatrains d'Al-Ghazali*. It is rather a process of opening up the signifying potential of the poem's central metaphor, so that it can work equally well in a medieval Iranian and in a modern French setting. This multivalence is most powerfully encapsulated by Desbordes-Valmore's use of the word 'robe', which can refer either to the robes worn by men in medieval times or to the dresses worn by women in the nineteenth century. Because the poem is written by a nineteenth-century woman, readers are far more likely to picture the latter, but this is due to our propensity towards biographical interpretation rather than any quality inherent to the text. Moreover, by avoiding the inclusion of any medieval, Islamic, or Iranian cultural markers in her poem, Desbordes-Valmore is focusing her readers' attention on the intellectual substance of Sa'di's writing, as opposed to its exotic provenance. In doing so, she was able not only to preserve the essence of Sa'di's reflections on language, but also to transmit them to a new audience. This is illustrated by Yves Bonnefoy's reading of 'Les Roses de Saadi', which grasps the metapoetic significance of the rose metaphor, without even knowing that it had first been formulated by Sa'di. This more subtle form of intertextual engagement has stood the test of time in a way that overt forms of cross-cultural poetic imitation have not: while Renaud and Cazalis's Persian poems are forgotten today, 'Les Roses de Saadi' remains one of the most famous poems of the French nineteenth century. Through the double mediation of translation and intertextuality, Sa'di's roses have entered the French canon.

Conclusion

Victor Hugo, Théophile Gautier and Anna de Noailles all associated Persian poetry with an imaginary Orient that was a haven from the disappointments of modern life in Europe. In doing so, they exhibit two key symptoms of Orientalism as defined by Edward Said: the binary opposition of Orient and Occident and the assumption that the Orient of the imagination is preferable to the real place. There is nonetheless a progression from the jumbled Orientalism of Hugo, where Persian poets are combined with a wide range of exotic figures and locations, in particular, the early nineteenth-century Ottoman Empire, and the cultural specificity of Gautier and Noailles's enthusiasm for things Persian. The literary and visual cultures of Iran grew in popularity over the course of the nineteenth century. As a result of this wider trend, 'Persia' became an increasingly specific and familiar signifier among the French, and in particular, Parisian, elite. The fact that Gautier and Noailles's Persian fantasies were based on the literature and arts of Iran is also of interest in so far as it tests Said's distinction between the Orient as a Western creation and the Orient as a real place. Cultural fantasies could be fuelled by cultural realities, and these realities could in turn be embellished. The line between the real and the imaginary Orient is therefore not as clear-cut as some of Said's rhetoric might suggest. The newfound availability of Persian literature in translation, longed for by William Jones in the late eighteenth century and alluded to by Hugo in the preface to *Les Orientales*, allowed for an intertextual engagement with Iranian culture which resulted in a more fluid understanding of the cultural divide between Orient and Occident. Hugo chooses an elegiac line from Sa'di as his epigraph for 'Novembre' because it shares the feeling of loss described in the poem. And, by including epigraphs from Hāfez and Sa'di alongside epigraphs from canonical Western authors such as Shakespeare and Virgil, he also implies that they all have a place within one same library. In doing so, the collection foreshadows Sainte-Beuve's famous essay 'Qu'est-ce qu'un classique?' [What is a classic?] published twenty years later, in which the critic argued that his ideal library included Ferdowsi and Valmiki alongside Homer.[110] Gautier, in turn, by depicting Goethe reading not the lyric poet Hāfez, but the epic poet Nezāmi, suggests a subtle parallel between Napoleon's recent invasion of Germany and Alexander the Great's far more distant invasion of

Persia, which was the subject of Nezāmi's *Eskandar Nāmeh*. Noailles's collection *Les Éblouissements*, finally, presents the author's highly biographical lyric I as being both French and Oriental, a woman who writes in alexandrines yet also follows in the footsteps of the great Persian poets. For all three then, Persian literature is as much a form of escapism as it is a mirror for their own poetic concerns.

The distinction between the world of medieval Persian poetry and that of nineteenth-century French poetry collapses further in the work of our two fin de siècle poets, Henri Cazalis and Armand Renaud, who wanted their poems to be identifiably Persian. They achieved this by employing Persian forms such as the *ghazal* and the *robā'e* and by exploring the themes associated with the Persian lyric, in particular, erotic and mystical desire. As I have shown, although Cazalis claimed to be inspired by the profound similarities between Al-Ghazali's spiritual autobiography and his own experiences of religion, the collection's engagement with its Persian sources is overall superficial. The quatrains all follow French versification. Moreover, Cazalis is mainly preoccupied with the promotion of his personal brand of religious syncretism, which leads him to reject Islam in a work dedicated to one of Islam's most important theologians. Renaud, in contrast, took far greater formal risks by following the structure and rhyme scheme of the Persian ghazal. He also did not shy away from framing his poems in an Islamic context and did so from the collection's very opening page, which mimics the Persian book convention of praising God at the beginning of a new work. But Renaud did not limit himself to imitation: he also used Persian forms and images to write about the condition of the poet in fin de siècle France. By combining elements from both French and Persian poetry, and openly showing the differences as well as the commonalities between these two traditions, Renaud follows the ambivalent logic of cross-cultural similarity, as described by Bhatti and Kimmich.

Our final poet Marceline Desbordes-Valmore also managed to produce poetry that was indebted to both literary cultures, but her approach is altogether different to that taken by Renaud. Whereas *Les Nuits persanes* includes elements of cultural difference, such as religion and poetic form, Desbordes-Valmore's 'Les Roses de Saadi' extricates Sa'di's rose metaphor from its culturally specific setting, making it more open to interpretation and consequently readable within a nineteenth-century French setting. Desbordes-Valmore's attentive rewriting of Sa'di both preserves the metaphoric content of the text (i.e. the powers and limits of language and the perishability of human experience) and removes all traces of its Persian origins. In doing so, it makes a universalist statement. In this poem, it matters little whether the 'robe' carrying the roses is a medieval robe or a modern dress; what matters is the question that this image poses about language. That being said, Renaud and Desbordes-Valmore do also have much in common, namely, a keen sensitivity to the Persian poetry that they read in translation, which led them to focus not on its exoticism, but on what it says and how it says it. These two French authors also have a strong poetic voice, which makes itself heard even when they are borrowing the words or images of others. Poems such as 'Délire' and 'Les Roses de Saadi' bear the mark of their author's individuality and as a result do not read as imitations, but as original poems in their own right.

As a genre, lyric poetry allows for a multiplicity of approaches to writing Iran. Intertextuality plays a central role in this. The precedent set by the Persian poets could be acknowledged in the paratext (preface, titles, endnotes) or it could be signalled through the imitation of a formal structure, such as the ghazal, or of a recognized trope, such as giving up material goods or even one's faith in exchange for the good graces of the beloved. Persian poetry could also be engaged with in more subtle ways, for instance, by borrowing a central theme or idea, but presenting it in a new context. Poets have always defined themselves in relation to those who came before them, as is foregrounded in Noailles's poem 'Le Jardin-qui-séduit-le-cœur', where she imagines herself walking behind Ḥāfez, Saʿdi and Khayyām. What is unique to the nineteenth century is that for the first time French poets are attempting to walk in the footsteps of non-European authors. Chételat's anxiety of influence before Hugo's *Orientales* is not based on an Oedipal rivalry,[111] but on a fear of cultural contamination: if one accepts as he does that the Orient is by definition barbaric, then Persian literature can only have a deleterious effect on French literature. While Chételat's imperialist and eurocentric belief in the inferiority of Middle Eastern peoples is absurd, there is one sense in which he was right to be afraid: the availability of Persian literature in translation made it far more difficult to uphold an ontological opposition between France and Iran and thus, by extension, Europe and the Middle East. Intertextuality undermines any clear-cut separation between different authors and their respective literary cultures. In comparison to prose, lyric poetry has an even greater potential to blur the lines of cultural demarcation because it is polysemic, which makes it easy for one word to hold several meanings – including the first-person pronoun. Indeed, when Desbordes-Valmore and Renaud write 'Je', this 'Je' is both their own lyric subject and an echo of the lyric subject of Saʿdi's *Golestān* and of Ḥāfez's *Ghazalyyāt*. Whereas Edward Said's account of 'strategic location' revolves around identities that are both fixed and separate, with the first-person belonging to the Western subject and the third person being used to describe and thus other Oriental subjects,[112] the poems studied here present us instead with a sense of alignment and identification between the lyric subjects of nineteenth-century French poetry and the lyric subjects of medieval Persian poetry. They also demonstrate how multifaceted French authors' relationship to Iranian culture was, since the poems covered here include many examples of exoticization as well as identification. As such, these poems offer a valuable introduction to the complex and ambivalent terrain that is French writing on Iran.

2

History and historical fiction

Rewriting human history

It all began with a translation from Persian into French. Published in 1771, Abraham Hyacinthe Anquetil-Duperron's *Zend Avesta, ouvrage de Zoroastre* was a translation by relay of Zoroastrian liturgy, originally composed in the ancient Avestan language.[1] Its publication was a watershed moment in European intellectual history: this was the first time that the reading public could consult an ancient text that bore no relationship to classical Europe or the history of Christianity. The lives and cultures of the people of ancient Asia – and, in particular, ancient Iran where Zoroastrianism originated – could now be approached through the texts that they had held sacred, rather than the sparse and often biased claims made by Greek authors. It is in this event, combined with William Jones's development of a method for learning Sanskrit,[2] that Raymond Schwab situates a major turning point in modern Europe's conceptualization of itself and its others: 'L'Occident s'apercevait, dans un âge avancé, qu'il n'était pas seul titulaire d'un admirable passé intellectuel.'[3] [At an advanced age, the West realized that it was not the only possessor of an admirable intellectual history.] This was the beginning of a vast body of research into ancient Asia that grew over the course of the nineteenth century. These findings trickled from academic circles to the wider French reading public, vastly altering their understanding of human diversity and of Europe's place in history. The traditional opposition between a civilized ancient Greece (and later Rome) and a barbaric Orient was no longer a given, since the people of Asia were now proven to have had their own moral codes, cultural practices and foundational myths. Not only that, but it was also becoming increasingly clear that these Asian civilizations long predated Western civilization, which seriously undermined the assumption that Europe was at a more advanced stage of development compared to the rest of the world. In the words of the great nineteenth-century historian Jules Michelet: 'Trente siècles de plus ajoutés à l'antiquité, […] plusieurs mondes oubliés qui reviennent juger celui-ci.'[4] [Thirty centuries added to antiquity, […] several forgotten worlds now returning to judge this one.] In Michelet's *La Bible de l'Humanité*, a key text in this chapter, Europe is not only dwarfed by the temporal and geographic weight of Asia, but it is also shown to be Asia's moral inferior.

In my introduction, I outlined the two competing views of human diversity that Tzvetan Todorov identifies as a constant in French thought, from the Renaissance to modernity: cultural relativism and universalism. The Oriental Renaissance, as accounted for by Raymond Schwab, shows strong affinities for both standpoints. On the one hand, the access gained to ancient Asian cultures via their sacred texts was a major victory for cultural relativism, since it proved that the world was made of countless different civilizations, rather than one single civilization and its barbaric others. In Schwab's poetic words: 'Maintenant finit l'ancient "merveilleux", celui des Lotophages et des Hommes-Poissons, et le dernier fabuleux sera celui des myriades humaines.'[5] [Here end the old 'marvels', those of the Lotus Eaters and Mermen, and the final wonder will be that of human diversity.] On the other hand, Schwab views the Oriental Renaissance as essentially humanist, a natural continuation of the first Renaissance. Indeed, nineteenth-century thinkers tended to approach ancient religions through comparison, seeking out parallels that would confirm the universality of human experience across time and place.[6] We often find this combined emphasis on cultural diversity and on universalism within one single text and even within one same paragraph. Michelet, for instance, who was quoted above on the newly discovered civilizations that have come to judge modern Western civilization, also writes: 'Identique en ses âges, sur sa base solide de nature et d'histoire, rayonne la Justice éternelle.'[7] [Identical throughout the ages, on its solid basis of nature and history, shines forth eternal Justice.] Before adding: 'Voici le genre humain tout entier qui se met d'accord.'[8] [The entire human race here finds itself in agreement.] Acknowledging cultural difference, but also seeking to prove the universality of human experience, many of the texts generated by the Oriental Renaissance can be framed through Bhatti and Kimmich's paradigm of similarity.[9] Yet, the profound changes in historiography that came about as a result of the Oriental Renaissance were not always as progressive as this combined emphasis on difference and commonality might suggest. Alongside the new insights brought by emerging research on ancient languages, religions and cultures, a new grand narrative was also developing, one that reaffirmed Europe's central role in the history of civilizations: that of the Aryan race. This narrative was so alluring that a vicious circle formed, where the academic research that had inspired its first proponents soon became inflected by this fiction and indeed organized according to it.

The Aryan myth, which will be the focus of this chapter's first section, was based on two theories established between the late eighteenth and early nineteenth centuries. The first was the linguistic theory of the Indo-European language family, first formulated by William Jones in a 1786 lecture and later substantiated by Franz Bopp, according to which the lexical and grammatical similarities between Persian, Sanskrit, Greek and Latin suggested that these languages had all originated from a common – and now lost – language, which is still referred to today as proto-Indo-European.[10] Secondly, the German Romantic belief (as formulated, in particular, by Herder) that language was intimately tied to culture, community and indeed nationhood was drawn on to posit that the links between the peoples that spoke Sanskrit, Persian and European languages went beyond language, and were in fact the expression of what we would today call a shared ethnicity. As summarized by David Motadel: 'the linguistic "Indo-European" relationship was soon taken as proof of the tribal and volkish kinship of the people who spoke that language. As a consequence, European scholars began to see the ancient Persians as their ancestors.'[11] Indeed, the term 'Aryan', which over the course of the nineteenth century began to be used interchangeably with 'Indo-European', was itself taken from ancient Iranian sources.[12] This appropriation of the ancient Persians as proto-Europeans went hand in hand with an othering of the peoples who spoke Semitic languages, a linguistic family that had developed independently from Indo-European languages and included Hebrew and Arabic. What we are presented with is a reformulation of the Europe versus Orient binary, which now takes the form of Europe's Oriental ancestors (the Aryans) versus the 'Semites', a category that included the ancient Babylonians, Phoenicians and Egyptians, as well as the ancient Jews. These people were not exactly presented as barbaric, since they had built important civilizations. However, they *were* associated with the negative stereotypes of Orientalism as defined by Edward Said. Whether the opposition was expressed along linguistic, cultural or racial lines – and often it was all three at once – it always served to glorify the Aryans.

The peculiarities of Iranian history and culture, however, did not always align with the grand narrative of an ancestral conflict between Aryans and Semites.[13] For one thing, the recasting of the ancient Persians into the noble role of ancestors of the West went against centuries of reliance on classical European sources, according to which the Persians were despotic, decadent and effeminate. The ancient Persians were Europe's first Other, the original 'barbarians',[14] and in this sense the first victims of what Said calls Orientalist discourse. Moreover, a further tension emerged when French writers attempted to account for Iran after the Arab conquest of the seventh century AD: on the one hand, the Persians were still viewed as Aryans, defined in opposition to their Semitic conquerors, but on the other hand, they were that most suspicious of all others: Muslims. Iran thus plays a mercurial role, both intimately tied with the origins of the Aryan myth, giving it its very name, but also revealing it for the fiction that it is, since its long and complex history as an ethnically, culturally and religiously diverse region resists the grand narratives of nineteenth-century historians.[15] The complexity of Iran's cultural identity would have been most obvious to readers of Ferdowsi's *Shāhnāmeh*, which appeared in complete French translation in instalments between 1838 and 1878.[16] Ferdowsi's poem was written after the Arab conquest and is dedicated to the God of Islam, yet it also celebrates the heroes of Iran's Zoroastrian past, making it ambiguous in certain passages which of the two religions is being referred to. The *Shāhnāmeh*, moreover, is a piece of historiography in its own right, since its subject matter is the history of Iran from creation to the Arab conquest. This made it an essential source for the authors studied in this chapter, who were deeply engaged not only with the history of Iran, but also with defining historiography as a modern academic field. Indeed, the texts analysed in this chapter have much to reveal not only about nineteenth-century French views on Iran, but also about the philosophies of history that were being developed at the time, an area that has been the subject of important studies by Lionel Gossman and Hayden White.[17] My focus on Iran will in fact allow me to revisit this field of study from a fresh perspective: one that is not centred on French history. Indeed, neither White nor Gossman include *La Bible de l'Humanité* in their discussions of Michelet's philosophy of history, even though the work's breadth and ambition – a history of world religions – make it a highly relevant case study.

The following section of this chapter compares the work of three different historians: the diplomat and racial theorist Arthur de Gobineau, the philologist and religious studies expert Ernest Renan and the aforementioned Michelet, the historian best known for coining the term *Renaissance*.[18] These thinkers are notable both for their contributions to the development of historiography as a field and also for their enormous influence on nineteenth-century French thought. The two things in fact went hand in hand, since their words were intended to reach 'as large and general an audience as possible'.[19] In mid-nineteenth-century France, to be a historian was to take on an important public and civic role as 'the educator of [one's] people, and a passionate participant in the political debates of the day'.[20] The reach and relevance of these authors' theories of history is demonstrated by the public debate occasioned in 1888 by Renan's account of Iran's role in the Islamic Golden Age. The Muslim political activist Jamal al-Din Al-Afghani responded to Renan's lecture with an open letter, in which he offered a different version of the history of medieval Islam and of Iran's place within it. The exchange, which will be included in my analysis, has been described as 'the first major public debate between a Muslim and a European intellectual'.[21] Moving from grand narratives to narrative, the two sections that follow consider works of historical fiction set in pre-Islamic Iran. The first of these analyses Judith Gautier's novel *Iskender: Histoire persane* (first published in the press in 1869 and then as a volume in 1886), and the latter analyses Jane Dieulafoy's novel *Parysatis* (1890) and diptych of novellas *Rose d'Hatra* and *L'Oracle* (1893). It is worth noting at this juncture that Gobineau did write fiction about Iran as well as histories, but his Persian short stories are all set in the mid-nineteenth century and are concerned with the mores and customs of contemporary Iranians and not with Iran's past. They are therefore not relevant to the present discussion.[22]

Readers may have noted the gendered split between the authors of 'history' and the authors of 'historical fiction' covered in this chapter. This is by no means coincidental. Not everyone had the prerequisite authority to publish a book which claimed to speak truths – 'vérité' is in fact the term that Renan brandishes the most frequently in the texts discussed here. This genre distinction should therefore be seen for what it is: a manifestation of the patriarchal exclusion of women from academic writing, making fiction their only option for delving into the history of Iran. But if we examine these texts independently from the categories under which they fall, it soon becomes clear that all five authors are writing historical fiction, albeit each in their own way. Jules Michelet is well known for his novelistic style and, indeed, Hayden White goes so far as to argue that it is Michelet's reliance on narrative strategies that makes his histories so compelling.[23] Gobineau and Renan's priority is the promotion of the Aryan myth, their entire process of selection and explanation of historical events is thus governed by a fiction. Judith Gautier mixes history and legend in a manner that deliberately mimics that of Ferdowsi's *Shāhnāmeh*. Dieulafoy's novels, finally, are the result of a combined study of classical literature and first-hand archaeological research, which placed the author in far more intimate contact with Achaemenid culture than most of their male counterparts. We should also bear in mind White's broader observation that historiography is primarily an act of writing and as such relies on the discursive strategies and literary tropes associated with 'literature' narrowly defined (i.e. fictional prose, theatre and poetry). Indeed, my approach to all five authors will be the same, the analysis of their style being essential to our understanding of the narratives that they propounded. Whether dilettantes or respected professionals, their writing on Iran was never detached or scientific: they all had a story to tell about Iran's place in the world and its relationship to Europe.

'Nos parents, les Aryas'[24] (Gobineau, Renan, Michelet)

Arthur de Gobineau and Ernest Renan are the most regularly featured nineteenth-century French thinkers in studies of racism and anti-Semitism.[25] Jules Michelet, the historian best known for his vast *Histoire de France* (1833–67) and seven-volume *Histoire de la Révolution* (1847–53), seems a less likely suspect. As I will demonstrate, however, all three authors played an important role in the debates surrounding, on the one hand, the relationship between race, culture and religion, and, on the other hand, the Asian origins of Western civilization. Iran was a pivotal case study in both arenas. The continuities across these three authors' works, as well as their areas of disagreement, are in equal measure revealing of the ways in which Iranian history was appropriated and repurposed to support new narratives surrounding France's place in the history of civilizations. I will begin by considering Gobineau's account of the ancient Persians in the infamous *Essai sur l'inégalité des races humaines* (1853), where they are identified as Aryan and serve to illustrate Gobineau's racialist theory surrounding the rise and fall of civilizations. Ernest Renan, while sceptical of physiological definitions of race such as that propounded by Gobineau, nonetheless embraced and indeed bolstered the Aryan/Semite binary. Renan projected this binary onto Christianity and Islam, deeming the former to exemplify the poetry and free thinking associated with the Aryan race and the latter to be the ultimate expression of the Semitic mind, which he considered limited and dogmatic, and he put Iran's history to the service of these claims. Finally, I will turn to Michelet's *La Bible de l'Humanité*, a book that was designed to refute Renan's vision of religion and yet, in spite of this, fully adopted the racialist opposition of Aryans and Semites proposed by Gobineau and Renan.

Arthur de Gobineau's *Essai sur l'inégalité des races humaines* [*Essay on the Inequality of Human Races*] is a one-thousand page historical essay that purports to explain the history of humanity on the basis of race. It divides humankind into three main races (white, black, yellow) and identifies sub-categories within each of these. Gobineau considers the 'white race' to be superior to all others, going so far as to call it 'la race civilisatrice' [the civilizing race].[26] The work repeatedly decries miscegenation, arguing that any mixing of the white race with others will dilute its excellence, leading to civilizational decline. Indeed, as noted by Robert Young, the originality of the essay resides in its combination of what had until then been two separate fields of study: 'the historical question of the rise and fall of civilisations' and 'the racial concept of degeneration'.[27] As we shall see, Gobineau's treatment of the ancient Persians entirely conforms to this principle.

The *Essai* argues that among the different sub-categories of the white race, the most superior is the so-called Aryan race, to which belong Indians, Iranians and Greeks.[28]

Gobineau writes that the 'Aryan family' originated over four thousand years ago in Central Asia, from where one branch moved south east to India.[29] These Aryan settlers would later descend into the Iranian plateau where some of its members stayed, becoming the Persians, while others carried on travelling west where they would become the Greeks. It was this latter 'branch' of the Aryan family that founded European civilization.[30] By formulating Europe's origin story as a migration myth, Gobineau establishes an overlap between progress over time, which since the Enlightenment had been considered a defining characteristic of the process of civilization,[31] and geographic movement westward. Thus, the progressive stages of the Aryans' westward migration function both on a literal level as a historical claim for the origins of the population of Europe *and* on a figurative level as a metaphor for the Aryans' progressive civilizational accomplishments.[32] To get a stronger sense of how compelling a narrative of Western superiority this geographic and temporal overlap creates, it is helpful to contrast Gobineau's migration narrative to that offered by William Jones, some sixty years earlier. '*Iràn*,' Jones writes, 'was the true centre of population, of knowledge, of languages, and of arts; which [...] were expanded in all directions to all the regions of the world.'[33] Instead of being a stepping stone in a narrative of progress leading from India to Europe, Iran is the originator of both, placing the Asian subcontinent and the European continent on a level footing as the coeval inheritors of this legacy. We can see why Jones's version of events was somewhat less appealing to those authors who wanted European civilization to be the final destination and achievement of humanity.

Although Gobineau associates westward movement with civilizational progress, his vision of history is however notable for its pessimism, according to which civilizational progress inevitably leads to miscegenation and thus decline. The ancient Persians' temporal distance from the industrialized West therefore by no means presupposes a racial or civilizational inferiority. Quite the contrary: in Gobineau's writing, the Persian Achaemenid Empire is a manifestation of the Aryan race in its most pure and unadulterated form, which by definition would make the ancient Persians superior to the people of modern Europe, Gobineau himself included. At the same time, the ancient Persians are appropriated by Gobineau as proto-Europeans, so that their military and cultural achievements reflect positively on their modern European descendants. (As we shall see, the same appropriative logic will also be adopted by Renan and Michelet.)

Gobineau's racial claims allowed him to revisit the historic military rivalry between the ancient Greeks and ancient Persians in terms entirely different to those of classical and neoclassical Western literature. These two peoples were not at war because of irreconcilable cultural differences: they were at war because they were made of the same cloth, that of noble warrior peoples – in other words, Aryans. Gobineau goes so far as to describe the Greeks and the Persians as 'frères turbulents' [turbulent brothers],[34] an epithet that functions both on a metaphorical level by highlighting their cultural similarity and on a literal level by foregrounding their shared Aryan blood.[35] Race and culture are indeed inseparable in Gobineau's writing: the *Essai* describes both the chivalric values that Persians and Europeans have shared, starting in the Achaemenid period and continuing well into the medieval period (exemplified, he argues, by the parallels between Ferdowsi's *Shāhnāmeh* and Ariosto's *Orlando furioso*),[36] as well as the physiological similarities the ancient Persians bore to Europeans, since they were – according to him – blond and rosy-cheeked.³⁷ For all the problems presented by Gobineau's dubious claims that the two ancient rivals essentially shared the same genetic make-up, what is notable is, first, that it does not presume that the ancient Greeks were culturally superior to the ancient Persians and, secondly, that it presents the two civilizations as coeval. By this I mean that by focusing on how the two cultures interacted, Gobineau is forced to address their temporal coexistence. This was by no means a given, since the migration narrative's imbrication of geographic movement and temporal progression meant that India, Iran and Greece were often not treated as coeval civilizations, but as separate stages on the Aryan's race's westward itinerary. This is the structure followed, for example, by Michelet's *La Bible de l'Humanité*, which considers India, Iran and Greece sequentially, confining each one to a separate book chapter. That said, while Gobineau shows a keen interest in the interactions between different civilizations and empires, when it comes to the Achaemenids, his narrative is repeatedly framed in terms of a protracted conflict between the two faces of the white race: that is to say, the Aryans and the Semites.

Gobineau's account of the rise and fall of the Achaemenid Empire is entirely founded upon his firm belief in the inherent superiority of the Aryans over the Semites and on the inevitable degeneration that will result from the Aryans mixing their blood with other races. The rise of the Persian Empire, beginning with Cyrus's conquest of the Assyrian Empire, is made possible according to him by the fact that the Assyrians, described as an earlier wave of Aryan migrants, had committed miscegenation and were so altered by 'le sang mélanien' [melanin blood] that they were 'presque à l'état des Sémites' [almost descended to the state of Semites].³⁸ As a result, Babylon was no match for Cyrus's army of pure-blooded Persians. In turn, the famous story of Darius the Great and the Noble Seven's dispatching of the impostor magus Smerdis/Bardiya is presented as Aryan Persia's heroic last stand against the Semitic onslaught – for Smerdis in this version is, naturally, a Semite.³⁹ In Gobineau's telling, the ancient Persians were beleaguered heroes, who for a time ruled over the Semitic peoples of the Middle East,⁴⁰ but eventually were swallowed up and contaminated beyond recognition:

> [À] l'époque d'Hérodote des sentiments de cette énergie n'existaient plus guère parmi les Perses, décidément déchus de leur primitive valeur ariane [...]. Après l'extinction de cette grande fierté, il y eut encore quelques années illustres; ensuite le désordre sémitique réussit à englober les Iraniens dans le sein croupissant des populations esclaves.⁴¹

> [At the time of Herodotus such powerful sentiments no longer existed among the Persians, who had decidedly fallen from their primitive Aryan valour [...]. After the extinction of this noble pride, there were still a few illustrious years. Then, the Semitic disorder engulfed the Iranians into the rotting fold of enslaved peoples.]

It is at this point, according to Gobineau, that the balance of power shifts from Iran to Greece, and that Athens and Sparta grow in influence as Aryan city-states, leading Gobineau to announce, in line with the westward motion of his civilizational narrative, 'Je vais donc quitter le groupe Iranien pour m'occuper du nouveau peuple arian' [I shall therefore leave the Iranian group to study the new Aryan people]. Gobineau here follows a common narrative in classical European literature, according to which the Achaemenid Empire entered a state of decline upon Xerxes's defeat, sealing its fate to be eventually conquered by Alexander.[42] But by formulating this decline along racial lines, Gobineau creates a vicious – or from his perspective virtuous – cycle: just as his racialist theories are used to justify historical events, so too historical events seem to justify the racialist theories, investing these with the aura of inescapable truths.

Gobineau would revisit and revise his account of the rise and fall of the Persians sixteen years later in his *Histoire des Perses*.[43] In this work, the emphasis is laid not on Alexander displacing Persian rule, but on his being adopted by the Persian elite as one of their own.[44] This follows Gobineau's racial logic in so far as they share an Aryan lineage. In contrast to his earlier account of events in the *Essai*, in this version the Persians have not yet been contaminated beyond recognition when Alexander arrives. The fall from grace is instead postponed by several centuries to the advent of the Sassanian Empire. The result, however, is much the same as it had been in the earlier telling: 'les Sassanides commencèrent l'Iran nouveau, celui où l'influence sémitique, celle des races de valeur secondaire, devint à jamais prépondérante.'[45] [The Sassanians created the new Iran, the one where the Semitic influence, that of races of secondary value, became forever dominant.] Gobineau's narrative voice in the *Histoire*, however, is more personal and therefore mournful than it had been in the *Essai*. He describes the 'Semitic influence' as a turning point in which the Persians go from being exceptional among the Orientals to being typically Oriental, only occasionally able to revive their ancestral qualities through the memory of their glorious past.[46] Thus must Gobineau bring his history of Iran to a premature close in third century AD: 'Je m'arrête au point où la proche parenté cesse d'exister entre nous et les dominateurs de l'Iran.'[47] [I stop here, at the point where the close familial tie ceases to exist between ourselves and the rulers of Iran.] This final sentence is telling, both in terms of Gobineau's motivations for writing about the Persians – Iran is mainly of interest in so far as it is considered Europe's ancestor – and in terms of the melancholy tone of the *Histoire*'s final paragraphs. It is as though Gobineau blames Iran for having robbed him of the noble ancestors that were so necessary to his feeling of self-worth as a modern European. The line in the sand that Gobineau draws here between the ancient Persians and the people living in Iran from the Sassanid period onwards also plays an important ideological function: that of distancing ancient Iran from modern Iran, the better to appropriate ancient Iran as proto-European, and by consequence, the purview of modern Europeans.[48] This very same ideological separation would later serve French archaeologists such as Jane Dieulafoy, a key figure in the coming pages, and their successor Jacques de Morgan in their moral claim over ancient Iranian artefacts – a claim that came before that of Iranians.

'Vous avez fait là un livre des plus remarquables, plein de vigueur et d'originalité d'esprit, seulement bien peu fait pour être compris en France […]: la France croit très peu à la race.' [You have written an absolutely remarkable book, full of vigour and original thinking, yet hardly made to be understood in France […]: France believes very little in race.] With these words, Ernest Renan praised Gobineau's enterprise in the *Essai sur l'inégalité des races humaines*, while also commiserating about the challenges they would both face in their quests to explain world history on the basis of race.[49] Their shared belief in racial predetermination indeed went against the universalism that had been enshrined in French culture in the Enlightenment period and was instead much closer to German conceptions of *volk*. But although Gobineau and Renan were early adopters, they were by no means the last French intellectuals to 'believe in race'.

Taking the absolute inferiority of the 'black' and 'yellow' races as a given, Renan devoted his work to the opposition between Indo-Europeans (or Aryans) and Semites. Renan did not believe that these two races could be distinguished in physiological terms, arguing that '[l']étude des langues, des littératures et des religions devait seule amener à reconnaître ici une distinction que l'étude du corps ne révélait pas'.[50] [The study of languages, literatures and religions alone could bring us to recognize a distinction that the study of the body here did not reveal.] In contrast to Gobineau's physiological racism, which is concerned with categories such as physical strength, as well as skin and hair colour, Renan views race as being an essentially linguistic, intellectual and cultural matter – at least when it comes to distinguishing between the two white races. In the language of Renan's philological racism, the opposition between the Aryan and Semitic races is therefore most often described in terms of 'esprit' and 'génie', words which in English roughly translate as 'mindset' and 'spirit'. To use an expression to which we shall return, race for Renan is to do with how one 'thinks and feels' and these two things were intimately tied to language.

The Aryans and Semites according to Renan are the world's only civilized races. The movement of human history is therefore governed by their confrontations and occasional collaborations. In his inaugural lecture as Chair of Hebrew at the Collège de France, Renan argued that the most significant result of the interaction between the two races was the birth of Christianity, a religion that was founded upon an Aryan reinterpretation of a Semitic religion (Judaism).

> En adoptant la religion sémitique, nous l'avons profondément modifiée. Le christianisme, tel que la plupart l'entendent, est en réalité notre œuvre. [...] La victoire du christianisme ne fut assurée que quand il brisa complètement son enveloppe juive, quand il redevint ce qu'il avait été dans la haute conscience de son fondateur, une création dégagée des entraves étroites de l'esprit sémitique. Cela est si vrai, que les juifs et les musulmans n'ont que de l'aversion pour cette religion, sœur de la leur, mais qui, entre les mains d'une autre race, s'est revêtue d'une poésie exquise [...].[51]

[In adopting the Semitic religion, we changed it profoundly. Christianity, as most understand it, is in reality our *oeuvre*. [...] The victory of Christianity was only ensured once it completely broke out of its Jewish shell, when it became once again what it had been in the high conscience of its founder, a creation liberated from the rigid restrictions of the Semitic mind. This is so true that Jews and Muslims feel only aversion for this sister religion, which in the hands of another race has assumed an exquisite poetry [...].]

Renan, having lost his faith in the 1840s, is not speaking here as a Christian. Indeed, by referring to Christianity as an 'œuvre', he is presenting this religion as something man-made rather than a divine revelation, a perspective that outraged French Catholics.[52] According to Renan, language is a manifestation of a race's inherent characteristics and, more importantly, language also plays a predetermining role in how the members of a racial-linguistic community think, since it structures their very thought processes. Due to his academic background, Renan approached religions primarily as textual entities. In doing so, he was able to substantiate his racial classification of the Abrahamic faiths on linguistic grounds: the New Testament is the superior text because it was written in an Indo-European language (the form of Greek known as *koine*), whereas the Old Testament and Quran were limited by virtue of being written in Semitic languages (Hebrew and Arabic). When Renan describes the sentimentality of Christianity as being 'l'opposé du génie sémitique, essentiellement sec et dur' [the opposite of the Semitic spirit, which is essentially dry and hard], he is simultaneously expressing a racial stereotype (about the rigidity and lack of creativity of Semites) *and* an aesthetic bias. It was a commonly held view among nineteenth-century French scholars that Indo-European languages were more beautiful and thus better suited to poetry than Semitic languages. Consider, for instance, the terms with which Casimir Barbier de Meynard contrasts Persian to Arabic in his own inaugural lecture as the Collège de France's chair of Persian:

> sonore, harmonieuse, souple, riche en termes composés, d'une construction facile et élégante, [la language persane] se plie à toutes les combinaisons de l'art; [...] une grâce, un charme que le caractère métallique des langues sémitiques ne peut revendiquer [...].[53]

> [sonorous, harmonious, supple, rich in compound words, of an easy and elegant construction, the Persian language lends itself to all artistic combinations; [...] a grace, a charm that the metallic character of Semitic languages could never claim to have [...].]

Not only is the Indo-European Persian language more beautiful, it is more *flexible*, an attribute in direct opposition to the rigidity associated with Semitic languages and peoples.

Renan's monolithic vision of language, religion and race as coherent entities served to construct a neat binary between a Christian Aryan West, which carried the legacy of the Greek classical period, and a Muslim Semitic Orient. Indeed, the ultimate targets of Renan's anti-Semitism were not so much Jews, as Muslim Arabs. This is most clear in passages such as the following one, where Renan single-mindedly ignores the fact that there exist non-Arab Muslims, non-Muslim Arabs and also non-Christian Europeans:

> L'Arabe du moins, et dans un sens plus général, le musulman, sont aujourd'hui plus éloignés de nous qu'ils ne l'ont jamais été. Le musulman (l'esprit sémitique est surtout représenté de nos jours par l'islam) et l'Européen sont en présence l'un de l'autre comme deux êtres d'une espèce différente, n'ayant rien de commun dans la manière de penser et de sentir.[54]

[The Arab at least and, in a more general sense, the Muslim, are more distant from us today than they have ever been before. The Muslim (the Semitic mind at present is mainly represented by Islam) and the European are in each other's presence like two beings from different species, having nothing in common in their way of thinking and feeling.]

Though phrased as an analogy, the reference to a different 'species' here is particularly loaded, since it harks to the racialist view known as polygenesis, according to which different human races were in fact different animal species – in other words, people of colour were not merely inferior to white people, they were *not even human*.[55] Renan's refusal to admit even the potential for similarity between the 'thoughts and feelings' of Europeans and Muslims or Arabs is much to the same effect. The passage thus reveals how easy it is to go from rejecting universalism to completely dehumanizing cultural others, which is precisely the danger that Todorov identifies in extreme forms of cultural relativism such as Renan's.[56] What had been introduced as a lecture on the nuances of the academic study of philology was in fact a virulent attack on Muslims, whose racial inferiority is presented by Renan as scientific fact.

Renan was not the first to view the linguistic distinction between Indo-European and Semitic languages as evidence of racial difference, but he was the first to apply the newly emerged racialist 'science' to the study of religions. There were many problems with this. First, as I have noted, there was the fact that linguistic, religious and racial categories often do not align. Iran as an ethnically diverse, Indo-European language-speaking, Muslim-majority country is a perfect example of this. Secondly, Renan's racialist views against Semites and in particular Arabs were extreme even for the time in which he was writing, leading several academics to express their scepticism towards them.[57] Twenty years later, Renan delivered a lecture that was designed to address these weaknesses in his work. This lecture, which was published in *Le Journal des Débats*, was entitled 'L'Islam et la Science' (1883) and centred on the Islamic Golden Age. This was a period in history when the Muslim world had a greater degree of scientific advancement than the Christian world, and thus was arguably more 'civilized' – scientific progress being in Renan's view synonymous with civilizational progress. It was also a chapter of history in which Muslim scholars had contributed greatly to the development of European thought, since it was they who gathered, expanded and shared the ancient Greek philosophical texts that would enable the Renaissance, one of Europe's greatest civilizational achievements. All this made the Islamic Golden Age an apt terrain for Renan to test his theories. Would he really be able to continue to claim, as he had done in his previous work, that Arabs and Muslims had contributed 'nothing' to the development of politics, art, poetry, science or philosophy?[58]

Like any good lecturer, Renan opens 'L'Islam et la Science' by announcing his teaching aim, which is to bring nuance and clarification to some common misunderstandings about history. What follows, however, is a far cry from nuanced: 'Toute personne un peu instruite des choses de notre temps voit clairement l'infériorité actuelle des pays musulmans, la décadence des États gouvernés par l'islam, la nullité intellectuelle des races qui tiennent uniquement de cette religion leur culture et leur éducation.'[59] [Any person who is at all informed on the issues of our time can clearly see the current inferiority of Muslim countries, the decadence of States governed by Islam, the intellectual nullity of the races who only draw their culture and education from this religion.] Rather than retracting, Renan is doubling down on the racial-religious pronouncements introduced in his earlier works, this time citing evidence from current affairs as well as history. But Renan soon adds a caveat to this blanket condemnation of the Muslim world: 'La Perse seule fait ici exception; elle a su garder son génie propre, car la Perse a su prendre dans l'Islam une place à part; elle est au fond bien plus chiite que musulmane.'[60] [Persia alone here is an exception. She has been able to preserve her own spirit, for Persia has found a place of her own within Islam; she is, in the end, far more Shi'i than Muslim.] While at first glance this appears to be a comment about Iranian cultural identity, which indeed remained strong even following the Arab conquest, there is something more at play here. As we saw earlier, 'génie' is one of Renan's favourite words when contrasting Aryans and Semites. If we acknowledge this racial subtext, then it becomes clear why Renan claims that Shi'ism does not fall within Islam: he is redeploying his foundational assumption that religion is an expression of race. Islam being a Semitic race and the Iranians being Aryans, they had to formulate their own version of the religion. This line of thinking after all has a precedent: Renan's argument that Christianity was born as an Aryan interpretation of a Semitic religion. But by suggesting in this lecture that Shi'ism is an Iranian-Aryan religion and that Sunnism is an Arab-Semitic religion, Renan ignores one important detail: during the historical period covered by his lecture, 'de l'an 775 à peu près jusque vers le milieu du treizième siècle' [from the year AD 775, give or take, until the mid-thirteen century],[61] the majority of Iranians were Sunni and the majority of Shi'i Muslims were actually Arab. Shi'ism was only introduced as a national religion in Iran in the sixteenth century AD, under the Safavid dynasty. Thus, we come to see that Renan, for all his claims of scientific method and intention to rectify misunderstandings, is conveniently sidestepping essential historical information in order to sustain his narrative of a conflict between the Aryan and the Semitic spirit. And it is this very same foundational narrative that will allow him to claim in 'L'Islam et la Science' that there exists no such thing as Islamic or Arab philosophy.[62]

Pursuant to his central distinction between the Semitic mind as dry, narrow and limited and the Aryan mind as creative and innovative, Renan argues that the true fathers of the Islamic Golden Age were not the region's Abbasid rulers, but the Persian members of their courts. These men of learning, crucially for Renan's argument, were neither Arab nor Muslim, thus they were Semitic in neither race nor religious belief: 'les conseillers intimes, les précepteurs des princes, les premiers ministres sont les Barmékides, famille de l'ancienne Perse, très éclairée restée fidèle au culte national, au parsisme [i.e. Zoroastrianism], et qui ne se convertit à l'islam que tard et sans conviction.'[63] [The intimate advisors, the princes' tutors, the first minister are Barmekids, a very enlightened family from ancient Persia, which had remained faithful to the national religion, Parsism [i.e. Zoroastrianism], and only converted to Islam later on and without conviction.] Renan's argument is that the Islamic Golden Age was effectively the work of reluctant Aryan converts, Islam in its true form being incompatible with intellectual inquiry.[64] Iran, which was first referred to as the exception that confirmed the rule, now takes on an even more pivotal role: it functions as a lightning rod attracting credit for all the achievements of the Islamic Golden Age so that Renan can claim that the Arab Muslim contribution was minimal. In a story similar to that told by Gobineau in his account of the fall of the Achaemenid Empire, Iran is a beleaguered Aryan outpost, which ultimately falls to the Semitic majority surrounding it, its positive influence on the region only lasting for a limited time. Renan's historical narrative is also emblematic of a recurring tendency among French authors to minimize the importance of Islam to Iranian culture, in order to strengthen a claim of proximity or kinship between themselves and their subject matter. As we saw in Chapter 1, this was the case for example with Henri Cazalis's treatment of Al-Ghazali.

Renan's claims against the Islamic Golden Age rest upon a binary opposition between enlightened Persian philosophers and the religiously orthodox Arabs persecuting them. But Renan's ultimate end in this lecture is to minimize even the role played by his Persian heroes, who are eventually revealed to be nothing more than the benevolent custodians of a European legacy: 'Tel est ce grand ensemble philosophique, que l'on a coutume d'appeler arabe, parce qu'il est écrit en arabe, mais qui est en réalité gréco-sassanide. Il serait plus exact de dire grec; car l'élément vraiment fécond de toute cela venait de la Grèce.'65 [Thus it is with this great body of philosophy that we are accustomed to calling Arab, because it is written in Arabic, but is in fact Greco-Sassanid. It would be more precise to say Greek; for the truly fruitful element in all of this came from Greece.] Iran, it turns out, had been a convenient stepping stone, in an argument that unfolded westwards, like most iterations of the Aryan myth do, towards Greece. Ancient Greece, idealized and ideologized as the bedrock of European civilization, emerges triumphant as the true hero of the story, the Persians having only played a supporting role. It is also further worth noting that Renan's choice of the adjective 'Sassanid' in this passage, rather than 'Persian', serves to further dissociate philosophy (and Iran) from Islam, since the Sassanians were Iran's last non-Muslim ruling dynasty. Renan's strategic use of the Sassanians in this lecture also illustrates the many different ways in which one same period of history can be told, based on its function in the wider narrative being constructed by the historian. Whereas in Gobineau's *Histoire des Perses*, the Sassanians stood for Iran's fall from grace, the moment when the nation's rulers became 'more Oriental than Persian', in Renan's 'L'Islam et la Science', they are pre-Islamic Iran's last hurrah, the one dynasty in Middle Eastern history to have contributed something to human knowledge.

The conclusion reached by Renan at the end of 'L'Islam et la Science' is a categorical one: 'L'islamisme a de belles parties comme religion [...]. Mais, pour la raison humaine, l'islamisme n'a été que nuisible.'66 [Islam has some beautiful aspects as a religion [...]. But, when it comes to human reason, Islam has only been detrimental.] Such a radical condemnation of one of the world's most widely practiced religions was not made to go unquestioned. Two months after publishing the lecture, *Le Journal des Débats* followed up with a response: an open letter penned by Jamal al-Din Al-Afghani, a political activist who lived a life of exile as a result of fighting Western imperialism and preaching pan-Islamic unity. Although he was known as 'the Afghan', it is believed that Al-Afghani was originally from Iran and had chosen this moniker so that the public would assume he was Sunni and not Shi'i, thereby giving his ideas broader reach.67

Today, Al-Afghani is remembered in particular for denouncing the Qajar monarchy's complicity with Iran's financial exploitation by the West and eventually conspiring to assassinate Naser ed-Din Shah.[68] His response to Renan's lecture, likely composed with the assistance of a translator, is a rhetorical masterpiece. It unravels Renan's entire argumentative thread, yet on the surface remains polite, conciliatory and succinct. In doing so, it offers a completely different vision of Iran's cultural identity.

Al-Afghani does not disagree with Renan's premise that the Middle East is less developed than the West, nor that religion can be a barrier to knowledge. Instead, he argues that Islam is a younger religion and therefore has not yet had the time to reach the same degree of liberalism that Christianity has done.[69] In doing so, Al-Afghani rejects the nineteenth-century view championed by both Gobineau and Renan that race predetermines the potential of a human group (in this case, Muslims) for civilization; he follows instead an Enlightenment understanding of civilization as referring to universally shared stages of temporal development. As noted by Robert Young: '[t]hough unilinear and hierarchical, such a view generally considered any hierarchy as a temporary one, merely a difference of stage at the present which could be transformed through education, not a constitutive basis of difference for all time.'[70] Al-Afghani's universalist understanding of civilization and scepticism towards any form of religious dogmatism comes across most strongly in his simple observation that: 'Toutes les religions sont intolérantes, chacune à sa manière.'[71] [All religions are intolerant, each in their own way.] The latter point is well taken given that Renan himself had been persecuted on religious grounds. The Minister of Education had warned him at the time of his appointment at the Collège de France that he should aim to 'exclure de mon enseignement toute opinion personnelle contraire aux principes fondamentaux de la religion chrétienne' [exclude from my teaching any personal opinion that goes against the fundamental principles of the Christian religion], and because Renan was deemed to have failed to do so, he was dismissed after less than three years in post.[72] These events not only explain why Renan was so personally invested in defending intellectual freedom against the pressures of religious orthodoxy, but they also demonstrate his hypocrisy in claiming that fundamentalism was an inherently Islamic trait.

Rather than explicitly referring to Renan's own experiences at the Collège de France, Al-Afghani tactfully chooses to focus on more distant examples of Christian intolerance, such as the Spanish Inquisition. He also shows more compassion than Renan by choosing to explore the psychological motivations that lie behind narrow interpretations of religion, rather than dismissing these as the product of cultural or racial inferiority. The crux of the matter, according to Al-Afghani, is the fact that humans are by nature torn between the conflicting lures of fact and faith, which while at odds, hold equal importance for how we view the world around us. He concludes: 'Il en sera toujours ainsi. [...] Tant que l'humanité existera, la lutte ne cessera pas entre le dogme et le libre examen, entre la religion et la philosophie.'[73] [It will always be so. [...] As long as humanity will exist, the battle will never cease between dogma and free thought, between religion and philosophy.] Al-Afghani's effort to show the parallels between Christianity and Islam and to present the human experience of religion in universalist terms is all the more powerful if we consider it in light of Renan's previous claims that Europeans and Muslims have 'nothing in common in their way of thinking and feeling'.[74] But this is only one part of Al-Afghani's case.

Alongside his universalist argument, Al-Afghani is also interested in picking apart the binary oppositions around which Renan had scaffolded his argument. Thus, counter to Renan's claim that philosophy is a Western pursuit, Al-Afghani wryly notes: 'Les Européens ont fait bon accueil à Aristote, émigré et devenu arabe; mais ils ne songeaient nullement à lui quand il était grec et leur voisin.'[75] [Europeans welcomed Aristotle once he had emigrated and become Arab; but they did not give him a second thought when he was Greek and next door.] As well as reiterating that it was the Arab-speaking world that made the European Renaissance possible, the image of an Arab Aristotle also suggests the porousness of cultural boundaries and the vacuity of any nationalist appropriation of human knowledge. The history of Western philosophy is both transnational and multi-religious, since pagan, Muslim and Christian thinkers all played a role in it. This lays the ground for Al-Afghani's critique of the other key binary in Renan's lecture, that of Arabs and Persians. Medieval Persian intellectuals spoke Arabic and wrote in Arabic, and had possibly done so even before the Arab conquest, writes Al-Afghani.[76] Renan's opposition between Arabs and Persians would therefore have held little currency in the eyes of medieval Islamic philosophers. To further drive this point home, Al-Afghani goes so far as to adopt Renan's own thesis that language is the one true marker of 'race', but turns it against him, observing that from the moment a group of humans shares one same language, the geographic origins of its various members are soon forgotten.[77] Counter to the monolithic vision of language, race and religion that Renan had weaponized against Muslims and Arabs, Al-Afghani thus offers a two-pronged response, arguing for the universality of the conflict between religion and science and foregrounding the multilingualism and layered identity that had characterized the medieval Islamic world. In such a context, Renan's racialized opposition of enlightened Aryans/Persians and regressive Semites/Arabs is shown to be a modern construction. But this was not one that Renan was prepared to relinquish.

On 19 March 1883, *Le Journal des Débats* published a brief response from Renan to Al-Afghani's open letter. It is, overall, a conciliatory one. Renan agrees with Al-Afghani's universalist case against the tyranny of all religions, prophesying that one day free thinkers such as themselves will win over the fanaticism of the 'rival fables', by which he presumably refers to Christianity and Islam, thereby ignoring that he himself had repeatedly presented Christianity as a superior faith.[78] Renan, therefore, seems to have embraced Al-Afghani's argument that the two religions are not so different in their repression of intellectual freedom. But this apparent recanting of his earlier views is only short-lived. In a surprising twist, Renan informs his readers that he has in fact met Al-Afghani: 'Peu de personnes ont produit sur moi une plus vive impression [...]. La liberté de sa pensée, son noble et loyal caractère me faisaient croire, pendant que je m'entretenais avec lui que j'avais devant moi [...] Avicenne, Avveroès.'[79] [Few people have made a stronger impression upon me [...]. His freedom of thought, his noble and loyal character led me to believe, as I was listening to him, that I had before me [...] Avicenna or Avveroes.] Whereas in his academic writing Renan had minimized the contributions of medieval Islamic philosophers, now they are presented as exemplary characters, the better to praise Al-Afghani as their modern descendant. But there is a reason, Renan tells us, why Al-Afghani is such a great mind 'in spite' of being Muslim: his race. 'Le Cheik Gemmal Eddin est un Afghan, entièrement dégagé des préjugés de l'Islam; il appartient à ces races énergiques du haut Iran, voisin de l'Inde, où l'esprit aryen vit encore si énergique sous la couche superficielle de l'islamisme officiel.'[80] [The Sheikh Jamal al-Din is an Afghan, entirely free from the biases of Islam; he belongs to those energetic races from the Iranian plateau, near India, where the energetic Aryan spirit lives on under the superficial layer of official Islam.] Renan describes Al-Afghani in the same way that he had described the Persian intellectuals that exerted a positive influence on the Abbasid court: only Muslim on the surface, by way of circumstance, the Semitic Islamic faith ultimately being incompatible with his race. Race thus remains the sole criterion for determining an individual's intellectual abilities. This move not only allows Renan to deny Al-Afghani's agency, it also turns the very strength of his counterargument into further evidence of the inescapable difference between Aryans and Semites: only an Aryan could have made such a compelling case against Renan. The fierce debater is thus reduced to a case study. Renan drives this point home by adopting the deeply dehumanizing language of scientific observation and classification, writing '[r]ien de plus instructif que d'étudier ainsi [...] la conscience de l'Asiatique éclairé' [nothing is more instructive than studying thus [...] the conscience of the enlightened Asiatic], and describing Al-Afghani as 'le plus beau cas de protestation ethnique contre la conquête religieuse' [the finest case of ethnic protestation against religious conquest].[81]

The conclusion of this debate illustrates both the resilience of nineteenth-century racialist theories and the malleability of the Aryan myth. Whereas for Gobineau the people inhabiting the Iranian plateau had ceased to be Aryan countless centuries ago (in the *Essai* at the end of the Achaemenid period and in the *Histoire des Perses* during the Sassanian period), for Renan they were still Aryan to this day – provided they attracted attention to themselves by critiquing his work. Renan's racialist argument remains despicable in its dehumanization of a large portion of humanity, but his claim that great Aryan minds have continued to be at work in the Middle East, from antiquity to the Islamic Golden Age to modernity, is worthy of note, since it presents a select few from India, Afghanistan and Iran as not just equal to Europeans, but similar in their racial make-up. In doing so, Renan is avoiding the denial of coevalness present in many other accounts of the Aryan myth, wherein Iran ceased to be Aryan – and indeed, to exist – from the moment the baton of civilization had been handed over to Greece.[82] At the same time, however, it is clear that these were exceptions that confirmed the rule of European greatness: the one true inheritor of the great ancient Aryan legacy was the Christian West. But the heroic role that Renan ascribed to Christianity as the ultimate Aryan faith, and thus the most superior of all religions, not only failed to placate his Catholic opponents, it also angered some of the period's most anticlerical thinkers. Among them was Renan's own former university lecturer, Jules Michelet, who had held the Chair of History at the Collège de France from 1838 until his suspension and eventual dismissal under the July Monarchy.[83] While Renan would later reflect in a letter to Michelet's widow that '[s]ur le christianisme, nous n'avons pu différer que sur des nuances d'opportunité' [on Christianity, we only ever differed on some small nuances],[84] Michelet's diaries tell a rather different story: namely, that his entire motivation for writing his book *La Bible de l'Humanité* was to take a stand 'contre Renan et le Christ' [against Renan and Christ].[85]

La Bible de l'Humanité [*The Bible of Humanity*] (1864) is one of Jules Michelet's most ambitious, if lesser-known works: it is a history of world religions, written as a cohesive narrative, starting with the birth of Hinduism in India and ending with medieval Christianity. Michelet's histories are known for their mastery of narrative, as well as their personal and even emotional tone, which differs so strongly from the conventions of contemporary historiography. Hayden White has noted in particular Michelet's predilection for binary oppositions, which allowed him to craft dramatic narratives of conflict and redemption – the conflict always being one between the forces of good and evil.[86] *La Bible de l'Humanité* is no exception to this and indeed goes much further than Michelet's other works, since it allows him to bring his philosophy of history to bear on a far wider geographic and temporal expanse than he had ever done before, known as he was for his expertise in French history. This, in turn, reveals a different side of Michelet, one that has gone largely unnoticed. Contrary to Lionel Gossman's claim that Michelet never questioned 'the preeminence of France and of the West in general in human history' and White's confident assertion that 'Michelet was unable, by the logic of his conception of history, to find virtue in anything except the one moment of pure conjunction that he thought he had seen in the history of France during a single year, 1789', *La Bible de l'Humanité*, and in particular its chapter 'La Perse', do just that.[87]

One of the greatest innovations of *La Bible de l'Humanité* is its approach to the study of religion, which runs against the philological method favoured by scholars such as Renan. Michelet argues that religion is inextricably tied to the everyday lives of ordinary people, making it a key facet of what we today call social history. 'Il se trouve souvent que c'est le plus profond qu'on oublia d'écrire, la vie dont on vivait, agissait, respirait.'[88] [It so often is the case that the most profound things are those that go unrecorded, life as it was lived, acted, breathed.] Rather than an end, the study of religion for Michelet is a means: it allows the historian to reconstruct an ancient people's moral codes, as well as their fears, desires and material conditions. This reflects Michelet's wider interest in accessing and writing the interiority of historical figures so that he and his modern readers may better identify with them.[89] Such a project is all the more radical and difficult to achieve when its subject is not a famous figure from French history, but an anonymous Iranian man going about his business over two millennia ago, which is the premise of the book's chapter entitled 'La Perse'.

The chapter opens by conjuring the religious beliefs of ancient Iranians through brief and evocative sentences, such as: 'La Perse n'a point de temples, point de cérémonies, de culte que la prière et la parole. Point de mythologie. Nulle poésie imaginative. Tout vrai, positif, grave et fort. L'énergie dans la sainteté.'[90] [Persia has no temples, no ceremonies, no cult but for prayer and the word. No mythology. No imaginative poetry. All is true, positive, grave and powerful. Energy within sanctity.] Michelet then begins *in medias res* describing a patriarch ('le chef de famille') getting up to tend the fire for the midnight prayer: 'Il se lève, prend ses vêtements, et il ranime le feu, lui donne sa nourriture. La maison resplendit.'[91] [He rises, takes his clothes, and rekindles the fire, feeds it. The home glows.] The use of third-person omniscient narration makes the chapter read like a nineteenth-century novel, with the present tense adding a sense of immediacy. The text indeed follows the conventions of historical fiction, by using a fictional character as a vehicle for feeding information to the reader. Thus, we are told that the patriarch is thinking about farming, which allows the narrator to quote passages from the *Avesta* referring to agriculture and to water.[92] Through the narration of the patriarch's day of work in the field, we then learn about Zoroastrianism's respect for nature and the personal sense of duty that inspires the faithful to act virtuously.[93] The character's harmonious relationship with nature and moral virtue bears more than a light resemblance to the eighteenth-century myth of the 'noble savage', but unlike this earlier figure, Michelet's protagonist is rooted in a highly specific religious context: his virtue is the product of nurture as much as nature. At the same time, the depiction of this ancient Iranian character is also deeply rooted in nineteenth-century morality, since Michelet uses him to sanctify the patriarchal structure of the nuclear family: 'ce chef de famille, levé en pleine nuit, quand la femme et l'enfant dorment, prononce, par-devant le Feu, les mots qui vivifient le monde, – en vérité cela est grand.'[94] [This head of the family, risen in the middle of the night, when the woman and child sleep, pronounces before the Fire the words that revive the world, – in truth, this is noble.]

The way in which Michelet introduces his readers to ancient Iran is undeniably original: he focuses not on great kings, but on a hardworking farmer. This is because a humble character of this kind is far better suited to illustrating Michelet's main point of interest in Zoroastrianism, which is the agency with which the religion invests its followers by placing the conflict between good and evil within every single person. According to Michelet, it is this sense of personal responsibility combined with its profound optimism that makes Zoroastrianism a vastly superior religion to Christianity – contra Renan.[95] Christianity since the medieval period had encouraged moral behaviour by instilling in its followers the fear of eternal retribution in Hell. As such, it was 'une éducation par le crime' [an education through crime].[96] Zoroastrianism, in contrast, is founded on a benevolent God and the belief that all humans are capable of good: 'Un Dieu bon et clément fait des hommes doux et magnanimes.' [A good and benevolent God creates kind and magnanimous men.][97] This distinction applies not only to how the religions treat their followers, but also how they treat the superhuman principle of evil: the Christian Satan has done nothing but grow in stature across the centuries and is ultimately invincible, but the Zoroastrian Ahriman is loved by Ahura Mazda (God) and the faithful pray for him to be redeemed.[98] Rather than dividing the world into the blessed and the wicked, Zoroastrianism thus aims to incorporate everyone and everything into one single totality of good. As such, the religion is closely aligned to Michelet's own philosophy of history which, as has been argued by Hayden White, is fuelled by a desire for humanity to be united into one single whole.[99] But whereas White suggests that the only moment in history in which Michelet thought that this ideal could be achieved was 'France during a single year, 1789',[100] *La Bible de l'Humanité* demonstrates that this is not the case. Michelet believed that his ideal had once existed and that the way ahead for France lay not in inventing new values, but in returning to the values of the past:

> La Justice n'est pas l'enfant trouvé d'hier, c'est la maîtresse et l'héritière qui veut rentrer chez elle, c'est la vraie dame de maison. [...] Elle peut dire: 'J'ai germé

dans l'aurore, aux lueurs des Védas. Au matin de la Perse, j'étais l'énergie pure dans l'héroïsme du travail. Je fus le génie grec […].'[101]

[Justice is not yesterday's foundling, she is the mistress and the heiress who wants to return home, the true lady of the house. […] She can say: 'I was born at dawn, in the light of the Vedas. In the morn of Persia, I was pure energy in the heroism of work. I was Greek genius […].']

The moral compass, in other words, lies with 'nos parents, les fils de la lumière, les Aryas' [our parents, the sons of the light, the Aryans].[102] Although Michelet wrote this book with the sole purpose of proving his former student wrong, his moral elevation of the ancient Indians, Persians and Greeks above all other societies follows the very same binary opposition that had been disseminated by Renan: that of the Aryans and the Semites.

There is a contradiction at the heart of *La Bible de l'Humanité*, which is summed up by the book's title and structure. This is a work predicated on a universalist assumption, that of 'humanity' as one single entity: 'L'humanité dépose incessamment son âme en une Bible commune. Chaque grand peuple y écrit son verset.'[103] [Humanity continuously lays its soul into a common Bible. Each great people adds its verse.] In Michelet's titular metaphor, the verses stand for the world's different religions, which together form a coherent whole and can thus be metaphorized as the many individual verses collectively forming a single Bible. The emphasis is therefore on commonality within difference, in line with Bhatti and Kimmich's paradigm of similarity. We find the same emphasis in Michelet's preface, which argues that recent developments in historical research offer 'le sens d'un passé fraternel et la joie de savoir qu'elle [la Terre] a vécu d'un même esprit!' [the feeling of a fraternal past and the joy of knowing that [the Earth] once lived of one mind!].[104] According to Michelet, the more one studies the world's religions, the more parallels one finds between them, confirming the essential unity of humanity. And yet, *La Bible de l'Humanité* is also a work that strictly adheres to the hierarchical opposition of Aryans and Semites promoted by Gobineau and Renan. Michelet invests the Aryan trinity formed by the Hindu Indians, Zoroastrian Persians and pagan Greeks with the foundational role of having laid the three moral pillars of European civilization: family values, work ethic and philosophy, respectively.[105] The people of ancient Carthage, Egypt and Judea in contrast form 'le sombre génie du midi' [the dark spirit of the South] and are 'sans nul doute le côté secondaire, la petite moitié du genre humain' [without a doubt, the secondary part, the minor half of the human race].[106] The opposition is further cemented by the book's structure, which is divided into two parts: Part I, which contains the chapters on India, Persia and Greece, is entitled 'Les peuples de la lumière' [The peoples of the light]; Part II, which covers the rest of Europe, the Middle East and North Africa, is entitled 'Les peuples du crépuscule, de la nuit et du clair-obscur' [The peoples of the twilight, night, and *chiaroscuro*]. Michelet does not use the term 'Semite' in his preface, but then he does not need to: the label is implied by its oppositional term 'Aryan' as well as the regions named by Michelet, which had already been categorized as Semitic by Renan. However, there is also a crucial difference between the former master and student.

Whereas Renan presented Christianity as the Aryan religion *par excellence*, Michelet relegates it to Part II, with the religions of darkness. According to him, the world's most just and benevolent religions are Hinduism and Zoroastrianism.[107] Michelet's idealization of these religions is not without its issues, being as it is underpinned by the Aryan myth and also, as was noted above, often close to the myth of the noble savage: the presentation of the Persian Zoroastrians as pure, innocent and close to nature can often reek of paternalism. That said, one cannot understate what a radical proposition it was in 1864 to be arguing that, on a global scale, Christian Europe was far from holding the moral high ground. As we saw, Renan himself had been dismissed from the Collège de France for his anticlericalism, even while arguing that Christianity was the superior religion. The greatest legacy of *La Bible de l'Humanité* therefore lies in its desire to introduce its French readers to religions with which they were unfamiliar and to challenge their Eurocentric bias in favour of Christianity. Paradoxically, then, Michelet's writing demonstrates highly progressive thinking, while being inflected by the racialist theories that circulated at the time that he was writing.

In 'La Perse', Michelet is keen not only to describe the virtuous lives led by the ancient Zoroastrians, but also their 'mortel dégoût pour les fables obscènes du monde noir, des peuples souillés d'Assyrie' [their mortal disgust for the obscene fables of the black world, of the sullied people of Assyria].[108] The lexical field of purity and impurity and the use of blackness as a marker of inferiority has strong echoes of Gobineau's account of the same historical period in the *Essai sur l'inégalité des races humaines*. But Michelet also embellishes, bringing to the history of the Achaemenid Empire his own flair for dualism: the Persians are united and the Assyrians divided; the Persians are embodied by the winged *faravahar*, the Assyrians by the crawling snakes and dragons that they worship; the Persians, finally, are 'le peuple du feu, un incendie en marche, qui veut épurer tout' [the people of fire, a marching blaze, that wants to purify everything], who will travel as far as Egypt, 'aux peuples noirs d'Afrique, ennemis nés de la lumière' [to the black people of Africa, born enemies of the light].[109] The Aryan myth and Michelet's love of dualist narratives of a struggle between good and evil here overlap so neatly that they bind into a cohesive whole. So much so that *La Bible de l'Humanité*'s central metaphor of light versus darkness in this passage becomes indistinguishable from the physiological opposition of light versus dark skin promoted by Gobineau. While Michelet aligns with Gobineau in his use of ancient Semitic peoples as foils for the heroic Persians, there are also some notable differences between their accounts of Iranian history: in particular, in terms of their ideals of masculinity. Whereas Gobineau praises the ancient Persians for being, like the Greeks, warriors by nature, Michelet praises instead the Persians' peaceful nature. His male role model is not a soldier, but a father and farmer. In Michelet's account, the expansion of the Achaemenid Empire was not an act of conquest but of self-defence: 'Les purs, les pacifiques, pour la défense ont pris l'épée.'[110] [The pure, the peaceful, took up the sword to defend themselves.] The two of them also differ in their understanding of the evolution of Iranian identity following the fall of the Achaemenids. Gobineau, as we saw, describes a fall from grace resulting from the Persians' progressive miscegenation with Semites, which robbed them of their Aryan vigour. Michelet challenges this account and tells a rather more interesting story.

Michelet signals that he is deliberately challenging Gobineau through the use of a rhetorical question, which asks what happens to Zoroastrianism once Islam becomes the dominant religion in Iran: 'Babylone l'avait-elle engloutie?' [had Babylon swallowed her?], words that directly echo Gobineau's claim that the Iranians were 'swallowed up' by the Babylonians.[111] This serves as a dramatic introduction to Michelet's rejoinder, which exhibits a far more flexible understanding of cultural identity than had been present in either Gobineau or Renan's work:

> Elle resta, sous tout empire, l'âme sainte et l'identité de l'Asie, se survivant et dans ses fils directs, les pauvres et honnêtes Guèbres ou Parsis, mais surtout, mais bien plus dans son ascendant indirect sur les Musulmans, ses vainqueurs, sur les innombrables tribus, les sultans et les dynasties de toute race qui passaient.[112]

> [She remained, under every empire, the holy soul and identity of Asia, surviving both through her direct descendants, the poor and honest Zoroastrians or Parsis, but especially, and even more so, in her indirect influence on her Muslim conquerors, on the innumerable tribes, sultans, and dynasties of all races that passed through.]

Radically demarcating himself from Renan's monolithic view of race, culture and religion, Michelet here argues that Zoroastrian values transcend the Zoroastrian religion: they remain present among Muslim Iranians and, in turn, influence non-Iranian Muslims too. When Renan had argued that 'Persia has found a place of her own within Islam',[113] his point was ultimately a racialist one that sought to deny Iranians' commitment to Islam. Michelet does not suggest that Iran's ancient Zoroastrian heritage makes it any less Muslim, but argues to the contrary that this heritage is 'especially' present through its indirect influences on Islamic culture. In this sense, it is Islam that sustains these ancient values and traditions. Michelet's phrase 'de toute race', furthermore, explicitly contradicts the notion that an individual's religious or moral beliefs should be predicated by their race.

Although Michelet is more flexible in his approach to religious and cultural identity, one should nonetheless acknowledge that he does share some of Renan's anti-Arab and anti-Muslim prejudice. The final section of 'La Perse' is, rather originally, devoted to the courage and agency of the female characters of the *Shāhnāmeh*.[114] Ferdowsi's positive treatment of women, according to Michelet, speaks to the poem's Zoroastrian values, which strongly differs from Judaism, where women are associated with original sin, and Islam, where they are treated like property.[115]

> Firdousi n'a nul souvenir de la femme musulmane, vendue et achetée, captive. Il n'a peint que la femme perse. Les héroïnes, dans son livre fidèle à la vraie tradition, sont d'une fierté, d'une grandeur antique. Si elles pèchent, ce n'est pas par faiblesse. Elles sont rudement fortes et vaillantes, d'initiative hardie, de fidélité héroïque.[116]

> [Ferdowsi has no memory of the Muslim woman, sold and bought, captive. He only depicted the Persian woman. The heroines of his book, which remains faithful to true

tradition, are of an ancient pride and grandeur. If they sin, it is certainly not out of weakness. They are tough and brave, show bold initiative, and are heroically faithful.]

Ferdowsi's poem in Michelet's view is the ultimate illustration of how the indomitable 'soul' of ancient pre-Islamic Iran lives on and in so doing 'elle avive l'esprit musulman, l'inonde de sa bonté féconde et de sa riche inspiration' [vivifies the Muslim spirit, fills it with fruitful goodness and deep inspiration].[117] The opposition between 'Persian' and 'Muslim' women in this passage clearly follows Renan's religious iteration of the Aryan/Semite binary. And yet, Michelet also goes beyond it, by viewing Islamic Iran, starting from Ferdowsi, as a successful cross-fertilization of pre-Islamic and Islamic cultures. This is a radical departure both from Gobineau's claim that once the Persians began mixing their blood with other peoples they were doomed to disappear and from Renan's firm belief that Islam and the Aryan spirit are ultimately incompatible. Oppositions can dissolve and formerly divided peoples can be united into one. Michelet's narrative desire for unity on this occasion triumphs over the rigid binaries of the Aryan myth.

La Bible de l'Humanité was not just written to contradict Renan's positive account of Christianity: it was also a work of great social ambition. Michelet believed that France had lost its way: 'Ils crient: Fraternité! Mais ils ne savent guère ce que c'est. Elle veut une sûreté et de moeurs et de caractère, une austérité pure, dont ce temps a peu l'idée.'[118] [They cry *Fraternité*! Yet they do not know what it is. It requires a confidence of morality and of character, a pure austerity, of which this time has little notion.] He had personal reasons for believing this: the French Second Republic (1848–52), which was created to restore the values of the First Republic, from which it had taken the motto 'Liberté, Égalité, Fraternité', had instead paved the way for Louis-Napoléon to seize power and establish the authoritarian Second Empire. This new government's conservatism had been the reason behind Michelet's ban from lecturing and eventual dismissal from the Collège de France in 1852, the same fate that would be experienced by Renan just over a decade later. Faced with such a disappointing present, it is perhaps unsurprising that Michelet took refuge in 'la haute Asie, le profond Orient' [great Asia, the deep Orient].[119] But his was more than escapism. It was a search for an alternative: an uncorrupted moral system that if adopted could make up for the failures of Christian Europe. In this context, the 'tendresse austère' [austere tenderness] of the ancient Persians was nothing less than a path to salvation.[120] Eighteenth-century philosophers may have considered the prelapsarian state of the noble savage as incompatible with the development of civilization, but in Michelet's eyes, ancient India and Iran were proof that moral purity and civilization could coexist. Utopia was attainable.

The Persian Alexander: Hybridity and queer (anti-)imperialism (Judith Gautier)

The literature surrounding the feats of Alexander of Macedon is as transnational as Alexander's life was, spanning Europe, the Arab world and Iran. In France, Alexander romances flourished in the Middle Ages and were mainly based on the pseudo-Callisthenes, a Greek life of Alexander written in the third century AD that merged historical events with fantastical adventures. But, following the early modern period's return to classical sources, it was the more sober biographies by authors such as Plutarch that gained favour among French readers. In the nineteenth century, Alexander became viewed as a proto-Western colonizer and symbolized the triumph of Europe in the clash of civilizations between East and West. This Alexander was a role model for the young Napoleon.[121] The picture is rather different in Persian literature, where under the Persianized name 'Eskandar' (often transliterated as Iskender), Alexander was adopted as one of the great kings of Iran. In Ferdowsi's influential telling of the legend, Alexander is not the son of Philip of Macedon, but the secret child of the king of Iran and Philip's daughter, which means he has both Greek and Iranian blood. The Persian Alexander is thus a hybrid, embodying the coming together of East and West. Over the course of the narrative, we also witness him undergoing a cultural transition from being king of Greece ('Rum' in Persian) to king of Iran. This change of status from foreign invader to righteous king is rendered both narratively in a scene where Alexander holds the dying King Darius (in Persian Dārā) and is acknowledged by Darius as his successor, and structurally in the transition from Chapter XIX 'Dārā' to Chapter XX 'Eskandār', which marks Alexander's entrance into the poem's long roster of Iranian kings. The fiction of Alexander's mixed blood thus ultimately functions as a metaphor for an alternative approach to the historiography of the Macedonian conquest of Iran, one that emphasizes the continuities between Alexander's rule and that of his Achaemenid predecessors. Contrary to modern European historiography's emphasis on the West's military and cultural supremacy, Ferdowsi's poem offers a flexible understanding of cultural boundaries and argues that one same person can go from identifying as Western to identifying as Iranian. It was this paradigm shift that drew Judith Gautier to the Persian Alexander, for she herself was a European who yearned to escape her cultural surroundings.[122]

Iskender: Histoire persane (hereafter *Iskender*) interpolates key events from Ferdowsi's poem with episodes of Gautier's own invention, and focuses in particular on the personal relationships between Alexander and Iranian characters. Whereas in the *Shāhnāmeh* Eskandar (Alexander) never learns that his true father is King Darāb, Gautier has this information revealed to him on the eve of his battle with Dārā (Darius).[123] This has the effect of heightening the stakes: on the one hand, Eskandar now knows that he is the legitimate king of Iran, which gives him even more motivation to take the throne, but on the other hand, he also knows that the man he is about to fight is his own brother. The *Shāhnāmeh* sets a precedent for the tragic story of two family members on opposing sides of a battle: the mythical hero Rostam (the Hercules of Persian literature) and his secret child Sohrab. This is the most famous episode of Ferdowsi's epic and its pathos stems from the fact that Rostam only realizes who Sohrab is after mortally wounding him. By allowing the characters to discover their kinship, Gautier invests Dārā's last moments with a similar pathos to that of Sohrab, transferring the cathartic release that had been present in Ferdowsi's telling of the death of Sohrab to her telling of the death of Dārā. In other words, it is a form of rewriting that remains very close to the spirit of the source text.

– C'est moi qui suis ton frère! s'écria Iskender, la voix pleine de larmes; moi, le cruel ambitieux qui cause ta mort et qui n'est pas digne de porter la couronne [...].

Toute la vérité vibrait dans la voix du roi de Roum, et Dara, lui saisissant la main, en plaça la paume sur ses lèvres.[124]

[– I am your brother! cried Eskandar, his voice full of tears; I, whose cruel ambition caused your death and who is not worthy of the crown [...].

The whole truth trembled in the voice of the king of Rum and Dārā, grabbing his hand, placed its palm on his lips.]

Dārā's death now comes with a sense of resolution. Not only were both men able to learn the truth, but after kissing Eskandar's hand in recognition, Dārā tells him that as the eldest brother he is the rightful heir to the throne of Iran. Eskandar's challenge will now be to convince both himself and the people of Iran that Dārā is indeed right and that he is not a usurper. After all, as the passage reminds us, to all intents and purposes, he is still 'King of Rum'. Eskandar's transformation from foreign invader to just ruler of Iran, marked by a chapter transition and dwelt on very little by Ferdowsi, will become a key thematic focus for Gautier. First appearing in serialized form in the newspaper *La Liberté* (10 November to 17 December 1869), *Iskender* was not published as a book until 1886, which is when it started to gain public attention through reviews in the press, leading to its reissue in 1894.[125] Gautier was therefore sharing the story of a Western character who assimilates into an Oriental society at the very height of French colonial expansion, when right-wing politicians were beginning to formulate the ideology of the *mission civilisatrice*, according to which it was France's moral duty to civilize its Oriental others, from Tunisia (colonized in 1881) to Annam (colonized in 1883).[126] Although the distant setting and the fantastical and sentimental elements of *Iskender* make it seem like an apolitical text, Gautier's revisionist choice to tell the story of Alexander along Persian lines was therefore a bold one, since it brought under question Eurocentric approaches to historiography, as well as the ideology underpinning contemporary imperialist discourse.[127] The cultural hybridity of the novel's protagonist is also matched by that of Gautier's writing, which cuts across the norms and traditions of Persian epic poetry and the French historical novel. *Iskender* is thus a highly original work in which theme and style are in perfect ideological alignment.

Judith Gautier's source text was Jules Mohl's complete translation of the *Shāhnāmeh*, *Le Livre des Rois*, which was the first translation of the poem into a European language. The *Shāhnāmeh* famously consists of two parts, the first being devoted to legendary kings and the second to historical rulers. Yet, even the latter part contains legendary elements, especially when it comes to the adventures of Alexander, many of which are inherited from the pseudo-Callisthenes. To the modern Western reader, the *Shāhnāmeh* is therefore a hybrid work that merges elements associated with fantasy novels, such as superhuman strength, talking animals and the quest for immortality, with real historical events. Gautier emulates Ferdowsi's mix of history and legend, which results in an unusual approach to the French historical novel, a genre that prided itself on its realism. The subtitle *Histoire persane* can therefore be read as a playful allusion to *Iskender*'s genre ambiguity: is this 'Persian history' or a 'Persian tale'? The precedent set by the

Shāhnāmeh would suggest it is both. On a more granular level, Gautier also draws on stylistic markers of the Persian epic, such as lists, simile and hyperbole, in particular, in the build-up to the battle between Dārā and Eskandar and in her descriptions of beautiful female characters.[128] Like Ferdowsi, Gautier calls the ancient Persian Empire 'Iran'. And as well as using the region's native name, she includes many calques on Persian, which range from literary Persian, as in 'pleurer du sang' (*to cry tears of blood*, a Persian figure of speech for *to weep abundantly*), to everyday language, as with the formulaic phrase 'qorbānet' rendered as 'Je suis ton sacrifice' (literally *I am your sacrifice*, figuratively *you are welcome*).[129] The texture of the novel is thus rich with stylistic echoes of Ferdowsi's poem and the Persian language more broadly, giving it a completely different style to contemporary works. This is most obvious if we contrast the magical elements and flowery metaphors of *Iskender* to the detached narrative voice and gruesomely detailed descriptions of ancient warfare and bodily harm in Flaubert's *Salammbô* (1862, reissued 1879), the most famous nineteenth-century French novel set in the ancient Orient.[130]

Gautier establishes from the outset that she is emulating a Persian narrative style by framing her novel as a performance by a *naqāl*. *Naqāls* are traditional storytellers who recite episodes from the *Shāhnāmeh* in Iranian coffee houses to this day. Gautier specifies that this particular *naqāl* is performing at a celebration held in honour of Naser ed-Din Shah, who ruled Iran at the time that she was writing. The *mise en abyme* thus breaks the reader's transition from nineteenth-century France to ancient Iran into two steps: first, we travel from France to Iran, and then, we travel back in time. The frame is returned to in the opening of each of the novel's four chapters, in which the *naqāl* invokes God to assist him in his performance, just as Ferdowsi in the *Shāhnāmeh* invokes God to help him compose his poem. This creates a slippage between the voice of Ferdowsi and the voice of the *naqāl*, which is typical of such oral performances, given that *naqāls* typically alternate between introducing the *Shāhnāmeh* passages in their own voice and reciting the poem as narrated by Ferdowsi. And to this we must of course add a third layer: that of the French context in which and for which Gautier was writing. Just as in Iran *naqāls* will call upon their audience to listen more attentively and react more strongly to the events that they are recounting, so too is Gautier calling upon her readers by using colloquial interjections typical of oral performance. The novel's most frequent colloquial interjection is 'tu aurais dit que' (literally *you would have said*, figuratively *it was as though*), which is a calque on the Persian *gofti ke* (you would have said that), but works well in French given its proximity to the set phrase 'on aurait dit que' (literally *one would have said*, figuratively *it was as though*). By explicitly identifying her narrator as a *naqāl*, Gautier signals her novel's affiliation to an Iranian storytelling tradition, as opposed to a Western one; a tradition that has oral roots, is prone to hyperbole and excels in uniting historical fact and popular legend. Approached in this way, the ornate style and fantastical plot elements of *Iskender* become evidence of an informed engagement with Iranian culture rather than markers of personal eccentricity. Indeed, although Gautier never travelled to Iran and therefore likely never attended a performance by a *naqāl*, she had two reliable sources: the Orientalist Charles Clermont-Ganneau, who was her Persian tutor, and her suitor and thereafter lifelong friend, an Iranian diplomat named Mohsen, to whom *Iskender* is dedicated.[131]

Gautier's friend and biographer Suzanne Meyer-Zundel writes that following her divorce with Catulle Mendès, Judith often expressed regret at how different her life might have been had she married Mohsen instead of the French writer, a match rejected by her parents no doubt due to the Iranian diplomat's religion and marriage history.[132] There is therefore an undeniable personal investment in the central plot of *Iskender*, which is the story of how Alexander went from identifying as Western to identifying as Iranian in great part due to his intimate friendship with an Iranian character. What is particularly original in Gautier's writing is that this loving bond is formed not between a man and a woman, but between two men. This is a queer friendship which, coupled with Persian literature's vision of a hybrid Alexander, powerfully subverts imperialist discourse by hacking at the very binaries that prop it up (self versus other, Western versus Oriental, civilized versus uncivilized), as well as the Orientalist trope of presenting the Orient and its people as feminized, the better to emphasize the heroic masculinity of the Western conqueror. By choosing to invent a storyline in which Eskandar befriends the most masculine and powerful of the *Shāhnāmeh*'s heroes, the Herculean warrior Rostam, Gautier establishes instead a relationship of equals, modelled on an Aristotelian ideal of friendship. By calling this a queer friendship I do not intend to claim that 'friendship' here is a euphemism for a sexual relationship, though I do believe that Eve Kosofsky Sedwick's claim that homosexuality and homosociality exist not in opposition, but on a continuum certainly applies to this novel.[133] I describe the friendship between Eskandar and Rostam as queer for two reasons: first, the erotically charged intensity of the love between the two characters, and secondly, because of the political consequences of this love. These two dimensions are present from their very first meeting.

As previously noted, Eskandar's military victory in chapter I of the novel is undercut by the sense that he is a usurper. On top of the guilt experienced when holding his dying half-brother in his arms, Eskandar also feels judged when upon entering the royal palace he is confronted with a statue of their father:

> Une émotion profonde enveloppa Iskender devant l'image glorieuse de son père; son cœur se serra et il connu le remords, car il lui sembla que ce front de pierre se ridait de courroux et que les lèvres froides de Darab lui reprochaient d'avoir été cruel et vorace de gloire.[134]

> [A profound emotion seized Eskandar before the glorious image of his father. His heart ached and he knew remorse, for it seemed to him that the stone forehead was furrowed with anger and that the cold lips of Darāb reproached him for being cruel and thirsting for glory.]

Similarly, the sight of the royal women in mourning 'rendaient sa poitrine pleine de soupirs et son cœur plein de regrets' [filled his chest with sighs and his heart with regret].[135] Eskandar's desire to find Rostam, Iran's greatest warrior, is thus introduced in chapter II as part of an agenda to prove himself worthy of the Iranian crown. In the *Shāhnāmeh*, the character of Rostam lived several centuries before Eskandar, but Gautier solves this narrative problem by giving Rostam a great great grandson, who bears the same name and to all intents and purposes is identical to his forefather. Devastated by the death of King Darā, the loyal Rostam has withdrawn to his magical castle, which is only accessible by riding Rostam's supernaturally powerful horse Rakhsh. 'L'insoumission de Rustem ferait une ombre sur ma gloire; il faut qu'il se soumette' [Rostam's insubordination would cast a shadow over my glory; he must submit], Eskandar tells himself.[136] And so he sets off alone to ascend Rostam's mountain, reaching the castle without Rakhsh. But while the episode begins as an exercise in imperialistic one-upmanship, in which the conqueror proves his superior physical prowess to that of the land's greatest native warrior, its tone changes altogether when Eskandar finally reaches his destination.

Eskandar finds Rostam crying, resembling 'la statue brisée d'un dieu' [the broken statue of a god], a highly evocative image that connects Rostam both to the statue of the Iranian king Darāb and to Eskandar himself, who is repeatedly described as 'godlike' in the novel.[137] This simultaneously makes Rostam a surrogate figure for Darāb and, by association, Darāb's son Darā, whom he is mourning and whom he will come to replace as Eskandar's metaphoric 'brother', and also introduces what will be a key component of Rostam and Eskandar's friendship: their similarity. Eskandar, before whom the conquered people of Iran had kneeled, kneels beside Rostam to console him, his posture symbolizing a change in status, as he moves to present himself not as Rostam's superior, but as his equal.[138] Indeed, Eskandar cannot help but mirror Rostam's emotional state and he begins to cry too.[139] Rostam does not realize who the man sympathizing with him is until Eskandar finally reveals his identity as 'Iskender, fils de Darab' [Eskandar, son of Darāb]. Upon discovering whom he is speaking to, Rostam attempts to prostrate himself, as Iranians historically did before their monarchs.

– O mon roi! murmura-t-il.
Mais Iskender ne le laissa pas s'agenouiller; il l'entoura de ses bras et le serra contre sa poitrine.
– Cette fois, tu es vaincu! dit-il en le baisant tendrement.[140]

[– O my king! he murmured.
But Eskandar would not let him kneel. He put his arms around him and clasped him to his chest.
– This time, you are defeated! he said, kissing him tenderly.]

Eskandar's words playfully redeploy the language of military victory to refer to the two men's nascent friendship: he has not won over – or against – Rostam, but rather, he has won Rostam over. Rostam is no longer submitting to the authority of his liege, but to the affection of a friend. The passage thus exhibits a very fluid treatment of identity: Rostam is simultaneously an alter ego for Darā and for Eskandar, and Eskandar is simultaneously Rostam's sovereign and his equal. This fluidity, which refuses both monolithic identities and fixed relationships, is just as queer a feature of this novel as Gautier's depiction of the effusive intimacy between the two male characters.

After kissing Rostam, Eskandar seizes him by the wrists and verbalizes their newly forged relationship as follows:

– Je suis bien récompensé de mes peines, cher Rustem, dit-il. Jusqu'à ce jour je me suis senti solitaire au milieu de ma gloire. J'étais si haut, que je ne pouvais pas avoir d'égal; j'avais des sujets innombrables et pas un ami. J'aurais été forcé de me courber pour aimer, et ma vanité n'imaginait pas qu'il existât un compagnon digne d'Iskender; mais toi, tu m'as donné cette joie de pouvoir aimer sans être généreux.

– Ne me rends pas fou, Iskender, murmura Rustem en pressant sur ses lèvres la main du roi.[141]

[– I am well rewarded for my efforts, dear Rostam, he said. Until this day I felt alone in the midst of my glory. I had climbed so high that I could have no equal: I had many subjects and not one friend. I would have had to bend in order to love and my vanity refused to believe that there could exist a companion worthy of Eskandar; but you, you have given me the joy of being able to love without being charitable.

– Do not drive me mad, Eskandar, murmured Rostam, pressing his lips to the king's hand.]

The language and emotional tenor of the scene is that of a marriage proposal: Eskandar tells Rostam that he wants him for his companion and Rostam enthusiastically accepts this proposal. Eskandar's proposal fulfils Aristotle's two criteria for ideal friendship: that is, that it be among two equals and that it be based on free choice.[142] At the same time, it is accompanied by an emotional intensity and physical intimacy that is highly erotic. While the act of kissing Eskandar's hand may denote political hierarchy rather than sexual attraction – indeed, it mirrors Dara's own kissing of Eskandar's hand upon recognizing Eskandar as his king – the same cannot be said of what follows: Rostam undresses, bathes and massages Eskandar, who declares: 'Tu as rendu la souplesse à mes membres, beau Rustem.'[143] [You have reinvigorated my limbs, beautiful Rostam.] They then ride down the mountain together on Rostam's noble steed Rakhsh, a position which by necessity involves close physical contact.[144] Indeed, later in the novel, Gautier will use the same device of having two characters ride upon one horse in order to initiate sexual contact between Rostam and a female character.[145]

What had begun as a private relationship in the seclusion of Rostam's castle is officialized upon the two characters' arrival in the Iranian capital city of Estakhr, where they 'go public' by ascending together the grand staircase leading to the royal palace, and pause on its top terrace so that the entire population can take delight in their appearance: 'Le peuple entier put alors le voir, appuyé d'une main sur l'épaule de Rustem; il put admirer ces deux jeunes hommes d'une beauté égale et qui semblaient les dieux réconciliés de deux religions enemies.'[146] [The entire population could then see him, with his hand resting on Rostam's shoulder; it could admire these two young men of equal beauty, who seemed the reconciled gods of two enemy religions.] Rostam and Eskandar's first public appearance has the tenor of a marriage cementing a new alliance between two families or in this case, two nations. But unlike the two (historically inspired) diplomatic marriages that Eskandar will pursue over the course of the novel, this is an alliance predicated on 'equality'. The two men share the same beauty, masculine prowess in matters of war and god-like grandeur, and these similarities are greater than their cultural differences as former enemies. The same bond cannot be forged between Eskandar and his two female partners, the Iranian princess Roxane and the Indian princess Indûmatî, because they lead an existence of seclusion in the harem. Moreover, such diplomatic marriages are tainted by *real politik*: any sexual intercourse between Alexander and his brides serves a (re)productive function: that of providing heirs to his empire and cementing his political alliances with the Iranian and Indian elite. Any sense of choice is thus severely compromised by the duties associated with Alexander's political role as king.

The Aristotelian criteria of equality and choice that characterize Rostam and Eskandar's relationship are also what makes it so queer: it exists beyond the hierarchical binaries of gender (man versus woman), empire-building (imperial power versus vassal state) and Orientalism (Western self versus Oriental other). The question of whether their friendship may or may not involve a sexual dimension is therefore only secondary to the fact that their love and companionship deeply troubles the Orientalist logic that would posit the Western character as masculine and dominant and the Oriental character as feminine and passive, in conformity with the West's conquering role as civilizer of the Orient. Gautier's choice to make a relationship between two men the emotional core of her novel resonates with Michel Foucault's observation a century later that it is not sex between men that threatens institutions, but the 'unlikely alliances' that result from love between men, '[c]es relations qui font court-circuit et qui introduisent l'amour là où il devrait y avoir la loi, la règle ou l'habitude' [those relations that create a short-circuit and introduce love where there should be law, order, or habit].[147] Eskandar may be the king and Rostam his vassal, but the love between them is so strong that it will lead Eskandar to put his friend's happiness before his diplomatic interest.

Eskandar and Rostam's relationship is put to the test when Rostam falls in love with Eskandar's prospective second wife, the Indian princess Indûmatî, whom he is charged with escorting from her homeland to her groom's palace. It has been argued by both René Girard and Eve Kosofsky Sedgwick that in Western literary representations of love triangles (which typically centre on two male rivals competing for a female character's affections), 'the bond that links the two rivals is as intense and potent as the bond that links either of the rivals to the beloved'.[148] In Gautier's novel, there is no doubt that the bond between the two male characters is more powerful than that which either of them share with Indûmatî. The beautiful princess is attracted to Rostam from the moment she first lays her eyes on him and initiates flirtation by asking if her prospective husband looks anything like Rostam.[149] The advance makes the hyper-masculine warrior crumble. With a voice 'pleine de sanglots' [full of sobs], he replies: 'Il ne ressemble qu'à lui-même. C'est un Dieu qui s'est fait roi. C'est mon frère, mon ami, mon maître. Je suis à lui, ma vie est à lui. Je l'aime autant qu'on puisse aimer, je l'aime par-dessus tout!'[150] [He resembles no one but himself. He is a God who made himself king. He is my brother, my friend, my master. I am his, my life is his. I love him as much as it is possible to love, I love him above everything!]

The cause of Rostam's suffering is not the fact that he cannot be with Indûmatî, to whom he is attracted, but the fact that in desiring her he is betraying Eskandar. Indûmatî does not grasp this, and as their journey to Estakhr proceeds she wonders to herself 'où donc puise-t-il la force de résister à mon regard qui le cherche?' [wherever does he find the strength to resist my gaze that goes searching for him?] The answer of course is: in his love for Eskandar. Even after an ambush from enemy warriors leads to a stolen kiss between Rostam and Indûmatî as they ride to safety on Rostam's noble steed, Rostam's thoughts remain first and foremost with Eskandar. And the same goes for Eskandar. Having safely escorted Indûmatî to the royal palace, Rostam falls ill as a result of his guilt at betraying his friend and his sadness at losing the woman he has fallen in love with. Upon discovering Rostam lying pale and unconscious, Eskandar 'le couvrit de baisers et de larmes' [covered him with kisses and tears], which has a healing effect upon the distressed hero: '[s]ous ces caresses ardentes Rustem revint à la vie et ouvrit les yeux' [under these burning caresses, Rostam returned to life and opened his eyes].[151] Concerned for his friend's well-being, Eskandar chooses to spend the night not with his new bride, but in Rostam's room.[152] And upon awaking the following morning, he jovially tells Rostam 'ma nouvelle reine sera jalouse de Rustem, car à cause de lui elle a passé la nuit sur une couche solitaire' [my new queen will be jealous of Rostam: because of him she had no one to share her bed with].[153] Gautier's references to 'burning caresses' and sexual jealousy certainly hint at a sexual relationship. But whether or not we choose to view Eskandar and Rostam's companionship in this light, what is clear is that their relationship comes before sexual relations with women. In doing so, it poses a challenge to the reproductive politics of alliance.

In *The Misfit of the Family*, Michael Lucey explores how queer relationships in Balzac's novels threaten the social order by contravening the system of family alliance and inheritance.[154] The desires of the bourgeois characters studied by Lucey have rather small-scale consequences in comparison to the alliances and rivalries between royal dynasties dramatized in the legendary world of Ferdowsi's *Shāhnāmeh*. But there is nonetheless a strong parallel between Gautier's novel and the cases analysed by Lucey in so far as Eskandar's love for Rostam does ultimately lead him to give up on his diplomatic marriage with Indûmatî, a choice that runs contrary to his social role as imperial ruler. Indeed, the novel's love triangle comes to a resolution when Eskandar, having finally discovered the secret passion that is leading his friend to distraction, decides to gift him his fiancée: 'aime-la, sois son époux; prends-là, je te la donne' [love her, be her husband; take her, I give her to you].[155] The directness of the language, though shocking to a modern reader, entirely conforms to the gendered social order. Indeed, Eskandar is following a patriarchal model of heterosexuality which Sedgwick, following the work of anthropologists, has described as 'the use of women as exchangeable, perhaps symbolic, property for the primary purpose of cementing the bonds of men with men'.[156] This particular exchange however goes against Eskandar's diplomatic interests, since it leads him to break the contract he had formed with Indûmatî's father, thereby sacrificing a bond that is far more politically valuable to him than his relationship with Rostam. Eskandar and Rostam's friendship is therefore queer in the social sense foregrounded by Lucey, since it limits Eskandar's ability to produce heirs and to hold on to the Indian provinces of his empire. Add to this the steadfastness of Rostam and Eskandar's feelings for each other, which endure until the very end of the novel – Rostam is the only person by Eskandar's side when he dies, a scene that mirrors that of Dārā's death at the beginning of the novel – and that their bond is predicated on reciprocity and equality, in spite of the fact that Eskandar is Rostam's political superior, and what we have is a relationship that truly defies the norms of both gender and imperialism.

As has been shown by Amanda Chapman in her study of Victorian adventure novels, queer male friendships were a common trope in imperialist literature, provided that the primary relationship was that between Western characters: the young male heroes of such novels were 'to resist the temptations of the erotic Other, to maintain their strongest erotic bonds with their fellow Brits'.[157] The novels analysed by Chapman offer an illuminating contrast to Gautier's *Iskender*, where the Western protagonist's primary relationship is with an Iranian. The erotic undertones of Eskandar and Rostam's relationship are never steeped in exoticism: the two men admire each other's beauty and physical strength without their different cultural origins ever being a matter for discussion. They belong to the same world: one that prizes chivalric ideals of courage and honour above all else. Gautier found in Persian literature her model for an Alexander who, by virtue of his mixed heritage and desire to take Dārā's mantle, is not a foreigner in Iran. But it was her invention of a queer relationship that allowed her to most powerfully dramatize the process by which Eskandar becomes Iranian. As Anne Vincent-Buffault notes in her study of friendship in nineteenth-century French culture, friendship, unlike institutional relationships such as marriage, allows individuals to 'affirmer une identité' [affirm an identity].[158] By choosing Rostam as his most intimate friend, Eskandar takes the first step towards affirming his Iranian identity, which only grows in importance over the course of the novel.

When his half-brother Dārā dies, Eskandar goes from being king of Rum (Greece) to being king of Rum *and* Iran, a political title that reflects his dual heritage, as well as the mixed composition of his royal court and army, which is made up of those men who accompanied him from the West and Dārā's former subjects.[159] But all this changes on the day when the 'Rumi' soldiers (the *Shāhnāmeh*'s term for Greek or Macedonian) refuse to pursue his military campaign into more distant territories, an event that offers the Iranian recruits a chance to prove that their loyalty runs much deeper.[160] The Iranians declare that they are ready to march on: 'O Roi des rois, [...] O Kéïani, nous sommes tes esclaves et la poussière sous tes pieds. Ne confonds pas dans ton courroux les fils de l'Iran avec les fils du Roum.' [O King of kings, [...] O Keyani, we are your slaves and the dust beneath your feet. Do not in your anger mistake the sons of Iran for the sons of Rum.][161] The emotional charge of the Iranian soldiers' words is further conveyed by Rostam, who kisses Eskandar's hand as they speak. But the soldiers in this scene are doing more than profess their loyalty: they are rewriting Eskandar's identity. The vocative addresses 'roi des rois' (the title given to Achaemenid kings) and 'Kéïani' (the name of the royal dynasty in the *Shāhnāmeh*) twice identify Eskandar as a member of the Iranian royal dynasty, an identification Eskandar is all too glad to confirm:

Le glorieux pays d'Iran est ma seule patrie! s'écria Iskender plein de joie; le sang d'Isfendiar coule pur et fier dans mes veines. Je suis l'héritier du royal héros, et je ferai prospérer sa gloire. Puisque j'ai Rustem pour pelewan et les Iraniens pour soldats, je m'assoirai sur le monde comme sur un trône.

Une clameur d'enthousiasme emplit l'air, et toute l'armée iranienne célébra le nom d'Iskender.[162]

[The glorious country of Iran is my only homeland! Eskander cried out full of joy; the blood of Esfandiyār runs pure and proud in my veins. I am the heir of the royal hero and I shall make his glory prosper. Since I have Rostam for my pahlavān and the Iranians for soldiers, I shall sit on the world as on a throne.
Cheering filled the air, and the entire Iranian army celebrated Eskandar's name with enthusiasm.]

The episode is the climax of the protagonist's journey of cultural transition from being Greek to being both Greek and Iranian, to being solely Iranian. Through the biological image of Keyani blood running 'pure' in his veins, Eskandar denies his mixed origins as the 'fils de Darāb, petit fils de Phileïkous' [son of Darāb, grandson of Filqus [Philip]].[163] Father and grandfather have been discarded in favour of one single Iranian ancestor: the legendary King Esfandiyār. Eskandar's intimate and public relationship with one Iranian individual (Rostam) thus lay the foundation for his broader relationship with the Iranian people, whose 'enthusiasm' matches his own 'joy' at declaring himself Iranian.

There is a parallel between Gautier's decision to make cultural identity a matter of personal choice and her queer treatment of the relationship between Eskandar and Rostam: both presuppose a fluid understanding of human identity and relationships. Thus, just as love for Rostam went against the reproductive politics of alliance, so too Eskandar's self-identification as Iranian defies the rules of biology and cultural predetermination: Eskandar may be half 'Rumi' and have grown up abroad, but he can still *choose* to be Iranian. In contrast to Gobineau's ideology of racial predetermination, the reference to 'blood' in Eskandar's speech is as much a performative speech act as it is a biological fact.[164] It is this queer fluidity, combined with Gautier's refusal to predicate the bond between Eskandar and Rostam as one of exotic-erotic attraction between a conquering Greek hero and a passive Oriental other, that gives this novel its virulently anti-imperialist streak. Gautier's Eskandar may be Rostam's political superior, but he is not so because he is Western; he is so because, just like in Ferdowsi's poem, his royal Iranian lineage and heroic deeds make him Iran's most worthy king. By closely engaging with the *Shāhnāmeh* and at the same time boldly innovating upon it, Gautier pulls off the incredible feat of making a novel about empire building go against the grain of the colonial ideology of her time.

Ancient history? Iran as a mirror to French feminism (Jane Dieulafoy)

'Les fouilles de Suse, de long pèlerinages en Orient provoquèrent mes visions, les auteurs classiques créèrent mes songes.'[165] [The dig at Susa and long pilgrimages across the Orient provoked my visions, the classical authors created my dreams.] This is how Jane Dieulafoy describes the inspiration for her first novel *Parysatis* (1890), which centres on the eponymous Achaemenid queen who, according to classical sources, fomented the succession conflict between her two sons Cyrus the Younger and Artaxerxes II. In interviews and press releases, Dieulafoy tended to emphasize the temporal and geographic distance of the settings of *Parysatis* and her subsequent diptych of novellas *Rose d'Hatra* and *L'Oracle* (1893).[166] But this was nothing more than a ploy. The novels all centre on one same theme: women's relationship to power. This was a fraught subject at a time when French first-wave feminists were campaigning for the right to vote and the right to divorce, two campaigns that were perceived as threats to social order. It was also a deeply personal matter. Before becoming a novelist, Dieulafoy was a travel-writer and archaeologist, assisting their husband in documenting pre-Islamic monuments (1881–2) and participating in the archaeological dig at Susa (1884–6), a mission that would earn them the legion of honour.[167] Dieulafoy not only pursued what were considered male occupations, they also *looked* like a man. On the occasion of their first journey to Iran, they cropped their hair and wore men's suits, claiming that this was more practical for life on the road. After that, Dieulafoy never went back to dresses or long hair – clearly, there was more to the sartorial choice than practicality: it was a matter of personal identity. Nineteenth-century scholar Rachel Mesch has argued that Dieulafoy's gender non-conformity is best understood as an example of transgender identity at a time when there was no word for this.[168] Dieulafoy resisted the gender binary, both passing as male and redefining what it meant to be a woman. In the words of one of their contemporaries, Dieulafoy 'rejected her sex without disavowing it'.[169] Mesch's biographical focus in her work on Dieulafoy has led her to favour the pronoun 'they' over 'she'.[170] As she explains, she does so 'not because I believe Dieulafoy would have identified this way, but because "they is a powerful, gender neutral way to refer to someone whose gender is unknown, irrelevant, or beyond classification"'.[171] In both this chapter and the following, I am more interested in Dieulafoy's authorial persona than in their historical identity and therefore find the ability to switch between the pronouns 'they' and 'she' to be an effective analytical tool. Indeed, I argue that Dieulafoy adopts different authorial, and consequently gender, positions based on the genre and subject at hand. And so, while I find the pronoun 'they' most appropriate when focusing on Dieulafoy as a historical individual and when analysing texts in which their narrative voice shifts between different gender positions (see Chapter 3), I favour 'she' when analysing Dieulafoy's novels set in ancient Iran, which foreground the female experience and create an association between their female protagonists and the figure of the author. If the autobiographical writings and two novels set in France studied by Mesch are where Dieulafoy 'rejects' her sex, her Iranian historical fiction is where she 'avows' it, referring to herself from the very first page as 'plus audacieuse que les auteurs classiques' [more audacious (NB: gendered feminine) than the classical authors (NB: gendered masculine)].[172] Using the ancient harem as metaphor, Dieulafoy shows in these works that women's perceived weakness is the product of social conventions and not of female nature. Pre-Islamic Iran therefore acts as a mirror for the condition of women in fin de siècle France. As Dieulafoy wryly noted in the draft version of the preface to *Parysatis*: 'Change le cadre, le tableau est toujours le même.'[173] [Change the frame, the picture is always the same.] The observation, which is neatly crossed out in the manuscript, never made its way to publication. Was Dieulafoy self-censoring or following editorial advice? We will never know. But the redaction is as telling as the sentence itself.

Dieulafoy's debut novel *Parysatis* is based on the classical histories of Xenophon, Plutarch and Ælian and the finds of the Dieulafoy mission at Susa. The novel recounts the troubled early reign of Artaxerxes II (404–397 BC), but centres on the political role of his mother Parysatis. The novel's main theme is announced early on, when, faced with the prospect of her ill-equipped son inheriting the throne, Parysatis tells her gloating daughter-in-law Stateira:

> Roi! que n'eussé-je pas fait de la Perse? Mais des coutumes sauvages me confinent dans le harem, et c'est du fond de cette prison éternelle comme le tombeau que je dirige le monde avec l'aide d'intermédiaires maladroits, parfois méprisables! Les hommes osent proclamer leur supériorité; j'ai dépensé plus de talent et de volonté pour mouvoir un grain de sable qu'il n'en faudrait à un souverain pour ébranler une montagne.[174]

> [King! what would I have not made of Persia? But savage customs confine me to the harem, and it is from the back of that prison, as eternal as a grave, that I run the world through clumsy and often despicable intermediaries! Men dare proclaim their superiority; but I have dispensed more talent and will power to move a grain of sand than it would take a king to crush a mountain.]

Women have to work twice as hard and find ways to overcome the incompetence of their male agents, yet they are still perceived as the weaker sex. By using an ancient Persian queen as her mouthpiece, Dieulafoy is able to condemn gender inequality in far stronger terms than she uses in her non-fictional writing. But she also makes her point through plot and characterization: in this novel, the male characters are not leaders, but unwitting pawns in the game of chess played by the old queen. What follows is a civil war and a series of murders through which Parysatis will eventually regain control of the empire. The transition of power from son to mother is conveyed symbolically in a scene in which Artaxerxes hands over the royal seal:

> [Artaxerxes] sentait auprès de lui *un conseiller viril*, au lieu des comparses toujours prêts à flatter le maître et à louer en termes hyperboliques ses projets et ses actions:
> 'Agissez, vos ordres seront mes lois: voici le sceau royal.'
> *Parysatis régnait enfin*. Ses crimes l'avaient chassée des conseils de l'empire, son génie l'y ramenait en souveraine.
> Elle se mit à l'œuvre sans retard [...] frémit du désordre et de l'incurie qui présidaient à la direction des affaires politiques. La reine s'émut, mais elle n'était pas *femme à pâlir* en face d'un pressant danger. Les difficultés semblaient plutôt accroître que paralyser ses talents.[175] (My emphasis.)

> [[Artaxerxes] felt *a virile counsellor* by his side, instead of the walk-on courtiers always seeking to flatter their master and praise his plans and actions in hyperbolical terms:

'Do as you must, your orders will be laws: here is my royal seal.'

Parysatis ruled at last. Her crimes had banished her from the empire's councils, her genius brought her back as a sovereign.

She set to work without delay [...] trembled at the disorder and negligence that presided over the direction of political affairs. The queen was upset, but she was not *the kind of woman* who pales in front of an urgent danger. The challenges seemed to increase rather than paralyse her talents.] (My emphasis.)

The short sentence 'Parysatis régnait enfin' [Parysatis ruled at last] informs us that Parysatis's longstanding desire to be a king and not queen has finally been fulfilled, the word 'enfin' carrying the weight of all the crimes that were committed to reach this outcome. Parysatis's ascension is symbolized by Artaxerxes handing over his cylinder seal, the instrument used to ratify royal decrees. The relinquishing of the seal is a more powerful sign of abdication than the relinquishing of any other sign of power – such as a crown – because the seal not only represents power, but it also enacts power. In Achaemenid Iran, cylinder seals were used to sign and ratify decrees. Whoever holds the royal seal is therefore effectively performing the role of king. Henceforth, Artaxerxes will be a figurehead and Parysatis, who holds the seal, will be the effective ruler. The passage makes a strong use of gendered terms: the weak king perceives his mother's authority as 'virile', but a few sentences later, Dieulafoy tells us that Parysatis was not 'the kind of woman to pale in the face of danger', thereby reminding us that one can be a woman and a brave ruler. In the pages that follow, Dieulafoy describes the diplomatic efforts through which Parysatis fixes Artaxerxes's mess and re-establishes the Persian Empire's position against the Greek city-states, making even the king of Sparta bow to her will.[176] Artaxerxes takes no interest in this diplomatic work, relieved that he no longer has to handle the responsibilities that come with ruling.[177] Artaxerxes's gender may have made him king, but he has neither the ability nor the will to do the job. For Parysatis, in contrast, politics is both a passion and a 'talent'. Biological sex is thus proven to be a completely arbitrary basis for power.

One year after Parysatis's return to court, peace has been achieved and a grand celebration is held in honour of her achievements, but all the credit for her work must go to Artaxerxes:

Une année avait suffi pour rendre à la Perse déchue *une autorité et un pouvoir incontestés*. [...] La vieille reine avait bien mérité de la patrie, mais elle n'eût pu, sans irriter *son fils impuissant* et orgueilleux, sans soulever les jalouses protestations des grands, savourer en public son triomphe et assister à la proclamation solennelle du traité de paix. On allait fêter un événement mémorable et elle ne devait point figurer à la réception royale. Seules des acclamations lointaines lui parviendraient, apportées par la brise au-dessus des hautes murailles du harem. Que lui importait d'ailleurs! On l'humiliait, mais elle mesurait son mépris de l'humanité à l'immensité de ses efforts et aux conséquences inespérées de la victoire: *on la traitait comme une reine, mais elle avait agi en roi*. Les moyens employés? Les résultats les justifiaient de reste. Le grand Darius ressuscitant de l'empire des morts, retrouverait plus que glorieux cet empire qu'il avait laissé sous l'échec de Marathon...[178] (My emphasis.)

[One year had sufficed to bring *an undisputed authority and power* back to fallen Persia. [...] The old queen had earned her homeland's gratitude, but could not, without irritating *her powerless* and proud *son*, without causing jealous protestations from the great, enjoy her triumph in public and attend the official proclamation of the peace treaty. She was not invited to the royal reception. Only the cries of celebration would reach her, carried by the breeze over the harem's high walls. What did she care! They were humiliating her, but her contempt for humanity was equal to the enormity of her efforts and the unhoped for consequences of victory: *they treated her like a queen, but she had acted as a king.* The means employed? The results more than justified them. Were the great Darius to return from the dead, he would find the empire he had left under the defeat of Marathon more glorious than ever...] (My emphasis.)

Dieulafoy tells her readers point blank that Parysatis's achievements are not acknowledged because this would hurt a man's ego. The contrast is striking between Parysatis, who brings 'authority and power', and her son, described through the antonym 'powerless', further establishing that between the two characters only one had what it took to rule. The harem's high walls, like the modern metaphor of the glass ceiling, also serve to figure the structural inequalities that continue to govern Parysatis life, even when she is ruling the world's greatest empire. This brings a bitter but realistic note to the novel's ending. Parysatis may have succeeded in acting like the greatest of kings, surpassing even Darius the Great, but she will never succeed in making her society recognize her accomplishments. And the fact that Parysatis's achievements are kept secret ensures that the social order that she had momentarily disrupted is perpetuated: power must be associated with men, not women.

The politics of gender and empire explored in *Parysatis* tap into what was a chief concern in fin de siècle France: the perceived causal relationship between France's decadence on the world stage and the changing role of women in society. France's humiliating defeat in the Franco-Prussian War in 1871 was seen as the first sign of this civilizational decline and considered by many to be the direct result of women's emancipation and men's emasculation.[179] Many novels published in the fin de siècle therefore centred on 'the myth of woman as a bestial, irrational, instinctively destructive being'.[180] This myth of the *femme fatale* was also invested with scientific credibility through the pathologization of women as 'hysterics', which had legal ramifications. Until 1914, it was possible in France for women to use hysteria to plead innocent when tried for murder.[181] Juries were all too happy to acquit women on the basis that they were simply 'too emotional' to commit a premeditated murder. The character of Parysatis clearly offers a counter example to these clichés: her acts of violence are all politically motivated and, in the case of the assassination of her daughter-in-law, carefully premeditated. This queen is Machiavellian, not hysterical and eschews the descent into madness typically associated with female killers such as Lady Macbeth. In the character's own words, rendered by Dieulafoy in *discours indirect libre*: 'Les moyens employés? Les résultats les justifiaient de reste.'[182] [The means employed? The results more than justified them.] Though a monster in many ways, Parysatis commands respect for her ability to rule the empire more effectively than any of the novel's hapless male characters. The novel shows two versions of women in power: up until Artaxerxes relinquishes the seal, Parysatis only has soft power and operates in the dark through manipulation and crime. But once she is given executive power, she is shown to be a capable ruler, surpassing all of her predecessors and bringing peace and security to her people. We thus discover that Parysatis did not just want to rule out of a delusional lust for power: she is actually good at it. All that was lacking was the opportunity. This is an altogether different interpretation of the historical events to that offered by male classical authors such as Xenophon and Plutarch, who tended to emphasize Parysatis's maternal love for her younger son Cyrus as her main motivation for acting against Artaxerxes. Dieulafoy, by contrast, considered this woman to be first and foremost a politician.

Women's enormous potential and the deleterious consequences of their confinement to passive and narrowly defined 'female' roles remains a major theme in Dieulafoy's diptych of novellas *Rose d'Hatra* and *L'Oracle,* published as a single volume in 1893. *Rose d'Hatra* is inspired by the story of the siege of the city of Hatra (in modern-day Syria) by the Sassanian king Shapour (*c.* AD 240–1) as chronicled in two Persian histories, Mirkhond's *Rowzat os-safā* and Ferdowsi's *Shāhnāmeh*, which were both available in French translation.[183] In Dieulafoy's version, the protagonist of the story is Nadirah, the princess of Hatra, who has caused the war by kidnapping a romantic rival out of spite.[184] She could end the siege at any moment by relinquishing her captive, but she would rather see her people die than give up on her petty revenge. When Shapour and his army attempt to storm the city, Nadirah glimpses the Persian king from the battlements and falls in love with him. As a result of her infatuation, she hates her father and brothers for fighting the war that she started and wants Shapour to win. That very night, Nadirah drugs her father and lets the enemy army into the city. And thus, a city that had resisted three Roman sieges is undone by an adolescent infatuation. Nadirah's family and people are massacred and she gets her heart's desire: a night with Shapour. But when the morning comes, Shapour regrets having been charmed by a woman 'who sold her father for a night of pleasure' [qui vendit son père pour une nuit de plaisir].[185] He has her executed. Nadirah's narcissim and self-interest make her a rather odious character, but Dieulafoy's narrator suggests that the young woman's betrayal of her people and untimely death are in fact the tragic result of her education. From a young age, Nadirah was 'grisée de flatteries capiteuses, pervertie par d'incessantes adulations' [intoxicated with heady flatteries, perverted by incessant adulations].[186] Her shallowness is thus the result of nurture, not nature, and the true culprits are those who raised her to aspire to nothing more than to be beautiful and to be loved. This raises the implicit question: what would have happened if she had been educated in the same way as the men in her family? Would she still have betrayed her people? The novella indirectly suggests that she would not, by alluding to a different path: that taken by Nadirah's paternal grandmother, whom the narrator tells us had been a brave warrior, just like her father.[187] What is only implied in *Rose d'Hatra* becomes explicit in the novella that follows it, *L'Oracle*, which centres on Artemisia of Caria, the female naval commander who fought for Xerxes in the Battle of Salamis (480 BC).

In the opening pages of *L'Oracle*, Artemisia is first introduced as a frail and timid girl enamoured with her heroic male cousin Agasiclès. Time passes, and Artemisia marries another man and becomes a mother. When we meet her again, she is a widow and has taken over as the ruler of Caria, a Greek vassal kingdom under Persian rule (in modern-day Turkey). Artemisia has grown into a wise woman and responsible politician. And so when the request comes for Caria to provide an army for Xerxes's campaign in Greece, 'elle ne mit en balance que les avantages et les inconvénients de l'obéissance' [she only weighted the pros and cons of obeying].[188] Like Parysatis, Artemisia always thinks strategically. A politician and a warrior, she will not only rally her people to the Persian cause, but also don her armour and personally command the new recruits. The Persian king Xerxes at first feels threatened by this woman who acts like a man, but he is soon won over by her beauty and spiritedness.[189] Dieulafoy proceeds to depict Artemisia as a Cassandra figure, who warns Xerxes not to engage at sea. Instead, Xerxes listens to his male advisors and loses the Battle of Salamis, though Artemisia courageously pursues an enemy Athenian ship even after it is clear that she is on the losing side. In the aftermath of the battle, Artemisia comes across her wounded cousin Agasiclès, who had fought on the opposing side. She saves him, turning the tables as she becomes the hero and he the damsel in distress. But before the pair can live happily ever after, Artemisia must first end Xerxes's infatuation with her without appearing to reject him, which she accomplishes by being perceptive and thinking on her feet.

While Parysatis was a complex character who had both admirable qualities and terrible faults, Nadirah and Artemisia are, respectively, objectionable and saintly. But what makes for far less entertaining reading undoubtedly pays off in political expediency. Read together, the novellas form a diptych: the first illustrates the bad that comes from raising women to cultivate their looks and be waited upon, and the second, the good that comes from allowing women to have a public life and take on serious responsibilities. Moreover, *L'Oracle* further illustrates how it is not enough to allow women to work alongside men: men also need to treat women as equals. Xerxes's choice to ignore Artemisia's military advice in favour of that of the men in the room costs him dearly. This thematic progression from negative to positive example of female behaviour is clearly intentional, since Dieulafoy goes against chronology by placing the novella set in the Achaemenid period after the novella set in the Sassanian period. Indeed, the author reserves her most impassioned critique of gender roles for a passage that comes at the end of *L'Oracle*, which in terms of the sequencing of the volume suggests that this is intended to come as a conclusion to the themes that had hitherto been explored through contrasting examples. But Dieulafoy covers her tracks by placing this critique in the mouth of Artemisia in a humorous scene in which she is tricking Xerxes, thus making it unclear to the reader not only whether these are the authors' personal views, but also whether these views are to be taken seriously.

Artemisia describes her progressive vision for women's education in the context of a marriage proposal. Having almost lost Artemisia in battle, Xerxes has realized that he is in love with her. He therefore reveals to her that he wants her to be his wife and to come live with him in Persia.[190] Artemisia at first demurs and Xerxes, furious, takes this as a slight against his manhood, assuming that she has lost interest because he lost the battle.[191] Changing strategy, Artemisia, who knows that Xerxes is tired of war, declares that she looks forward to fighting beside him as his wife: 'De la Perse nous formerons un vaste camp retranché, car deux guerriers tels que nous doivent asservir le monde.'[192]

[We will turn Persia into a vast entrenched camp, for two warriors such as us must subjugate the world.] She then adds that she will personally avenge the death of Cyrus the Great, who was killed by another female warrior: the Scythian Queen Tomyris.[193] Xerxes is horrified by the prospect of a life at war. And this is when Artemisia delivers the *coup de grâce*. When Xerxes asks her what will become of his 'women', by which he means his multiple wives and concubines, while he and Artemisia are away on campaign, Artemisia replies,

> Vos filles, vos sœurs, voulez-vous dire? Toutes me béniront. A moi de déchirer leur voile écrasant, d'ouvrir les palais où, comme des plantes privées d'air, elles pâlissent et s'étiolent. C'est par l'austérité de la vie et l'exemple de la vertu qu'on élève les esprits et qu'on forme les grands cœurs. Dès l'enfance, nous endurcirons les corps selon les lois de Lacédémone afin que, vigoureux, ils portent des âmes fortes.
>
> Nulle vierge ne deviendra l'épouse d'un prince du sang qu'elle ne sache poursuivre la gazelle à la course, abattre l'hirondelle au vol capricieux et se jeter joyeuse dans la mêlée, telle qu'un vaillant capitaine.
>
> Je veux régner sur des héros.
>
> Xerxès n'en était plus à regretter le trop prompt aveu d'une flamme déjà morte.[194]

[Your daughters and sisters, you mean? They will all sing my praises. I shall be the one to tear off their heavy veil, to open the palaces where, like plants deprived of air, they pale and wither away. It is through an austere lifestyle and the example of virtue that one elevates the minds and forms noble hearts. From childhood, we shall toughen their bodies according to the laws of Sparta, for powerful bodies carry strong souls. No virgin will marry a prince of royal blood without having first learned to chase after gazelles on foot, strike down the swallow in its capricious flight and throw herself happily into the fray, like a courageous captain.

I want to rule over heroes.

All that Xerxes could do now was regret having confessed too soon a flame that was already dead.]

Women's emancipation is the ultimate turn-off. The scene is clearly intended to have comical undertones since it comes in a long tradition of stories in which sly individuals outwit self-important fools, not least La Fontaine's fable 'Le Corbeau et le Renard' (1668). There is the added element that men's desires are shown to be base and predictable, which is why they can be played like fiddles: Artemisia knows what Xerxes means when he says 'mes femmes', but she pretends not to because she knows no man is going to enjoy the prospect of losing access to unlimited sexual partners. She also knows that he derives sexual pleasure from the soft flesh of these women and will therefore be appalled at the thought of them becoming 'tough' and muscular. Finally, the sheer speed with which Xerxes goes from professing his undying love for Artemisia to literally fleeing from her is in itself farcical:

> Sans lui répondre il se leva, s'enfonça dans la profondeur de la tente réunie à d'autres tentes et, de très loin:

– Au revoir… au revoir…
Artémise eut un sourire que ne vit pas Xerxès pressé de fuir.[195]

[He rose without a word, and disappeared into the depths of the tent, which was connected to several other tents, and from afar:
– Goodbye… goodbye…
Artemisia had a smile that Xerxes did not see, rushing as he was to escape.]

And yet, although Artemisia's education reforms come from a place of deception and are spoken in a humorous scene, in the context of the novella and, more broadly, the volume, there is substance to them. The scene comes after Artemisia has proven herself as the wisest of Xerxes's advisors and the bravest of his naval commanders. Does this not suggest that had Xerxes had more women like Artemisia on board, he might have won his battle against the Athenians? Secondly, in the context of the volume as a whole, Artemisia's words come after the example of the hyper-feminine Nadirah, the pale and sheltered 'rose' of the novella's title, who emblematizes the women that Artemisia compares to 'plants deprived of air'. Too shallow and selfish to consider the consequences of her actions, Nadirah illustrates what goes wrong when women are not given a chance to 'elevate their minds' and 'form great hearts'. Thus, by the time that Artemisia makes these proposals, she has already been proven right. We also know from Dieulafoy's travel-writing that she considered women's veiling and physical confinement in Qajar Iran to be forms of oppression.[196] She had personally relished the opportunities to travel across Iran and work in the field as an archaeologist, even when it put her life at risk. Moreover, Dieulafoy had also fought in the Franco-Prussian War by disguising herself as a man and firmly believed that women should be allowed to serve in the military.[197] It is therefore clear that Artemisia's provocative suggestions for the education of princesses mirror Dieulafoy's own feminist ideals. By expressing these views in a scene that is intended to make us laugh, Dieulafoy chooses to gently invite her readers to consider her point of view, rather than preaching at them. But there is also another dimension to Dieulafoy's choice of Artemisia as a mouthpiece, one that speaks to a certain conservatism.

Unlike the character of Parysatis who was ambitious and motivated only by her desire to rule, the character of Artemisia only takes on a leadership role by circumstance, following her husband's death. Although she serves the Persian Empire, Artemisia is also ethnically Greek, making her less of a cultural other in the eyes of fin de siècle French readers. Moreover, for all her courage in military combat, Artemisia will lay down her weapons for the man whom she truly loves. In doing so, she shows herself willing to re-establish the gender binary. Indeed, the novella contains two highly symbolic scenes of disarmament. The first takes place during Artemisia and Xerxes's first meeting. In this episode, the narrator homes in on the highly gendered contrast between the two characters' appearances: 'Étrange contraste entre l'homme fardé, couvert de bijoux et d'étoffes précieuses, comme embaumé dans sa majesté royale et la femme bardée de fer poli, debout, prête à combattre.' [Strange contrast between the man in make up, bejewelled and bedecked in precious fabrics, anointed by his royal majesty and the woman encased in polished iron, standing, ready to fight.]

The narrator adds: 'L'Achéménide en eut conscience, et une jalousie secrète mordit son cœur.'[198] [The Achaemenid realized this, and a secret jealousy bit at his heart.] Xerxes sees that Artemisia performs masculinity far more successfully than he does and envies her for it.[199] Suspecting that she is in fact a man and not a woman, Xerxes asks Artemisia if she wears a helmet to conceal a beard. Artemisia allays his fears: 'Passant ses armes à des esclaves, Artémise releva le casque. Un hasard intelligent, aidé d'un geste brusque, dénoua la lourde torsade ramenée sur la nuque et, le long de la cuirasse, se déroulèrent des boucles brunes, en spirales alanguies.'[200] [Handing her weapons to one of her slaves, Artemisia raised her helmet. A serendipitous chance, aided by her sudden gesture, undid the heavy coil on her nape and her long brown locks unfurled unto her breast-plate, in languorous spirals.] The long hair restores her femininity and kindles the desire of Xerxes, whom she allows to touch her face. There is a delicious ambiguity in the power dynamics of this scene. Xerxes is in a position of authority over Artemisia both in terms of gender and political hierarchy, yet he is intimidated by her and envious of her. By kneeling and letting him touch her face, Artemisia puts herself in a submissive position. But she also laughs out loud at the thought of being mistaken for a man and seems to let him touch her face in jest.[201] Whereas Artemisia remains coolly detached throughout this scene, Xerxes is overcome with emotion: 'Jusque-là Xerxès avait tout eu, tout méprisé. A cette heure il éprouvait un plaisir ignoré, il pressentait des émotions nouvelles.'[202] [Until then Xerxes had had it all and despised everything. In this moment he felt an unknown pleasure and could foresee new emotions.] Romantically, then, she has the upper hand.

The second scene of disarmament comes at the end of the novel and this time there is no ambiguity. Artemisia appears before her cousin Agasiclès for the first time since the Battle of Salamis. She prepares for the interview by donning her armour, in order to resemble the goddess Athena, whom she had considered a rival to his affections when they were young.[203] When Artemisia appears before him, Agasiclès is terrified, since he is convinced that she has come to punish him for having once spurned her – after all, 'Hell hath no fury'. 'Soit humaine' [be humane] he begs, fearing for his very life.[204] But the words also have another meaning: 'be human', as in, do not be a goddess. When Agasiclès continues to tremble despite her many reassurances, Artemisia teases him by referring to his athletic successes during their youth: 'Qu'est devenu le vainqueur des jeux triopiens? En ceignant l'épée lui aurais-je légué ma quenouille?' [What happened to the winner of the Triopian games? Did I hand him my spindle when I girded my sword?] To which he responds that even Hercules had to bow before the Amazonian queen Omphale.[205] The power until here is clearly in Artemisia's hands, even more so than it was with Xerxes. And so she proceeds to surrender it. When Agasiclès recognizes her multifaceted identity as both a kind and loving woman and a war hero ('l'héroïne de Salamine'), she responds: 'D'accord avec Circé, Eros changea les hommes en bêtes; aujourd'hui, repentant, il a transformé pour te plaire une femme timide en une vaillante amazone. Oublieras-tu Pallas Athéna, ma rivale de jadis?'[206] [Working with Circe, Eros turned men into beasts; today, repenting, he transformed a timid woman into a brave Amazon, so that you might like her. Will you forget Athena, my old rival?] She only changed herself in order to win his heart. Of course, this does not follow: as we saw, the narrator had previously stated that Artemisia chose to fight for Xerxes because it was the wisest political move.²⁰⁷ Moreover, at the time she had no idea that Agasiclès, who had been living in exile for a decade, would participate in the war. Her explanation is therefore untruthful. But it does succeed in diminishing her achievements. As a result, Agasiclès is now the one doing the reassuring: 'Tu es aussi belle que la déesse; mieux qu'elle tu sais pardonner.'²⁰⁸ [You are as beautiful as the goddess, and you know even better than her how to forgive.] The comparison between the woman and the goddess, which was in itself problematic in so far as it created a female rivalry that had never existed, is now recast in terms of physical beauty and kindness, the ultimate feminine qualities, when in fact the qualities Artemisia and Athena really share are wisdom and military prowess. Now that Artemisia has diminished herself in Agasiclès's eyes, the pair can finally profess their love for each other. To celebrate, Agasiclès removes Artemisia's armour: 'L'ayant dépouillée de son armure, il la contemplait avec des yeux pleins d'extase où se peignaient le ravissement et l'amour!'²⁰⁹ [Having removed her armour, he admired her with eyes full of ecstasy, rapture, and love!] Artemisia has been many things: the queen of Caria, a military general, an adviser to Xerxes, a mother and a woman in love. But the novella reduces her to that single final attribute, no doubt the most sympathetic in the eyes of Dieulafoy's readers.

Parysatis was a poor saleswoman for fin de siècle women's empowerment because she did not seek the approval of any man: 'Le monde entier connaissait son nom. Du fond de son harem elle maniait les hommes et les choses avec une égale fermeté, avec un égal dédain; ses mains pétrissaient l'univers comme un statuaire pétri la glaise.'²¹⁰ [The whole world knew her name. From the back of her harem she manipulated men and objects with equal firmness and disdain; her hands moulded the universe just like a sculptor moulds clay.] When her husband is on his death bed, Parysatis does not fear the loss of her life partner, but the loss of her conduit to power: 'Cette femme si forte, si dominatrice, habituée depuis vingt-cinq ans à gouverner la Perse avec des rois pour instruments, subissait la torture de ses terribles pensées.'²¹¹ [This woman, so strong and dominant, accustomed for twenty-five years to governing Persia with kings for instruments, suffered the torture of terrible thoughts.] Artemisia's authority, in contrast, is tempered by the fact that she will bow to the will of her lover and, presumably, soon-to-be husband. She may rule a kingdom and command a navy, keeping her cool in battle when her male peers flee in distress, but when Artemisia arrives home, she is all too happy to restore social order by removing her armour and letting a man take charge. The effect is comparable to the redeeming power of Dieulafoy's own status as the doting wife of Marcel Dieulafoy, which combined with their political conservativism, made their gender non-conformity far more acceptable. As a Catholic, Dieulafoy was staunchly opposed to the legalization of divorce, which was a key feminist cause of their time. This made them a poster child for a less threatening vision of feminism, which claimed that women could have careers while still living up to their wifely duties.²¹² A caption accompanying a photograph of Dieulafoy in the women's magazine *Femina* reads: 'Mme Dieulafoy est pour son mari la plus dévouée et la plus active des collaboratrices. Après l'avoir suivi dans tous ses voyages scientifiques, elle continue à l'aider à Paris dans ses nombreux travaux, ce qui ne l'empêche pas d'écrire des romans émouvants.'²¹³ [Madame Dieulafoy is her husband's most devoted and active collaborator. After having followed him on his scientific journeys, she continues to assist him in his numerous projects in Paris, which does not prevent her from writing moving novels.] The syntax of this passage reflects the presumed hierarchy within the Dieulafoys' marriage: the husband leads and the wife follows. Dieulafoy's first duty is always to assist Marcel in his work; her own work comes second. The article is also keen to stress that putting their husband first does not 'prevent' women from having their own interests, in this case, writing novels. The adjective 'émouvant' [moving] here is deeply gendered: by alleging that Dieulafoy's historical fiction is sentimental, the magazine downplays the research that went into these novels and, more generally, misrepresents Dieulafoy's narrative voice and choice of subject, which are far from sentimental. Only Marcel's work is worthy of the far superior label of 'scientific'. This was in great part due to the different genres that their respective publications fell under. By writing travelogues and novels, rather than academic essays or histories, Jane remained within two genres that were deemed acceptable for women, who were not qualified to have a scientific voice. And yet, although Dieulafoy played by the gendered rules of genre, women's pursuit of equal status to men remained at the forefront of their writing. All three of their Iranian novels centre on strong independent women. Even Nadirah, for all her selfishness, is a bold and ingenious character who twice defies patriarchal order: first by disobeying her father and then by acting as the pursuant in her love affair. Dieulafoy's concern with their own authority, moreover, runs as a rich thread throughout their fiction and non-fiction. In their first-person travelogues, to which we shall turn in Chapter 3, Dieulafoy seeks to establish their status as an intrepid explorer, who was as brave and played as active a research role as their male companions, identifying with them in a manner that they could never do with women. Dieulafoy's historical fiction also strives to establish the author's scientific authority, though without presenting them as male. By questioning patriarchal hierarchies and showcasing their expertise within the literary genres available to women writers, Dieulafoy was thus playing a careful balancing act, analogous to the one they performed in society as the doting gender-non-conforming wife of Marcel Dieulafoy.

The third-person narration in Dieulafoy's Iranian novels is replete with references to the architecture and material culture that Dieulafoy had played a key role in reconstituting. This is most obviously the case in *Parysatis*, which contains detailed descriptions of the palace of Susa,[214] as well as of the archers in the royal guard, who match the ceramic figures excavated by the Dieulafoy mission down to their very shoelaces.[215] The connection would have been clear to Dieulafoy's readers: even if they had not personally viewed the frieze at the Louvre, they would have seen images of it in the numerous illustrated press articles that marked the inauguration of the Susa finds (see Figure 3.4). Dieulafoy's narration thus establishes a direct link between the author's ability to write the Achaemenids and her participation in the excavation. In the years that followed the publication of *Parysatis*, Dieulafoy would repeatedly make the case that inspiration for the novel came to her during the archaeological dig. The 'resuscitation' of Parysatis (Dieulafoy's own term) was thus the natural counterpart to the reconstruction of the ancient queen's residence.[216] References to the Susa finds also continue to feature in her later fiction. In *Rose d'Hatra*, the description of the Persian soldiers mentions 'l'or qui attirait les regards jusque sur la pomme de leur javeline' [the gold that drew the eye to the very pommel of their javelins], which is another (anachronistic) detail taken from the archers' frieze.[217] And when Xerxes tries to convince Artemisia to marry him in *L'Oracle*, the palace of Susa is the most alluring part of the offer: 'Viens en mon palais de Suse; suis-moi dans cette plaine adorable où les fleurs s'ouvriront sous tes pieds.'[218] [Come to my Susa palace; follow me into this adorable plain where the flowers will open under your feet.] Dieulafoy's narration similarly showcases her expertise by referring to the Persian language,[219] Zoroastrian liturgy,[220] and aspects of human and physical geography noted during her travels in Iran.[221] But Dieulafoy's most overt reference to her personal authority comes in the preface of *Parysatis*:

> Xénophon, Plutarque, Elien dévoilent d'une main discrète une femme qui paraît avoir joué un rôle immense pendant la période où la Perse, en relation constante avec la Grèce, rayonne d'un dernier éclat. Plus audacieuse que les auteurs classiques je me suis efforcée de ressusciter devant toi la reine Parysatis, de te la montrer animée de passions terribles, assez puissante pour s'y livrer sans contrainte. J'ai voulu te faire suivre pas à pas son génie, triomphant – Dieu sait au prix de quels efforts et de quels crimes – des obstacles semés sur sa route, déchirant impitoyablement les coeurs de tous les siens et les immolant à la grandeur de la monarchie.[222]

> [Xenophon, Plutarch, and Ælian reveal with a discrete hand a woman who seems to have played an enormous role during the period in which Persia, in constant relations with Greece, shone with a final splendour. More audacious than the classical authors, I endeavoured to resuscitate before you Queen Parysatis, to show her animated with awful passions, and powerful enough to devote herself to them unabated. I wanted to make you follow, step by step, her genius, triumphing – God knows through what efforts and crimes – over the obstacles planted on her path, crushing without mercy the hearts of her own family in order to sacrifice them to the glory of monarchy.]

The author, who is gendered in the feminine, compares herself to the male classical historians who wrote 'discretely', stating that she is bolder than all of them. For a woman to write authoritatively on history was in itself transgressive. To state that in doing so, she was surpassing canonical male authors was to do so self-consciously. Dieulafoy also proclaims her authority by using the informal 'tu', instead of the formal 'vous', to address her readers, which would have already been a bold move coming from a man (as is the case in Baudelaire's poem 'Au Lecteur'), and is therefore even more provocative coming from a woman author. In speaking within one same breath of her own 'audacity' and Parysatis's 'power' and 'genius', Dieulafoy creates an implicit parallel between herself and the Achaemenid queen. The parallel becomes all the more clear if we read the preface alongside the novel's ending (analysed above), in which Parysatis is described as having surpassed Darius the Great, much as Dieulafoy describes herself in the preface surpassing her male predecessors Xenophon, Plutarch and Ælian. And is there not also an echo of the author in the queen who must stay in the shadows while her son takes all the glory? After all, Dieulafoy herself had watched her husband receive the greatest accolades for their work at Susa, including membership of the Institut de France, accolades that were denied to her as a woman. 'They were humiliating her, but her contempt for humanity was equal to the enormity of her efforts and the unhoped for consequences of victory.'[223]

Dieulafoy would cover her tracks, redacting the preface's final sentence ('Change the frame, the picture is always the same').[224] In the years that followed, she would go on to depict rather less threatening queens: Artemisia puts down her weapons and Parysatis, in her 1902 stage incarnation, is transformed into a concerned mother (see Chapter 4). Twenty years after *Parysatis* was first published, however, Dieulafoy returned to the novel's theme in a lecture entitled 'La femme roi' (1910). The gender clash in this title serves to question the gendered division of labour in much the same way as *Parysatis* had done through phrases such as 'they treated her like a queen, but she had acted as a king'.[225] In the lecture, Dieulafoy argues that the powerful women of history are not solitary exceptions, but emblems of female power and thus role models for the modern woman. She concludes: 'The time will come without a doubt when Woman […] will stand up from the kind of humiliation that the centuries seem to have given her, and that by virtue of being usurped has degenerated into a natural order, passing as a natural state.'[226] The lecture's bold frankness in comparison to the more measured approach adopted in Dieulafoy's novels suggests the progress that French feminism had made between 1890 and 1910. Dieulafoy now had the confidence to explicitly use antiquity as a mirror for the modern age, something that had only been implicit in her fiction. Three years after delivering 'La femme roi', Dieulafoy wrote an open letter to the Minister of War arguing in favour of women's right to serve in the military. The very same cause that had been shrouded in comedy when spoken by the character of Artemisia in *L'Oracle* was now a serious matter, and the author was finally prepared to defend it under her own name.[227] For Jane Dieulafoy, Iranian history was never a place of escapism: it was about the present of the women of France, a present that was in urgent need of change.

Conclusion

The nineteenth-century Oriental Renaissance challenged European views of world history by locating the origin of Western civilization in Asia. To quote Leconte de Lisle's prefatory sonnet to Judith Gautier's *Iskender*, the Orient was now 'la patrie antique' [the ancient homeland], whose 'vivant souvenir' [living memory] populated the dreams of these writers and their intended readers.[228] The problem, of course, was that France had for centuries identified with Greek and Roman antiquity, following a narrative that cast the Orient as Europe's ontological other. The myth of the Aryan and Semitic races, actively promoted by Gobineau and Renan and adopted uncritically by Michelet and Dieulafoy,[229] solved this problem by dividing the ancient Middle East into a superior Orient, from which Europe was descended, and an inferior Orient, from which Jews and Arabs were descended. This racialist theory worked hand in hand with Islamophobic bias, as is most evident in Ernest Renan's debate with Jamal al-Din Al-Afghani: Iranians were elevated above all other Oriental peoples by virtue of being linguistically Indo-European, racially Aryan and religiously the most reluctant of converts to Islam. It was this combination of features that made Iran seem culturally closer to France than any other Oriental nation … this and the undisputed might of its ancient empires. As a result, pre-Islamic Iran became the most attractive historical period for historians seeking to study the origins of Western civilization. A strict focus on Iran's past, rather than its present, was also a necessary condition in a narrative constructed upon the premise of an ancestral relationship. As I have shown, the Aryan migration myth tightly associates civilizational progress over time with geographic movement westwards, leaving contemporary Iranians out of the remit of the story. The kinship that authors such as Michelet expressed towards the Persians thus rested upon a strict temporal separation. French authors' keen interest in Iranian ancient history therefore adds a further facet to what has been described by Johannes Fabian as the 'denial of coevalness', that is to say the imperialist refusal to view non-Western cultures as contemporary, locating them instead at a temporal remove, so that the notion of 'development' may be employed to simultaneously other the colonized and justify the colonizer's civilizing mission.[230] In the case of Iran, the modern nation was indeed denied coevalness, something that we shall further explore in the coming chapter, but at the same time, Iran's history and cultural heritage was presented as coeval to that of the West. We might think back, for instance, to Gobineau's parallels between the ancient Persians and the ancient Greeks, and between Ferdowsi and Ariosto. Characters from ancient Iranian history also became coeval to nineteenth-century French readers through recuperative and creative acts of history-making, whether that be Michelet's day-in-the-life of an ancient Iranian farmer or Dieulafoy's exploration of the psychological motivations of Queen Parysatis. There is a marked contrast between how easily these authors identified with figures from Iran's ancient history and how rarely they viewed contemporary Iranians as similar or equal to them.

The intellectual appropriation of ancient Iran as proto-European served imperialist aims, most notably the physical appropriation of the Susa finds, which was justified as research into 'les origines de la race aryenne'.[231] But it could also lend itself to boldly non-Eurocentric perspectives, such as Michelet's claim that Zoroastrianism was a superior religion to Christianity and Gautier's depiction of an Alexander who did not Westernize Iran, but on the contrary, was willingly made Iranian. Moreover, for all its appropriative logic, the idea that modern French values could be found in ancient Iran was nonetheless a subversive one: it challenged both the temporal narrative of progress that had placed modern Europe as the pinnacle of human civilization *and* the Orientalist cliché that the ancient Persians were decadent and despotic, and thus morally dubious. Indeed, this is a trope that even Dieulafoy falls prey to: for all the psychological depth of characters such as Queen Parysatis, her portrayals of Kings Xerxes and Artaxerxes II are replete with such clichés, which the author directly inherited from Western classical sources. The publication over the course of the nineteenth century of French translations and commentaries of works such as Ferdowsi's *Shāhnāmeh* and Mirkhond's *Rowzat os-safā*, as well as of Zoroastrian scripture, played an enormous part in opening French historians' eyes to an other ancient Iran: one that was not filtered by the political biases of the ancient Greeks. The influence of Iranian historiography is particularly notable in the case of Dieulafoy and Gautier's portrayals of head-strong female characters, which owe a lot to the *Shāhnāmeh*. There is certainly something of Ferdowsi's Tahmineh and Manijeh in Gautier's Indûmatî, the young princess determined to make Rostam hers even if it means disobeying her king and fiancé. Dieulafoy based *Rose d'Hatra* on the story of Malekeh and Shapour, and there are also hints of Ferdowsi's character Homai, the warrior queen who gives away her son so that she can rule Iran in his stead, in the portrayal of Parysatis and Artemisia. Thus, the very aspect that we associate with French modernity, that is, strong female characters embodying the ideals of first-wave feminism, was in fact already present in the medieval Persian source material. On other occasions, the perceived similarities between ancient Iran and modern France seem rather to be a case of authorial self-projection, as with Michelet's obsessive conflation of Zoroastrianism and the 1789 French Revolution.

These five French authors all agreed on Iran's central role in the history of human civilization, but Iran also held an entirely different personal significance for each one of them. For Arthur de Gobineau, Iran provided irrefutable evidence that the rise and fall of civilizations resulted from the adulteration of the white civilizing race's blood. Ernest Renan too bought into the myth of the Aryan race, casting Iranian history as one of resistance against a nefarious Arab–Muslim–Semitic influence, an oppositional framework that he applied even to contemporaries such as Jamal al-Din Al-Afghani. For Judith Gautier, the historiography of the *Shāhnāmeh* offered a model for her own blend of realism and fairytale and Ferdowsi's vivid characters offered a way into a world in which desire – both queer and heterosexual – mattered more than the borders between nations and empires. Indeed, there is an unexpected parallel between Gautier's fluid understanding of cultural identity and Al-Afghani's description of the layered and multiple identities that formed the medieval Islamic world. Gautier and Al-Afghani's transcending of dualism also resonates with Michelet's argument that Islam incorporated and upheld certain Zoroastrian values. This, in turn, brings us back to Ferdowsi's *Shāhnāmeh*, which is Michelet's key case study for reaching this conclusion. For Dieulafoy, finally, ancient Iran was the domain in which they could prove that they were equal – if not superior – to any male Orientalist. Its history was as much a subject of fascination as a pretext for the ultimate performance of authority.

3

Travel-writing

'Tout chemin ne conduit pas en Perse'[1]

Characterized by a yearning for lands untainted by industrialization and the various mundanities of modern Parisian life, the *Voyage en Orient* [Oriental voyage or journey to the Orient] was a staple sub-genre of French Romantic literature and went on to outlive it. A French canon of Oriental voyages would have to include René de Chateaubriand, Alphonse de Lamartine, Gustave Flaubert, Gérard de Nerval and Théophile Gautier. Unlike Victor Hugo, whom we left in Chapter 1 daydreaming at his Parisian window, these authors all travelled to the Middle East and wrote accounts of their journeys.[2] None of them, however, made it as far as Iran – though Flaubert had intended to do so. Compared to North Africa and the Levant, the two dominant Orients of nineteenth-century French travel-writing, Iran was a more unusual destination. This was first of all due to its greater distance: travelling from France to Iran required one to first cross several other territories in order to reach either the Caspian Sea or the Persian Gulf, the two maritimes points of entry into the country. Once in Iran, those travelling to cities south of Tehran – and these are the accounts that I will be focusing on – had to cross several deserts, which was a gruelling experience for anyone unaccustomed to travelling off road and in extreme weather conditions. Due to its position on the frontiers of the Russian and British Empires, Iran, finally, was a site of competing and shifting geopolitical allegiances.[3] Although the Qajar aristocracy tended to look favourably upon France and French culture, French travellers in Iran were not guaranteed the level of protection and preferential treatment that they would have in a French colony such as Algeria. Travelling to Iran was thus a far more arduous process, which explains why the *Voyage en Perse* is a minor sub-category of the *Voyage en Orient*. Jane Dieulafoy, an author whom we already encountered in Chapter 2 and who provides the title for this chapter's introduction, reports the warnings they received upon planning their itinerary: 'Dans le sud comme dans le nord nous courions au-devant d'un désastre; le moins qu'il pût nous arriver était d'être hachés en menus morceaux.' [Whether we took the southern or the northern route, we were running into a disaster; the least that could happen to us was to get chopped into tiny pieces], before wryly adding: 'L'exagération évidente de ces prédictions fut cause que nous leur accordâmes médiocre créance.'[4] [The obvious exaggeration of these forecasts led us to only afford them the slightest credence.] Dieulafoy was right to be sceptical: while it remained a challenging enterprise, travelling to Iran was easier than it had ever been before.

Unlike their predecessors, French travellers in the second half of the nineteenth century could depend on travel by train and steamboat, communication via telegraph, and the support and shelter offered by European diplomatic outposts. This led to an increased number of European travellers in Iran. Iranian seasonal workers learned to cater to their needs, forming a small tourist economy. All of the authors studied in this chapter depended on the Iranian men whom they hired to be their guides, translators, grooms and domestic servants. While benefiting from the growing European presence in Iran, French travellers were also often suspicious of it, especially when it came to their imperial rivals, the British. As we shall see, French imperial anxiety vis-à-vis the British is a recurring theme across the travelogues studied in this chapter and, in the cases of the state-funded missions undertaken by Flandin, Gobineau and Dieulafoy, imperial anxiety is the journey's very *raison d'être*. Travel-writing thus emerges as a genre that is tightly intertwined with the politics of empire on two levels: first, on a material level, because of the political context that made these journeys possible, and secondly, on a textual level, in terms of how French authors positioned themselves in relation to the places that they visited and the people whom they met. In her influential study *Imperial Eyes*, Mary-Louise Pratt argues that travel-writing was 'a key instrument […] in creating the "domestic subject" of empire', since it offered European readers a sense of ownership over the lands and individuals that were being described.[5] Pratt's claim closely aligns with Edward Said's argument that the very act of describing the Orient served to assert the West's dominance over it. Indeed, as I noted in my introduction, English and French travelogues play a prominent role in Said's *Orientalism*, offering potent illustrations of the position of distance that Western observers sought to cultivate between themselves and their Oriental objects of study, which Said refers to as one of 'strategic location'. And yet, there is also much here to disentangle.

Unlike the other genres studied in this book, travel-writing derives its authority not from academic knowledge or literary prestige, but from personal experience. This makes it an idiosyncratic genre which encompasses many different forms of writing: geographic and ethnographic description, historical disquisition, political analysis, anecdotes ranging from the suspenseful to the farcical, recorded conversations and personal musings. Individual authors will adopt, adapt and combine these different modes of writing based on their own interests, subjective experiences and stylistic preferences. As such, travel-writing can be described as a 'genre composed of other genres', as a 'lawless' and 'slippery' genre, or even as a 'frontier' genre, which sits at the crossroads of description and narrative, fact and fiction, and science and literature.[6] This gives travelogues a patchwork-like texture, where the only connecting threads are the use of first-person narration and the linearity provided by the itinerary's progression through time. The openness or 'lawlessness' of travel-writing offered writers a great deal of freedom since they could choose which information to include and how this information was conveyed. In Alain Guyot's words: 'le "faire-savoir" au public passe nécessairement par un savoir-faire du relateur' [what is made known to the public is necessarily filtered by the know-how of the writer].[7] This is one way in which travel-writing, for all its claims of objectivity, is a deeply subjective genre. But even before an author puts pen to paper, travel-writing is also subjective in the sense that no two travellers' experiences and understanding of these experiences will be the same. In Iran, travellers' experiences differed based on such factors as their itinerary, preparatory reading, linguistic abilities, finances, social class and gender, to name only the most obvious. One particularly illuminating contrast is that between Claude Anet and Marthe Bibesco, two authors who travelled together to Iran and who both published accounts of this journey. Each of them brought their own perspective, areas of interest and literary style to their account, and as a result, their two travelogues are completely different. Were it not for the fact that Anet names Bibesco in his travelogue and that their journey was publicized due to their celebrity status – Anet was a jet-setting journalist and tennis-player and Bibesco was a Romanian princess – their readers would have had no way of telling that these two books were actually referring to the same trip.

Travel-writers' positions in relation to the Iranians whom they meet are equally varied. The examples studied in this chapter cover a wide spectrum, ranging from the superior sense of distance referred to by Said as strategic location, to cultural comparisons motivated by a desire to find common ground, and finally moments of personal interaction in which Iranians are not described as cultural or racial specimens, but as hosts and companions. Gender and class were of enormous significance on these occasions. Bibesco and Dieulafoy were invited to experience the domesticity of the harem because their status as women trumped their status as foreigners. And, as we shall see, their reactions to this hospitality differ entirely as a result of their different relationships to their own gender identity. Overall, French travellers' warmest interactions are those with the young men of the Qajar elite because these aristocrats were French-speaking and in many cases had studied in Paris. This provided them with a *lingua franca* and common references. At the same time, however, French travellers could often be very patronizing and cutting towards these Iranian aristocrats' idealization of European culture. As this brief survey shows, any categoric pronouncement that travel-writing is by nature imperialist in both its intent and its style ignores the diverse range of perspectives represented by Iranian travelogues and the variety of stylistic approaches that authors adopted to communicate their experiences with readers at home. For this reason, I will begin by introducing my cast of travellers and the respective contexts of their journeys to Iran, as this will provide essential background to my comparative analysis of their writings. In selecting my corpus, I have limited myself to travelogues published as volumes (as opposed to press articles) and where Iran is the intended destination rather than a stopover. A further criteria is that travellers should have made it at least as far south as the city of Esfahan, since many Western travellers never made it further than Tehran, the Qajar capital city, which lies in the north of the country. This leaves us with a dozen travelogues, out of which I shall focus on seven.[8] The motivations for the journeys recounted in these works fall under three categories: diplomacy, research and tourism.

Eugène Flandin's *Voyage en Perse* (1851) and Arthur de Gobineau's *Trois Ans en Asie* (1859) both recount French diplomatic missions to rekindle the alliance between France and Iran that had first been formed by Napoleon, with the ultimate aim of counteracting British influence in the region. Flandin, a painter by training, was also charged with completing a broader survey of the geography and ancient art of Iran. This gave him and his partner, the architect Pascal Coste, their own brief: one of state-funded research. Flandin's account is divided into two volumes. In the first, he describes his and Coste's journey among the French ambassador's escort, a highly regimented tour full of pomp and ceremony. Things change in the second volume, when Flandin and Coste remain in Iran alone and explore regions that were less known to Europeans. Free from the French ambassador and the diplomatic escort, the two travellers could now go 'off-piste', travel at their own pace, and interact with ordinary Iranians, rather than being confined to the highest rungs of the aristocracy. Gobineau, in contrast, never ventures out of the diplomatic cohort, nor deviates from their itinerary from the Persian Gulf to Tehran. This results in a much shorter travelogue that features only limited interactions with the local population. These two journeys took place in 1840–1 and 1855, respectively.

Jane Dieulafoy, whose historical fiction was discussed in Chapter 2, is the author of two of the travelogues studied in this chapter. I noted then that Dieulafoy had a complex relationship with their gender identity, and this is particularly obvious in their travel-writing. Dieulafoy's journeys to Iran, documented in their travelogues *La Perse, la Chaldée et la Susiane* (1887, hereafter *La Perse*) and *À Suse: Journal de fouilles* (1888, hereafter *À Suse*) were an occasion for them to reject their biological sex and assert a masculine identity. We see this both in terms of how they chose to present themself (cropped hair and men's suits) and in terms of their writing. In these travelogues, Dieulafoy repeatedly stressed their non-identification with women – French or Iranian – and also found ways to refer to themself through nouns and adjectives in the masculine plural, an ambivalent choice since the masculine plural holds two functions in French grammar: it can refer either to a group of men or it can be a gender neutral expression used to include both men and women. At the same time, Dieulafoy still passes as female in Iran and exploits this to gain access to the private sphere of Iranian women. Dieulafoy also shows a keen interest in the condition of women in Iran, which, for all their protestations that they are not like other women and perhaps are not even a woman at all, shows a level of personal investment and identification with the plight of women. To do justice to the complexity and ambivalence of Dieulafoy's relationship to gender in their travel-writing, I will therefore be favouring the pronoun 'they' when referring to their authorial persona in this chapter.[9] From 1881 to 1882, Dieulafoy spent a year travelling around Iran with their husband Marcel, an engineer with an interest in art history, who wanted to prove the influence of pre-Islamic Iranian architecture on the European Gothic. Marcel obtained a year's leave and a letter of introduction to French emissaries in Iran, but no funding. The pair therefore travelled alone and with modest means. Jane had learned Persian and photography before the journey. As a result, *La Perse* stands out from other travelogues for its inclusion of many lengthy passages in direct speech, which recount the conversations they were able to have in Persian, as well as numerous etchings reproducing the photographs that they took. Dieulafoy's voice in *La Perse* is also witty and sardonic, and they often draw on the comedic potential of moments of culture shock and miscommunication. Shortly after their return from Iran, the Dieulafoys were able to convince the director of the Louvre Louis de Ronchaud to intercede in their favour and were put in charge of France's first archaeological mission in Iran, which took place from 1884 to 1886 at the site of the ancient city of Susa. Dieulafoy's relationship with the local population and Iranian authorities in this second account differs markedly from the first, since they are now viewed in an antagonistic light as obstacles to France's appropriation of ancient Iranian artefacts.

At the tail end of this book's chronological coverage are three travelogues that recount touristic journeys to Iran. Pierre Loti's *Vers Ispahan* (1904) is one of the lesser known works in the long list of travelogues spanning from Morocco to French 'Indochina', which were a product of his career as a naval officer (real name: Louis-Marie-Julien Viaud). Loti took advantage of the fact that he had been posted in India to take a scenic detour across Iran on his way home to France in 1900. Escorted by his loyal footman, the confident Loti knows how to barter in third languages (in this case Turkish) and buy his way into places, and often feels like a caricature of the Western imperialist, though he is on occasion humbled by the beauty and scale of sites such as Persepolis and Qom. Claude Anet and Marthe Bibesco, two international Parisian socialites, travelled in 1905 together with Marthe's husband Georges Valentin Bibesco and other friends to visit Esfahan. Anet's itinerary and descriptions tend to repeat a lot of the same material we find in previous travelogues. The main novelty of his work is that it describes an attempt to travel across Iran by automobile. As it happened, the cars broke down in the desert between Tehran and Esfahan, and the travellers had to switch to a horse-drawn cart. This did not stop Anet from titling his book *Les Roses d'Ispahan: la Perse en Automobile* (1906). Marthe Bibesco took a few more years to publish her account of the journey, following encouragement from Anet who knew she had kept a diary during their travels. *Les Huit paradis* (1908) is exceptional among the travelogues studied in this chapter for being entirely unpreoccupied with the material aspects of the journey. We are not told whom Bibesco travels with nor by what means of finance or transportation. Instead, we are treated to a series of carefully selected and crafted scenes: Iran as seen from the Caspian Sea, a beautiful garden, a feast, meeting the wives of a local dignitary, a child beggar, a religious ceremony. These scenes, which often feel like pictures in an album, are devoid of any context and are interspersed with Bibesco's personal musings on her favourite Persian poets. Our final travelogue therefore defies the conventions of a genre that prided itself on factualness, typically signalled through the inclusion of details such as dates, miles travelled per day, names of people encountered and cost of living. By eschewing such details, Bibesco ushers in a new approach to travel-writing that we might label modernist, earning herself the admiration of Marcel Proust who upon reading *Les Huit paradis* declared its author 'un écrivain parfait' [a perfect writer].[10]

These seven travelogues span half a century and present us with many different perspectives on Iran, yet they nonetheless share some recurring themes: defining the 'Persian character', the condition of women in Iran, Shi'i religious customs, local art and architecture (both ancient and Islamic), and the deleterious effects of Western interventionism. These continuities arguably make the *Voyage en Perse* a sub-genre of its own, which benefits from being studied independently from the wider genre of the *Voyage en Orient*. In order to account for these crossovers, the chapter will not confine authors to individual sections, but remain comparative throughout. Different authors however will come to the fore in each section as a result of the nature of the issue being discussed: for example, the section on the harem focuses on Bibesco and Dieulafoy because these two authors had the most access to this space. The chapter as a whole will be guided by three overarching questions: First, to what degree do the literary conventions of the travelogue, in particular, the author's strategic location as observer, lead to the othering of Iranians? Secondly, how should we interpret French authors' use of similarity and analogy in their descriptions of Iran? Finally, what can these authors tell us about the difference between travelling to Iran and reading about Iran at home in nineteenth-century France? The use of comparative readings will allow me to answer these questions in a layered manner, doing justice to the surprising variety that exists within the minor sub-genre that is the *Voyage en Perse*.

Defining the Persians

The experience of the foreign encompasses many aspects, from differences in climate, landscape and architecture to those in language, religion and cuisine. But it is the encounter with individuals who are similar to the writer in their humanity, yet different in their customs, that elicits the greatest interest. The nineteenth century was an age fond of the generalizations made possible by grand narratives, as well as being obsessed with classification. As we saw in Chapter 2, these two urges came together in the newly emerged racialist discourse exemplified by Gobineau and Renan, which would come to influence the formation of the field of anthropology at the end of the century.[11] The travel-writers studied in this chapter were all too keen to stake out their own contribution to the growing effort to classify the societies and races of the world and would often venture their own definition of the Persian character.

Although they are no doubt essentializing, these attempts to define 'Persian-ness' are striking in that they reveal a complex use of the category of the 'Oriental'. Such definitions often involve a comparison between the Persians and Europeans, or the Persians and other Asian nations and ethnicities, with the Persians alternatively emerging as typical or atypical of the Orient. Neither self-evident nor sufficient, 'Oriental-ness' thus becomes a quality among many others as authors strive to get to the heart of what makes the Persians Persian.[12]

The six authors studied in this chapter are consistent with each other in considering the following traits to be Persian: politeness, intelligence, humour, fortitude, freedom of debate, a great love for both poetry and anecdote, and superstition. With the exception of superstition, these qualities are overwhelmingly positive and often met with effusive praise. Flandin, for example, writes: 'On pourrait presque dire qu'il n'y a pas un Persan inintelligent, comme il n'y en a pas de complètement illettré.'[13] [It could almost be said that there is no such thing as an un-intelligent Persian, just as there is no completely illiterate Persian.] Politeness (*ta'arof* in Persian), however, receives mixed reviews, making it a particularly interesting example of culture shock. French travel-writers all agree that *ta'arof* makes the inhabitants of Iran exceptionally easy and pleasant to interact with. Flandin, Gobineau and Dieulafoy also argue that because *ta'arof* is practiced by all Iranians irrespective of class, it also has the highly positive effect of effacing social hierarchies. This, in Dieulafoy's words, makes working-class Iranians 'très supérieurs aux hommes des classes inférieures de nos pays' [very superior to the men of the lower classes in our countries].[14] Claude Anet goes even further in his assessment, writing of the Persians: 'Je crois qu'il y a entre eux une égalité plus réelle qu'entre nous.' [I believe there exists a far truer equality among them than among ourselves.][15] Anet's comment is all the more pointed given the importance of 'égalité' in the Third Republic's self-mythologization. *Ta'arof*, however, was a double-edged sword, since at times French travellers could no longer tell if their hosts were acting out of kindness or mere social form. This ambivalence is best illustrated by Flandin, who will on different occasions argue that *ta'arof* is evidence that 'les Persans sont les gens du monde les plus habiles à déguiser le fond de leur pensée' [of all the people of the world, the Persians are the most adept at disguising what they truly think] and also that *ta'arof* proves that 'les Persans sont sans méchanceté et naturellement portés à la bienveillance' [the Persians are without malice and naturally kind to others].[16] On both occasions, Flandin uses the same style convention: the third-person statement in the present indicative. This suggests scientific authority (the present indicative being used for definitive truths), while also placing the author at a remove from the people whom he is describing through the use of the third person. However, the fact that these two assessments of Persian politeness directly contradict one another reveals that this is nothing more than a façade: the language of scientific authority is mainly there as a veneer, to cover up the fact that authors were only ever sharing personal impressions and conjectures. The one author to openly acknowledge this is Claude Anet, who states 'je n'en juge que d'après l'idée que je me fais des Persans, c'est mon seul critérium et il ne faut pas m'en demander d'avantage' (1905: 162). [I only judge according to my own idea of the Persians, that is my only criterium and one should not ask more of me.] Yet no matter how unreliable these generalizations were, they remained prevalent among travel-writers.

Distinguishing the Persians from their neighbours was an essential part of any attempt to define them. Was Iran exemplary of or exceptional to the Orient? French travellers by and large seem to have thought the latter, and any difference of opinion was a matter of nuance. Thus, whereas Flandin believes that the 'natural intelligence' of the Persians marries perfectly with the dignified attitude that they share with their fellow Orientals, the Arabs and the Indians, Dieulafoy argues that 'cette brillante intelligence particulière à un grand nombre d'Iraniens' [this brilliant intelligence that belongs to a great number of Iranians] is 'contrair[e] au caractère oriental' [contrary to the Oriental character].[17] Dieulafoy similarly cites the exceptional intelligence of the Persians when explaining why the art of the Achaemenids is of a greater sophistication than that of the ancient Egyptians and Assyrians: 'Ce n'est pas l'habileté de main qu'il faut louer seulement chez les Iraniens: les Perses sont surtout redevables de leur supériorité artistique à leur intelligence.'[18] [One should not only praise the manual dexterity of the Iranians: the Persians mainly owe their artistic superiority to their intelligence.] Thus, while for Flandin Oriental and Persian qualities can work together, making the Persians simultaneously exemplary of the Orient and purveyed of their own national traits, for Dieulafoy the positive qualities of the Persians are predicated upon their difference from all other Orientals. Moreover, Dieulafoy's comments on the Achaemenids directly link the superiority of contemporary Iranians over their neighbours to Iran's ancient imperial history. This presents the Persian character as essentially immutable, having maintained the same qualities for over two millennia. Flandin's more fluid perspective on the Oriental-ness of the Persians might therefore be explained by the fact that he was writing before the emergence of the racialist theories that would class the Persians as 'Aryans' and define them in opposition to the 'Semitic' Arabs and ancient Assyrians (see Chapter 2). That being said, Flandin is not immune to the urge to assert the Persians' superiority over their neighbours and, in the absence of a racial opposition, religion serves equally well.

Shi'ism has been one of the defining aspects of Iranian culture since the Safavid period. In contrast to eighteenth-century writers who seemed little aware of the distinction between Sunni and Shi'i Muslims,[19] nineteenth-century writers were curious to learn more about how the Persians' interpretation of Islam might differ from that of their Sunni neighbours, the Ottomans and the Arabians. I shall be taking a closer look at how these writers reacted to Shi'i rites later in this chapter, but for now, it is interesting to note that Shi'ism was often cited as further evidence of the superior intelligence of the Persians. Thus, Flandin writes of Shi'i Iranians that

> leur fanatisme a quelque chose de plus intelligent, de moins brutal que celui des Turcs. Ainsi, les Sunnites ne souffrent pas qu'on mette en discussion un seul des dogmes de leur religion; les Persans, au contraire, se plaisent dans la controverse; loin de l'éviter, ils la recherchent avec cette assurance que donne une foi vive et un esprit délié.

> [Their fanaticism is more intelligent, less brutal than that of the Turks. While the Sunnis cannot suffer to have a single one of their dogma put under discussion; the Persians, on the contrary, enjoy controversy; far from avoiding it, they seek it with the confidence of a strong faith and a nimble mind.][20]

Dieulafoy compares the Persians to the Arabs and the Turks on religious grounds as well, suggesting that while both Shi'i and Sunni Muslims believe in polygamy and predestination, Sunnis do not believe in free will, which makes them more likely to behave in a corrupt, lazy and immoral fashion.[21] This comparison is so forceful that it even takes on a biblical tone: 'Aussi, dans tous les pays où Turcs et Arabes ont posé les pieds, la fertilité de la terre semble s'être tarie à leur contact.'[22] [Thus, in all countries where Turks and Arabs have set foot, the land seems to have turned barren at their touch.] Although French writers' highly positive account of the Persian character had at first seemed to offer a promising challenge to the negative stereotypes of Orientalism, the fact it is often accompanied by vitriolic comments about other Muslim communities demonstrates that it does not entirely escape them. Rather, we are dealing with a repurposed binary opposition: instead of serving as a foil to the West, the Arabians and Ottomans now serve as a foil to the Persians, who emerge as the superior Orientals.

Although they were at great pains to establish what made the people of Iran unique and distinct from their neighbours, French writers were also often brought to realize that certain human traits are universal. Dieulafoy, in particular, punctuates anecdotes with the admonishment that what the reader might call 'barbaric' or 'savage' about Iran happens in Europe too.[23] They conclude: 'Vivez en Orient, vivez en Occident, et partout vous trouvez l'esprit humain également détraqué: toujours amoureux de surnaturel, de nouveautés, de contradictions absurdes.'[24] [Live in the Orient, live in the Occident, everywhere you will find the human mind equally deranged: in love with the supernatural, novelty, and absurd contradictions.] Dieulafoy also enjoys identifying similarities between rural France and rural Iran, both in terms of landscapes and customs:

> Chaque jour nous constatons avec surprise des *analogies* d'habitudes et des *similitudes* de caractère entre les paysans persans et les habitants de nos villages méridionaux. Ce sont, avant de traiter une affaire, les *mêmes* cris, le *même* marchandage, […] la *même* habitude du vendeur de demander le triple de la valeur de sa bête alors que l'acheteur en offre le quart, et que tous deux savent à cinq centimes près à quel prix ils s'accorderont. Enfin, toujours *comme* dans nos campagnes, quand l'achat est conclu, les deux parties se donnent la main et ratifient ainsi leurs conventions verbales. (My emphasis.)[25]

> [Every day we notice with surprise *analogies* of habit and *similarities* of character between the Persian farmers and the inhabitants of our southern villages. It's *the same* cries, *the same* haggling before agreeing on a deal, […] *the same* habit the seller has of asking the triple of the animal's value while the buyer offers a quarter, when both of them know to the penny on what price they will agree. Finally, *just like* in our countryside, when the deal is made, the two parties shake hands and thereby ratify their verbal agreement.] (My emphasis.)

Dieulafoy's admission of their 'surprise' at these 'similarities' reveals travel-writing's bias towards difference: when far from home, one expects things to be different. Cultural differences are a key selling point of a travelogue and, in a sense, the travelogue's very *raison d'être*. This bias in favour of difference is here counteracted by the passage's detailed description of a sheep market, in which the same interactions take place, whether one is in Iran or the south of France, where Jane and Marcel grew up. This has a profoundly familiarizing effect.

While Dieulafoy is able to make room for both cultural difference and similarity, other writers are uncomfortable with the idea that the Persians might be similar to them. This anxiety towards similarity is palpable in the lines that follow Flandin's praise of the Persians' dignified demeanour and lively intelligence:

> On a dit d'eux que c'étaient les Français de l'Orient. S'ils se rapprochent de nous par quelques-unes de leurs qualités, il faut cependant convenir que nous ne leur sommes pas semblables par leurs défauts et leurs vices. Ils sont, à la vérité, spirituels, aimables, polis, bienveillants, hospitaliers, braves, alertes; leur imagination brillante aime la poésie, la peinture, les arts de toute espèce et se passionne pour la gloire militaire. Mais nous ne saurions admettre que leur ressemblance avec

nous se complète par la ruse qui leur est naturelle, la vénalité de leur conscience, leur cruauté, leur fourberie et l'habitude de mentir, plus forte souvent que leur volonté […].²⁶

[It has been said that they are the French of the Orient. If they resemble us in some of their qualities, we must nonetheless admit that we do not resemble them in their flaws and vices. They are, in truth, witty, friendly, polite, kind, hospitable, brave, alert; their brilliant imagination loves poetry, painting and all of the arts, and is passionate about military glory. But we could never suggest that their resemblance to us includes their natural cunning, the venality of their conscience, their cruelty, their deceitfulness and the habit they have of lying, often in spite of themselves […].]

The suggestion that the Persians resemble the French in their qualities but not their flaws makes Flandin's motive transparent: French cultural superiority must be preserved at all costs, even if this means veering from the most extreme praise to the most extreme criticism. Defining the Persian character is thus a negotiation, which requires that the Persians remain on the middle of a spectrum running from a nefarious Orient embodied by the Arabs and Turks to a glorious Europe embodied by France, 'le pays de la liberté par excellence' [the country of freedom *par excellence*].²⁷ Flandin may be prepared to admit that the Persians have positive qualities and even some affinities with the French, but he does not want his readers to think of them as equals either: they may be better than the Arabs and Turks, but at the end of the day, they are still Orientals.

Among women: Scenes from the harem

Muslim women are by far the most consistent subject of fascination for European travellers in the Middle East. The facts that Islam permitted polygyny and that Muslim women could not be seen by male strangers combined to fuel European fantasies of the harem as a space populated by beautiful women whose only role was to pleasure their husband and master, a common theme in Orientalist paintings. Catching a glimpse of unveiled Muslim women became a titillating challenge for travellers, first and foremost because it was practically impossible. But there was also an unspoken analogy between unveiling the Oriental woman and unveiling the mysteries of the Orient: the colonial desire for knowledge as dominance was projected onto these women's bodies.²⁸ When out in public, Shi'i Iranian women of the Qajar era would wear a combination of a dark chador and a white face mask referred to as *rubandi*, making their faces and bodies indiscernible (see Figure 3.1). At home, they resided in the *andaruni*, the most private section of a domestic building, into which no strange man was allowed. How then was a Frenchman to regale his friends at home with descriptions of alluring Oriental women?

One of the most dramatic episodes in Eugène Flandin's travelogue is when the French-speaking Iranian aristocrat, 'le prince Malek Khassem Mirza', agrees to sneak

Figure 3.1 Street scene by Eugène Flandin showing two women in outdoor clothing.

Source: Eugène Flandin, 'Bazar et entrée de mosquée, Casbin', *Voyage en Perse. Perse moderne: Planches* (Paris: Baudry, 1851).

Flandin into his *andaruni* to meet his wives.²⁹ Flandin shrouds the entire episode in suspense and secrecy: the visit takes place after the city's curfew so that no one can see him. He must walk in complete darkness first through the streets and then through the house's many corridors: a torch would alert onlookers of his presence. Suddenly, he reaches a brightly lit dining room where the prince and his wives are having an evening of music, dancing and feasting:

> une vingtaine de femmes, surprises par mon apparition, poussèrent des cris d'effroi en cherchant à cacher leur visage. Le prince Malek-Khassem-Mirza […] partit d'un grand éclat de rire en voyant ma stupéfaction qui, à vrai dire, n'était pas moins grande que celle de ces dames. ³⁰
>
> [About twenty women, surprised by my entrance, cried out in fear trying to hide their faces. Prince Malek-Khassem-Mirza […] burst out laughing when he saw my stupefaction which, to be entirely honest, was equal to that of the ladies.]

Although Flandin presents this as a humorous moment, there is also an uncomfortable voyeurism to the scene, since it suggests that the prince did not inform his wives of Flandin's visit, thus robbing these women of the right to consent to being seen by an outsider. The tension, however, is soon dispelled as the women forget about Flandin's presence and go back to playing music and dancing.³¹ There follows a detailed description of their features, make-up and clothing.[32] When festivities come to a close, Flandin writes that he returns home 'aussi content de ma soirée que fier de pouvoir raconter à mes camarades les féeries que j'avais vues' [as delighted by the evening as I was proud to be able to tell my companions about the enchanting visions (*féeries*) that I had witnessed].[33] Flandin has indeed achieved a rare feat for a European man. Our other male travellers have no local accomplices. Their excitement will therefore be limited to the hope of glimpsing a woman's face as her veil is being rearranged or lifted by a breeze.[34]

The curiosity of male travellers is predominantly erotic: Iranian women are only considered in terms of the pleasure that their appearance can bring to European men. In contrast, the curiosity of Dieulafoy and Bibesco is often directed towards understanding Iranian women's lifestyles: it is less their bodies than their perspectives that they wish to unveil. As has been compellingly argued by Billie Melman and Bénédicte Monicat, European women were able to identify with Oriental women on one basic, but important, level: they too were man's inferior Other in their home society.[35] This could often elicit feelings of sympathy, though of a Eurocentric nature, since the assumption was that Oriental women must have it 'even worse'. Dieulafoy and Bibesco's writing on the condition of Iranian women indeed exhibits a complex interplay between exoticization and identification, which in Dieulafoy's case is further complicated by the fact that even though they were considered a woman in both French and Iranian society, they were gender non-conforming and therefore reacted against this label. Indeed, Dieulafoy's dissatisfaction with the role assigned to them by nineteenth-century French gender conventions is one of the dominant themes of the opening pages of *La Perse*. Whereas Dieulafoy cannot contain their excitement about their approaching departure for Iran, their female friends discourage them from leaving, suggesting instead that it would be preferable to stay at home and take advantage of the time afforded by their husband's absence to undertake domestic chores and social activities more befitting of a middle-class French woman. Dieulafoy rejects these propositions with the lapidary and sarcastic statement: 'Je sus résister à toutes ces tentations' [I was able to resist all these temptations].[36] The journey recounted in *La Perse* was Dieulafoy's first step towards a successful career as a writer, archaeologist and public speaker, for which they were awarded the Legion of Honour, becoming in professional terms 'one of the boys'. And yet, Dieulafoy was also seen as a woman, both due to their biological sex and their social role as the wife of Marcel Dieulafoy. Their travel-writing records that in Iran they were addressed by locals as 'khanoum' (the Persian for Miss or Mrs) and that they were always admitted into the women-only space of the harem. Thus, despite the fact that they could, and at times did, pass as a man as a result of their appearance (cropped hair and suits) and their behaviour (riding astride, shooting, sitting around the campfire late at night with men),[37] Dieulafoy also never lost their female status in Iranian society. And, although their writing suggests that they did not personally identify with the category of woman, at the same time, they were all too keen to exploit the fact that being categorized as a woman granted them access to the female spaces that had proven so elusive to their male predecessors. Indeed, I argue that it was precisely because of the precedent set by male travellers that Dieulafoy's descriptions of Iranian women are engaging and competing with. Dieulafoy's treatment of Iranian women is therefore complicated, and at times even conflicted, since it oscillates between the eroticized othering typical of male-authored Oriental travelogues and the strong feelings of anger that are elicited by Iranian women's lack of social emancipation. Nowhere is this tension more evident than in Dieulafoy's criticisms of the veil.

Throughout *La Perse*, Dieulafoy complains of how Iranian women's outdoor clothes conceal their 'feminine forms', noting

> Quand une femme est ainsi empaquetée, fût-elle jeune ou vieille, grasse ou maigre, imberbe comme l'enfant qui vient de naître ou barbue comme un sapeur, bien jaloux serait celui qui la reconnaîtrait.[38]

> [When a woman is packed up like this, young or old, fat or thin, as hairless as a newborn or as bearded as a sapper, only the most jealous of men would be able recognise her.]

Not only is the colloquialism *empaquetée* derogatory and dehumanizing, the passage also reduces Iranian women to a taxonomic list of their level of physical attractiveness, focusing entirely on a male gaze: that of the jealous husband. There is something disingenuous here since Dieulafoy chose to conceal their 'feminine forms' in order to present as a man. The choice to mock women who hide their bodies and to refer to the figure of the bearded lady, who is a subject of revulsion precisely because she does not conform to the physiology associated with her sex, therefore, seems a denial of the author's own identity as a gender non-conforming individual. Dieulafoy's objectification of Iranian women in such passages thus serves to convince readers that they are reading a book by a 'regular' male heterosexual travel-writer, rather than a trans person. This becomes all the more clear if we consider the gendered use of language in two episodes that are centred on Dieulafoy's gaze on Iranian women.

Early on during their stay in Iran, Dieulafoy spots two women who are talking to a male member of their family in the privacy of their courtyard and have, therefore, not covered their faces:

> Un gros chat noir s'avance prudemment et seul paraît flairer la présence d'un étranger: je me dissimule derrière un pan de mur, demande à mon mari les appareils photographiques et les dispose au plus vite, ravie de dérober à la jalousie persane une aussi jolie scène d'intérieur. [...] Le larcin commis et les châssis enveloppés, nous allons courir la ville.[39]

> [A fat black cat advances cautiously and seems the only one aware of the presence of a stranger: I hide behind a wall, ask my husband for my cameras and set up as quickly as I can, delighted to steal such a pretty interior scene from Persian jealousy. [...] Once the theft has been committed and the chassis packed, we go explore the city.]

Although the reference to a husband and the feminine adjective *ravie* ultimately gender Dieulafoy as female, it is striking that they choose to introduce this scene of voyeurism by referring to themselves with the masculine noun *un étranger* (a stranger), thereby signalling that the European spying on – and capturing – unveiled Middle Eastern women is an inherently male role. It has indeed been argued by the art critic Linda Nochlin that Orientalist paintings of women always imply the presence of the male colonizer, who as a figure is absent from the scene, but present because it is his gaze that the female body is on display for.⁴⁰ The combination of the male term *étranger* and the lexical field of robbery to refer to the photograph taken by Dieulafoy presents them in the same light: the Western voyeur who derives pleasure from breaking local moral codes. The stolen photograph is as exciting as a stolen kiss because both are non-consensual. The subtext of this scene is therefore one of male sexual domination. Moreover, the fact that the illustration does not match the text's version of events – far from having been caught unawares, the women are gazing back at the photographer and smiling – further suggests that this was a very deliberate stylistic choice on Dieulafoy's behalf.⁴¹ This exemplifies Guyot's observation that travel-writing is always filtered by an author's narrative intentions.⁴²

The second episode recounts Dieulafoy being invited to dinner by a Baha'i family. Granted access to the female space of the kitchen, they make conversation with the mother, while watching the daughter prepare the meal:

> La déesse du pilau porte une chemisette de gaze rose dont les minces plis dessinent avec fidélité un buste développé qui ne connut jamais la tutelle du corset; sa petite jupe de cachemire de l'Inde, à palmes, est attachée très bas au-dessous de la chemisette et laisse au moindre mouvement le ventre nu. C'est la toilette d'hiver. J'aurais bien voulu prolonger ma visite et faire connaissance avec les ajustements d'été, mais les heures des voyageurs sont fugitives.⁴³

> [The pilau goddess wears a chemisette of pink gauze, the fine folds of which offer the faithful outline of a developed bust that has never known the tutelage of the corset; her little skirt of Indian cashmere is pleated and fastened very low under the chemisette so that every movement reveals her naked belly. This is the winter style. I would rather have liked to prolong my stay and acquaint myself with the summer outfits, but travellers have few hours to spare.]

The young Baha'i woman is exoticized from the outset through the patronizing use of the term 'goddess' in combination with the vernacular term *pilau* to describe the ordinary task of cooking rice. The lengthy sentence itemizing the woman's clothes and body conveys the leisurely pace with which Dieulafoy's gaze wanders over her body. The titillating descriptions of her breasts and occasionally revealed midriff makes the reader forget who is speaking, and think only of the eroticized body. The passage ends on a salacious remark: not only does Dieulafoy explicitly say that they would like to see this woman with even fewer clothes on, but the expression 'acquaint myself' (*faire connaissance*) sounds like a euphemism for a sexual encounter. At a heteronormative time, in which Middle Eastern women were frequently sexualized by European men, this reads like a sentence from a typical male traveller, and a rather forward one at that. And just as in the previous passage Dieulafoy had referred to themself through the masculine noun *étranger*, so too they adopt here the masculine-neutral pleural *voyageurs*, rather than the feminine *voyeugeuses*. Having been granted access to the feminine sphere on the basis of being identified as female, Dieulafoy offers their French readers what they most desire: unveiled Muslim women as seen through an erotic male gaze. One might counter that Dieulafoy, as a gender non-conforming person, should be understood as having a queer gaze that eludes the oppressive binary of male colonizer/ female colonized. But even if we did assume that Dieulafoy was writing from a position of personal attraction towards this woman – of which we have no evidence – this does not change the fact that Dieulafoy wrote for an audience that relished the erotic fantasy of the harem, a fantasy framed both in travel-writing and the visual arts as the Western man's illicit penetration into the inaccessible world of Muslim women. Dieulafoy's personal contact with Iranian women was the travelogue's greatest selling point, and this would remain the case long after their death: in 2011, *La Perse* was reissued by Phébus with the new title *L'Orient sous le voile*.[44] Dieulafoy knew what they were selling.

As well as critiquing the veil because it prevents onlookers from admiring Iranian women's bodies, Dieulafoy also argues that the veil serves as an instrument for Iranian men to exert control over women. Whereas the first complaint is predicated on the pleasure of the Western traveller and thus objectifies Iranian women, the latter critique is of a rather different nature, since it is motivated by an identification with Iranian women on a human level. According to Dieulafoy, the chador and women's seclusion in the *andaruni* is motivated not by religion, but by male sexual possessiveness. This possessiveness could even put women's lives at risk, as was exemplified by the unsafe mode of transport referred to as the *kadjaveh*, a box precariously balanced on a horse's back, into which Iranian women were crammed in order to be hidden from sight whilst travelling.[45] This, then, was a society in which the desires of men came before the safety and happiness of women, which gave Dieulafoy serious reservations about the Muslim faith. Dieulafoy's condemnation of gender inequality is most vivid in a conversation that they have with a local religious authority, the 'mouchtéïd' (*mojtahed*) of Tabriz, about the afterlife. After the priest has described the sixty-two *houris* that make men's sojourn in heaven 'pleasing', Dieulafoy interjects: what about women when *they* go to heaven? Are they still subjected to polygyny? Are they still kept in an *andaruni*? Must they still wear the veil?[46] Relishing as they are the newfound freedom brought to them by travel, Dieulafoy cannot help but note the stark contrast between their lifestyle and that of these women. Not only that, but Dieulafoy's faith in Catholicism meant that they firmly believed in monogamy and the sanctity of marriage. As such, they could only imagine that practices such as polygyny and temporary marriage must cause Iranian women great suffering.[47] Dieulafoy does, however, also acknowledge that in some exceptional cases Iranian women were able to benefit from these customs. This is the case of a working-class woman known as 'Anizeh Doouleh', who after a temporary marriage to the Shah became his favourite concubine and was able to exert soft power.[48]

Dieulafoy's criticism of the veil and gender seclusion could be condemned from today's perspective as an imperialist ideology masquerading as women's emancipation: after all, if Dieulafoy was really so invested in these women's rights, why describe them in a manner designed to fuel Western readers' sexual fantasies? Inge Boer has described this contradiction as one between text and image: whereas

Dieulafoy's writing expresses a desire to liberate Iranian women, the illustrations of *La Perse* exploit their bodies.[49] But, as I have shown, both of these dimensions in fact exist within the text itself. The tension between them reveals the challenges that Dieulafoy faced in grappling with their authorial persona in this text. They want to be considered 'one of the boys', and if sexist and Orientalist tropes can guarantee them a male identity, then they are all too happy to exploit these. But, as we saw in Chapter 2, for all their exceptional achievements, Jane Dieulafoy was also regularly belittled and denied the same level of opportunity that was offered their husband Marcel. And so it was only natural that Iranian women's confinement to the domestic sphere would have elicited a strong emotional response from them. Dieulafoy's critiques of Islamic customs certainly come with a high level of bias – Eurocentric, Christian and personal – and thus expose the risks of universalism which, as argued by Todorov, can often serve as a mask for ethnocentrism.[50] But, had Dieulafoy not voiced their anger at the forms of gender discrimination that were sanctioned by religion, we would have only been left with erotic descriptions of these women, which would have resulted in a far more dehumanizing account of Iranian women. Dieulafoy's travel-writing thus aptly illustrates the double bind presented by universalism and cultural relativism, both of which have their pitfalls: the former can be a self-projection, and the latter can be a form of othering. Dieulafoy, it seems, was aware of this, since they explore the double bind of cultural difference in an engaging episode of role reversal, where humour proves to be the key to striking a rare balance between relativism and universalism.

The role reversal takes place in the *andaruni* of the wife of the governor of Kashan, who has sneaked Dieulafoy inside to have her photograph taken. The secrecy surrounding Dieulafoy's visit has the effect of presenting the harem as a forbidden space, much like the harem episode in Flandin's travelogue, but the difference here is that the rule-breakers are not intrusive men, but women taking charge of their own space. In contrast to the episode of the stolen photograph, the governor's wife has personally requested the photography sitting, even though it means disobeying her husband who has not given her permission to do this.[51] This leads to a comical set up, in which Dieulafoy has their credentials examined by the sitter, whom they are anxious to satisfy:

'Vous savez faire l'*ax*? M'a dit à mon arrivée la femme du gouverneur (*ax* est le nom persan donné à la photographie, il signifie 'opposé, à l'envers'). Vous êtes *ackaz bachy dooulet farança* (littéralement: 'retourneur en chef du gouvernement français')?
– Certainement, ai-je répondu sans hésitation, car il ne s'agit pas ici d'avoir l'air d'un photographe sans clientèle.[52]

[You can take the *ax*? Enquired on my arrival the governor's wife (*ax* is the Persian name given to photography, it means 'opposite, upside down'). You are the *ackaz bachy dooulet farança* (literally: 'the chief turner of the French government')?
– Certainly, I replied without hesitation, for I did not want to appear to be a client-less photographer.]

The exposition of the Persian word 'ax' is significant. First of all, it draws attention to the fact that the conversation takes place in Persian, giving the episode an air of veracity. Although we can assume that there are embellishments, the neologism 'ackaz bachy dooulet farança' and interjection 'Allamdoullah' used later in the passage are expressions that Jane as a non-native speaker would have picked up, but not invented. Secondly, the word *ax* is of thematic significance, since its etymology ('opposite, upside down'), is announcing the passage's main theme: things are about to be turned upside down, as Dieulafoy and the Iranian women's roles are reversed. In order to avoid answering any further questions, Dieulafoy retreats 'sous les voiles noirs' [under the black veils] of their camera covers, a far from innocent turn of phrase in a work that has repeatedly described the dark chadors worn by Iranian women. Silent and veiled, the author is now in the position that they have put these women: an object of curiosity, described and discussed without being consulted. They have gone from being the observer, a status emphasized both formally and symbolically by the fact that they are the narrator and the one holding the camera lens, to being the observed party.

'Dans le Faranguistan, dit la femme du gouverneur à l'épouse de l'imam djouma, qu'elle paraît traiter comme une naïve provinciale, les femmes sont bien moins heureuses qu'en Perse: les hommes les obligent à travailler. Celle-ci est *ackaz bachy* (photographe en chef), d'autres sont *mirzas* (écrivains) ou *moallem* (savants); quelques-unes même, comme la fille du *chah des Orous* (le roi des Russes), ont obtenu le grade de général et font manoeuvrer des armées.
— Tu te ris de mon ignorance? répond l'autre avec un air de doute.
— *Allamdoullah*! (grâces soient rendues à Dieu) je t'ai dit la vérité, amie chérie. Non seulement dans le Faranguistan il y a des femmes qui commandent des régiments, mais il y en a une qui est chah. Interroge *khanoum ackaz bachy*: elle te dira que cette princesse a un ambassadeur à Téhéran. Enfin, ajoute-t-elle comme information supplémentaire, si la fille du roi des Orous porte un casque et des épaulettes, la khanoum chah possède en outre de longues moustaches.'
[...]
La femme de l'imam djouma est tenace et désire s'instruire.
'La khanoum chah a-t-elle plusieurs maris dans son andéroun?' Demande-t-elle après quelques minutes de profonde réflexion.
Ici je juge opportun de dégager ma tête des voiles [...]. Il est temps d'intervenir et d'assurer que la reine d'Angleterre est imberbe d'abord, n'a eu qu'un seul époux, et que dans sa vie privée elle a toujours donné l'exemple de toutes les vertus domestiques.[53]

['In Farangestan,' the governor's wife explains to the imam's wife, whom she appears to treat like a naive provincial, 'women are far less happy than in Persia: their men make them work. This one is *ackaz bashy*, others are *mirzas* (writers) or *moallem* (scholars); and some even, like the daughter of the *shah of Orous* (king of the Russians), have reached the status of general and command armies.
— You are mocking my ignorance? says the other, with an air of doubt.

– *Alhamdollellah*! I am telling you the truth, my dear friend. Not only in Farangestan do they have women commanders, they also have a woman shah. Ask *khanoum ackaz bachy*: she will tell you that this princess has an ambassador in Tehran. And,' she adds as further information, 'the *khanoum shah* also has a big moustache.'

[...]

The imam's wife is both eager to learn and persistent.

'Does the *khanoum shah* have several husbands in her *anderoun*?' she asks, after a few minutes of reflection.

I decide that the time has come for me to remove my head from under the veil [...] and to reassure them first of all that the queen of England has no facial hair and secondly that she has only ever had one husband and is a model of all domestic virtues.]

The scene is clearly intended to be comical: Dieulafoy emerging from 'under the veil' in order to defend Queen Victoria's honour is a punchline if there ever was one. But beneath its humorous tone, the passage is doing a lot of heavy lifting. First, it sounds a profoundly relativistic message, which is that one should never assume that any one culture is by nature more desirable than others: Dieulafoy may not envy the lives of Iranian women, but that does not mean that these women envy theirs. At the same time, Dieulafoy and the Iranian women's mutual disregard for each other's cultures is also a profession of universalism, since it shows that humans in general are suspicious of foreigners and enjoy gossiping about them. Indeed, the relationship between the two Iranian women discussing Dieulafoy is one that could be encountered anywhere: the shy, lower status friend (wife of the religious authority) and the bossy show-off friend (wife of the political authority) are universal types, which Dieulafoy would have encountered just as easily in their hometown of Toulouse. One of the most subversive aspects of the passage is that the Iranian women explain the situation of European women in terms of gender oppression: European women work because 'their men make them'. This is the very same logic that had been used by Dieulafoy to explain Muslim customs such as the veil, which they had suggested were worn by Iranian women because of their 'jealous husbands'. If the governor's wife is mistaken in her assumption, then perhaps Dieulafoy is as well. Pushing the parallel further, we might also note that the hearsay, exaggeration and exoticization present in the Iranian woman's description of European women mirrors the clichés that circulated in France about Oriental women.

What may at first seem like a moment of comic relief thus plays the subversive role of holding a mirror up to Dieulafoy and her readers' attitudes towards the Islamic world. The passage acknowledges cultural relativism, while also reminding us that some behaviours are universal. In doing so it resolves (albeit only temporarily) the travelogue's oscillation between othering and identification. If the passage succeeds in doing so, it is in great part thanks to its use of dialogue, which lets the Iranian women speak for themselves. Dieulafoy's knowledge of Persian is a key factor here, since it allows them to include exchanges in direct speech. It would be naive to assume that Dieulafoy is recording the conversation as it happened: their knowledge of Persian had its limits, their memory was as unreliable as anyone else's and their priority was to tell an entertaining story, not to offer an accurate transcription. But direct speech does nonetheless hold a powerful symbolic value, since, as has been argued by Billie Melman, 'instead of an ethnocentric discourse *on* the Orient, [it] suggests an exchange of information between active, equally articulate participants'.[54] By writing a scene in which two Iranian women openly voice their biases against Western societies, Dieulafoy shows us that differences and commonalities can coexist, discarding Orientalist binaries in favour of the paradigm of similarity.[55]

Although Dieulafoy is on this occasion able to reconcile difference and commonality, it must be said that overall they hold Iranian women at a remove. Yet there is more to this distance than what Said termed strategic location: Dieulafoy's position at a remove has as much to do with the Iranian women's gender identity as with their culture. Indeed, from the travelogue's opening pages, Dieulafoy is defined in opposition to the women surrounding them, in the first instance the friends from home advising against travel.[56] The women in Kashan in fact have a lot in common with Dieulafoy's female friends: both groups are equally suspicious of their choice to lead what was then considered a male lifestyle. Thus, although Dieulafoy occasionally aligns themself with women in political terms by critiquing their unequal status in society, they often struggle to identify with them. The episode of the photography sitting exemplifies this: whereas the governor's wife bemoans Dieulafoy's situation as a working photographer, Dieulafoy is very much enjoying this activity and would struggle to understand women who prefer to lead a domestic life. In contrast, Dieulafoy finds it easy and enjoyable to converse with men, no matter their nationality or religion, since their professional lives provide them with a greater range of topics for discussion. Dieulafoy writes particularly warm accounts of their conversations with 'Mirza Nizam de Gaffary', a young Iranian man descended from a long line of Shi'i clerics who studied mining and engineering in France, the French 'Docteur Tholozan', who is the Shah's personal physician and Father 'Pascal Arakélian', who is the only Catholic Minister in Djolfa, the Armenian quarter of Esfahan.[57] Dieulafoy's distancing of Iranian women becomes all the more manifest when we compare their travel-writing to that of Marthe Bibesco in *Les Huit paradis* (1908). Bibesco's burning desire to identify with Iranian women can come across as gauche and naive. However, it also enables her to write what is possibly the most positive account of the Islamic veil in French literature.

Bibesco's first meeting with Iranian women takes place in the harem of an unnamed Qajar prince, to which Bibesco has been invited along with an unnamed female travel-companion –this is typical of *Les Huit paradis*, which is generally sparse on practical information. After the prince has made introductions, the two European visitors and his three wives can do nothing but stare at each other in silence, since they do not share a common language. This inability to communicate is described by Bibesco in a passage that mixes the language of sympathy and that of othering:

Elles baissent les yeux, un peu farouches, osent à peine avancer leurs petites mains gantées de blanc. Je voudrais leur prouver par mon regard que je les considère avec douceur, afin qu'elles soient envers nous sans défiance et sans envie…

Je me souviens des dimanches où j'allais voir jadis une petite amie qu'on avait mise au couvent. Je craignais toujours que les couventines ne s'attristassent à ma vue, par la pensée que je pouvais m'en aller [...] quand je le voudrais [...]. Dans ces âmes de sérail, quels sentiments se seront agités durant notre visite? [...] Je regarde leurs impénétrables figures aux yeux sans cesse baissés, leurs visages, si pâles d'être perpétuellement dérobés au jour, et je pense à toute leur vie.

Quelles petites filles, quelles adolescentes furent-elles?

Dans les chambres basses des harems, dans les jardins murés, au fond des carrosses à portières closes, leur enfance s'est écoulée si différente de la nôtre que nous pouvons à peine l'imaginer. [...] Je regarde ces créatures soumises pour quelques heures à mon observation. Le secret des âmes limitées m'apparaît dans leurs yeux, insondable, autant qu'en des prunelles d'animaux, et je sens ma pensée s'arrêter au vide de leur regard, prise de ce même vertige d'incompréhension qui me penche quelquefois sur les yeux d'un chien ou d'un nouveau-né.[58]

[They lower their eyes, a little wild, and barely dare bring forward their little white-gloved hands. I would like to prove to them through my gaze that I regard them with kindness, so that they might not feel any distrust or envy towards us...

The Sundays when I once used to visit a childhood friend who had been put in a convent come to mind. I always feared that the convent girls would be saddened by my sight, by the thought that I could leave [...] when I pleased [...]. In these seraglio souls, what feelings might be stirred during our visit? [...] I look at their impenetrable faces, eyes constantly lowered, those faces, so pale from being perpetually hidden from the light of day, and I think of their entire existence.

What little girls, what adolescents were they?

In the low rooms of the harem, in the walled gardens, in the back of closed carriages, their childhood went by so differently to our own that we can barely imagine it. [...] I look at these creatures submitted for a few hours to my observation. The secrecy of limited souls transpires in their eyes, which are inscrutable like those of animals, and I feel my thoughts stop before the emptiness of their gaze, seized by the same dizziness of incomprehension that leads me sometimes to peer into the eyes of a dog or of a newborn.]

Bibesco yearns to understand these women and to interact with them, but this is impossible. Even her attempt at non-verbal communication is presented as futile, as is suggested by the conditional *voudrais* [I would like to]. The passage is structured around an opposition between surface and substance: Bibesco can stare at these women as much as she likes, an act that is foregrounded through the repetition of the noun *regard* and verb *regarder*, as well as the self-aware statement that these women are being 'submitted' to her gaze, but she will never access their interiority. This realization is presented as overwhelming through the evocative phrase *vertige d'incompréhension* [dizziness of incomprehension]. Bibesco's 'dizziness' has serious ramifications for the genre: if one admits that foreign populations cannot be understood via observation, then what is the purpose of describing them in travelogues? This point, however, is marred by Bibesco's extremely dehumanizing comparisons of these women to animals and newborns, which are combined with the derogatory assumption that they have 'limited souls'. Her language, rather than expressing that the interiority of these women is inaccessible, here suggests that they possess no interiority at all. Bibesco's convent analogy, in contrast, is both humanizing and familiarizing. By comparing the prince's wives to nuns, Bibesco suggests that these women are merely difficult to relate to because their relationship to religion and to the opposite sex places them in different circumstances to her own. Their differences are thus existential and not ontological, a point which Bibesco further develops later in the passage.

> Elles sont là, assises en rang, ces trois femmes d'un même mari qui en possède encore plusieurs autres. [...] Avec des chances de plaire si mal réparties, les imagine-t-on vivant chaque heure du jour en commun, dans une même maison, sous les regards d'un seul homme? L'aimeraient-elles [...] ? En ce cas, il faut les supposer exemptes de cette volonté de la suprématie qui engendre la haine, les fureurs jalouses et jusqu'à l'idée simple et nette du meurtre. Est-il possible de concevoir une différence aussi profonde entre leur humanité et la nôtre?[59]

> [Here they are, sitting in line, these three wives of one same husband who has several others besides them. [...] With such unevenly distributed chances of appealing to him, can one imagine them living every hour of the day together, in one same house, under the gaze of one only man? Might they love him [...] ? In that case, one must suppose that they are exempt from that will to supremacy that engenders hatred, jealous fury, and even the simple and clear idea of murder. Is it possible to conceive of such as profound difference between their humanity and ours?]

Bibesco is effectively asking, what does it mean to be human, but differently? This is a question too vast to be answered by anyone alone, but by posing it, she is acknowledging that definitions of humanity vary based on cultural context. Although jealousy is considered a natural feeling in monogamous societies, this might not be the case in polygamous societies. The challenge, then, is to conceive of a different definition of humanity. In this instance, this would require imagining a marriage that is not premised on sexual exclusivity. In order to do so, one would have to leave aside one's own cultural biases. Dieulafoy, who speaks Persian, never entertains the possibility that Iranian women might feel differently about polygyny than they do. They assume that this must be a humiliation for them because they would experience it as one. Bibesco, in contrast, is willing to admit that, as hard as it is for her to imagine, Iranian women might not feel the same way about polygyny as she does. Despite her initially dehumanizing language, Bibesco thus seems capable of greater cultural relativism than Dieulafoy. This becomes all the more obvious in a later section of *Les Huit paradis*, which is entitled 'De la condition des femmes en Perse' [Of the condition of women in Persia].[60]

Bibesco opens this section with a description of the chador and *rubandi* worn by Shi'i Iranian women. She comments:

> Européenne, j'ai cru d'abord qu'il était bon de plaindre ces enlaidies volontaires. Mais, à force d'en voir, et de les bien regarder je n'ai plus trouvé qu'elles fussent attristantes. Et même j'ai fini par comprendre qu'elles riaient sous cape.[61]

[As a European woman, I thought at first that I should pity these women who voluntarily make themselves ugly. But, the more I saw them and the closer I looked, I ceased to find them saddening. And I even came to realise that they were laughing up their sleeves.]

Bibesco here frames her opinion in terms of cultural bias, making explicit what Dieulafoy only hints at in the scene of the photography sitting. Her use of the idiom 'laughing up one's sleeve', which in French literally translates to 'laughing under one's cape', points directly to the chador, which is now suddenly presented as a garment that puts Iranian women at an advantage. Indeed, in the pages that follow, Bibesco explains that the chador enables freedom of movement, creates a greater level of social equality and protects women's anonymity when conducting romantic liaisons.[62] It also shields them from sexual harassment: 'À l'abri des sollicitations importunes [...]. Elles ne seront ni surprises ni dominées.'[63] [Safe from unwanted advances [...]. They will be neither taken by surprise nor dominated.] This final point is particularly striking for its implication that Iranian women have greater control over their relationships with men than European women do. Indeed, Bibesco argues that by being able to observe a man without being seen by him, Iranian women can take longer to assess the nature of their feelings: 'Elles pourront se sentir lentement attirées vers lui, au lieu de n'être que les victimes de sa volonté plus forte.'[64] [They will be able to slowly develop an attraction for him, rather than merely being the victims of his stronger will.] What is most notable about this comment is that it treats Iranian women as desiring subjects, when other authors had only ever viewed them as objects of desire. As well as listing what she considers the practical advantages of the veil, Bibesco praises the exclusivity that it creates between husband and wife, using terms entirely sympathetic to Islamic cultural norms:

[Le voile] assure à celles qui aiment la possibilité de garder pour leur époux tous [sic] le charme émané d'elles. L'aimé ne partagera jamais avec la foule des autres hommes, avec les passants jeunes ou vieux, étrangers ou non, la joie que procurent aux yeux les lignes de leur corps de femme, la couleur de leur regard, la surprise de leur sourire.[65]

[The veil guarantees women in love the possibility of keeping for their husband all the charm that emanates from them. Their beloved shall never share with countless other men, with passersby young or old, foreign or local, the joy brought to the eyes by the contours of their female body, the colour of their gaze, the surprise of their smile.]

Bibesco also notes that there is a tendency in Europe to negatively exaggerate the condition of Iranian women:

Si l'emprisonnement au harem est encore permis, du moins, n'est-il guère pratiqué. En Perse, comme ailleurs, la loi donne à l'homme des droits dont il ne fait plus usage.[66]

[While imprisonment in the harem is still legal, it is hardly practiced. In Persia, like anywhere else, the law affords men certain rights that are no longer in use.]

As well as suggesting that Europeans are ill-informed about the condition of women in Iran, Bibesco also places a universalizing emphasis on how common it is for a country's mores to evolve faster than its laws, an observation designed to have a familiarizing effect upon the reader.

The positive treatment of the veil in *Les Huit paradis* is notable for its explicit taking to task of cultural bias. Bibesco writes openly that she had arrived in Iran convinced that her way of life was superior, but then came to realize that she had been wrong. However, Bibesco is so keen to sing the praises of Iranian women that she falls into another extreme: instead of making the veil a focal point for debates over the backwardness of the Muslim world, she fetishizes it as the ultimate expression of an untroubled existence. According to her, Iranian women lead a charmed life devoted to endless play. This leads Bibesco to form the fantasy of staying in Iran and becoming one of them:

être une hanoum persane!
    Toute conscience étouffée, toute passion s'étiolant, ne vivre qu'une longue enfance, protégée par l'ombre triple des voiles, des arbres et des murs.
    Ne plus jamais regarder le monde qu'à travers des mailles de soie; n'avoir que de petits plaisirs, alternant avec de petites peines: être une dame d'Ispahan…
    O mes sœurs des cloîtres parfumés! Tous vos amusements deviendront les miens.⁶⁷

[To be a Persian *khanum*!
    All conscience dampened, all passion vanishing, to live only a long childhood, protected by the triple shade of veils, trees, and walls.
    To only ever see the world through a silk mesh; to have only small pleasures, alternating with small sorrows: to be a lady of Esfahan…
    Oh my sisters of the perfumed cloisters! All your amusements will become mine.]

Bibesco speculates that if this dream were to come true, then her current life as a European aristocrat would vanish, only to be remembered as a nightmare:

Aussi, plus tard, […] si je venais à me souvenir d'un autre monde où les villes noires que la foudre illumine, hurlent et fument vers le ciel […], où des machines de feu se précipitent en sifflant […] où des centaines de maisons n'ont pas de jardins; […] où l'on voit errer des femmes, le visage nu, montrant leurs cheveux et leur front, des femmes que pas un homme ne garde! si je me souvenais, si je venais à me souvenir, je croirais avoir dormi, et que peut-être les balsamines du verger ont une odeur qui donne des rêves…⁶⁸

[And if later […] I came to remember another world where black cities, illuminated by lightning, scream and smoke towards the sky […], where fiery machines rush forward whistling [...] where hundreds of homes have no gardens; [...] where one sees women wandering bare faced, showing their hair and forehead, women that not one man guards! if I remembered, if I came to remember, I would believe I had been asleep, and that perhaps the balsams in the orchard have a dream-inducing smell...]

Bibesco, like her cousin Anna de Noailles had done in her poem 'L'Occident' (see Chapter 1), describes modern European metropolises such as Paris through a defamiliarized gaze. But whereas Noailles did so to reclaim and celebrate the Occident over the Orient, Bibesco does the very opposite: Europe here is a threatening Other. Bibesco's effort to describe European cities as seen through the eyes of a 'hanoum persane' is, however, inherently flawed because it is predicated on a distorted vision of life in Iran. Bibesco takes her experiences as a European princess hosted in the palaces of the Qajar aristocracy, which were mostly located in the green outskirts of cities, and claims that these reflect the lives of all Iranian women. Gardens are a traditional part of high-status residences in Iran: they surround such building complexes and are also present internally as the centrepieces of large-scale private courtyards. Ignoring the fact that these luxurious gardens were the preserve of the ruling classes, Bibesco presents these as evidence that life in Iran truly is paradise on earth, making it imminently preferable to the vicissitudes of life in Europe: 'Les Persanes ont mille raisons d'être heureuses. Elles sont enfantines et leur vie se passe à jouer dans des jardins' [Persian women have a thousand reasons to be happy. They are child-like and spend their lives playing in gardens].[69]

Travelling to Iran ten years apart from one another, Dieulafoy and Bibesco are the only authors in this book to have been hosted by Iranian women. Yet they drew entirely different conclusions from these visits. Dieulafoy considers Iranian women to be oppressed and has an impersonal relationship with them. However, they also acknowledge their cultural bias by quoting two Iranian women's negative opinion of their lifestyle. Bibesco, who does not speak Persian, idealizes the condition of Iranian women, proving herself utterly unaware of social inequalities. But although her view of Iran is distorted by privilege, Bibesco is notable for explicitly confronting her cultural biases against the veil and polygyny, and ultimately transcending them. Her travelogue tracks a progression, showing how her opinion on the veil changes over the course of her time in Iran. Moreover, Bibesco's list of the veil's benefits for Iranian women, which include marital exclusivity, shows a rare level of empathy towards a cultural practice that was viewed with deep suspicion in the West. It is possible that Bibesco's international existence between Paris and Budapest may have been a factor in her more generous perspective on cultural difference. Dieulafoy's gender fluidity and Bibesco's female identity not only granted them physical access to the harem, but they also led them to form far more layered opinions on the condition of Iranian women than those expressed by the male authors' studied in this chapter. They thus confirm the insights of critics such as Monicat and Melman, who have argued that women travel-writers' position at the intersection of the hierarchies of imperialism and patriarchy offers them a more complex perspective on the Middle East. At the same time, the differences between these two authors demonstrate that women's writing – if we can even class Dieulafoy as a woman writer – is far from unified.

Understanding Shi'ism

The Islamic practices of the veil, gender segregation and polygyny were all great sources of fascination for European travellers, and Iran was no exception. But there were also other aspects of Iranian Islamic culture that arrested the attention of travellers, and these were not all to do with the eroticization of women.[70] In this section, I will compare travellers' accounts of two facets of Shi'ism: first, the mourning rituals of the month of Muharram, and secondly, the religious seminary of Esfahan, one of the most important historic Shi'i institutions in Iran. The month of Muharram commemorates the death of Hossein, son of Ali and grandson of the Prophet Muhammad at the battle of Karbala on the tenth of Muharram 680. It is marked by public mourning rituals, including weeping, chest beating, flagellation and passion plays (*ta'zieh* in Persian). In French travel-writing, the violent nature of these rituals becomes totemic of Shi'i Iranians' 'fanaticism', an assessment that ignores the many examples of religious laxity that these same travellers encountered during their travels, most notably, Shi'i Iranians' consumption of wine. The Madreseh (seminary) of Esfahan, in contrast, is treated in positive terms across all travelogues. The distinct treatment of the mourning rituals and of the seminary illustrate how French travel-writers could alternate between following the well-trodden path of presenting Muslims as irrational, and even dangerous, and rare moments of openness that went beyond such stereotypes.

Our earliest account of the rituals of Muharram is that of Eugène Flandin, who includes descriptions of self-mortification, *ta'zieh* and effigies of Omar being insulted and beaten until they release sweets, as per the Spanish piñata.[71] While not averse to the term 'fanatical', Flandin does seek to offer alternative explanations for the rationale behind Shi'i practices. According to him, self-mortification is practiced by 'les hommes les plus fanatiques, ou ceux qui ont quelque grande pénitence à faire' [either the most fanatical men or those who have a great penance to make].[72] This implies that when it is done for penance, self-mortification can be a reasonable act, perhaps because it equally exists in Christian culture. Indeed, Flandin's interest in making analogies between Shi'i and Christian practices becomes explicit when he describes the blood-stained shirt worn by Hossein when he was killed, which is preserved in the Masjed Shah (royal mosque) of Esfahan. Flandin states that the preservation of this shirt follows the same logic as that behind the Christian worship of relics, such as the cloak of St Martin kept in the Basilica of St Martin in Tours.[73] By identifying commonalities between Christian and Shi'i practices, Flandin moves away from the trope of dehumanizing Muslims by presenting them as inherently more 'fanatical' than Christians. Comparison here serves a levelling purpose, foregrounding the similarities between the two religious cultures.

The Muharram ritual to which Flandin devotes the greatest attention is a *ta'zieh* performance. He highlights the realism of the re-enactment of the battle of Karbala:

> Ce simulacre prit une telle animation, un tel aspect de vérité, qu'il y eut un moment où l'on put croire que des coups sérieux allaient être portés. Les combattants s'animaient de plus en plus et s'exaltaient au point qu'il fallut employer la force pour leur faire cesser un combat qui allait devenir meurtrier.[74]

> [This simulacrum became so animated, and seemed so real, that there was a moment in which one could truly believe that serious blows would be brought. The warriors were increasingly animated and exalted, to the point where one had to resort to force to interrupt a combat that was about to become deadly.]

Flandin also notes that during Muharram, Sunnis in Iran must keep a low profile, since the frenzied state of the Shi'i population means that disagreements can easily escalate to violence.[75] Despite the hatred that it incites, Flandin appreciates the *ta'zieh* performance on an artistic level:

> Quelques passages qui nous en furent traduits nous parurent pleins de sentiment et d'énergie. Les acteurs les chantent et les déclament avec une accentuation bien sentie, et les gestes dont ils accompagnent leur déclamation contribuent à produire un grand effet sur la foule, qui répond aux strophes les plus pathétiques par des sanglots déchirants.[76]

> [A few passages that were translated to us seemed full of feeling and energy. The actors sing and perform these with a truly felt accentuation and the gestures with which they accompany their performance contribute to producing a great effect on the crowd, which responds to the most tragic verses with heart-rending sobs.]

The audience's strong reaction is thus not explained in terms of religious fanaticism, but on the basis of the quality of the performance, which is designed to elicit emotion. Flandin is also delighted by the fact that the only Christian character in the *ta'zieh* is presented in a positive light as an ally of the sons of Ali. The French legation even becomes involved in the production by lending the actors some personal items of clothing for this character's costume.[77] While not rejecting the cliché of Islamic 'fanaticism' wholesale, Flandin thus seeks to temper his account through the use of analogies with Christianity and alternative explanations for the faithful's behaviour. The fact that he and his companions personally assist the production by sourcing costumes also makes it clear that the ritual is not perceived as being threatening.

The rituals of Muharram have no such redeeming qualities in the eyes of Dieulafoy and Loti. For Dieulafoy, not only are these practices to be condemned for their incitation of violence against Sunnis, but they are also aesthetically disappointing. In contrast to Flandin, they find the *ta'zieh* performance that they attend to be of the lowest amateur level and the audience's emotional reaction to be insincere:

> Les femmes laissent échapper des hoquets de douleur ou des paroles de commisération à l'adresse des victimes, frappent leur poitrine et leurs épaules;

puis, [...] reprennent la conversation enjouée interrompue quelques instants auparavant.⁷⁸

[The women let out sobs of pain and words of commiseration for the victims, beat their chest and shoulders; then, [...] pick up the jovial conversation that had been interrupted a few moments ago.]

The person in charge of the *ta'zieh* is not spared either: 'un gros homme assis sur un siege de bois trône avec la satisfaction d'un *impresario* présentant au public une troupe de choix' [a fat man sat on a wooden stool as though it were a throne, with the smug look of an impresario offering the audience a first-rate theatre company].⁷⁹ Dieulafoy's biting sarcasm keeps them at a distance from the ritual. They are a detached and amused observer, for whom these religious practices are both vapid and absurd. The tone is radically different in Loti's account of the Muharram rites that he witnessed, which emphasizes the danger that Western travellers exposed themselves to by attending Shi'i mourning ceremonies.

Loti finds two men who are willing to sneak him into a Muharram ceremony at the local mosque for a price. The journey to the mosque is shrouded in darkness and secrecy, but unlike Flandin's visit to the harem of prince 'Khassem Mirza', the secrecy is chilling rather than exciting, deploying the Dantesque imagery of a descent into the underworld. The streets are 'un dédale sinistre' [a sinister labyrinth], made up of 'précipices et oubliettes' [cliffs and dungeons] and their walk feels like 'une course crépusculaire dans des catacombes abandonnées' [a crepuscular race through abandoned catacombs].⁸⁰ In turn, the mourners at the mosque are described through consistently dehumanizing similes. They are compared on three occasions to a sea storm and are also likened to wild animals: the men let out 'un rugissement continu' [an uninterrupted roar] and smell of 'la sueur et le fauve' [sweat and wild beasts], while the women standing on the mosque's walls are 'perchées, immobiles et muettes, semblent un vol d'oiseaux noirs qui se serait abattu sur la ville' [perched, still and silent, like a mischief of black birds that has fallen upon the city].⁸¹ The male mourners all seem to be having a seizure: '[o]n voit le blanc de leurs yeux, ouverts démesurément, dont la prunelle trop levée semble entrer dans le front' [one can see the white of their excessively open eyes, their pupil is rolled so far back it seems to enter their forehead];⁸² 'un vieillard [...] frappe comme un possédé' [an old man [...] strikes as though possessed];⁸³ 'il y a un muezzin en délire' [there is a delirious muezzin].⁸⁴ Loti is not describing a scene of worship, but a generalized hysteria, which incites extreme forms of self-harm. Loti conveys the violence of the self-mortification by homing in on the noise created by the blows and the blood being spilt as a result of them. This emphasis on the senses of sight and sound, combined with Loti's use of the present tense, serves to create an immersive horror spectacle for his readers:

[D]es poings cruels s'abattent sur toutes les poitrines, d'un heurt caverneux qui couvre le son du tambour. Des hommes qui ont jeté leurs bonnets se sont fait au milieu de la chevelure des entailles sanglantes, la sueur et les gouttes de sang ruissellent sur toutes les épaules; près de moi, un jeune garçon, pour s'être frappé trop fort, vomit une bave rouge dont je suis éclaboussé.⁸⁵

[Cruel fists fall on to every chest, with a cavernous thud that covers the sound of the drum. Some men who have removed their hats have carved bleeding wounds into the middle of their hair, sweat and drops of blood run down everyone's shoulders; near me, a young boy, for having hit himself too hard, vomits a red drool that splatters on to me.]

Loti's personal contact with the bodily fluids of one of the mourners serves as the climax of the episode's abjectness, which had been built up through his liberal use of dehumanizing similes and emphatic adjectives such as 'terrible', 'monstrueux', and 'affreux' [awful].[86] The presence of these fluids on Loti's very body breaks down the separation between the clean dispassionate observer and the bloodied mass of mourners. It is also a climactic point in the narrative because it is at this very moment that the crowd finally notices the presence of an intruder and seems about to turn on Loti – a terrifying prospect, given how much time the author has devoted to establishing their bestiality:

une minute de silence et de stupeur... 'Viens!' disent mes deux hommes [...] et nous sortons à reculons, face à la foule, commes les dompteurs, lorsqu'ils sortent des cages, font face aux bêtes... Dans la rue, on ne nous poursuit pas...[87]

[A minute of silence and shock... 'Come!' Say my two men [...] and we leave walking backwards, facing the crowd, like tamers, when they leave cages, face the beasts... Out in the street, we are not pursued...]

The fact that no one follows Loti out of the mosque suggests that he was never at risk of being killed; indeed, as Flandin and Dieulafoy make clear, the target of the mourners' hatred are Sunnis, not Christians. But Loti prolongs the sense of danger through his use of ellipses, as if at any moment this might change. The violence of the acts of self-flagellation, which are shown to visit serious damage upon those performing them, go from being a shocking spectacle to a personal threat, since they adumbrate the violence that may be visited upon the Western intruder. Loti thus presents us with the most negative account of Shi'i rituals, pushing the emphasis on difference to such an extreme that it becomes an existential threat: no longer human, the mourners are wild beasts who may tear the author to shreds at any moment.

Marthe Bibesco's interpretation of the rituals of Muharram could not be more different to Loti's. According to her, Iranians are 'un peuple prodigieusement sentimental et avide de poésie' [a people prodigiously sentimental and hungry for poetry] and have 'un furieux appétit de tristesse' [a furious appetite for sadness] that must be satisfied in order to safeguard their faith.[88] Far from being repulsive, the mourning rituals of Muharram serve a cathartic purpose:

Après s'être fait mal ainsi pendant trente jours, ayant épuisé toutes les voluptés du martyre, le peuple persan revient à la vie contemplative. Il lui fallait sa Passion: il l'a eue.[89]

[After having harmed themselves thus for thirty days, having exhausted all the voluptuous pleasures of martyrdom, the Persian people return to the contemplative life. They needed their Passion: they got it.]

The language adopted by Bibesco makes it clear that the performance of these rituals is both salutary and pleasurable to the mourners. Her reference to the Passion of the Christ also reveals the analogy that she perceives between the martyrdom of Hassan and Hossein and that of Jesus Christ, which has a rich ritual tradition within Catholicism. This parallel is further explored by Bibesco in an episode where she asks a group of Iranian women to re-enact a mourning ceremony for her:

> Pour savoir si j'aurais, moi aussi, grand'pitié d'Hassan et d'Hoceïn, j'ai dit à des femmes de me parler d'eux comme elles en parlent toute la nuit, au temps de leur pieux chagrin.[90]

> [To find out whether I too would feel great pity for Hassan and Hossein, I asked some women to talk to me about them as they do throughout the night, during their period of holy mourning.]

What is striking about the introduction of this episode is that unlike our previous travel-writers, who present themselves as observers unaffected by the (fanatical) passions of the locals, Bibesco wants to experience the mourning for herself. Moreover, the fact that she asks the women to speak *as though* they were performing a religious ceremony, rather than attempting to sneak into an actual ceremony as Loti does, suggests a far greater level of respect than we encountered in other authors: first, because this requires the women's consent and, secondly, because it maintains a boundary between a real ceremony, which remains the preserve of believers, and a private re-enactment of such a ceremony, which Bibesco can attend because it does not hold the same religious weight. Bibesco provides the women's lamentations in direct speech, over three pages that read like a transcript.[91] She then concludes the episode by describing the ambiguous sensuality that characterizes ritualized mourning when it is practiced by women:

> Longtemps elles soupirèrent comme des amantes et se plaignirent comme des mères. [...] Et qu'importe si la victime adorable eut le flanc déchiré par la dent du sanglier, le cimeterre du Kalife ou la lance du centurion?
> Quand des femmes reçoivent un Dieu mourant sur leurs genoux [...] nous devons reconnaître en elles des servantes de l'Adônis.[92]

> [For a long time they sighed like lovers and lamented like mothers. [...] And what does it matter if the adorable victim had his side teared by the tusk of a boar, the scimitar of the Caliph or the lance of a centurion?
> When women receive a dying God upon their knees [...] we must recognise in them the servants of the Adonis.]

Bibesco's tripartite analogy between the Shi'i women mourning Hossein, the Virgin Mary and Mary Magdalene retrieving Christ's body from the cross and Aphrodite holding the dying Adonis suggests the universality of women's experiences of religion, in which mourning plays a central role irrespective of their cultural background. In her own words: 'Une religion sans martyrs n'est pas faite pour plaire aux femmes'.[93] [A religion without martyrs is unlikely to attract women.] This in turn suggests that it was easy for Bibesco to understand and share the emotions of the Iranian women lamenting the deaths of Hassan and Hossein. Given the ubiquity in Christian art of scenes depicting the 'Descent from the Cross' and 'Our Lady of Sorrows', Bibesco's analogy between the mourning rituals of Shi'i women and the two Marys mourning Christ would have strongly resonated with her European readers. Her perspective on the month of Muharram thus emerges as exceptional in two ways. First, because she is the only travel-writer who wants to participate in the ritual rather than merely observing it with emotional distance. Secondly, Bibesco is the only author to have avoided presenting ritualized mourning as representative of the otherness of Islam. Her emphasis on mourning's universality is expressed in much stronger terms than Flandin's occasional comparisons. This makes her the only author in this chapter to view Islam and Christianity as similar in the flexible sense described by Bhatti and Kimmich.

While the rituals of Muharram are typically viewed as a manifestation of all that is undesirable about Islam, the reverse is true of the seminary of Esfahan founded by the Safavid Shah Hossein, alternatively known as the Madreseh Mādar-e Shāh or Madreseh-ye Chahār Bāgh, which French travellers consistently present as one of the highlights of Esfahan. For Loti, the pleasure is purely aesthetic: the Madreseh has 'une magnificence digne de ce peuple de penseurs et de poètes, où la culture de l'esprit fut en honneur depuis les vieux âges' [a magnificence worthy of this people of thinkers and poets, where the culture of the mind was honoured from the oldest times].[94] The students, however, still have that inevitable air of 'fanaticism',[95] and a closer look reveals that the school is falling into disrepair: 'tout cela s'en va sans espoir, s'en va comme la Perse ancienne et charmante, est à jamais irréparable' [all of this is disappearing without hope, disappearing like the old charming Persia, forever irreperable].[96] Loti's admiration for the Madreseh thus ultimately comes from a place of nostalgia. His idealization of the lost golden age of the Safavids serves to further highlight the shortcomings of the country that he is visiting.

Flandin, Gobineau and Dieulafoy, in contrast, are delighted by the seminary as a contemporary institution that supports learning through its exquisite architecture, room for the small pleasures in life and freedom of debate. Ever interested in the effects of architecture, Flandin writes:

> Le plan et la disposition de ce *Medressèh* n'offrent aucune différence avec une mosquée ordinaire. Il n'en a cependant pas l'austérité habituelle; on y a donné quelque chose aux jouissances de la vie.[97]

> [The plan and layout of this Madreseh are no different from an ordinary mosque. Yet it is free from the usual austerity; room has been made for the pleasures in life.]

Between classes, students can consume moderately priced food and shisha pipes in the Madreseh's beautiful gardens, leading Flandin to conclude that: 'Dans ce lieu l'étude est un plaisir, et les jeunes Persans qui viennent l'y chercher s'y oublient volontiers.'[98]

[In this place study is a pleasure, and the young Persians who seek it happily forget themselves here.] For the same reasons, Gobineau calls it 'pour l'étude et la méditation un lieu d'asile' [an asylum for study and meditation],[99] adding

> Je comprends à merveille qu'on puisse s'y livrer avec passion à la vie contemplative; mais c'est bien le plus mauvais endroit du monde pour se convaincre que les biens terrestres ne sont rien; on dirait qu'il a été bâti pour prouver le contraire.[100]

> [I completely understand how one could devote oneself with passion to the contemplative life here; yet it is the worst place in the world if one wants to convince oneself that worldly goods are worthless; it seems that it has been designed to prove the contrary.]

Dieulafoy, who was educated in a convent, is just as enthusiastic, going so far as to praise the Madreseh above all European religious institutions:

> Tout ce que j'avais rêvé n'est rien auprès de la réalité. [...] je ne connais pas en Europe de monument susceptible de produire une impression analogue à celle que l'on éprouve en présence de la médressè de la Mère du Roi.[101]

> [All my dreams were nothing compared to this reality [...] I do not know of any monument in Europe that is susceptible to producing an analogous impression to that which one experiences in the presence of the Madreseh Mādar-e Shāh.]

Their words again illustrate – pace Said – that not all comparisons between the West and the Orient were in favour of the former.

Dieulafoy visits the seminary in the company of their husband and of their host, Father Pascal, the Catholic minister of Djolfa (the Armenian suburb of Esfahan). During this tour, Father Pascal stops to give his regards to some of the seminary's instructors, who cannot resist the opportunity for a theological debate.[102] The debaters are soon surrounded by a curious crowd, made up not only of students, but also of food vendors. This leads Dieulafoy to observe:

> Les Persans [...] traitent en général sans aucune acrimonie des sujets dont la discussion soulève au milieu de nos sociétés civilisées d'inévitables conflits; plusieurs fois déjà j'ai eu l'occasion de constater cette modération des chiites dans des circonstances où leur fanatisme excessif pouvait faire redouter de bruyants éclats: chacun ici parle à son tour, attaque la thèse de son interlocuteur, parfois avec une grande justesse d'arguments, et toujours avec une parfaite tranquillité d'esprit et de gestes.[103]

> [The Persians [...] usually discuss without any acrimony topics that raise inevitable conflicts in our civilised societies. I have already had the opportunity on many occasions to note the moderation of the Shi'i in circumstances where their excessive fanaticism might make one fear heated arguments. Here everyone

speaks in turn, attacks their interlocutor's thesis, sometimes with extremely sound arguments, and does so always with a perfectly calm mind and demeanour.]

The passage contrasts the 'fanaticism' that Dieulafoy expects from Shi'i Muslims to the calm tone and reasoned arguments that actually characterize religious debate in Iran, thereby revealing the limits of the stereotype of the fanatical Muslim. The comparison between Shi'i Iranians and 'civilised societies' such as France, where this type of calm and lucid debate is impossible, also casts a doubt on the very label of 'civilised'. Flandin, as we saw above, had praised the freedom of religious debate in Iran by contrasting the Persians to the narrow-minded Turks.[104] Here, Dieulafoy goes much further, making Christian Europeans the negative term of the comparison, rather than falling into the predictable trope of using other, 'inferior' Orientals, such as Arabs and Turks, as foils to the Persians. The presence of Father Pascal is instrumental in this episode. As a devout Christian living in Iran, he can act as a cultural intermediary between Dieulafoy and the Shi'i seminarists and clerics. Indeed, a few days after the visit to the Madreseh, Dieulafoy asks Pascal how he can be close friends with mullahs, and in particular saïds (descendants of the prophet), given that they are 'incorrigible fanatics'. Father Pascal replies by citing the example of one such cleric: 'J'aime de tout mon cœur seïd Mohammed Houssein, parce que cet homme de bien a sauvé un chrétien d'une mort certaine.'[105] [I love Said Mohammad Hossein with all my heart, because this good man saved a Christian from a certain death.] Far from being a 'fanatic', it turns out that the cleric intervened to rescue an evangelist who had angered the local Muslim population. Although Dieulafoy's negative view of Islam remains entrenched, their experiences in Esfahan in the company of Father Pascal add an important dimension to their travelogue. In this episode, the Orientalist opposition between reasonable Christians and fanatical Muslims is displaced in favour of a more accepting perspective, one that allows Dieulafoy to show the – admittedly rare – friendships that can exist between Muslims and Christians and, for once, to make a comparison in favour of the former.

'Esfahān, nesf-e jahān'

It is no accident that Flandin, Gobineau, Dieulafoy and Loti all visited and described the same religious seminary. The city of Esfahan, which houses the Madreseh Mādar-e Shāh, was the Iranian capital under the Safavid dynasty and is the jewel in the crown of Iranian Islamic architecture, so much so that an Iranian saying goes '*Esfahān, nesf-e jahān*': Esfahan is half the world. The city's beauty had already been extolled by early modern European visitors to the Safavid court, so that by the nineteenth century French travellers knew that Esfahan should be a key stopping point on their itinerary. Pierre Loti and Claude Anet even name their travelogues after the city (*Vers Ispahan* and *Les Roses d'Ispahan*), making it their ultimate destination. In this section I will focus on Flandin, Gobineau, Dieulafoy and Loti's descriptions of Esfahan's most famous architectural feature: the central square known as the Meidān Shāh or Naqsh-e Jahān Square (Figure 3.2). Built between the late-sixteenth and early-seventeenth

Figure 3.2 Vista of Esfahan's Naqsh-e Jahan Square by Eugène Flandin.

Source: Eugène Flandin, 'Meidan-i-Chah ou Place Royale, Ispahan', *Voyage en Perse. Perse moderne: Planches* (Paris: Baudry, 1851).

century, Naqsh-e Jahān Square is a vast open space (160 by 560 metres), its sides formed by the city's most symbolically important buildings: two mosques (the Masjed Shāh on the south side and the Sheikh Lotfollah Mosque on the north side), the royal palace (on the west side) and the bazaar (on the east side). This means that the square's architecture encompasses all key aspects of public life: religion, commerce and governance, with the first being awarded the greatest importance.

The scale of the square and the architectural harmony between the four buildings that it connects make it one of the most memorable sights that Iran has to offer, inspiring ekphrastic descriptions and attempts at comparisons between European and Iranian architecture. A consistent theme in French travel-writers' accounts of Naqsh-e Jahān Square is that it is like nothing that a European has ever seen before. In the words of Eugène Flandin,

> Il va sans dire que ce n'est pas par nos temples européens de style grec ou gothique, qu'on peut deviner le genre des mosquées persanes. On peut encore avoir vu celles de Constantinople ou du Kaire, que l'on aurait aucune idée de celles de la Perse. Dans ce pays, l'art et les milles détails qui forment l'ensemble de ses productions architectoniques ont un caractère particulier, une essence originale que l'on ne commence à pressentir que de l'autre côté du Tigre.[106]

> [It goes without saying that it is not through our European temples, neither in the Greek nor Gothic style, that one can picture the type of the Persian mosque. Not even the mosques of Constantinople or Cairo, would give you any idea of those of

Persia. In this country, the artistry and endless details that form the whole of its architectural productions have a particular character, an original essence, that you can only begin to experience on the other side of the Tigris.]

Flandin emphasizes the uniqueness of Esfahan's architecture not only by way of contrast with Europe, but also with other Muslim countries. The same rhetorical strategy, that is to say, an emphasis on the limits of analogy, is employed by Jane Dieulafoy, who states that 'aucune ville d'Europe ne présente un ensemble de constructions comparable au Meïdan Chah d'Ispahan' [no city in Europe boasts an ensemble of buildings comparable to the Meidān Shāh of Esfahan], before admitting: 'La première fois que j'ai traversé l'esplanade, je me suis pourtant souvenu [sic] de la place Saint-Marc.' [The first time I walked across the esplanade, I was nonetheless reminded of Saint-Mark's Square.][107] However, they soon abandon the comparison between Esfahan and Venice on the grounds that 'il ne serait pas à l'avantage de l'Italie' [it would not be to Italy's advantage], and proceed instead to list that which can only be found in Esfahan.[108] Dieulafoy's hesitation between difference and similarity dramatizes the cognitive process of familiarizing oneself with new surroundings, which typically relies on analogies with that which one has encountered before. As a rhetorical strategy, moreover, it allows them to simultaneously give the reader an idea of what the square might look like, while conveying that it surpasses what the reader is imagining. This exemplifies how rhetorical figures of comparison offer a fruitful compromise between the twin risks posed by descriptions of unknown places, as identified by Alain Guyot: on the one hand, suggesting a complete equivalence between the foreign location and the known location would destroy any sense of specificity; on the other hand, the absence of comparison would render the description too opaque, preventing the reader from perceiving anything at all.[109] By dramatizing a personal hesitation that ends with a renewed emphasis on Esfahan's uniqueness, Dieulafoy makes their panegyric to the city all the more rhetorically convincing. Loti, in contrast, conveys the uniqueness of Naqsh-e Jahān Square by comparing it not to other cities, but to an imaginary setting: that of the *Mille et Une Nuits* [*Thousand and One Nights*], the collection of Arabic tales of Persian origin that was popularized in Europe through Antoine Galland's eighteenth-century French translation. Under Loti's pen, Esfahan is the materialization of this fairy-tale world, its blue architectural features appearing to be made not of ceramic tiles, but of precious stones: 'cette ville de turquoise et de lapis' [this city of turquoise and lapis].[110] Gobineau goes even further, suggesting that there is a reason behind Esfahan's resemblance to the palaces described in the tales of the *Mille et Une Nuits*: 'Ispahan n'a pu être conçu et exécuté que par des rois et des architectes qui passaient leurs jours et leurs nuits à entendre raconter de merveilleux contes de fées' [Esfahan could only have been conceived and executed by kings and architects who spent their days and nights listening to marvellous fairy tales].[111] In other words, it was these orally transmitted tales that gave them the ambition and imagination necessary to build such a spectacular city.

Esfahan's main mosque, the Masjed Shāh, was off bounds to Christian Europeans, accessible only in exceptional circumstances and with the support of local religious authorities. European travellers would therefore find themselves pausing before the thirty-metre tall portal leading from Naqsh-e Jahān Square into the mosque complex, admiring its rich decorations and attempting to imagine how luxuriant the mosque inside must be, given the beauty of the gate guarding it. Loti writes: 'la porte gigantesque, tout là-bas, m'attire comme l'entrée magique d'un gouffre bleu' [the gigantic gate, over there, draws me like the magical entrance to a blue cave], calling to mind the magical caves of Aladdin's genie and Ali Baba's thieves.[112] Flandin pairs enthusiastic praise with architectural jargon, so that his readers know that his admiration is founded on an expert appreciation of the portal's technical and aesthetic feats.[113] By lavishing praise on each of its architectural features, Flandin also conveys to the reader that every element of the portal is of equal beauty and quality. His description emphasizes how all these different elements 'marry' together, so that there is order within its variety. The scale and three-dimensionality of the portal, finally, are conveyed through a use of active verbs, which provide the description with a sense of depth (*découpée* [carved out of], *s'entrelacent* [interlace]) and movement (*s'élancent* [soar up], *courent* [run], *redescend* [descends again]). Less technical in his description, Loti combines instead two metaphors, one natural and the other man-made: running water (*cascade* [waterfall], *gouttelettes* [droplets], *coulent* [pour]) and the textile decorative arts (*brodées* [embroidered], *broderies* [embroideries]).[114] Like Flandin, Loti expresses awe at how the variety of patterns and colours achieves a sense of order, but his language is even more emphatic, privileging the use of oxymorons to convey the tension between order and chaos. The portal's decorations are *régulières* [regular] and *symétriques* [symmetrical], but also a *fouillis* [mess] and an *enchevêtrement* [tangle]. And yet, for all its 'complications', the portal instils 'une impression d'unité et de calme' [a sense of unity and calm].[115] Whereas Flandin's ekphrasis maintained a technical and detached tone in order to describe the portal as an impressive feat of human ingenuity, Loti is keen to stress the emotions and associations evoked by this architecture. His use of adverbs (*merveilleusement*, *délicieusement*) suggests the sensual pleasure that he derives from the conflicting impressions of chaos and order. He is also arrested by its overwhelming scale, describing its proportions as *écrasantes* [crushing]. The passage, moreover, makes an effective use of deictics to put the reader in the position of the traveller. Having first seen the portal from a distance within the broader context of the square, Loti introduces his more detailed description of its features with the words 'Lorsqu'on arrive sous ce porche' [When one arrives under this porch], inviting his readers to picture themselves standing beneath the portal and looking up with him.[116] The description ends on the portal's most understated feature, its wooden door, which is fetishized by Loti as an unsurmountable obstacle:

> impénétrable pour les chrétiens, la porte du saint lieu [...] plonge dans des parois épaisses, revêtues d'émail couleur lapis; elle a l'air de s'enfoncer dans le royaume du bleu absolu et suprême.[117]

> [Impenetrable to Christians, the door to the holy place [...] is buried in the thick walls covered with lapis-coloured enamel; it seems to sink into the kingdom of absolute and supreme blue.]

There is a slippage here, in which a door that leads to a real religious building now seems to open onto an imaginary world, the blue-coloured 'kingdom' evoked by the decorative tiles, which harks to the *Mille et Une Nuits*. Loti thus brings a sense of magical exoticism to his ekphrasis, presenting the buildings of Esfahan as a materialization of the landscapes evoked by Galland's Oriental tales.

Across these descriptions of Naqsh-e Jahān Square, French authors' emphasis on the otherness of Esfahan does not serve to belittle it: on the contrary, what makes Esfahan different to European cities is precisely what makes it the most admirable. The positive value ascribed to such differences is most obvious when authors draw explicit comparisons between Naqsh-e Jahān Square and the French royal palace of Versailles. Gobineau writes that whereas the imagination of those who designed Versailles was 'un peu prétentieuse' [a tad pretentious], Esfahan by contrast is 'le triomphe de l'élégant et le modèle du joli' [the triumph of elegance and the model of the agreeable].[118] Dieulafoy and Loti both note that Naqsh-e Jahān was built an entire century before Versailles, observing that Shah Abbas opted for symmetry and open spaces at a time when Europeans were still building narrow squares and winding streets.[119] In architectural terms, then, France had historically lagged behind Iran. In a later essay, Dieulafoy revisited this comparison between Abbas's Naqsh-e Jahān and Louis XIV's Versailles and argued that the monarchs' architectural legacies were symbolic of their wider attitudes towards governance:

> c'est autour d'une mosquée splendide qu'Abbas fait graviter groupa [*sic*] ses palais, ses jardins et les bazars où se coudoyèrent les représentants de toutes les races. Louis XIV ne construisit que des palais à sa royale divinité, Abbas autrement déiste couvrit l'empire [...] de monuments consacrés au bien être du peuple.[120]

> [It is around a magnificent mosque that Abbas anchored grouped [*sic*] his palaces, his gardens and the bazaars where members of all races crossed each other's paths. Louis XIV only built palaces to his own royal divinity, Abbas who was otherwise deist covered his empire [...] with monuments dedicated to the wellbeing of the people.]

Flandin too considers the architecture of Esfahan to be symbolic of the country's wider attitudes towards religion and society:

> En Europe, les palais des rois, les musées, les hôtels de ville, les maisons des particuliers même, rivalisent [...] avec les temples chrétiens [...]. Chez les peuples musulmans, les architectes ont employé tout leur savoir, appliqué les inventions les plus élégantes de leur imagination à la construction et à la décoration des mosquées.[121]

> [In Europe, the palaces of kings, museums, city halls, and even private houses, rival [...] with Christian temples [...]. In Muslim countries, architects have employed all their skill, applied the most elegant inventions of their imagination to the construction and decoration of mosques.]

Walking across Naqsh-e Jahān Square, the eye cannot avoid but fall on one of the two mosques that face each other on its northern and southern side. This leads Flandin to observe with admiration : 'Partout l'idée de Dieu domine; partout son culte frappe le regard, la pensée religieuse s'élève au-dessus du vulgaire.'[122] [Everywhere the idea of God prevails; everywhere His worship catches the eye and religious thought rises above vulgarity]. Such is the impression made by the religious architecture of Esfahan that the very same writers who had critiqued the centrality of Islam within Iranian culture as a matter of 'fanaticism' find themselves praising a society that ranks the spiritual above the material.

Although nineteenth-century travellers are united in their admiration for Naqsh-e Jahān Square as a feat of architectural design, the maintenance of the city's buildings had suffered greatly since the time of Shah Abbas. As a result, authors are divided as to whether Esfahan should be described in terms of its continuity with its historic legacy or whether it should be declared a shadow of its former self. The former writers, which include Flandin, suppose that 'l'effet qu'elle [la place] produit aujourd'hui, doit être le même qu'elle produisait au temps de sa plus brillante splendeur' [the effect that the square has today, must be the same that it had at the time of its greatest splendour].[123] They also describe the square as a centre of activity: the bazaar is as busy as ever, as are the two mosques, and at every sunrise and sunset musicians perform a salute to the sun on the terrace of the royal palace, a tradition which Dieulafoy and Loti suggest dates back to Zoroastrianism.[124] The vast open surface of the square itself is also used by food and tea vendors, storytellers and people taking the air on foot and on horseback.[125] Far from being a relic, the square thus continues to provide the same essential functions (commerce, religion, socializing) that it had done when it was first built, with the one exception of the royal palace, as the capital has since been relocated to Tehran. Gobineau and Loti, by contrast, find it important to stress the damage suffered by the square, suffusing their accounts with the theme of decadence. Gobineau identifies a clear political explanation for this decline: local corruption. Officials are pocketing the funds regularly sent by the shah to support the city's renovation, without carrying out any of the agreed restoration work. Gobineau cynically notes: 'on les touchera [les sommes allouées] longtemps après que la mosquée n'existera plus' [they will still be receiving (the allotted funds) long after the mosque has ceased to exist].[126] Loti's description of the city's disrepair is even more hyperbolic than Gobineau's. Having at first been amazed by the beauty of Naqsh-e Jahān Square, he notices upon closer inspection that many of the edifices' decorative tiles have fallen off, leaving them 'rongés d'une lèpre grise' [eaten by a grey lepracy].[127] The image of a plagued body (in reference to the areas in which the stucco has become exposed) is particularly vivid and foreshadows Loti's later pronouncement that the square is condemned to die: 'cette place unique au monde, qui a déjà plus de trois cents ans, ne verra certainement pas finir le siècle où nous venons d'entrer' [this world-unique square, which is already three hundred years old, will certainly not see the end of the twentieth century].[128] Whereas Gobineau had identified a practical cause for the square's decline and thus a potential solution to it – were it not for local corruption, the city could effectively be restored to its former glory – Loti presents this decline as fatal and irreversible. Not only does he accuse 'the Persians' of ignoring the square's state of disrepair, but he also suggests that they would not be capable of restoring it even if they wanted to because they have forgotten how to produce the blue pigment that was used to craft the original decorative tiles. The damage is thus 'irréparable',[129] the very same adjective that Loti uses when describing Esfahan's Madreseh as a testament to Iran's lost golden age.[130]

Loti ultimately presents Esfahan as a feat never to be repeated, a momentary slip in a long history of 'incurie orientale' [Oriental negligence].[131] In doing so, he effectively cordons the city off from the rest of Iran's history and architecture, writing 'ces ruines font l'effet d'une anomalie sur cette terre persane' [these ruins feel like an anomaly on Persian territory].[132] This is the exact opposite argument to that of Flandin, who, as we saw, argued that Esfahan was exemplary of Iranian architecture. The sentence also surreptitiously rewrites Loti's previous description of Naqsh-e Jahān, turning what had previously been described as a busy and beautiful square with a few missing tiles into 'ruins'. This is an overstatement if there ever was one, and one that will become Loti's signature. Indeed, Loti concludes his travelogue by revisiting his earlier description of Esfahan, commenting that the most memorable sight of the entire journey was

> une ville en ruines […], une ville d'émail bleu qui tombe en poussière sous ses platanes de trois cents ans, […] d'exquises faïences qui s'émiettent sans recours, […] cet Ispahan de lumière et de mort, baigné dans l'atmosphère diaphane des sommets…
>
> [a city in ruins […], a city of blue enamel which falls into dust under the three-hundred-year old plane trees, […] exquisite ceramics crumbling without remedy, […] this Esfahan of light and death, bathed in the diaphanous atmosphere of its summits…]

The passage describes a dying and crumbling city which has more in common with the desert ruins of Persepolis than the bustling – and indeed fully standing – city of Esfahan. The manner in which Loti keeps rewriting Esfahan, from being a magical city out of the *Mille et Une Nuits* to a historic capital in need of renovation work, and finally a set of abandoned ruins, should alert us not only to the subjectivity of travel-writing but also to its highly deliberate use of narrative strategies and rhetorical devices. Loti's priority is not to offer an accurate description of Esfahan, but to craft a compelling story: an elegy to a lost world, one that he would like his readers to believe he was the last European to witness.[133] Ironically for him, Gobineau had portrayed himself in the exact same way half a century earlier and Anet would do the same a decade after Loti.[134] And Esfahan still stands today, renovated and resplendent, destined to outlive these authors' attempts to aggrandize themselves.

Remembering 'the great of the earth'

Having established just how artificial Loti's elegy to Esfahan is, the time has come for us to turn our attention to some real ruins: the two-and-a-half-millennia old remains of the ancient cities and necropoles of Susa and Persepolis. These edifices, which were built under the Persian Achaemenid dynasty, leave a lasting impression on all

Figure 3.3 Vista of Persepolis by Eugène Flandin.
Source: Eugène Flandin, 'Vue des ruines de Persépolis', in *Voyage en Perse. Perse moderne: Planches* (Paris: Baudry, 1851).

those who visit them, from the early-modern travel-writers Jean-Baptiste Tavernier and John Chardin to the authors studied here.[135] Nineteenth-century travellers were struck in particular by the technical ingenuity, sense of the aesthetic and opulence suggested by the remains of the Achaemenids. Persepolis, the ceremonial capital of the Achaemenid Empire, was destroyed by Alexander of Macedon, but the city's terraces and many of the royal palace's pillars, statues, staircases and bas-reliefs survived both Alexander's fire and the passage of time, so that visitors get a direct sense of the scale, extent and beauty of the lost city (see Figure 3.3). Susa by contrast was completely buried. Its remains were brought to light by the archaeological mission led by Marcel Dieulafoy, for which Jane Dieulafoy wrote the dig diary. While the site was not as impressive as that of Persepolis, whose monuments remain standing to this day, the Susa finds revealed the polychromy of Achaemenid art, exemplified by the enamel tile work that once decorated the palace's walls. The Dieulafoys appropriated the vast majority of these artefacts and transported them to the Louvre, where they are still displayed today.[136] I will return to the imperialist implications of the Susa mission later in this chapter. For now, I shall focus on these writers' descriptions of Achaemenid art and architecture, the elegiac meditations that these inspire and the strategies that these authors adopted to envision and understand the people who once walked these ancient cities.

All those who visited the site of Persepolis were astonished at the longevity, scale and beauty of its ruins. For Flandin, Persepolis

> inspire un sentiment de religieuse admiration pour une civilisation qui a su créer de si pompeux monuments, leur imprimer un tel caractère de grandeur, et leur

donner une solidité qui a permis aux parties les plus importantes de résister jusqu'à nos jours, à travers vingt-deux siècles et tant de révolutions qui ont dévasté la Perse.[137]

[[Persepolis] inspires a feeling of religious admiration for a civilisation that was able to create such imposing monuments, to impress in them such a grandiose character, to give them a hard-wearing quality which has enabled the most important sections to resist all the way to our times, through twenty-two centuries and the many revolutions that have devastated Persia.]

Flandin homes in, in particular, on the bas-reliefs decorating the palace, which according to him are governed by two concepts designed to reflect the character of the Achaemenid dynasty: power and elegance.[138] Based on his observation of Persepolis alone, Flandin confidently declares the Achaemenids the most advanced and sophisticated civilization of the 'old world', ranking them above both the ancient Egyptians and the Indians on the grounds that

rien dans ces palais des princes achéménides, n'est sauvage ou barbare; [...] à Persépolis tout est art, tout est élégance; [...] les compositions des artistes perses se distinguent toujours par le goût, l'originalité et la richesse.[139]

[Nothing about the palaces of the Achaemenid princes is savage nor barbaric; [...] in Persepolis, all is art, all is elegance; [...] the compositions of Persian artists are always recognisable by their taste, originality, and richness.]

The choice of the adjective *barbare* is particularly apposite, since etymologically, the word was first used by the ancient Greeks to refer to the ancient Persians. To see Persepolis was to realize that the ancient Persians were anything but barbarians. Loti is equally struck by the longevity of Persepolis, expressing his awe through the adjective *éternel* and its cognate verb *éterniser* [to eternalise],[140] and the use of rhetorical questions: how is it possible for all these long, tall, slim pillars to still be standing?[141] Or for the polish of the bas-reliefs not to have faded?[142] The longevity of the Persepolitan bas-reliefs, according to Loti, is all the more impressive when compared to the façades of medieval European churches and ancient Greek marbles, which all show signs of erosion.[143] As with the comparisons between Esfahan and Saint Mark's Square or the palace of Versailles discussed above, the European point of reference serves to illustrate the superior quality of Iranian architecture. But whereas Loti's descriptions of Esfahan had relied on magical exoticism, his description of the scale of Persepolis is practical rather than hyperbolical: the stairs are wide enough to let an army march up and the terrace is large enough to support an entire city.[144] The site speaks for itself.

For all the awe-inspiring buildings that they had left behind them, the Achaemenids themselves however had long disappeared. In a passage that draws heavily on the language and style of Ecclesiastes, Dieulafoy writes of those who ruled the world's first great empire:

Aujourd'hui la loi des puissants n'est plus qu'un coup de tonnerre évanoui dans le passé, leur nom un éclair. Le froid impitoyable de la mort a raidi les bras des rois et des esclaves; les vers ont fait leur pâture de la chair des orgueilleux et des humbles; il n'y a pas un atome de cette terre foulée de nos pieds qui n'ait vécu et souffert.[145]

[Today the law of the powerful is nothing more than a long-vanished burst of thunder, their name a flash of lightning. The merciless cold of death has stiffened the arms of kings and slaves; worms have eaten the flesh of the proud and of the humble; there is not one atom of this earth we tread that has not lived and suffered.]

For Dieulafoy, the fact that no part of the Susa palace is left standing means that its loss is even more complete than that of Persepolis: 'Pas même des ruines ne sont restées debout pour raconter une mélancolique histoire.'[146] [There aren't even ruins left standing to tell a melancholy story.] Indeed, the ruins of Persepolis tell the story of a conflict between presence and absence: the structures and art are still standing, yet the civilization that built them has disappeared and very little is known of it. And although the longevity of the ruins is impressive, these are but a paltry reminder of how great the city would have been before its destruction. Loti's elegiac description of Persepolis captures the 'indicible mélancolie' [unspeakable melancholy] that this conflict between presence and absence inspires, juxtaposing the sights before his eyes with what was once there: quiet meadows where once epic battles were fought, wild flowers cropping up in the place of sumptuous carpets and goats grazing on the very spot where the throne room once was.[147] Loti's most poetic moment comes when he describes seeing his own reflection on the polished stone of a bas-relief, and realizes with shock that: 'ces plaques polies sont les mêmes qui, à cette même place, reflétèrent des figures […] évanouies depuis plus de deux mille ans' [these polished plaques are the same which, in this very spot, once reflected faces […] that vanished over two thousand years ago].[148] His words eloquently capture the sense of being simultaneously as close as he will ever be and yet irreparably distant from the people who once lived and worked among these walls.

In the absence of the Achaemenids and with very little information to go by, the challenge for travel-writers is to imagine what their lives might have been like. Flandin does this by cross-referencing ancient Iranian practices with modern Iranian practices. For example, he explains the gift-bearing scenes in Achaemenid Persian art as depictions of the festival of Nowruz.[149] The rigid postures of the men depicted in the bas-reliefs are similarly explained as the result not only of the artwork's formal character, but also of its realism, since to this day 'Orientals' affect 'une dignité froide et compassée dans leur maintien' [a cold and composed dignity in their demeanour].[150] Flandin thus proposes that in order to understand the Achaemenids, he need only look around himself, since the people of Iran have not changed. A similar suggestion is made by Claude Anet, who however restricts himself to the Zoroastrian community: they are the ones who have not changed, sharing with the bas-reliefs of Persepolis 'ce visage régulier, ces yeux larges, ce nez droit, la barbe bien plantée et la dignité […] de la plus vieille race persane' [that regular face, those wide eyes, that straight nose, that thick beard and the dignity […] of the oldest race of Persia].[151] Anet's claim assumes that other Iranians have mixed their blood with that of their Arab conquerors and are therefore not as closely related to the ancient Persians. This suggests that his notions of race were influenced by those of Gobineau, whom he read ahead of his journey.[152] Dieulafoy, by contrast, argues that the polychromy of Achaemenid art belies a powerful ancient race, whose aesthetics disappeared along with them. 'Est-ce une œuvre barbare?' [Is this the work of barbarians?] they ask rhetorically, before indirectly answering in the negative: 'Combien notre goût, fait de sensations pâles, né sous un ciel triste, me semble rachitique et mesquin auprès du grand sentiment qui inspirait les maîtres anciens!'[153] [How terribly scrawny and petty does our taste, made of pale sensations and born under sad skies, seem to me compared to the great sentiment that inspired the ancient masters!]

Dieulafoy is not the first to argue that the label of 'barbarian' is unfit for the ancient Persians. Their assessment of modern French aesthetics as meagre when compared to that of the Achaemenids however introduces a new binary into the discussion: instead of opposing the ancient Greeks to the ancient Persians, they are contrasting the power of ancient art (be it Greek or Persian) and the etiolated colours of modernity. This negative assessment of modern aesthetics aligns with Gobineau's definition of the Persians as Aryans, which went hand in hand with a fatalistic narrative of civilizational decline (see Chapter 2). By emphasizing the primal vigour of Achaemenid art, Dieulafoy makes it speak to a narrative of degeneration, according to which the once powerful Aryan race (which included both the ancient Greeks and the ancient Persians) has been weakened and diluted over time, and consequently lost its original vision and energy, as made manifest by its dull sense of the aesthetic.[154] Loti does not bring race into the equation. He does however, like Dieulafoy, believe that Achaemenid art offers a gateway into understanding the ancient Persians. The *lamassu* statues guarding the entrance to the royal palace

> révèlent sur leur souverain des choses intimes que je ne m'attendais point à jamais surprendre. En les contemplant, mieux qu'en lisant dix volumes d'histoire, je conçois peu à peu combien fut majestueuse, hiératique et superbe, la vision de la vie dans les yeux de cet homme à demi légendaire. [155]

> [reveal intimate things about their sovereign, which I never expected to discover. More informative than ten history books, their contemplation allows me, little by little, to conceive of how majestic, hieratic, and superb this semi-legendary man's conception of life was.]

And, Loti adds, once the cuneiform script is fully deciphered, the ancient Persians will speak for themselves through the texts they have etched on to the bas-reliefs.[156]

If ancient art and inscriptions offered vital clues, these were not sufficient for bringing the Achaemenids back to life. To do so required an effort of the imagination of the type that had been modelled by Jules Michelet in *La Bible de l'Humanité* (1864), when he used excerpts from Zoroastrian scripture as the starting point for a creative reconstruction of a day in the life of an ancient Iranian (see Chapter 2). Dieulafoy and Loti both take a leaf out of Michelet's book, inserting within their descriptions of the sites of Susa and Persepolis a momentary 'vision', in which they are able to witness the Achaemenid capitals as they once were. Dieulafoy's vision comes to them during a nocturnal walk around the archaeological site:

> [M]on imagination vagabonde s'envolait sur l'aile de la fantaisie jusqu'aux siècles où il me semblait avoir vécu une autre vie.
> Je les voyais ces souverains dont la grandeur inspirait l'effroi; ils se mouvaient solennels comme des statues d'ivoire, les muscles de leur face ne tressaillaient pas quand l'univers s'écrasait à leurs pieds.
> Là-bas souriait la volupté. Sous l'or, les bijoux et le fard des femmes anxieuses se disputaient le regard du maître du monde.
> Plus loin, toute une ville prosternée devant le temple d'une divinité humaine.[157]

> [My wandering imagination flew on the wings of fantasy to the centuries where it seemed to me that I had lived another life.
> I could see them, these sovereigns whose grandeur inspired fear; they moved as solemnly as ivory statues, the muscles of their face did not tremble when the universe came crashing at their feet.
> There, smiled sensual pleasure. Beneath the gold, jewels, and make-up, anxious women fought over the gaze of the master of the world.
> Further away, an entire city was prostrated before the temple of a human divinity.]

Dieulafoy's imagination is here characterized as a flying time-travel machine, which transports the author back to another millennium and homes in, in particular, to how the royal court and the people of Susa viewed their king. In doing so, Dieulafoy was adopting the same imaginative method that would inspire their novel *Parysatis*, which was discussed in Chapter 2:

> Chaque jour je respirais cette atmosphère de ruines vivantes, à tout instant apparaissaient des bas-reliefs, des vases, des pierres gravées, des émaux d'une couleur merveilleuse, peu à peu j'identifiai ma vie avec celle des grands de la terre pour qui on les avait créés.[158]

> [Every day I would breathe this atmosphere of living ruins, at every instant there appeared bas-reliefs, vases, carved stones, enamels of marvellous colours, little by little I identified my life with that of the great of the earth for whom they had been created.]

The notion of 'identifying' with the lives of others to such an extent that the author felt as though they had 'lived another life' is a powerful one. Moreover, it erases any sense of cultural or ontological difference between the people of ancient Persia and of nineteenth-century France. The examples of *La Bible de l'Humanité* and *Parysatis* show us how cultural fragments, be they of liturgy, pottery or palaces, could be a starting point around which a nineteenth-century author would scaffold an entire world.

Loti uses the trope of the imaginary vision for elegiac purposes too, though his vision is even more dramatic than Dieulafoy's: it recounts the destruction of Persepolis. The vision is triggered by a carbonized piece of wood, which Loti claims is a fragment of one of the beams that once supported the palace's roof and thus physical evidence of the fire set by Alexander of Macedon.[159] The historical significance that Loti attributes to the object invests it with a talismanic power: at its very touch, Loti is transported back to the event branded upon it:

> Pendant un instant, les durées antérieures s'évanouissent pour moi; il me semble que c'était hier, cet incendie; on dirait qu'un sortilège d'évocation dormait dans ce bloc de cèdre. [...] presque en une sorte de vision, je perçois la splendeur de ces palais, l'éclat des émaux, des ors et des tapis pourpre, le faste de ces inimaginables salles, qui étaient plus hautes que la nef de la Madeleine et dont les enfilades de colonnes, comme des allées d'arbres géants, s'enfuyaient dans une pénombre de forêt.[160]

> [For an instant, the periods between us vanish before me; it feels as if it were yesterday, this fire; it is as though an evocative spell lay dormant in this block of cedar. [...] almost in a kind of vision, I perceive the splendour of these palaces, the lustre of the enamels, the gold and the Tyrian purple carpets, the pomp of these unimaginable halls, which were taller than the nave of the Madeleine church and whose rows of columns, aligned like gigantic trees, disappeared into a forest's half-light.]

Loti describes the horrific sounds and sights of the grand edifices catching flame and crashing down, all before the eyes of the screaming people of Persepolis, as though he had personally witnessed it.[161] Loti remembers having been bored when he first read Plutarch's account of the burning of Persepolis as a schoolboy; now, he sees the beauty and scale of what Alexander destroyed.[162] Now that he stands among the ruins of Persepolis, he can finally see this act of vandalism for what it is: an 'irrémédiable sacrilège' [irredeemable sacrilege], which casts a doubt on the neat binary of civilized West and barbaric Orient.[163] Dieulafoy too cannot help but refer to Plutarch's text when attempting to make sense of the site of Persepolis. Physical and written sources are set side by side in a passage of *La Perse* where Dieulafoy sits reading a French translation of the *Life of Alexander* 'en présence de ces pierres calcinées, de ces colonnes rongées par les flammes, de ces débris de poutres carbonisées' [in the presence of these charred stones, of those columns gnawed by the flames, of these fragments of carbonised beams].[164] They too are forced to conclude that the man they once idealized committed a terrible crime. The melancholy inspired by the ruins of Persepolis is thus double, stemming not only from what has been lost, but also from the wanton nature of the site's destruction.

When we compare Flandin's description of Persepolis to the elegiac accounts of Loti and Dieulafoy, what emerges most clearly is the former's lack of sentimentality. Whereas the latter two seek to imaginatively reconstruct the world that once was, Flandin contributes to its erasure by defiling one of the tall slender pillars that defied both time and gravity by remaining erect for over two and a half millennia. Flandin carves a long and pompous graffiti into the pillar, an act of vandalism that he justifies with the fact that he and his travel companion Pascal Coste are 'explorateurs sérieux, envoyés par le gouvernement de France' [serious explorers, sent by the French government].[165] As he carves 'l'étendue de nos découvertes, de nos travaux' [the extent of their discoveries and studies] into the pillar, Flandin irreparably damages the very subject over which he is claiming expertise: ancient Iran.[166] The act reveals not only a lack of regard for conservation, but also the political implications of Flandin's surveying, which, like the graffiti, claims a vicarious sense of ownership over that which is described (or inscribed.) These subtle forms of appropriation are premised on the casting of the French travellers as protagonists and of Iran as the canvas upon which their scientific authority can be asserted. Whereas for Dieulafoy and Loti the Achaemenid capitals were home to imaginary ancestors and alter egos, for Flandin they are an arena in which French explorers can shine, revealing their superior understanding of antiquity – superior, it is implied, to that of the explorers from other European nations who also inscribed their names upon the ruins. It is no coincidence that Flandin chooses to carve his and Coste's names on 'l'un des piliers les plus élevés et les plus solides, […] aussi haut que possible' [one of the tallest and most stable pillars, […] as high as possible], in other words, above the names of others.[167] Iran was an accessory in an imperialist game of one-upmanship in which the players were all European. Flandin's graffiti was only the precursor to a far more large-scale act of appropriation: that of the remains of Susa for the Louvre, initiated by none other than the Dieulafoys.

Plagued by the West

Despite their desire to promote a positive image of French civilization and France's influence on the global stage, travel-writers were regularly confronted with the realities of European interventionism in Iran, which took the form of a British and Russian policy of undermining Iran's military power and agency (described by Flandin, Loti and Anet) and the exploitation of local resources and infrastructures by the British, Russians, French and later the Belgians (described by Flandin, Dieulafoy and Anet). Although it was never colonized, Iran was subjected to a far more insidious form of imperialism. To quote Anet's sardonic summary: 'La Perse a deux voisins qui s'intéressent vivement à sa santé: la Russie et l'Angleterre. / La Perse est malade.'[168] [Persia has two neighbours who are very interested in her health: Russia and Britain. / Persia is sick.] The process of Iran's financial exploitation by the West with the complicity of the Qajar and later Pahlavi Monarchy was famously denounced by the Iranian intellectual Jalal Al-e Ahmad in his 1968 political essay *Gharbzadegi*, from which this section takes its title. Translated alternatively as 'plagued by the West', 'West-struck-ness', and 'Westoxification', the titular term *gharbzādegi* is a neologism used by Al-e Ahmad to refer simultaneously to Iran's financial exploitation by the West as a rentier state and to the nation's Westernization, which Al-e Ahmad argued were both manifestations of Iran's internalized belief in Europe's cultural superiority. Flandin and

Dieulafoy's travelogues are of particular interest in this regard because their economic analyses foreshadow that of Al-e Ahmad. Other travellers' negative impressions of Western influence were, by contrast, rather superficial: Gobineau, Loti and Bibesco, for example, all criticize the popularity of Western artefacts and styles at the expense of local arts and crafts, but only do so because this undermines their experience of the exotic.[169] They do not consider the political and social ramifications of such trade arrangements.

As a member of a French diplomatic mission, Eugène Flandin witnessed firsthand France's efforts to bring Iran within its sphere of influence. As Flandin explains in his preface, Napoleon Bonaparte had initially forged an alliance with Iran to counteract British influence expanding westward from India, but there was also a strong commercial incentive for the journey: the mission hoped to open a new market for France to export its goods to.[170] Once in Iran, however, Flandin is dismayed to discover that such trade deals have successfully been used by the British to decimate local industry:

> Il s'y trouve [à Kachân] plusieurs fabriques d'où sortent des étoffes [...] d'un très-beau travail et d'une solidité parfaite. On y fait aussi des velours et des châles ordinaires; mais les importations anglaises [...] ont porté aux manufactures de Kachân un coup mortel. [...]
>
> Les producteurs persans ont ressenti les bienfaits de la civilisation européenne. Le contact des Anglais surtout a eu pour eux ce funeste résultat de répandre, dans tous leurs bazars, des quantités considérables de marchandises qui se vendent à un prix inférieur à celui des produits nationaux.
>
> – Il faut bien le dire, c'est là le fruit des traités de commerce obtenus par les agents diplomatiques, qui, sous les dehors d'une amitié protectrice et d'une alliance politique, cachent toujours l'arrière-pensée de tuer l'industrie du pays assez confiant pour leur ouvrir ses portes. Ils se font, pour ainsi dire, les commis-voyageurs en grand du commerce européen; [...] pour eux seuls, il n'y a plus ni douanes, ni patentes, ni impôt d'aucune espèce. L'inondant alors de marchandises qui se vendent au-dessous des cours établis pour celles des fabriques nationales, ils arrivent promptement à faire abandonner les unes, et, par suite, fermer les autres.[171]

[There are in Kashān several workshops that produce fine fabrics [...] that are of excellent workmanship and perfectly hard-wearing. Some even make velvet and everyday shawls; but English imports [...] have brought a mortal blow to the factories of Kashān.

Persian producers have felt the benefits of European civilisation. Contact with the English in particular has had for them the fatal consequence of filling their bazars with a considerable quantity of goods that are sold at a lower price than local products.

– It must be said, this is the fruit of the commercial treaties obtained by diplomatic agents, who, under the appearance of a protective friendship and a political alliance, always disguise the intention of killing the industry of the country trusting enough to open its doors to them. They become, so to say, the large-scale door-to-door salesmen of European commerce; [...] for them alone, there are no customs, no patents, no taxes of any kind. Thus they flood the country with goods that are sold beneath the prices set by local factories, and soon succeed in having many of these abandoned and, soon thereafter, closed.]

Flandin does not doubt for a second that the undercutting of local prices is designed to close down local industry, thereby rendering Iran dependent on European exports. The callousness of this strategy is made clear by the use of the lexical field of murder. By focusing on British financial imperialism, Flandin also creates a false dichotomy between the French as 'good colonisers' and the British as 'bad colonisers'.[172] The same tactic will later be adopted by Loti, who on several occasions portrays Iranians complaining to him that they are under the influence of the British, when they would much rather be under the influence of the French – it is never suggested that independence and self-sufficiency might be an even more preferable option.[173] Flandin's accusations, however, reach beyond Britain, inculpating the whole of Europe. This is demonstrated by his sarcastic reference to the 'benefits of European civilisation' in the passage above and becomes even more explicit in his conclusion:

Le voyageur [...] se demande avec tristesse si ces grands mots de civilisation européenne, portés pompeusement sur tous les points du globe, ne sont donc autre chose que le moyen de faire écouler les produits surabondants de certains pays. [...] Les pavillons, quelle que soit leur couleur, n'abritent-ils donc plus que des ballots de marchands? – Rome conquérait des territoires barbares, et y portait réellement sa civilisation dont nous saluons encore les nobles vestiges.[174]

[The traveller [...] wonders with sadness whether these great words of European civilisation, pompously carried across the four corners of the earth, are nothing more than a means to sell off the over-produced goods of certain countries. [...] Do all pavilions, whatever colour they may be, carry nothing more than the packages of merchants? – Rome conquered barbaric territories, and truly brought them a civilisation of which we can still admire the vestiges.]

While the Roman Empire had offered something to its imperial subjects, nineteenth-century superpowers sow only destruction. Not only that, but this modern form of destruction is insidious and manipulative, lacking the heroism of war. Flandin must centre his attack on the British because he works for the French state. But by referring to pavilions of all colours, he makes it clear that his observations apply to all European superpowers. Moreover, Flandin refers for a second time to 'European civilisation' being a false pretext that barely conceals the West's capitalist agenda. By foregrounding the term civilization, he presciently points the finger at the French ideology of the *mission civilisatrice* (civilizing mission), a phrase that would not gain currency until the 1880s, which is when Dieulafoy wrote their financial analysis of trade agreements between Iran and Europe.

Forty years after Flandin's visit, little has changed. Dieulafoy writes that whereas Iranian merchants transporting unprocessed cotton are subject to endless customs charges by corrupt local officials, these officials do not prey on European traders. As a result, unprocessed cotton is shipped to textile factories in France and Britain for a fraction of the price that it costs in Iran. This creates a perverse situation where although Iran is the cotton producer, it purchases processed cotton from France and Britain, rather than producing its own.[175] Dieulafoy here is describing the very same market dynamic outlined a century later by Al-e Ahmad, who argues in *Gharbzadegi* that the world is not divided into East and West, but into the countries that produce raw materials and the countries that become rich by refining these raw materials and selling these back to their producers.[176] Dieulafoy concludes:

> Cet état de choses est fort regrettable, car, s'il est à désirer de voir l'influence européenne s'établir en Orient à un point de vue moralisateur, scientifique ou même industriel, il est fâcheux que les avantages faits aux comptoirs étrangers soient pour l'Iran une source d'appauvrissement et de ruine.
>
> A dire vrai, je ne puis comprendre vers quel but tend le gouvernement persan en opprimant ses sujets au profit des étrangers. [...] j'aime mieux attribuer des mesures injustes à la rapacité des gouverneurs qu'à l'indifférence du souverain. Quoi qu'il en soit, le commerce ispahanien lui-même, si prospère et si puissant sous chah Abbas et ses successeurs, est à peu près mort aujourd'hui [...].[177]

> [This state of affairs is deeply regrettable, since, while it is desirable to see European influence established in the Orient from a moralising, scientific, or even industrial point of view, it is unfortunate that the advantages given to foreign traders are for Iran a source of impoverishment and ruin.
>
> To be honest, I cannot fathom what the Persian government's end could be in oppressing its own subjects to the benefit of foreigners. [...] I would rather attribute these unjust measures to the greed of local governors rather than the indifference of the sovereign. Be it as it may, commerce in Esfahan itself, once so prosperous and powerful under Shah Abbas and his successors, is more or less dead today [...].]

Dieulafoy here echoes Flandin, comparing the ruination of Iranian industry under the Qajars to its heyday under the Safavids and blaming Europe for this deterioration, an accusation that they also bring home through the lexical field of death. Yet, they cast the ultimate blame on Iranian officials as the ones betraying their own people. In other words, although Dieulafoy temporarily empathizes with the perspective of the native population, referring to Europeans as *étrangers*, they avoid confronting the root of the problem: financial imperialism. At this stage in the travelogue, Dieulafoy is not opposed to Western influence in the region, which they consider 'desirable'. Rather, they oppose the pernicious form that it has taken on the ground. For both Flandin and Dieulafoy, then, the problem lies not in the ideology of the *mission civilisatrice*, but in France's failure to execute it. Were the French Empire to live up to the model set by the Roman Empire, then Iranians would benefit from French interventionism.

While initially being in favour of Westernization, Dieulafoy however has a change of heart after spending more time in Iran. This change of opinion is formulated through the, by now, well-worn trope of contrasting the Iranians with inferior Orientals, in this case the Ottomans. However, whereas this opposition had previously been used to suggest that the Ottomans were more fanatical or immoral, this time they have committed an altogether different sin: that of being too Westernized.

> Ce n'est pas en s'efforçant de calquer, en tout ou en partie, les coutumes européennes, que les peuples musulmans progresseront, mais en suivant l'esprit de perfectionnement et les méthodes politiques caractéristiques des grandes nations de l'Orient. Combien je préfère à la Turquie de la réforme la vieille Perse avec ses satrapes et sa féodalité! [...] la Perse, avec ses institutions immuables, reste attachée à des gouverneurs assez puissants et assez respectés pour assurer, sans tribunaux et sans gendarmes, la sécurité matérielle et la bonne police du pays.[178]

> [It is not by trying to copy European customs, either completely or partially, that Muslim peoples shall progress, but by following the spirit of improvement and the political methods characteristic to the great nations of the Orient. How I prefer to reformed Turkey old Persia with her satraps and her feudality! [...] Persia, with her eternal institutions, remains attached to governors that are powerful and respected enough to ensure, without tribunals or gendarmes, the material security and the good policing of the country.]

Iran's local governors may be corrupt, but they are effective. Dieulafoy's tone here is certainly patronizing. Yet their strong stance against Westernization constitutes a dramatic rejection of the ideology of the *mission civilisatrice*, which had remained unquestioned by them until this point. Premised as it is on ethnocentrism masquerading as universalism, the claim that Western culture could and should be imposed on others fails to take into account the cultural and historic specificities of different regions. In suggesting that it is counterproductive for 'Muslim peoples' to adopt 'European customs', Dieulafoy pronounces themself in favour of cultural relativism. Little would they have known, but their call for Muslim nations to resist Westernization and remain true to their historic cultural identity and systems of governance would be at the heart of Al-e Ahmad's *Gharbzadegi* and, subsequently, the 1979 Revolution.[179] This, however, would not be Dieulafoy's last word on the West's role in Iran.

When Jane and Marcel Dieulafoy returned to Iran in 1884 to lead the archaeological dig at Susa, they were no longer civilians, but agents of the French state. As a result of this change in status, Dieulafoy's dig diary *À Suse* (1888) depicts an entirely different relationship between the author and the Iranian population than *La Perse* (1887). The indigent men hired as workers, the local authorities who view the dig with suspicion and Naser ed-Din Shah himself are now antagonists, who might hinder the French state's acquisition of the remains of the palace of Darius the Great. A politically revealing aspect of Dieulafoy's account of this antagonism is that the local officials who hinder the mission do not do so out of a desire to protect their ancient heritage, but as a bargaining chip to demand official decorations from the French state.[180] By using Prince Mozaffar el-Molk's dream of receiving the legion of honour to their advantage, the Dieulafoys are able to bring the entirety of the finds back to Paris. The fact that the Qajar aristocracy valued French recognition over the safeguarding of a priceless cultural heritage demonstrates the far-reaching consequences of cultural imperialism, without which the Dieulafoys would not have been able to bring the Achaemenid artworks to the Louvre. This shows Al-e Ahmad's shrewdness in arguing that the cultural prestige of the West was instrumental to its exploitation of Iran.

The Dieulafoy mission's appropriation of the Susa finds was just as exploitative as the French and British appropriation of Iranian resources such as cotton and oil. Indeed, as well as seducing local officials with the promise of French titles, the Dieulafoys misled them by disguising the quality and quantity of their finds. The contract between the two nations stated that any recovered artefacts would be evenly split between France, in reward for carrying out the search, and Iran, given that the search had been conducted on Iranian territory. The Dieulafoys, however, told the Iranian government that the most valuable items they had found were funerary urns,[181] and that aside from these, all they had found were 'pierres cassées' [broken rocks] and 'terre colorée, brisée, pilée' [coloured, broken, ground earth].[182] This was a bold-faced lie, as Naser ed-Din Shah himself would come to discover upon visiting the Dieulafoy exhibits at the Louvre, where the grandiose capital carved in the shape of a double-headed bull and the beautifully intricate ceramic friezes of archers can still be admired by visitors today.[183] The Dieulafoy mission was also the first step in France's move to obtain exclusive rights to archaeological searches on Iranian territory, a system that mirrors that of the concessions that would later give Britain exclusive rights to drill for oil. Yet, the ethical problems surrounding the appropriation of the artefacts are a blindspot for Dieulafoy, who remains convinced that Iranians cannot appreciate – let alone care for – their cultural heritage. When faced with a momentary obstacle in the transportation of the finds to France, Dieulafoy writes: 'Il est désespérant de penser que les greniers du Chah vont s'emplir de trésors archéologiques uniques au monde.'[184] [It is infuriating to think that the Shah's attics will be filled with world-unique archaeological treasures.] Dieulafoy's belief that the Shah would store the artefacts in his palace rather than exhibiting them in a public place may have been well founded, but what is most telling about the comment is its underlying assumption that the native population of Iran cannot be trusted with the finds. This serves the narrative function of painting the Dieulafoys as the saviours of ancient Susa and the local authorities as the antagonists who stand in the way of their heroic mission.

Dieulafoy only comes close to admitting the imperialist implications of the Susa mission on one occasion, when they deplore the French government's order to end the search while it is still underway, an order which comes with the instruction to extract as many artefacts as possible:

> Il ne pouvait entrer dans les idées de mon mari de rechercher de petits monuments, comme le fait un marchand d'antiquités. Les grandes lignes d'une architecture, l'art constructif, suprêmes manifestations du développement intellectuel et économique d'un peuple, lui paraissaient seuls dignes de ses efforts. [...] Peu importe à l'État [...] que l'on jalonne un chemin que des Français ne parcourront pas! Enrichissons nos musées, moissonnons la récolte semée l'hiver dernier.[185]

Figure 3.4 Inauguration of the Susa finds, showing Jane Dieulafoy (leaning over the display case) and Ernest Renan (foreground, bottom right).

Source: 'Inauguration des collections Dieulafoy, au Louvre, par M. Le Président de la République', *L'Univers Illustré* (16 June 1888): 376.

[It could not enter my husband's mind to search after small monuments, like an antiquities merchant does. The governing lines of an architecture, the construction techniques, supreme manifestations of the intellectual and economic development of a people, seemed the only worthy subjects of his efforts. [...] The State does not care [...] if we trace a path that the people of France will never walk! Let us fill our museums, let us reap the harvest we sowed last winter.]

The passage draws a clear opposition between the antiquities merchant, a figure solely motivated by cupidity, and the archaeologist, who seeks to expand human knowledge. The French government, it is implied, thinks like a merchant, since it is only interested in immediate gains and cares little for the scientific implications of the search. Dieulafoy's assessment is correct: the mission was funded with the intention of allowing the Louvre to compete with the British Museum, which until then had been unrivalled for its possession of 'Oriental antiquities'. The competition between the two national museums was a proxy war for France and Britain's imperial rivalry. Indeed, the French press was all too glad to trumpet that the Dieulafoy mission had succeeded where an earlier British mission had failed and to note that the Louvre had gallantly offered the British Museum casts of the artefacts now in its possession.[186] As such, the inauguration of the Susa finds was a triumph for the French nation, attended by both the scholarly community and the president of France himself (see Figure 3.4). It was also a personal triumph for the Dieulafoys, after whom the collection was named.

Cheap Iranian cotton had added to the profits of France's textile industry, now the freely obtained Susa finds could add to France's cultural and imperial prestige on the global stage. Dieulafoy, preoccupied as they were with their newfound fame, as well as their enduring pursuit of a level of scientific authority that was at the time reserved for men, never drew the connection between the forms of financial exploitation that they had bitterly decried in *La Perse* and the appropriation of priceless artefacts that they proudly reported in *À Suse*.

Books versus reality

The relationship between the Orient of European literature and the Middle East as an actual geographic location, in other words, that between books and reality, is at the heart of Edward Said's *Orientalism*. Said argues that the Western writers who travelled to the Middle East placed greater authority on Western-authored texts about the region than their own first-hand experience of it.[187] Any admission that the real place was nothing like what they had read would be accompanied by bitter disappointment, since the imaginary Orient was 'preferable, for the European sensibility, to the real Orient'.[188] According to Said, then, Orientalism is at its heart a misguided attempt 'to apply what one learns out of a book literally to reality', which he calls a 'textual attitude'.[189] Said's emphasis on the intertextuality of travel-writing is valuable since it reminds us that there is no such thing as an unmediated encounter with a foreign culture. However, in arguing that such texts erased and replaced 'the real Orient', Said rather overstates his case. Written sources could enhance European authors' experiences abroad, leading to a better understanding of local cultures and a more sympathetic outlook. One might cite, for example, of Dieulafoy's ability to have conversations with Iranians from all levels of society, which is the direct result of their study of Persian prior to travelling – though Dieulafoy will also learn that there are important differences between written and spoken Persian.[190] In turn, Claude Anet recognizes a *ta'zieh* performance when he sees one because he has read descriptions of these by Gobineau.[191] And, as we saw above, familiarity with the work of classical historians such as Plutarch provided essential context for apprehending the ruins of Persepolis.

The examples that I have cited suggest a rather straightforward relationship between books and reality: the former function as repositories of information that will later serve the traveller on the ground. In this section, I will focus instead on a more complex type of intertextuality: that of references to Middle Eastern literature. Indeed, the two most common literary citations in nineteenth-century French travelogues about Iran are Antoine Galland's *Mille et Une Nuits* [*Thousand and One Nights*, better known in English as the *Arabian Nights*] and classical Persian poetry. Such works were considered a valuable resource for readers seeking to familiarize themselves with the cultures and customs of the Middle East. Gobineau even went so far as to claim that, in this regard, the *Mille et Une Nuits* was the single most instructive book ever published.[192] Of course, there are many issues with Gobineau investing such ethnographic value into a medieval collection of tales that existed in various versions and was accessed by him in a translation that took great liberties – Galland worked before the professionalization of Oriental Studies and is well known for his elisions, additions and bowdlerizations. Moreover, the source text of Galland's translation was itself a translation: the stories of the *Thousand and One Nights* originated in pre-Islamic Iran, but were only preserved in Arabic translation, which adds yet another layer of mediation to the transmission of the stories. As I will show, however, the ultimate function of the *Mille et Une Nuits* in nineteenth-century French travel-writing is not so much ethnographic as rhetorical. The *Nuits* function as a shorthand for expressing French authors' wonder and delight at experiencing in real life what had until then been the stuff of dreams, a shorthand that was legible to readers who had never been to Iran, but were familiar with the tales popularized by Galland. This rhetorical function flies in the face of Said's account of Oriental travel-writing as a tale of 'disenchantment', in which the place could never measure up to the bookish fantasy: in Iran, the enchantment is so strong that authors need to refer to fairy tales to make sense of it.[193] Intertextual references to classical Persian poetry play a different role. In some instances, these citations are used to support a rather extreme identification of reality with literature; this would be the 'textual attitude' referred to by Said, except that it is based on an Iranian source and not a European one. In other cases, comparisons between Persian and European literature are useful devices in the formulation of a more subtle understanding of cultural difference. The use of intertextuality in these travelogues is thus far more dynamic and multifaceted than Said's account would lead us to believe. Literature, indeed, can serve many functions.

Whereas Persian poetry was predominantly read by an educated elite, the tales of Antoine Galland's *Mille et Une Nuits* were fully embedded into the popular culture of nineteenth-century France. By the end of the century, there had been over eighty editions of the collection, including several versions aimed at children.¹⁹⁴ The stories and characters of the *Nuits* were also a frequent subject for *féeries*, popular plays relying heavily on special effects, known in French as *trucs*. The appeal of Galland's collection for such stage adaptations is obvious: the tales' exotic and luxurious settings gave scope for striking costume and set design, and the plots' reliance on magic offered a good pretext for the use of special effects. Beyond the page and the stage, we get a sense of how the imagery of the *Mille et Une Nuits* had entered the everyday material culture of nineteenth-century France from Marcel Proust's *À la recherche du temps perdu*, where plates decorated with illustrations of stories from Galland's collection feature prominently in the narrator's childhood memories of his Aunt Léonie's provincial home.¹⁹⁵ Out of all the tales of Galland's *Nuits*, it was the tales told him by the Syrian Hanna Diyab (now referred to as the 'orphan tales') that became the most popular.¹⁹⁶ These included the tales of 'Aladdin and the Magic Lamp', 'Ali Baba and the Forty Thieves' and 'Prince Ahmed and the Fairy Princess Peri Banu'. Paulo Lemos Horta has shown that Diyab's tales pay particular attention to 'the marvellous, in the sense both of material riches and the supernatural'.¹⁹⁷ Indeed, they feature detailed descriptions of treasures (such as that kept in the genie's cave in Aladdin and the thieves' cave in Ali Baba) and their plots centre on supernatural elements, such as the genie in the lamp, the magical cave opening with a password and Prince Ahmed building an entire palace in one night. Another feature of these orphan tales, Horta argues, is the prominent role played in them by characters of humble origin, such as Aladdin and Ali Baba. It is precisely these three features (riches, magic and ordinary protagonists) that make the orphan tales of the *Nuits* a key point of reference for our travel-writers.

The primary function of intertextual references to the *Mille et Une Nuits* is visual. The illustrations and stage adaptations of the collection provided French readers with rudimentary notions of Islamic architecture and decorative arts, which were typically associated with fabulous wealth. It is therefore unsurprising that the highest concentration of references to the *Nuits* are found in descriptions of the beautiful and sumptuous architecture of Esfahan, discussed above. According to Flandin and Loti, the palaces inhabited by the Esfahani elite are lifted straight out of the *Nuits*.¹⁹⁸ But more than these residential buildings, it is the ceramic domes and façades of Naqsh-e Jahān Square that inspire wonder. Upon first sight, Loti declares the city to be 'invraisemblable et charmante autant qu'un vieux conte oriental' [as unlikely and charming as an old Oriental tale].¹⁹⁹ The blue tile work of the portals and domes of the mosques are 'si puissants et si rares que l'on songe à des pierres fines, à des palais en saphir, à d'irréalisables splendeurs de féerie' [so powerful and rare that one thinks of fine gemstones, palaces made of sapphire, impossible splendours out of a fairy tale (*féerie*)].²⁰⁰ Esfahan's resemblance to the magical world of the *Nuits* is so strong that Loti finds himself doubting that he is looking at a real place, something he brings across through the use of negative adjectives (*invraisemblable, irréalisable*). Loti's references to the *Nuits*, and in particular to the tale of Aladdin, continue in his descriptions of the Masjed Shāh's entrance portal, which is compared to 'l'entrée magique d'un gouffre bleu' [the magical entrance to a blue cave];²⁰¹ a corridor in the Madreseh Mādar-e Soleiman, which seems to lead to 'quelque palais de féerie' [some palace out of a *féerie*];²⁰² and the mosque of the Madreseh, which resembles 'quelque palais du Génie des cavernes' [some palace belonging to the Genie of the cave].²⁰³

The oral storytelling tradition from which the tales collected in the *Nuits* were born was one that sought to inspire wonder, in Arabic *ʿajāʾib*. We can recognize the very same pursuit of *ʿajāʾib* in nineteenth-century travellers' comparisons between what they witness and the magical world of the tales, as encountered through Galland's translation. When Flandin writes that he and Coste have been 'transportés, par une bonne fée, dans un de ces palais enchantés des contes arabes' [transported, by a good fairy, into one of those enchanted palaces of Arab tales],²⁰⁴ and when Loti speaks of 'irréalisables splendeurs de féerie' [impossible splendours out of a *féerie*], they are both expressing their surprise and delight, in other words, their wonder, at the physical realization of what had until then been imaginary landscapes. This feeling of wonder is expanded on in Loti's description of the golden dome of the Fatemeh Shrine in Qom, which, like the architecture of Esfahan, he characterizes with 'invraisemblance' [unlikelihood].²⁰⁵

> [L]e dôme étincelant nous réapparaît enfin, tout proche, trônant au milieu d'un décor qui a l'air arrangé là par quelque magicien, pour nous éblouir. Le long d'une rivière desséchée, au lit de galets blancs, que traverse un pont courbe à balustres de faïence, un panorama de féerie se déploie […]. Mes yeux, qui ont vu tant de choses, ne se rappellent rien d'aussi étourdissant ni d'aussi fantastique, rien d'aussi éperdument oriental que cette apparition du tombeau de la sainte Fatmah, un soir de mai, au sortir d'une nef obscure.
>
> Il existe donc encore en Perse des choses qui ne sont pas en ruines, et, de nos jours, on peut donc construire ou restaurer comme aux temps des *Mille et Une Nuits*!²⁰⁶

> [The gleaming dome reappears at last, close to us, towering over a scenery which seems arranged there by some magician, to dazzle us. Along a dry river, with a bed of white pebbles, crossed by a curved bridge with a ceramic banister, a panorama from a *féerie* lies before us […]. My eyes, which had already seen so much, do not remember a single thing more astonishing or fantastical, nothing so madly Oriental, as this apparition of the mausoleum of Saint Fatemeh, an evening in May, stepping out of a dark nave.
>
> So there still exist in Persia things that are not falling apart, and, in the present day, one can thus still build or restore like in the times of the *Thousand and One Nights*!]

Loti's references to magic in this passage serve the purpose of expressing the view's breathtaking beauty and his sense of surprise at the changes in perspective and passage from darkness to light. Indeed, the same analogy between a dramatically lit sight in Iran and a special effect from the French stage is used by Claude Anet to express his surprise at coming across illuminated private gardens during a nocturnal walk: 'ces jardins étincelants qui paraissent amenés dans notre promenade comme un truc de féerie' [these gleaming gardens which seem to have been brought into our walk, like a stage effect in a *féerie*].²⁰⁷ Loti, however, goes beyond analogy, presenting Qom as both the physical realization of a theatre set ('un décor', 'un panorama de féerie') and a confirmation of the tales of the *Nuits*. The exclamation that one can still build like 'in the times of the *Thousand and One Nights*' is multilayered. On a literal level, Loti is noting that Qom, unlike Esfahan, has recently been renovated. But he is also referring to Galland's tale of Prince Ahmed, who builds a palace for his fairy princess in only one night. In associating the renovation of Qom with the construction of Prince Ahmed's palace, Loti blurs the distinction between fairy tale and reality. And if any sight should challenge that distinction, it is perhaps the dome of Fatemeh, for while the blue domes of Esfahan only *seemed* to be made of precious stones, the dome in Qom is actually coated in gold. The hesitation between fairy tale and reality makes Loti declare that he has never seen anything 'so madly Oriental'. But what does he mean by this? The phrase is best understood in light of an earlier description, that of the landscape surrounding Hāfez's tomb in Shiraz, which Loti calls 'idéalement oriental' [ideally Oriental] on the grounds that it looks just like a scene out of Persian miniature art.[208] In other words, the landscape is so beautiful that it resembles an aestheticized representation of a perfect landscape. Instead of art imitating reality, reality imitates art. The phrase 'éperdumment oriental' in the description of Qom ups the ante on 'idéalement oriental'. Fatemeh's gold dome is the crystallization of Loti's Oriental fantasies, making him question his very own eyes, as encapsulated by his description of its gleam: the phrase 'rayonne avec invraisemblance' [shimmers with unlikelihood] is as much a metaphor for his general disbelief as a description of the effect of the light.[209] The true wonder, for Loti, is not that the architecture and landscapes of Qom, Shiraz and Esfahan are breathtakingly beautiful, but that they should so closely resemble his fantasies.

For Bibesco, it is not a beautiful building, but a walk through a bazaar that brings back childhood memories of Galland's *Mille et Une Nuits*. This is because the sight of the different trades- and craftsmen reminds her of the characters of the stories, who are often referred to by their profession:

> À travers les quartiers actifs où s'exercent, selon d'immuables règles, toutes les professions d'autrefois, devant le spectacle de cette Asie trafiquante, je me souviens à tout instant des contes orientaux que j'écoutais dans mon enfance, et dont le merveilleux, bien différent de celui des légendes du nord, présente un curieux mélange de réalisme et d'ironie.
>
> On y parle du fils 'd'un riche marchand de Bassorah' et non d'un prince enchanté. [...] Et les noms magiques de Damas et de Bagdhad [*sic*] traversaient ces récits, oppressant de désirs nos cœurs d'enfants prédestinés aux voyages.[210]

[Through the active neighbourhoods in which the professions of the past are performed according to immutable rules, before the spectacle of this bustling Asia, I remember at every moment the Oriental tales that I listened to in my childhood, and whose wonder, very different to that of the legends of the North, offers an original mix of realism and irony.

They tell of the son 'of a rich merchant of Basrah', not of an enchanted prince. [...] And the magical names of Damascus and Baghdad would run through these stories, oppressing with desire our hearts of children predestined to travel.]

Bibesco writes of a fascination long predating her journey and places emphasis on the evocative power of names. As has been noted by Horta, Galland had a tendency to remove material details in his translations of the tales. As a result of this preference for abstraction, the names of cities and professions are often the only remaining clues to the stories' Middle Eastern origins. Bibesco is therefore right to home in on these names as the tales' most evocative details. Moreover, her reference to the activities of the bazaar having changed little over the course of the centuries should not be understood as an 'Orientalist' distortion of reality: traditional Iranian arts and crafts, such as carpet weaving and copper beating, do follow ancestral practices and are performed under the eyes of the public in open bazaar stalls to this day. One can therefore see why these activities would have been viewed by Bibesco as an illustration of the professions named in the *Nuits*, since she was discovering for the first time how the crafts that she only knew by name were actually practiced.

Like Flandin and Loti, Bibesco refers to 'magic' in order to convey her sense of wonder: the names of Middle Eastern cities are mysterious and alluring because they are the only thing she knows about them. Bibesco returns to this idea that a name alone is enough to fuel fantasy in Esfahan. Addressing the city, she writes that she is one of those people whom 'votre seul nom rendait prématurément nostalgiques' [your name alone made prematurely nostalgic].[211] Her words echo those of her travel companion Claude Anet, who writes: '"Je suis à Ispahan." / Ces seuls mots évocateurs me suffisent pour l'instant' ['I am in Esfahan.' / These evocative words alone are all I need for now], suggesting that the name of a place can be just as exciting as the place itself.[212] Indeed, whenever Anet finds too many commonalities between his new Iranian surroundings and old familiar European landscapes during his travels, he relies on the talismanic power of the words 'Je suis en Perse' [I am in Persia] to rekindle the sensation of exoticism.[213] In doing so, he acknowledges that the otherness of Iran is as much to do with one's perspective as it is to do with any concrete cultural or geographic differences. This self-awareness with regards to the psychological nature of exoticism is symptomatic of early-twentieth-century writing: it characterizes Bibesco's cousin Anna de Noailles's poem 'L'Occident', which was discussed in Chapter 1, and is a major theme in their personal friend Marcel Proust's *À la recherche du temps perdu*.[214] But whereas Proust and Noailles explore the disappointment that is experienced when a place is nothing like the fantasies that its name had evoked, Bibesco presents her journey as the confirmation of all her fantasies. Moreover, while Flandin and Loti express surprise at the continuities between reality and the imaginary world of books, Bibesco seems to take these entirely for granted.

Of all the travelogues discussed in this chapter, Bibesco's is the most heavily mediated by literature. In her preface, she explains that she titled her travelogue *Les Huit paradis* and divided it into eight chapters devoted to different cities as an allusion to the eight gates of the Islamic heaven, which is described in the Quran as being made of gardens with flowing water. This information is introduced through citations from two Islamic texts: the Quran and the *Pendnāmeh*.[215] Bibesco also cites as her epigraph an extract from Ernest Renan's *Vie de Jésus*, which reads:

Un vieux mot, Paradis, que l'hébreu, comme toutes les langues d'Orient, avait emprunté à la Perse, et qui désigna d'abord les parcs des rois achménides, résumait le rêve de tous: Un jardin délicieux où l'on continuerait à jamais la vie charmante que l'on menait ici-bas.[216]

[An old word, Paradise, which Hebrew, like all Oriental languages, had borrowed from Persia, and which referred at first to the parks of the Achaemenid kings, encapsulated everyone's dream: a delicious garden where one would continue for eternity the charming life led on earth.]

Through this patchwork of texts, Bibesco foregrounds the central leitmotiv of her travelogue: Persia as paradise on earth, a notion that she is so committed to that it results in an idealization of life in Iran that goes to the point of distortion, as was shown in the section 'Among women: Scenes from the harem'.

When it comes to Persian literature, Bibesco is the most widely read of our travellers, citing Ferdowsi, Sa'di, Khayyām, Hāfez, Rumi and Jāmi.[217] She is also the only travel-writer to portray herself as having a strong personal relationship with Persian poetry by using vocative interjections such as: 'Écoute, vieux Khàyyàm' [Listen, old Khayyām] and 'N'ayez crainte, Hafiz!' [Fear not, Hāfez!].[218] Sa'di features in pride of place in the epigraph on the book's cover, which reads ' "Je ne suis qu'une argile sans valeur / Mais j'ai demeuré quelque temps avec la rose." SAADI.' ['I am but a piece of clay without value / Yet I have lived some time with the rose.' SA'DI.] In the source text, the *Golestān*, the humble clay witnessing the beauty of the rose is a metaphor for Sa'di witnessing God. Recast into the context of Bibesco's writing, the epigraph's first-person now reads as Bibesco's voice, who via this intertext presents herself as a humble witness to the eight beautiful Middle Eastern cities that she visited. Sa'di's centrality to *Les Huit paradis* is particularly fitting given the travelogue's focus on Persian gardens: Sa'di's two books are entitled *Golestān* (the Rose Garden) and *Bostān* (the Orchard). Bibesco's frequent references to Persian poetry serve a dual purpose: they confirm her idealized portrayal of Iran and this idealized Iran, in turn, reflects positively on her authorial persona. Bibesco informs her reader that over the course of her journey she 'recognises' the plants and gardens described by Sa'di,[219] Khayyām[220] and Hāfez,[221] and that the pottery shop that she visits is 'similar' to the one that inspired Khayyām's poems.[222] In doing so, she presents herself as being 'in touch' with the spirit of Iran, by virtue of being deeply acquainted with its literature. This rose-tinted identification of real places with the pages of poetry appears all the more affected when we compare it to Gobineau's reaction on the occasion that he visits a site described in Persian poetry:

le fameux ruisseau de Roknabad, si célébré par Hafyz et les poètes de Schyraz. J'y entrai jusqu'à la cheville, et cette onde poétique ne m'apparut que sous l'aspect d'un trou bourbeux.[223]

[the famous stream of Roknābād, celebrated by Hāfez and the poets of Shiraz. I stepped in ankle-deep, and the poetic waters appeared before me under the aspect of a muddy hole.]

Bibesco's identification of real places with Persian literature includes not only poetry, but also the illustrations in books of Persian literature. After writing several ekphrases of the beautiful miniatures that adorn a copy of the *Golestān* lent to her by her host in Esfahan, Bibesco writes:

> J'ai fermé le livre. [...] Mais pour retrouver le décor d'une idylle persane, je n'ai qu'à repousser les rideaux de ces fenêtres. La voilà, l'herbe plus verte qu'un dos de perroquet! L'arbre en fuseau, la rose grimpante, les voici!
>
> Et derrière le mur qui sépare cet Eden d'un Eden pareil, se dérobent des mondes de jardins! Tous ombreux, tous beaux...
>
> Des amants littéraires s'y promènent; de vieux hommes s'y désolent encore auprès d'enfants boudeuses.[224]

> [I closed the book. [...] But to find again the scenery of a Persian idyll, all I have to do is draw the curtains. There it is, that grass greener than a parrot's back! The spindly tree, the climbing rose, here they are!
>
> And behind the wall that separates this Eden from another Eden, hide worlds of gardens! All of them shady, all of them beautiful...
>
> Literary lovers walk there, old men still pine after sulking girls.]

The passage combines references to Persian miniature art, which frequently features stylized cypress trees and roses, with the language of Persian poetry, for instance, the simile of the parrot to evoke the colour green. The adjective 'literary' is also ambiguous: is Bibesco referring to real-life lovers who enjoy literature or to lovers who seem to be straight out of a work of literature?

By stating that the book that she is reading and the city outside her window are equivalent, Bibesco dissolves the boundaries between representation and reality. This emerges most clearly if we contrast her use of definitive statements to Loti's use of simile and approximation on the one occasion where he does compare an Iranian landscape to a Persian miniature. Admiring the landscape surrounding Hāfez's tomb, he writes: 'On est comme dans le cadre d'une ancienne miniature persane, agrandie jusqu'à l'immense et devenue à peu près réelle.'[225] [It is as though one is inside the frame of an old Persian miniature, which has been enormously enlarged in order to become almost real.] There is no 'à peu près' for Bibesco, who steps into the miniature, just like Mary Poppins jumps into a chalk drawing. Indeed, Bibesco not only describes the gardens within her eyesight, but also those that she imagines lie 'behind the wall'. This leads her to conclude: 'Ah! secrète Ispahan! / Nous l'habiterions vingt ans sans la connaître, si notre imagination ne s'élevait au-dessus des vergers clos" [Ah! secret Esfahan! / We could live there for twenty years without knowing her, if our imagination did not rise above the closed orchards].[226] Thus, as well as presenting an idealized pictorial representation and a real place as interchangeable, Bibesco is also ascribing imagination and empirical observation the same level of authority. A similar process takes place later in the Esfahan chapter, when having been denied entrance to the Masjed Shāh, Bibesco imagines visiting it by flying in on the back of the Simorgh, the mythical giant bird who raises the hero Zāl in Ferdowsi's *Shāhnāmeh*.[227] Through this narrative device, Bibesco describes a building that she has not seen. The description is lacklustre and does no justice to the mosque, based as it is on a vague and generic understanding of Islamic architecture.[228] At the same time, however, the passage is made lively by the fact that Bibesco portrays herself as a heroine out of Ferdowsi's epic poem. The episode thus takes intertextuality to an entirely new level, inserting into the account of Bibesco's journey a section of fiction that pastiches medieval Persian literature.

Bibesco's preference for an idealized Iran based on literature over the realities of the place that she is visiting comes to the fore when we compare her first visit to a bazaar, in which she had happily recalled the *Mille et Une Nuits*, to a later visit to another bazaar, where literature and reality clash uncomfortably:

> À mesure qu'on avance dans le Bazar, les boutiques se font plus pressées, la foule augmente. Avec les parfums, les condiments, les herbes à sachets, on vend, paraît-il aussi, d'inavouables drogues; le marchand d'aromates ne laisse pas que d'être un peu magicien, s'il n'est déjà empoisonneur.
>
> Et, dans un malaise imprécis, j'ai la vision d'un Orient encore inconnu qui me trouble et m'écœure.[229]

[The more one advances into the Bazaar, the more the shops become crammed, and the crowd increases. Along with the perfumes, condiments, pouches of herbs, they sell, it is said, shameful drugs; the herb vendor indeed could well be a bit of a magician, if he isn't already a poisoner.

And, in a vague malaise, I have the vision of an as of yet unknown Orient, which troubles and nauseates me.]

No longer the subject of old tales, poison has become a reality, along with (one presumes) aphrodisiacs. This dangerous and sexualized Orient has a long history in the West, but it is diametrically opposed to the idealized Orient that Bibesco had crafted out of her favourite Persian poems. Her nausea is not so much caused by the immoral implications of the activities that she is describing, but by the realization that her ideal Persia may not survive, threatened as it is by the reality of a different 'unknown' Orient – unknown because she has purposefully avoided it. If the rose-tinted veil that she has delicately wrapped around the country is torn, what will be left?

Rather than bringing her a more intimate understanding of the place that she is visiting, Bibesco's selective references to Persian poetry and the *Mille et Une Nuits* serve to keep unpleasant realities at bay. Whereas Flandin and Loti's references to the *Nuits* served to better convey their sights and experiences in Iran, Bibesco will happily close her eyes on what is in front of her in order to better describe her personal fantasies and her favourite poems. *Her* Persia ('ma Perse'),[230] as she calls it, is a 'Fraîche oasis où l'art respire' and a 'Jardin-qui-séduit-le-coeur', to quote the poems by Théophile Gautier and Anna de Noailles discussed in Chapter 1. Indeed, for Bibesco, as for these poets, Iran is not so much a geographic location as a canvas of poetic allusions that allows the lyric subject to escape the mundanity of France, both as a geographic location and as a literary tradition. This Persia is an idealized space, in which the lyric subject can reimagine herself. The continuities between the treatment of Persia in French poetry and in Bibesco's travel-writing should not surprise us: as a literary work, *Les Huit paradis* is written in a style that is heavily influenced by lyric poetry. This lyric dimension is most obvious in Bibesco's frequent addresses to individuals who cannot speak back, including Khayyām, Iranian women, the Shah and a child beggar.[231] Triangulated address is a quintessentially lyric trope, in the words of Jonathan Culler: 'To invoke or address something that is not the true audience, whether a muse, an urn, Duty, or a beloved, highlights the event of address itself as an act.'[232] Bibesco's references to Persian literature therefore are not so much points of entry into a local culture as they are instruments of self-expression and self-fashioning. Bibesco is certainly the most extreme example of what Said calls a 'textual attitude', but it would be a mistake to consider this the result of Western ignorance or 'Orientalist' indoctrination. Bibesco's unique approach to travel-writing, which merges fact with fantasy and views reality through the prism of literature, is a self-conscious device. The Bovarysme of *Les Huit paradis* is essential to the author's self-presentation as an eloquent and eminently sensitive individual. Bibesco's rejection of the established praxis of travel-writing and deft use of literary allusion thus results in a highly aesthetic and innovative piece of writing, one that would earn her the recognition of the Académie Française.[233] Moreover, what Bibesco lacks in precision and objectivity, she makes up for in those moments where her enthusiasm for Iran and emotional openness allow her to engage with local cultural practices, be it the veil or ritual mourning, in a manner that is not coolly observational, but sympathetic.

In contrast to Bibesco's strong sense of identification with the Persian poets, Loti and Dieulafoy tend to approach classical Persian poetry from the perspective of cultural relativism. According to Dieulafoy, the Persian lyric's liberal use of metaphors and the hyperbolic qualities that it tends to ascribe to the beloved all strike a French reader as somewhat excessive, which suggests the two cultures have an altogether different sense of the aesthetic.[234] Dieulafoy is also shocked by the explicit references to sex and homosexuality in works such as Saʿdi's *Golestān*.[235] But despite these reservations, French authors generally consider the enduring popularity of medieval poetry in modern Iran to be cause for praise, especially in comparison to Europe. In the words of Loti: 'Chez nous, à part des lettrés, qui se souvient de nos trouvères, contemporains de Saadi, qui se souvient seulement de notre merveilleux Ronsard?'[236] [In France, apart from the learned, who remembers our troubadours, who were contemporaries of Saʿdi, who even remembers our wonderful Ronsard?] As well as noting the aesthetic differences between the literary cultures of Iran and Europe, travel-writers also sought out examples of cultural equivalence. Dieulafoy refers to ghazals 'sortes de sonnets' [a kind of sonnet] and Flandin explains that Ferdowsi's Rostam, the legendary hero of the *Shāhnāmeh*, is 'l'*Hercule* ou le *Roland* des Persans' [the *Hercules* or the *Roland* of the Persians], thereby formulating a parallel between medieval Persian, classical Greek and medieval French epic poetry.[237]

Over the course of their time in Iran, French travellers could also gain a new perspective on Persian poetry. As he admires the vista from Hāfez's tomb, Loti writes:

> Il y a vraiment quelque chose, dans ce pays de Chiraz, un mystère, un sortilège, indicible pour nous et qui s'échappe entre nos phrases occidentales. Je conçois

en ce moment l'enthousiasme des poètes de la Perse, et l'excès de leurs images, qui seules, pour rendre un peu cet enchantement des yeux, avaient à la fois assez d'imprécision et assez de couleur.²³⁸

[There truly is something, in this land of Shiraz, a mystery, a spell, indescribable for us since it escapes our Occidental phrases. I conceive in this moment of the enthusiasm of these Persian poets, the excess of their images, which alone, can do justice to this enchantment of the eyes, since they are both sufficiently imprecise and sufficiently colourful.]

Loti admits that his previous assessment of Persian poetry had been unfair because it had been formulated from a European perspective. Now, he can see that the intensity of Persian poetry is in fact perfectly attuned to the landscapes in which it originated. This may be a rather naive understanding of how literature works, but it does nonetheless lead to a profound shift in perspective: having previously deemed Persian poetry to be excessive, Loti now suggests that it is the French language that is insufficient, since it cannot capture the landscape's effect on the author. Though their enthusiasm never reaches the same level as that of Loti, Dieulafoy too changes their outlook on Persian poetry over the course of their stay, going from calling Hāfez 'overwrought'²³⁹ to quoting him to better explore the similarities and differences between themself and the Iranian travellers with whom they share the shelter of a caravanserai:

Au milieu de la nuit j'ai été réveillée par un bruit infernal: après deux jours de repos la caravane reprend sa marche. Tandis que je me prélasse mollement allongée sur une paillasse fraîchement garnie, je me prends à répéter avec un bonheur égoïste les vers du poète:
Suave, mari magno, turbantibus aequora ventis,
E terra magnum alterius spectare laborem;
Non quia vexari quenquam est jucunda voluptas,
Sed, quibus ipse malis careas, quia cernere suave est.
Je me repose et mes compagnons de route grimpent mélancoliquement sur leurs montures ou s'effondrent dans les kadjavehs en se rappelant peut-être, de leur côté, le célèbre passage d'Hafiz: 'Lorsque nous fendons dans une nuit obscure des vagues terribles et des gouffres effrayants, combien de ceux qui habitent en sûreté le rivage peuvent comprendre notre situation?'²⁴⁰

[In the middle of the night I was awoken by an infernal racket: after two days of rest, the caravan is back on the road. As I lazily lounge on my freshly garnished straw mattress, I find myself repeating with selfish joy the verses of the poet:
Pleasant it is, when on the great sea the winds trouble the waters,
To gaze from shore upon another's great tribulation:
Not because any man's troubles are a delectable joy,
But because to perceive what ills you are free from yourself is pleasant.
I lie in bed and my journey companions climb sadly on to their horses or crash into their *kadjavehs* [boxes in which women travel] remembering perhaps, at their

end, the famous passage from Hafez: 'In the dark night, amid terrifying waves and whirlpools, what do they know of our state, those who remained at shore, free from care.]²⁴¹

On the one side are those who remain, and on the other ('de leur côté'), those who are leaving. Both groups, Dieulafoy suggests, consider one another. Dieulafoy's ingenuous use of intertextuality here relies on the pairing of two texts from different cultures with related content: the Latin poet Lucretius's didactic poem *De rerum natura* and the opening ghazal of Hāfez's *Divān*. The effect of this is twofold. On the one hand, it emphasizes cultural relativism: Dieulafoy and the Iranian travellers each have their own (different) cultural points of reference. Indeed, when Dieulafoy refers to Hāfez's Ghazal n°1 as 'famous', they speak for Iranians and not the French public, who were more likely to have come across the works of Sa'di, Khayyām and Ferdowsi and would probably not have recognized the quotation. On the other hand, the similarity between the two quotations undermines the binary of Occident versus Orient, here embodied by Dieulafoy versus the Iranian travellers, since both sides are portrayed as sharing the same universal experiences: the danger of the journey, the safety of home and literature's ability to help individuals articulate their emotional state and offer solace. This cross-cultural literary parallel allows Dieulafoy to establish an emotional proximity between themself and the Iranian travellers, while also acknowledging their inability to completely understand them. Indeed, the limitation of their perspective is indicated by the 'peut-être' [perhaps] that introduces their act of ventriloquism: this is only a supposition. The limits of Dieulafoy's perspective as a cultural outsider are brought across even more powerfully by the dialogue that is created by the two quoted fragments of poetry. The speaker in the verses by Lucretius, with whom Dieulafoy identifies, claims to see the pain of those who are travelling; a claim that is undercut by Hāfez's verses, which state that those who are at home *cannot* understand what travellers go through. It is as though the sailors in Hāfez's verses are answering back, telling Lucretius/Dieulafoy 'you have no idea what you are talking about'. The passage is thus ambivalent. While it makes an effort to demonstrate the commonalities between two different cultures, the Hāfez intertext also reminds us that one can never fully understand the predicament of others. In the original text, Hāfez had adopted this metaphor to describe the pains of heartache: only a person who has experienced them can sympathize with the anguished lover. Removed from the context of this love poem, Hāfez's seafaring metaphor takes on a new significance in Dieulafoy's text. Here, it can be interpreted as pointing to the cultural chasm between the travel-writer and the people whom they seek to describe: what can a French person know of the state of being Iranian?

To conclude then, the intertextual presence of Middle Eastern literature in French travel-writing can serve a range of functions. With Bibesco, we have a rather literal identification of reality with literature: her experiences in Iran are only valued in so far as they confirm the fantasies that she had formed by reading the *Mille et Une Nuits* and the classical Persian poets. For Flandin and Loti, the imaginary landscapes of the *Nuits* function as a visual aid for readers who have never travelled to the Middle East. The magic associated with these tales also helps express French authors' sense of wonder at Iran's exquisite architecture and landscapes. Intertextuality can also function as a narrative structuring device, as is the case in *Les Huit paradis* where dispersed descriptions and musings are presented as a literary pilgrimage to the origins of Persian poetry and of the concept of paradise. Finally, intertextual references could serve as starting points for a reflection on the travel-writer's own work. Dieulafoy and Loti, who first considered Hāfez's poetry to be too hyperbolic and overwrought, develop an entirely different relationship to it after spending time in Iran. Loti comes to see the limitations of French language and literature, which cannot do justice to his experiences in Shiraz. And Dieulafoy, by staging a dialogue between Lucretius and Hāfez, implicitly admits the limitations of their attempts to speak on behalf of Iranians. The variety of ways in which French travellers engaged with Persian poetry is thus deeply revealing of how they negotiated their own position in relation to Iranian culture.

Conclusion

When it came to Iran, nineteenth-century French travel-writers shared many areas of interest, namely, the Persian character, the condition of women, Shi'i rituals, the city of Esfahan, the ruins of the Achaemenids, Western influence in the region and the role of literature in making sense of the place. Yet, a close comparison of these authors' treatments of these themes reveals that they each held different opinions about them, opinions that were communicated to the reader through a variety of rhetorical and narrative strategies. The account of one same reality thus varies entirely from author to author: the *ta'zieh* performance that is so captivating to Flandin is farcical to Dieulafoy, and the natural environment that disappoints Gobineau can inspire enthused comparisons with Persian literature and the *Mille et Une Nuits* from Loti and Bibesco. As well as having diverging perspectives, travel-writers also had to employ a variety of styles and modes of writing in order to do justice to the wide range of subjects covered by their writing: one does not describe the architecture of Esfahan or the politics of financial imperialism in the same manner as one recounts a visit to a harem. Moreover, such a visit may hold an entirely different narrative function based on whether it is secretive (as with Flandin), formerly arranged (as with Bibesco) or both, as is the case with Dieulafoy's photography sitting, requested by the sitter, but unsanctioned by the sitter's husband. Travel-writing may have derived its authority from empirical observation, but this did not prevent authors from being deeply subjective in their impressions and artful in their expression.

The fact that travelogues are organized chronologically as the sequential narration of an author's experiences over the course of their itinerary also enables the genre to dramatize the evolution of an author's perspective over time. This is the case, for instance, with Bibesco's journey towards appreciating the veil and Dieulafoy's growing scepticism towards Westernization. In other cases, travelogues might through their contradictions simply illustrate the unreliability of the human subject as a source and guarantor of information about Iran: consider for instance Flandin's fluctuating pronouncements on *ta'arof* (Persian politeness), which is presented as evidence of genuine kindness and of hypocrisy. As such, travel-writing reveals the human mind to be contradictory, flexible and changeable, especially in its negotiation of cultural difference, an aspect that had been absent from the more cohesive and consistent vision of Iran presented by poems, histories and historical novels.

Travel-writers' fascination with the lives of contemporary Iranians brings into sharp relief the extent to which other literary genres focus on Iranian figures from the past, be it the rulers of the Achaemenid Empire, the mythical Aryans or the medieval Persian poets. French poets, historians and playwrights' presentation of such figures as their ancestors or alter egos results in a blindspot when it comes to contemporary Iranians, who are not part of the picture. As I noted in Chapter 2, such a silence may be seen as a 'denial of coevalness', a phrase coined by Johannes Fabian to refer to the trope of claiming that non-Western societies are at an earlier stage of development, thereby refusing to acknowledge their contemporaneity and by extension their very existence.[242] With Iran, however, the denial goes in the opposite direction: rather than suggesting that Iran is at an earlier stage of development, French poetry, narrative writing and performing arts' focus on historical subjects to the exclusion of contemporary Iranians suggests that the nation is past its prime, which is why the present is not worth writing about. This is indeed a trope that we can also encounter in travel-writing, for instance, when Gobineau and Loti emphasize Esfahan's past glory. Yet, travel-writing by and large acts as a corrective to the erasure of contemporary Iranians by the other literary genres studied in this book. The most memorable experiences for travellers were those where they were able to spy, and in some cases experience, a day in the life of an Iranian. More than anything, it is moments of personal interaction and indeed culture shock that bring such accounts to life, whether it is Flandin being sneaked into his Iranian friend's harem, or Dieulafoy eavesdropping on two women gossiping about the West or, rather more graphically, Loti being splattered with the blood of Muharram mourners. On some occasions, these experiences could even lead French travellers to question their prior assumptions. Was the Islamic veil really such a bad thing if it protected women from sexual harassment? How could Alexander burn down Persepolis, that breathtaking testament to human art and ingenuity, and still be considered 'great'? Was it really in order to export its 'civilisation' that Europe interfered with foreign markets? And why was it that French people did not value their literary heritage like the Iranians did? Travellers' interactions with Iranians gave them an experience that would forever elude the poets, historians and playwrights writing from the comfort of their home: that of being oneself someone else's other. For these authors, cultural relativism was no longer a theory, but a lived reality.

4

Performing arts

Orientalism and the stage

This chapter differs from the previous three. Up until this point, I have discussed works that had reached their final stage of completion: texts written to be consumed as texts. The texts I shall be analysing here (libretti and dramatic scripts), in contrast, were only one element of a production. In order to make sense of them, we therefore need to approach them in the context of their performance, and this requires a certain amount of reconstruction. My primary sources will be a combination of scripts, sketches for costume and set designs, musical scores (and, where they exist, contemporary musical recordings), the correspondence between members of production teams and reviews. With the exception of Félicien David's opera *Lalla-Roukh* (1862), which returned annually to the Opéra Comique until the end of the nineteenth century, the productions studied here were short-lived affairs, which only ran for one or two seasons. The archival materials from their première, therefore, give us an accurate idea of the definitive form that they took on stage. As we shall see, the multi-sensory nature of the performing arts allowed for a layered representation of Iran which encompassed such aspects as plot, dialogue, choreography, costume and set design, and – last but not least – music. Indeed, it was in the nineteenth century that musical Orientalism as we know it (and as it is still practised) was invented and codified.[1] The combination of all these different elements would give the audience an immersive experience of *dépaysement* (literally: of being transported to another country). Hector Berlioz describes the overwhelming sensory experience of the première of *Lalla-Roukh* by referring not only to what he heard and saw, but also what he imagined he could touch and smell:

> C'est un voyage au pays des roses, où tout chante, où tout sourit, où Bulbul, le chantre ailé des nuits, s'épuise en soupirs mélodieux. L'ombre y est douce, le soleil caressant, l'onde tiède et parfumée.[2]

> [It is a journey to the land of roses, where everything sings, everything smiles, where Bolbol, the winged singer in the night, exhausts himself in melodious sighs. The shade is soft, the sun caressing, the water warm and perfumed.]

The value of these works thus lay in their power to transport audiences to a land far away. But did this faraway bear any relationship to the places that could be experienced through travel, as our authors did in Chapter 3, or was it pure fantasy?

Gilles de Van, in his article on the exotic in fin de siècle opera, argues that stage representations of the 'elsewhere' existed at the intersection of realism and fairy tale. On the one hand, the new availability of information about distant countries, in particular through travel-writing, meant that late-nineteenth-century French audiences were no longer satisfied with spatiotemporal vagueness. The demand was now for works in clearly established settings that came with precise details and local colour. But on the other hand, what made these operas most attractive to audiences was the escapism that they offered from the boredom of 'bourgeois civilization'. The world that they depicted therefore had to be more beautiful than the audience's own world.[3] Historical Iranian settings thus offered an ideal compromise to French librettists: they were sufficiently documented by historians, archaeologists and travel-writers to be grounded in reality, while being visually sumptuous and temporally removed enough to leave room for embellishment. *Lalla-Roukh* is a perfect example of the combination of local colour and fantasy described by de Van: it is set at a precise time and in a specific region of Asia, yet Berlioz in his review does not declare himself transported to another country or city (i.e. India or Samarkand), but to the 'land of roses' and 'Gol o Bolbol'. In other words, to an imaginary place associated with Persian poetry. Berlioz's words thus suggest that audiences knew that what they were seeing was not a realistic portrayal of a foreign country, but an invention designed to entertain them. Indeed, another reviewer of *Lalla-Roukh* describes the title character dining on flowers 'comme on se nourrit peut-être dans une planète moins grossièrement conçue que la nôtre' [as one feeds oneself perhaps on a planet less vulgarly constructed than our own].[4] By venturing that the actions of the princess might be plausible on another planet, the reviewer is openly admitting that he knows that no human behaves like this, not even in Asia. De Van's analysis is thus a useful reminder that one same production typically included both elements of local culture, for example, through set designs which could be extremely accurate recreations based on documentation from travellers, and the evocation of Western fantasies of a purer, simpler, more beautiful elsewhere.[5] Indeed, the productions studied here combine elements drawn from Iranian culture, which range from characters from Iranian history and literature to imitations of fashions and architectures from Iran, with a more generic and fantasy-driven exoticism, which tends to be rooted in the clichés of Orientalism, as defined by Edward Said. Studied chronologically, however, these dramatic works do reveal a growing interest on behalf of creators to find more original and culturally specific ways of staging Iran. Of particular note are Maurice Bouchor's attempt to present Omar Khayyām's philosophy through the medium of puppetry (1892), the painstaking reconstruction of the architecture and material culture of the Achaemenids in the outdoor stage version of Dieulafoy's *Parysatis* (1902) and the pairing of a libretto inspired by the *Shāhnāmeh* with set and costumes derived from Persian miniature art in Dukas's *La Péri* (1912).

Compared to the other genres studied in this book, where we find efforts to go beyond Orientalist stereotype as early as 1852 with the poetry of Desbordes-Valmore (Chapter 1) or 1869, when the serialized version of Judith Gautier's novel *Iskender* was first published (Chapter 2), the performing arts lag behind. This is in great part due to the formal and cultural parameters of the genre, on which I shall say more in a moment. But it is equally important to emphasize that the performing arts, in contrast to other forms of literature, are profoundly collaborative ventures and that, consequently, the librettists and dramatists studied here only controlled one aspect of the production that they were contributing to create. The vision of Iran conveyed by a production was the result of the combination of script, set and costumes, music and performers, as well as such deciding factors as programming and venue. Thus, even if a writer was personally invested in representing Iran *qua* Iran, rather than repeating tired clichés regarding the Islamic Orient, the production could still take a completely different direction on stage. The collaborative and multi-layered nature of the performing arts is therefore an aspect that shall be returned upon throughout this chapter. But before we examine the productions that make up our case studies, I find it essential to state my own theory for the prevalence of Orientalist tropes in the performing arts over all other genres studied in this book. De Van makes a convincing case for the ideology behind the combination of local colour and fantasy in Orientalist opera, but I find the practical and material aspects of the performing arts to be equally important. I venture that Orientalist binaries and essentializations are encouraged, first, by the physical experience of attending performances and, secondly, by the financial cost associated with large-scale productions, which places them under greater pressure to conform to the expectations of the public.

 The binary opposition of self and other, or France and Iran, was made a physical reality by the performing arts in two ways. First, because sets, costumes and music materialized cultural difference through sight and sound in a manner that could not be ignored. This is in complete contrast to the written text, which invites readers to form their own picture. Consider for example the use of the word 'robe' in Marceline Desbordes-Valmore's poem 'Les Roses de Saadi', which was analysed in Chapter 1. To the poem's reader, the word could refer either to the robe of a medieval Persian sage or to the dresses worn by modern French women, and even both things at the same time. The poem's lyric I is malleable, open to interpretation and indeed identification. There is no such openness to interpretation in a stage production in which characters stand before the audience in exotic costumes. Add to this the boundary between audience and performers, known as the fourth wall, which in larger venues took the form of a very wide physical gap, and the separation between the 'us' of the audience and the 'them' of the foreign characters on stage could not have been more clear. A nineteenth-century French audience member would sit among a community of people who looked and behaved like them, gazing together upon a physically removed group of people who looked and sounded different to them. Of course, the individuals on stage were for the most part fellow French-men and -women in make-up and costume, and in the case of star opera singers were identifiable as such, but the suspension of disbelief encouraged by theatrical performances meant that for the time they were on stage, they were identified with the characters that they played. As such, they were experienced as cultural others and defined in opposition to the group formed by the audience. Some works strove to bridge this divide, for example by choosing a music devoid of exotic markers or by emphasizing the universality of the characters' predicament – for example, Zoroaster the man in love, as opposed to Zoroaster the prophet of a distant religion. Other works, on the contrary, exploited the distance created by the stage to write two-dimensional characters who function as sources of laughter or horror, offering the audience the smug satisfaction of having nothing in common with such despicable figures – we see this for instance with the characters of the eunuch and the slave merchant in Gautier's libretto for *La Péri*. The exception that confirms this rule is the musical genre known as song ('mélodie'), which was typically experienced in a private domestic setting, either by playing and/or singing the piece oneself, or by listening to a friend or relative doing so. The words of songs such as Fauré's setting of 'Les Roses d'Ispahan' (1884) were suggestive of exotic locales, but the performer was a familiar person and, moreover, the music was devoid of exotic markers. This meant that the distant setting was instantly domesticated.[6]

The considerable financial cost associated with stage productions, in particular operas which required a large number of performers and typically featured ambitious sets, costumes and lighting designs, and the large auditoriums that they needed to fill in order to meet these costs, is the second reason why they would have privileged Orientalist clichés over more innovative approaches to cross-cultural representation. Deviating too widely from audience expectation was a risk, which could result in financial losses and the embarrassment of bad reviews, empty seats and an early end to the run. And while there were Iran experts or at least enthusiasts among the members of a large opera audience, the majority would have had a more limited knowledge of the region, largely based on Western codes of representation. This is most true of music. Orientalist music as it developed in the nineteenth century relied heavily on stylistic features that became associated with the Orient, which I shall refer to as 'Oriental markers'. The most prominent of these features for the musical corpus under consideration here are musical scales that use the augmented second interval (sometimes known as the 'Arabic' scale), ornamentation (also known as arabesque), metallic percussion and the use of the oboe as a surrogate for 'Eastern' wind instruments. The same modus operandi can be found in nineteenth-century Orientalist ballet, which 'featured traditional western classical dance movement, occasionally punctuated by exotic gestures and dances'.[7] Some of the features used as Oriental markers did resemble aspects of the musical traditions from Asia and the Middle East; for example, Persian and Arabic modes once transposed into Western scales do include augmented second intervals, but the use of these features became so codified in nineteenth-century French music that they were reified into a language of their own. Composers were not trying to imitate other musical cultures: they were imitating one another, creating and bolstering a set of musical codes which, to a European ear, were evocative of the Orient. Thus, while in the realms of poetry, history and travel-writing, I have had cause to disagree with Said's suggestion that the West created the Orient; when it comes to the music and choreography studied in this chapter, the point is certainly well taken that: 'We need not look for correspondence between the language used to depict the Orient and the Orient itself, not so much because the language is inaccurate but because it is not even trying to be accurate.'[8] Building on Said's claim, the musicologist Derek Scott has argued that the purpose of such music 'is not to imitate but to represent', and as such, it had to be intelligible to a Western audience. In other words, had composers included actual Persian music in their scores, audience members, who had never been to Iran and thus not been exposed to local musical traditions, would not have understood this music as 'Persian', but as incomprehensible.⁹ This explains why even productions that overtly engaged with Iranian sources never did so through music: their sources were always textual (history, literature, religion) or visual (architecture, fashion, miniature art), and as such, intelligible to audiences. If, however, we abandon the lost cause that is searching for Persian music on the nineteenth-century French stage, and focus on the latter two dimensions (i.e. the textual and the visual), it is clear that as the century unfolds, we find a growing interest in depicting Iran in terms of its cultural, historical and regional specificity. The fact that the most experimental approaches to staging Iran are concentrated at the tail-end of the period covered by this book is indicative of the French public's growing familiarity with Iran's distinct identity within the Middle East. By the 1890s, French readers had access to the texts studied in Chapters 1, 2 and 3 of the present book. They had been able to attend the Paris World Fairs of 1878 and 1889, which both featured Persian Pavilions, and from 1886 they could visit the Dieulafoy rooms at the Louvre, the inauguration of which had garnered much attention from the press. This is why one critic could confidently declare in 1902: 'nous sommes mieux renseignés sur la Perse au temps des Achéménides que sur des époques et des pays beaucoup plus rapprochés de nous' [we are better informed about Achaemenid Persia than we are about historical periods and countries that are much closer to us].¹⁰

This chapter covers a range of genres within the performing arts: ballet, opera, puppetry and outdoor musical theatre, exploring in each case the interaction between text, music, set and costume. Ballet offers a dramatic point of entry, since it presents us with two works from opposite ends of the period studied in this chapter and with completely contrasting approaches to staging Iran, all the while sharing the same purported subject matter. These two ballets are both entitled *La Péri* and centre on the female mythological creature of the same name (in Persian *pari*). Théophile Gautier and Burgmüller's *La Péri* (1843) completely amalgamates Iran with the Islamic Orient of the French imagination. Paul Dukas's *La Péri* (aborted production 1911, première 1912), in contrast, is immersed in the world of the *Shāhnāmeh*. Are these two opposing approaches to be explained on the basis of the temporal span between them? In other words, is it a matter of cultural evolution, from unbridled Orientalism to interest in Iran *qua* Iran? Lest we should jump too hastily to positive conclusions, I compare the visual aesthetics that were developed for the two different productions of Dukas's *La Péri*. The contrast between them reveals, on the one hand, the enduring allure of Orientalism well into the early twentieth century, and on the other, the consequences of the collaborative nature of the performing arts: one same libretto and musical score can be made to signify entirely different things through the addition of visual language. The section that follows is on opera and compares three works: Michel Carré, Hippolyte Lucas and Félicien David's wildly successful *opéra comique Lalla-Roukh* (1862) and two more austere grand operas: Jean Richepin and Jules Massenet's *Le Mage* (1892) and Louis Gallet and Louis-Albert Bourgault-Ducoudray's *Thamara* (1892). My focus shall be on the representation of Iranian men as lead characters in these three works and I will be showing in particular how these operas go against Ralph Locke's model of the archetypal nineteenth-century Orientalist opera. Such operas, according to Locke, typically centre on a male Western hero (with whom the audience is encouraged to identify) who intrudes into the exotic world of an alluring Oriental woman.[11] But what happens when the cross-cultural romance at the centre of an Orientalist opera is not between East and West, but between East and East – in our case, Iran and its Asian neighbours? Is the audience intended to see all characters as equally distant Oriental Others? Or is there a hierarchy of difference? And if so, where does Iran fall on this ladder of otherness? Having dealt with the most large-scale form of popular entertainment of the French nineteenth century, we will then move on to somewhere much smaller: the marionette stage. The chapter's penultimate case study is a play entitled *Le Songe de Omar Khèyam* (1892) written for the puppets of the Petit-Théâtre de la Galerie Vivienne by the poet and dramatist Maurice Bouchor. What were the implications of replacing human actors with these small mechanical figures? And did this gel with the play's source text, the quatrains of Omar Khayyām? Finally, I will end by examining a production led by a writer with whom you have by now grown familiar: Jane Dieulafoy. At the turn of the century, Dieulafoy initiated a new creative experiment: a collaboration with star composer Camille Saint-Saëns and Southern industrialist-turned-producer Fernand Castelbon des Beauxhostes to produce a stage version of their novel *Parysatis*, which premièred in 1902. How did Dieulafoy approach writing for a new genre? And how did they manage the conflicting demands of the feminist spirit of the source novel, their scientific mission to disseminate Achaemenid visual culture to the wider public and the commercial pressures of working in the performing arts?

Each of the four performing arts studied in this chapter (ballet, opera, puppetry, outdoor theatre) presents us with a different set of formal rules, combination of media and performance context. They must therefore be analysed on their own terms, in light of the particular tools that they had at their disposal for staging Iran. At the same time, it is also worth studying these four performance genres together, since they all contribute answers to a common set of questions. Did the French public's growing familiarity with Iran's distinct cultural identity challenge the clichés of Orientalism? Or are all stage depictions of Iran inevitably essentializing and othering, by virtue of the material considerations raised above? Do scripts and librettos favour any one narrative of Iran or were all five of the narratives outlined in the introduction equally popular? And how does this narrative change once the text is paired with the aural and visual dimensions of the performing arts? Do the different elements of a stage production (plot, dialogue, choreography, set, costume, music, cast, venue) typically coalesce into one vision of Iran? Or are they rather in conversation with one another, with the potential to disagree and thereby offer the audience multiple visions of Iran within one same production? These are the questions that shall guide us as we journey through the reconstructed world of the French stage between 1843 and 1912.

A tale of two *Péris*: Iran, the imaginary Orient, and ballet (Théophile Gautier, Paul Dukas)

The long nineteenth century saw the creation of two French ballets entitled *La Péri*. The first *Péri*, which had a libretto by Théophile Gautier, music by Friedrich Burgmüller and choreography by Jean Coralli, premièred at the Paris Opera on 17 July 1843.[12] It was originally subtitled 'ballet oriental' and finally retitled 'ballet fantastique',[13] thus confirming de Van's insight into the close association between exotic settings and fairy tale. The music and libretto of the second *Péri*, subtitled 'poème dansé', were written by one same person: Paul Dukas. This ballet was due to première at the Théâtre du Châtelet on 13 June 1911 as part of Diaghilev's Ballets Russes season with Nijinsky in the lead male role, but due to internal disagreements the production was cancelled at the last minute. The ballet was revived through the efforts of its lead ballerina Natalya Trouhanova, who assembled a new creative team, and it finally premièred on 22 April 1912.[14] These two ballets have nothing in common aside from the fact that they both centre on the relationship between a male character and a *pari* – that is, a nymph or fairy from Persian mythology (from the old Persian *pairikā*).[15] The profound differences between the two ballets' treatments of this theme are of interest in themselves, since they present us with the two opposite ends of the spectrum referred to above: Iran as an ingredient among others within the Orient of the imagination (Gautier) and Iran as a culturally specific setting (Dukas). The seventy-year gap between the two productions can go some way towards explaining this striking opposition, since the early twentieth-century public was better educated with regard to Iran's distinct cultural identity within the wider Middle East than the mid-nineteenth-century public. This would also explain why Dukas did not find it necessary to gloss in his libretto that the male protagonist 'Iskender' is the Persianized name of Alexander the Great.[16] Another important reason for this divergence, aside from the temporal gap, is the context of the venue: the Ballets Russes were known for experimentation; the Paris Opera was not.

Before we take a closer look at these two works, it is worth considering the nature of the relationship between text, music and visuals (by which I mean choreography, costume and set) in nineteenth-century French ballet. Nineteenth-century ballet libretti were more than pre-production materials: they were printed and circulated as part of performance programmes, which meant that audience members typically consumed text and ballet in conjunction.[17] For this reason, their authors put great care in their style and presentation. Gautier was no exception, going through several draft versions of *La Péri* before being satisfied. His libretto contains not just description, but also narrative devices such as dialogue and *discours indirect libre*. It reads like a lively short story, in a similar vein to Gautier's other shorter narratives with Oriental settings.[18] The libretto, moreover, circulated beyond the context of the production and could therefore be purchased as a book by readers who did not attend a performance. We find the same attention to language in Dukas's libretto, which is much shorter than Gautier's, mirroring the respective durations of the ballets: at roughly twenty minutes, Dukas's ballet is a third of the length of his predecessor's. While Gautier's libretto is comparable to a short story, Dukas's succinct style is more reminiscent of the prose poem as practised by Charles Baudelaire in his collection *Le spleen de Paris* (1869); indeed, Dukas himself referred to his text as a 'poem' in its subtitle. The libretto is also packed with details that would have been impossible to communicate through performance, most notably similes that name sites in Iran and characters from Persian literature. It is therefore clear that Dukas considered reading the libretto to be an integral part of experiencing the ballet performance.[19] He also included the libretto as a frontispiece to the published musical score, which suggests that the text was essential not only to an appreciation of the ballet by the audience, but also to instrumentalists wishing to perform its music.[20] The relationship between the ballet's textual dimension, on the one hand, and its music and visuals, on the other, was in fact reciprocal: the libretto guided composers, choreographers, designers, dancers and musicians in crafting the performance, as well as the audience in following the plot; but, conversely, the performance also shaped the audience's reception of the libretto, since they were being consumed together. In this section, I will therefore be exploring what these two libretti came to signify through their interaction with such elements as music, costume and choreography. One aspect of particular note will be both ballet composers' choice to eschew the Orientalist markers that I listed above, which has different implications in the context of each production.

Théophile Gautier's libretto tells the story of 'Achmet', an Ottoman lord who lives in Cairo in a 'harem d'une riche architecture arabe' [a harem of lavish Arabic architecture] decorated with 'vases de Japon' [Japanese vases] and who has grown bored of the pleasures offered by his numerous concubines, which include both Oriental and European women. In a dream, Achmet has a vision of a *pari* residing in heaven with her friends. Luckily for him, the *pari* sees him too, and they fall in love. But before inviting him to live happily ever after with her, the *pari* sets out to test Achmet's love by appearing before him under the guise of a harem slave: if he loves her in this mortal coil, then he is worthy of her. Achmet proves his loyalty by going against the local *pacha* who wants the slave for himself. As a consequence, he is thrown into a prison with 'Arceaux mauresques, murailles sombres bariolées de versets du Koran' [Mauresque arches, dark heavy walls painted with colourful Quranic verses] and featuring a deadly torture device lifted straight out of a painting by Decamps.[21] But, on the day of Achmet's execution, the *pari* saves him and carries him to heaven, where they live happily ever after. From the opening scene with its 'odalisques occupées à leur toilette' [odalisques washing themselves] to the 'discussion animée et comique' [animated and comical discussion] between a eunuch and slave merchant haggling over women, and finally the violent ending where a man is condemned to death for contravening another man's lust, the libretto serves us with all the stock characters and premises of Orientalism. Gautier's only innovation here is the introduction of the magical character of the *pari*, who comes to symbolize the male protagonist's aspiration towards a pure and ideal love, which an earlier draft indicates is born from Achmet's passion for poetry.[22] Despite having centred his libretto on a character from Iranian folklore, Gautier shows no interest in setting the ballet in Iran. The story takes place instead in Cairo, but more than that, it takes place in a generic Islamic Orient. Indeed, aside from the titular 'péri', the characters in the ballet all seem to have stepped out of the imaginary Orient of Victor Hugo's collection of poems *Les Orientales* (see Chapter 1). Two of them even share their names with the titular characters of Hugo's poems: Achmet (after 'Sultan Achmet') and 'Nourmahal, la sultane favorite' (after 'Nourmahal la rousse' and 'La sultane favorite').[23]

Although Gautier's libretto sought to regale audiences with an exotic spectacle, the composer, choreographer and costume designer seem to have been content with only gesturing to this sense of elsewhere in discrete ways. Burgmüller's musical score is not exoticizing by any means: were the audience to close their eyes, they would simply hear the familiar sounds of Western classical music. As such, it illustrates how in the early- to mid-nineteenth century, French composers had not yet broken away from an older tradition, exemplified by ballets such as Rameau's *Indes galantes* (1735), in which exotic settings were conveyed visually, but not musically. The choreography and costumes of *La Péri* did make some attempt at injecting a sense of elsewhere into the production, but this was only done superficially, so that the performance would not deviate from the norms of French Romantic ballet. In terms of dancing, as has been reconstructed by Amanda Lee, Oriental markers would have involved altering standard ballet postures by jutting the hips or inclining the torso. In other words, the Oriental characters danced in a slightly more relaxed manner than the poised European characters.[24] According to Nerval, who had actually been to Cairo, the choreography of *La Péri* was not only Westernized, but also terribly tame compared to the performances that he had attended during his travels.[25] He was also deeply disappointed by the costumes, and understandably so: all of the female dancers in the production, whether they portrayed European or Oriental characters, wore tutus. Costume sketches show even the supernatural *pari* herself to be wearing the white skirt typical of Romantic ballet. Her magical quality is only sparingly suggested through a tiara adorned with stars (hinting at her celestial abode) and her Oriental origins through a bodice designed to imitate an Indian sari outfit (cropped blouse and diagonal fabric across the chest).[26] All levels of the production then, textual, musical and visual, worked together to divorce the figure of the *pari* from her origins in Iranian folklore, transforming her into a metonymy for the generic Orient of Western fantasy.

It is interesting at this juncture to contrast the erasure of Iran in Gautier's 1843 libretto with the foregrounding of Persian literature in his 1852 poem 'Préface', discussed in Chapter 1. Nerval argued that while Gautier's ballet had completely failed to provide any realism in its portrayal of North Africa, it had nonetheless succeeded in depicting an ideal Orient.[27] 'Préface' too presents us with a privileging of the poet's imagination over reality: the lyric I chooses to ignore what is happening outside his window and immerse himself in the world of poetry. But whereas in *La Péri*, the favoured imaginary world is a culturally unspecified Orient built from an accumulation of Western stereotypes, in 'Préface' it is classical Persian literature and its European reception via Goethe's *West-östlicher Divan* that offers an escape from the disappointments of the real world. Perhaps this pivot towards the world of Persian poetry was motivated by Gautier's journey to Algeria, on which he embarked just after *La Péri* premièred in Paris. Witnessing the brutal realities of French colonialism no doubt made it impossible for Gautier to continue idealizing North Africa as an exotic setting. The ideal Orient lay instead within the pages of medieval Persian literature: works predating French colonialism and composed in a region that was never part of the French Empire. It was the same literary culture that would come to inspire Dukas's *La Péri*, a ballet that was all about Iran.

Dukas's libretto (1911) opens as follows: 'Il advint qu'à la fin des jours de sa jeunesse, les Mages ayant observé que son astre pâlissait, ISKENDER parcourut l'Iran, cherchant la Fleur d'Immortalité.'[28] [It came to pass that in the final days of his youth, the Magi having observed that his star was paling, ESKANDAR travelled around Iran, searching for the Flower of Immortality.] From its very opening sentence, then, the libretto is explicitly set in Iran: the country is referred to by its native name and the plot centres on figures from Iranian history, the Magi (Zoroastrian priests) and Alexander the Great, who is referred to by his Persian name Eskandar (often transliterated as 'Iskender'). As we saw in Chapter 2, Eskandar was an important heroic figure in medieval Persian culture, integrated by Ferdowsi into the roster of great Iranian kings of the *Shāhnāmeh*. By the time that Dukas penned his libretto, the French public had already been introduced to this Persian Alexander through Judith Gautier's novel *Iskender: Histoire persane* (serialized version 1869, single book edition 1886). In Dukas's version of the story, Iskender finds the Flower of Immortality in the hands of a sleeping *pari*. He steals it and she wakes up. 'Cependant ISKENDER, la considérant, admira son visage qui surpassait en délices celui même de Gurdaferrid. / Et il la convoita dans son cœur.' [Yet ESKANDAR, considering her, admired her face which surpassed in delight even that of Gordafarid. / And within his heart he desired her.] At first the *pari* fails to take the flower back from the 'Seigneur Invincible' [Invincible Lord]. Then, she decides to perform 'la danse des Péris' [the dance of the *paris*]. Seduced by her dance, Iskender willingly returns the flower. 'ISKENDER la vit disparaître. / Et comprenant que, par là, lui était signifiée sa fin prochaine, / Il sentit l'ombre l'entourer.' [ESKANDAR saw her disappear. / And understanding that this was a sign that his end was near / He felt the darkness close in on him.]

Dukas's principal source for this ballet is most definitely Ferdowsi's *Shāhnāmeh*, which devotes two chapters to Alexander/Eskandar's conquest of Iran. Dukas even signals this affiliation when he compares the *pari*'s beauty to that of Gordafarid, who is one of the *Shāhnāmeh*'s female characters. At the same time, the libretto also includes allusions to the portrayal of Alexander in the European tradition: he is the 'Seigneur Invincible', a reference to the epithet 'unconquered' which is associated with Alexander in classical literature. The libretto's inciting event (i.e. the Magi warning Alexander) does not take place in the *Shāhnāmeh*, where Alexander is warned of his impending death by a talking tree, but it does correspond to Western biographies of Alexander, such as Plutarch's, where we are told that the Chaldean priests of Babylon made one such prophecy.[29] Because the protagonist's name is never glossed by Dukas, these details functioned as subtle clues that 'Iskender' and Alexander the Great are one same person, clues that only an educated reader would have been able to discern. Dukas makes it very clear that the story is set in Iran not only by referring to Iranian characters (Eskandar, Gordafarid) and Iran itself in the opening sentence, but also by naming specific regions of Iran: 'les forêts du Ghilan' [the forests of Gilan] and 'la cime de l'Elbourz' [the summit of the Alborz mountains, i.e. Mount Damavand]. From the outset then, Dukas's approach to the mythological character of the *pari* is diametrically opposed to that of Gautier, since he associates her with Iran's unique geography and literary culture.

In the *Shāhnāmeh* we are first introduced to Eskandar as the foreign conqueror who displaces King Darā.[30] After Eskandar has become king of Iran, the poem covers his many quests and adventures, which are mostly mythical. One such quest is Eskandar's search for the waters of immortality, in which he fails because he loses his guide, Khezr. The episode had already been adapted by Judith Gautier, who includes it in her novel *Iskender*, though she modifies it in two ways: first, by writing that the key to immortality is a magical pearl which once dropped into a lake converts its waters into an elixir, and secondly, by having her protagonist intentionally renounce his immortality.[31] Gautier's approach was no doubt a source of inspiration for Dukas, who mirrors it: he too changes the form of the elixir, which is now a lotus flower – most likely in reference to the iconography of kingship in Achaemenid art – and he too has Eskandar deliberately choose to relinquish his immortality. But whereas in Gautier's adaptation, Eskandar does so because he has the philosophical realization that death is the greatest adventure of all, in Dukas's version, the protagonist sacrifices his immortality out of love. Although the Eskandar chapters of the *Shāhnāmeh* do not feature a meeting with a *pari*, they do include other events of a supernatural nature and, moreover, *paris* are referred to in other chapters of the poem.[32] The story, though of Dukas's own invention, is thus consonant with the rules of the world of the *Shāhnāmeh*. This approach is very similar to that of Judith Gautier, who had combined existing characters from the *Shāhnāmeh* into new configurations and woven elements of Ferdowsi's plot with events of her own invention, all the while aiming to emulate the tone and style of the Persian epic. One of the most original aspects of Dukas's *La Péri* is its ambivalent portrayal of the title character. Although she appears as a beautiful and ideal creature, she manipulates Eskandar's desires and, once she has obtained what she wanted from him (i.e. the flower of immortality), she leaves him to die without a second thought. This ambivalence is in fact reflective of the mixed history of *paris* in Persian folklore. Although by the modern period they had come to be viewed as benign fairy or nymph figures, in ancient scripture, *paris* (under the old Persian name of *pairikās*) were demonic beings akin to the figure of the succubus in Christian cultures. James Darmesteter in the introduction to his translation of the *Zend Avesta* for Max Müller's *Sacred Books of the East* series had defined these *pairikās* of Zoroastrian scripture as 'demoniac nymphs, who rob the gods and men of the heavenly waters'.[33] Darmesteter also considered the modern *pari* to have retained some of the negativity associated with the ancient *pairikā*, defining her as a 'fée belle et dangereuse' [beautiful and dangerous fairy].[34] Darmesteter's work on the *Zend Avesta* thus seems a likely source for Dukas, who was known to have an interest not only in Persian literature, but also in the study of sacred texts.[35] Indeed, Dukas explicitly situates his libretto within a Zoroastrian context, both by referring to the Magi and by invoking twice 'Ormuzd', which is the Zoroastrian name for God (Ahura Mazda). As well as having an explicitly Iranian geographic setting, Dukas's libretto thus also draws on a variety of sources, including Iranian history, literature, folklore and religion, as well as the broader reception of these in European literature and scholarship, from Plutarch to Judith Gautier. How, then, was Dukas's keen interest in Iran reflected in his musical composition?

Dukas does not borrow from the musical traditions of Iran, nor does he overly rely on the musical markers typical of Western evocations of the Islamic Orient. The musical language that he is closest to is that of Russian composer Nikolai Rimsky-Korsakov, whose ballet music had been showcased in Paris by the productions of the Ballets Russes, most notably *Schéhérazade* (1909). Indeed, the musical style of *La Péri* has been defined as a combination of features associated with fin de siècle Russian composition ('divided strings, punctuating chordal brass and sweeping, high register woodwind') and French 'instrumental combinations and textural layering'.[36] This results in a music that possesses an eerie and otherworldly quality, which has a defamiliarizing effect on the listener. Rather than communicating a change in geographic location, the aural strangeness of *La Péri* is more suggestive of mystery and magic, and thus of a displacement into a world where different rules apply: that of fairy tale. This is largely due to the musical theme of the *pari*, which is played on high register instruments (flute and violin) and uses a rapid rhythm, ascending chromatic scales and a circular melody to convey the image of a light aerial creature, who flutters around us in circles and is always able to evade us by ascending just out of our reach. The high register and chromatic scales also convey a sense of precariousness and risk, which makes the listener sit on the edge of their seat. Dukas's music thus communicates the *pari*'s ambivalence as a magical figure that is both charming and dangerous, in line with the historic ambivalence of *paris* in Iranian folklore. This ambivalence can also be linked to French spectators' wider feelings towards the Orient, which, like Dukas's 'Péri', was considered alluring, and even magical, but also dangerous. Indeed, as well as being eerie and otherworldly, the musical theme of the *pari* features two Oriental markers: chromatic scales and flute arabesques. The association between the *pari*'s magical powers, seductiveness and Oriental-ness would have been evident to Dukas's listeners, evocative as it was of the world of the *Mille et Une Nuits* [*Thousand and One Nights*], which as we saw in Chapter 3 remained a popular cultural reference throughout the nineteenth century. One admirer even defined the *pari*'s theme as 'orientaliste et vénéneusement sensuel' [Oriental and poisonously sensual].[37] Fairy tale and exoticism thus remained as intertwined in the first decades of the twentieth century as they had been three centuries earlier when Galland's *Mille et Une Nuits* first entered the French literary scene. Eskandar's musical theme, in contrast, is in a low-to-middle register and its main instrument is the French horn. It differs from the *pari*'s theme both in rhythm, since it is noticeably slower and steadier, and scale, since it is diatonic rather than chromatic. The contrast between the two themes encapsulates the opposing natures of the characters: Iskender is human, reliable and earthly; the *pari*, otherworldly, capricious and aerial. We may also infer from this that Eskandar is, musically speaking, more 'Western'. That being said, it is important to note that the character of Eskandar in Persian literature is Iranian both by extraction and by adoption (see Chapter 2). Given that the libretto is so heavily invested in the *Shāhnāmeh* as a source text, it is therefore unlikely that Dukas would have viewed Eskandar as a Western character. The Persian Alexander is best understood as a transcultural figure, who bridged East and West. And indeed, Dukas's instrumentation respects this quality.

As well as being the perfect foil to the *pari*'s theme, the register and instrumentation of Eskandar's theme is an excellent fit for the qualities associated with the historic Alexander, as well as the ideals of masculinity shared by classical Greek literature and medieval Persian literature. Indeed, in both literary cultures, war and hunting were considered masculine activities *par excellence*, since they combined prowess in horse riding and the wielding of weapons. The historic Alexander was not only known for his mastery of war, but also for his love of hunting, and these are two activities in which he is frequently depicted in Western art. Battles and hunting scenes were also favoured subjects in Persian miniature art, including *Shāhnāmeh* illustrations. Both the advance into battle and the pursuit of a quarry are traditionally accompanied by the sound of blaring horns, making these wind instruments the ideal metonymy for the masculine universe of Alexander. Indeed, Dukas would later emphasize this association by composing a brass 'Fanfare' (1912) to be performed as a prelude to his ballet. As well as illustrating Iskender's earthliness through its lower register, the French horn's regal and military associations therefore serve to bolster his characterization as an unconquered hero who is physically unstoppable, yet allows his heart to be conquered by a female, rendering his self-sacrifice all the more dramatic. What emerges from this musical analysis is that the exoticism of Dukas's music is secondary to its narrative function. In the *pari*'s theme, Oriental markers are used selectively in a manner that bolsters the character's portrayal as otherworldly, charming and dangerous; they are a means rather than an end. These markers are also layered with musical textures and tropes drawn from both French and Russian music, making their evocation of the Orient far from conventional. In Eskandar's theme, Oriental markers are abandoned in favour of an instrumentation that evokes scenes of hunting and military pomp, which results in a portrayal of Alexander that is consistent with both the *Shāhnāmeh* and Western classical literature. It was rare for a librettist and a composer to be one same person and the result of this shows: in Dukas's *La Péri*, music and storytelling work of one accord. But what of the ballet's choreographers, designers and performers?

Comparing the archival materials of the aborted 1911 production and those of the 1912 première of *La Péri* proves particularly illuminating at this juncture, since the differences between these two productions reveal the important role played by creative collaboration and artistic programming in determining the vision of Iran communicated by a performance. Although there are no extant choreography notes for either production, we can surmise from the fact that the original Ballet Russes production was choreographed by Michel Fokine with Vaslav Nijinsky in the lead role that the dance would have been characterized by the freedom, expressivity and iconoclasm that had so surprised, fascinated and even scandalized the French public, accustomed as it was to Romantic ballet. The shock effect of the Ballets Russes also explains the predilection that its creative director Sergei Diaghilev showed for ballets with historical and Oriental settings, since these served to justify any provocative aspects of the productions as belonging to distant and less civilized societies.[38] The Ballets Russes programme in fact pairs the première of *La Péri* with a revival of its successful ballet *Schéhérazade* (1909, music by Rimsky-Korsakov). The two ballets were due to be performed consecutively, with *Schéhérazade* coming first. Thus, even though Dukas's libretto seeks to pay homage to Iranian literature and folklore, centring on characters that were still relatively new in a French context, the programming framed his ballet through the lens of the old and familiar Orient of Galland's *Mille et Une Nuits*. This pairing may have been justified by the fact that the characters of *Schéhérazade* were also Iranian: the ballet centres on the framing story of the *Mille et Une Nuits*, in which the Sassanian Persian king Shahryar discovers his wife cheating on him with a slave and as a result becomes a cruel killer of women. Despite the misleading title, the ballet in fact ends before Schéhérazade ever enters the scene. As a result, the audience never meets this resourceful heroine. Instead, it is simply treated to orgiastic scenes of sexual licentiousness and extreme violence. The story and tone of Dukas's ballet contrast markedly with these popular Orientalist themes. Instead of a tale of lust, jealousy and brutal revenge, we are presented with a story of unrequited love, which ends with the male character choosing to sacrifice himself for his beloved. Moreover, death in *La Péri* is brought not by a dagger plunged to the heart, but by a discarded flower, a delicate symbol of man's mortality. Does this mean that *La Péri* was programmed as a corrective to *Schéhérazade*? Or was it there as a continuation – perhaps a further illustration of the seductive powers of Oriental females? A look at the production's costume designs most definitely suggests the latter.

The costumes and sets of both *Schéhérazade* and *La Péri* were designed by Léon Bakst, the Ballet Russes's star designer, known for his breathtaking use of colour, vivid imagination and attention to the performer's comfort. These costumes did not feature tutus. For the title character of *La Péri*, Bakst created a costume nothing like what any French audience would have seen before, thereby conveying the *pari*'s otherworldly quality (see Figure 4.1). The outfit features contrasting colours, a pair of wire wings with jewel-like decorations, an elaborate head piece which includes two antennae, necklaces hanging off anywhere but around the neck (specifically: from the head piece, from the chest, from the legs) and flesh revealed in unusual places: the upper cleavage is covered but the breasts themselves are bare, and the costume also features black leggings with slits.[39] While the *pari*'s costume is profoundly original, it also bears internal continuities with Bakst's earlier work for *Schéhérazade*, namely, the use of block jewel colours overlaid with geometric patterns, as well as the enormous colourful veil that the *pari* holds about her in a manner suggestive of choreography. When we look at the costume for 'Iskender' (Figure 4.2), the continuities are even more obvious. It is in fact a more polished version of the 'first eunuch' costume from *Schéhérazade* (red fabric embellished with blue and white geometric patterns, blooming trousers and a tall red hat, also bearing a geometric pattern and adorned with a piece of light fabric).[40] The slightly revealed midriff where the trousers meet the blouse is also a more demure version of the costume previously worn by Nijinsky in *Schéhérazade*, in the role of the golden slave.[41] Had the production gone ahead as planned, no audience member could therefore have missed the visual statement that *La Péri* was cut from the same cloth as the familiar exotic world of the *Mille et Une Nuits*. Bakst's designs, though beautiful, bear little relation to the arts and costumes of Iran, aside from one element: the men's tall hats, which imitate those worn by the Qajar aristocracy, including Naser ed-Din Shah. The numerous decorations on the red version worn by Iskender make it rather different to the Qajar model, which was black, and in the case of the shah only adorned with a single jewel and plume. Yet, the original designs for *Schéhérazade* leave us with no doubt that this was Bakst's source. Indeed, these aquarelle sketches include a male and female figure that manifestly imitate Qajar portraiture not only through their clothing, but also their facial features.[42] The male figure sports a tall navy hat with a single white jewel embellished with feathers, a style entirely consonant with portraits of Qajar men. These early Qajar-inspired drawings for *Schéhérazade* could not be more different from the final designs that were adopted for the production: golden blooming trousers and a bikini top in the case of Nijinski. This stark contrast, as well as the gradual evolution in Bakst's hat designs, which become more and more brightly coloured and adorned, and thus distinct from their original Qajar models, reveal the

Figure 4.1 Natalia Trouhanova as 'La Péri' in Dukas's *La Péri*, design by Léon Bakst (1911).

Source: Bibliothèque nationale de France, département Bibliothèque-musée de l'opéra, AID-931 (1, 144–212). 'Programme officiel des Ballets russes, Théâtre du Châtelet, juin 1911' [deuxième spectacle 13 et 15–17 juin 1911]: 181.

Figure 4.2 Nijinsky as 'Iskender' in Dukas's *La Péri*, design by Léon Bakst (1911).

Source: Bibliothèque nationale de France, département Bibliothèque-musée de l'opéra, AID-931 (1, 144–212). 'Programme officiel des Ballets russes, Théâtre du Châtelet, juin 1911' [deuxième spectacle 13 et 15–17 juin 1911]: 145.

wider aims of the design. The priority was not to recreate the styles of clothing worn in Iran (contemporary or historical), but to bring to life the Orient of Western fantasy; a world where fashion is always colourful, bejewelled and scandalously revealing. Bakst had pulled off the rare feat of inventing a visual language that was unique to him, yet at the same time was legible as 'Oriental' to a French audience. Sadly for him, his costumes for *La Péri* would never see the stage.

As has been shown by Helen Julia Minors, the eventual première of Dukas's *La Péri* in 1912 was a labour of love led by Natalya Trouhanova, the Russian ballerina who performed the title role of the *pari*. After the Ballets Russes cancelled the production, she assembled a new team, while also keeping Dukas in the loop and insisting that he conduct the music himself. The production's choreographer was Ivan Clustine (transliterated today as Khlyustin), who had trained in Russia but succeeded in becoming part of the French dance establishment as the master of ballet of the Opera, the same role that had been held by Coralli, the choreographer of Gautier's *La Péri*. One can therefore assume that his choreographic style, in contrast to the sensational Ballets Russes, had found a way to adapt Russian ballet to a French audience. Trouhanova collaborated closely on the choreography, her priority being that it follow Dukas's libretto as closely as possible. Bakst was replaced by French designer René Piot, who rather than inventing a new visual language, chose instead to evoke the setting by imitating Iranian art. The resulting set and costumes look just like a Persian miniature (see Figures 4.3 and 4.4).[43]

The backdrop is a stylized landscape, with mountains and a cypress tree to the left. In the foreground are a tree and a bush in blossom. This directly mimics Persian Safavid miniature's approach to landscape, which tends to combine a stylized and flattened background, against which pop details painted in excruciating detail, most often flowers. The choice of colours (hues of pink and blue) is more unusual, since

Figure 4.3 Trouhanova and Bekefi in *La Péri*, costumes and set by René Piot (1912).
Source: *Comœdia illustré* (24 May 1912): 1.

Figure 4.4 René Piot's set for *La Péri* in a later production of the ballet.

Source: *Comœdia illustré* (1 July 1921): 494.

green would typically predominate in miniature landscape; however, we do find this same combination of colours in miniatures depicting mountain landscapes.[44] This backdrop was framed along the top and along the sides of the stage by rectangular hangings decorated with foliage patterns, in a manner reminiscent of the page margins of illuminated Persian books. The desired effect of this is evident: framed just like a page from a book, this ballet performance is an illustration that has sprung to life. Indeed, the costume design for the character of Eskandar conforms entirely with the male outfits depicted in Safavid-era illustrations of the *Shāhnāmeh*, the work that had introduced the Persian mythology of Alexander in France.[45] He wears a white turban and a long patterned robe, with short sleeves revealing an undershirt of a different colour. Two plumes have been attached to his turban, which is also typical of portraits of Alexander in Persian miniatures from across the ages: because he is never depicted as ethnically distinct from the other characters in the image, the only detail that is ever used to differentiate Alexander from other characters is the addition of two plumes to his headwear – a visual reference to the two plumes that adorned the historical Alexander's Macedonian helmet. Piot's costume design thus depicts the character of Eskandar/Alexander in the exact same way that he had historically been depicted in Iranian art: traditional Iranian clothes (in this case, of the Safavid period) combined with two feathers. As well as being suggestive of a wider desire to provide an element of cultural authenticity to his work – something absent from Bakst's designs – this approach is indicative of Piot's commitment to creating a visual language that matches the language of Dukas's text. What better illustration could there be for a libretto inspired by the *Shāhnāmeh* than a set and costume design inspired by illustrations of the *Shāhnāmeh*? Despite being programmed to run in combination with two other ballets with Oriental settings (as the 1911 production had equally intended to do),[46] the 1912 production of *La Péri* was thus able to retain its own distinct identity: that of a French interpretation of Iranian book culture. As such, it offered audiences a degree of cultural specificity that had eluded Théophile Gautier's *La Péri* and the Ballets Russes' *Schéhérazade* in their pursuit of the worn Orientalist trope of the tyrant in the harem.

Of poets, prophets and kings: French opera's love affair with Iranian men (*Lalla-Roukh, Le Mage* and *Thamara*)

Opera was the most important and popular form of large-scale entertainment in nineteenth-century France and indeed the period is considered the golden age of French opera. I shall be focusing here on three works: *Lalla-Roukh* (1862), *Le Mage* (1891) and *Thamara* (1891), which all centre on a love story between an Iranian man and a woman from a community distinct to his. These operatic treatments of Iran are of particular interest because they combine the widest range of art forms: on top of the textual dimension of the libretto, the visual dimension of set, costume and choreography, and the use of music, all of which we just encountered in ballet, opera also comprises acting and singing. As well as encompassing a wide array of artistic mediums, the operas studied here also showcase the multifaceted nature of French representations of Iran. In these three works alone, we encounter all five of the narratives outlined in the book's introduction, sometimes even in contradiction: the Persia of poetry (*Lalla-Roukh*), ancient Iran as original Other (*Le Mage*), ancient Iran as ancestor (also *Le Mage*), Iran as modern Islamic nation (*Thamara*) and Iran as generic Islamic Orient (all three, to varying extents). A further interesting aspect of these three operas is the fact that they all break with the archetypical Orientalist opera plot as defined by Ralph Locke. Locke argues that Orientalist operas typically feature a white male European character (sung by a tenor) who intrudes into a strange and foreign land where he falls in love with – or is seduced by – a local woman. Their relationship ends tragically, typically because the elders of the woman's community oppose the relationship. These elders (sung by bass or baritone) tend to be depicted as religious fanatics.[47] Locke also suggests that this formula presupposes that the male European character stands for the audience's perspective. The three operas studied here, however, do not include a single European character: the star-crossed lovers are all from Asia. In diverging from the formula outlined by Locke, these operas therefore pose interesting questions: Who is the audience encouraged to identify with – if anyone – if all of the characters are cultural others? Does dispensing with the plot opposition of East and West allow for a more flexible perspective, in which French audience members can identify with any character, be they Iranian, Indian or Uzbek? Or do these operas in fact replace the

East/West binary with new oppositions, as the field of philology had done with the Aryan/Semite binary (see Chapter 2)?

Before delving into these works, we must distinguish between the two different operatic styles into which they fall: *opéra comique* and *grand opéra* (hereafter grand opera), which are guided by different storytelling conventions. *Lalla-Roukh* falls under the former category: it premièred at the Opéra-Comique, a venue primarily dedicated to staging works in French of broad popular, and even family-oriented, appeal, which often meant that these were humorous – though this type of humour should not be confused with the slapstick humour of boulevard theatres. *Opéras comiques* typically had less demanding singing parts than grand operas and could even include spoken sections. Most importantly, the plots of *opéras comiques* would result in a happy outcome. This is in direct contrast to the tragic plots favoured by grand operas such as *Le Mage* and *Thamara*. Grand operas, which were deemed more sophisticated than *opéras comiques*, had their origin in the Gluckist *tragédie lyrique* and were performed at the Paris Opera, an institution which changed its name over time ('Académie nationale de musique' and later 'Théâtre National de l'Opéra'), and also venue: in 1875, its main venue became the especially constructed Palais Garnier, where *Le Mage* and *Thamara* premièred. As well as the differences in music, plot and venue, a further difference was that grand operas were characterized by enormous sets and large crowd scenes, two features that are costly and technically challenging to stage. Over the course of the century, however, these distinctions faded as the productions of the Opéra-Comique began to include increasingly lavish sets and to address increasingly serious themes. *Lalla-Roukh* (1862), the first opera to be analysed here, does possess the ambitious sets and costumes associated with grand opera, as well as an ensemble ballet, but its playful tone and happy ending sit squarely within the traditions of *opéra comique*. The grand operas *Le Mage* (1891) and *Thamara* (1891), in contrast, are both set in the context of a war between the two protagonists' communities, and while in *Le Mage* the two lovers survive, in *Thamara* they both die tragically. This difference in tone may be one of the reasons behind *Lalla-Roukh*'s enduring success: it was still running at the Opéra-Comique in 1891, thirty years after its première, and continued to be performed in the following years, when the more sombre *Le Mage* and *Thamara* were already starting to be forgotten in Paris.[48] But how do these tonal differences manifest in these three works' treatment of Iran? In order to answer this question, I shall be focusing on these operas' characterizations of their male protagonists. Our cast of characters (in order of appearance) is as follows: a king of Timurid descent masquerading as a poor poet, the prophet Zoroaster and a merciless conqueror who proves to be a tender lover.

Michel Carré and Hippolyte Lucas's libretto for *Lalla-Roukh*, which is based on Thomas Moore's prose and verse narrative of the same title,[49] tells the story of the eponymous heroine, a Mughal princess travelling from Delhi to Samarkand, where she is intended to marry the king of Bukhara (the province of which Samarkand is the capital). During the journey, she is seduced by Noureddin, a 'poor poet', who has fallen in love with her and follows her caravan serenading her. This is to the great displeasure of Baskir, the ageing minister who is in charge of ensuring that Lalla-Roukh reaches her betrothed intact (i.e. a virgin). As Baskir, who is more comedic than threatening, tells the audience on multiple occasions: 'C'est moi qui répond du moindre dommage!'

[I am answerable for any damage!].⁵⁰ But Baskir is no match for Noureddin, who plies the guards with wine and lures Baskir himself away with the prospect of a sexual encounter with Lalla-Roukh's maid. The coast is finally clear to Lalla-Roukh's tent. 'O nuit d'amour, nuit parfumée! Nuit d'ivresse et d'enchantement!' [Oh night of love, perfumed night! Night of drunkenness and enchantment!] sings the no longer virginal heroine the following day.⁵¹ When Baskir learns that the damage is done, he tells the young lovers to hold their tongues: better a cuckolded monarch than an angry one. To his great distress, however, Lalla-Roukh insists that she will tell her future husband the truth. All's well that ends well, then, when upon arriving at Samarkand they discover that 'l'humble poète était roi!' [the humble poet was the king!] As Noureddin explains to his beloved: 'Je voulais ne devoir mon bonheur qu'à toi-même! Me pardonneras-tu cette ruse?' [I wanted to owe my happiness only to you! Will you forgive my deceit?] The answer, of course, is: 'Je t'aime'.⁵² Lover and mistress become husband and wife and the threat of sexual impropriety is thus averted through the post hoc sanctification of marriage. This outcome would no doubt have reassured those audience members' whose virtue was offended by the fact that the opera is otherwise a rather overt celebration of female sexuality: as Lalla-Roukh's maid knowingly sings before and during the princess's seduction: 'un vieux roi pour les moins folles ne vaut pas un jeune berger' [an old king, for more sensible women, is nowhere as good as a young shepherd].⁵³ At the same time, it should be noted that despite its sexual content, the opera never descends into bawdy farce: the music throughout remains sophisticated and the love songs and duets between Noureddin and Lalla-Roukh in particular are of a refined sentimentality. These no doubt were the qualities that Berlioz was referring to when he wrote in his review: 'La passion y murmure tendrement et ne rugit point.'⁵⁴ [Passion here murmurs tenderly, it does not roar.] In the context of this chapter, in which we shall meet altogether less pleasant kings than *Lalla-Roukh's* Noureddin, it is also worth noting that the other threat averted by the opera's resolution is that of the jealous Oriental despot-cum-husband, a figure introduced into French popular culture by the *Mille et Une Nuits*, the inciting incident of which, as we saw above, is King Shahryar's decision to execute his wives rather than live with the risk of infidelity. *Lalla-Roukh* subverts this trope by turning the feared figure of the Persian king into a tender and playful young lover.

The increasing popularity of Persian poetry in France at the time that the opera was written certainly played an important part in its positive treatment of desire, and also provided a context from which French audience members, such as Berlioz, could apprehend it. By writing that *Lalla-Roukh* transports him 'au pays des roses, […] où Bulbul, le chantre ailé des nuits, s'épuise en soupirs mélodieux' [to the land of roses, […] where Bolbol, the winged singer of the night, exhausts himself in melodious sighs], Berlioz is making a reference to the Persian poetic trope of the rose and the nightingale, in Persian '*Gol o bolbol*' (which is also the title of a section in Armand Renaud's *Les Nuits persanes*, see Chapter 1).⁵⁵ The fact that neither Berlioz nor his editor felt the need to gloss the term 'Bulbul' is indicative of how familiar the Parisian cultural elite was with Persian literature. Appreciation for *Lalla-Roukh* however went far beyond the intelligentsia. The morning after the première, throngs of people crowded the box office, spilling out into the Opéra-Comique's corridors and even the surrounding neighbourhood, to vie over the remaining seats. One journalist described the victorious among them brandishing their tickets in the air, while the losers 'les mains dans leurs poches et la tête inclinée, s'en allaient tristement, déçus et irrités' [left sadly, their hands in their pockets and their heads hanging low, dejected and annoyed].[56] Although the setting of *Lalla-Roukh* was foreign to nineteenth-century Parisians, it was at the same time familiar and recognizable to many among them as the idealized Orient of Persian poetry. The seed for this association was in fact sown in the opera's opening aria which announces to the audience 'C'est ici le pays des roses' [this is the land of roses]. These roses could only be those of Sa'di and Hāfez, which had featured prominently in such recent poems as Marceline Desbordes-Valmore's 'Les roses de Saadi' (1860) and Théophile Gautier's 'Préface' (1852), which includes the line 'comme Goethe [...] d'Hafiz effeuillait les roses' [like Goethe [...] plucked the roses of Hāfez] (see Chapter 1). Though set in the seventeenth century, the opera in fact harks back to the age of these poets through its association with the Timurid Empire (fourteenth-century Iran). The characters are travelling to Samarkand, which was the capital of this empire, immortalized in Hāfez's famous 'Shirazi Turk' ghazal. Moreover, the opera's male protagonist Noureddin is a fictional descendent of the Timurid kings who once ruled over Sa'di and Hāfez. The opera's heroine Lalla-Roukh, whose name means 'tulip-cheeked' in Persian, is a fictional Mughal princess and therefore an Indian native speaker of Persian. The choice is unusual for the French context, where Persian-ness is typically understood through the lenses of geography and ethnicity, rather than language. It is, however, symptomatic of the source text's English context: British writers and intellectuals were introduced to the Persian language and, most importantly, to classical Persian literature not in Iran, but in India. For them, then, Persian literature was not primarily tied to a place, but to a language and written style. It is this language and style that are emblematized by the character of Noureddin, the king masquerading as a poet, whose 'Persian-ness' is foregrounded in the operatic adaptation in a manner that it had not been in Thomas Moore's work.

In Moore's *Lalla Rookh* (1817), the character of Noureddin, who is not called Noureddin but 'Feramorz', is a storyteller. Moore adopts the structure of the *Thousand and One Nights*, but reverses the gender roles: he uses the narrative of Lalla-Roukh's journey as a frame for four tales narrated by Feramorz, who wins the princess's heart through his storytelling talent, just as Scheherazade wins over Shahryar. By transforming Feramorz into Noureddin, the French opera replaces the storyteller with a poet. This alteration serves the conceit of opera, since lyric poetry is better suited to being sung than prose narrative. Further to this practical function, it also conjures by association the world of Persian poetry. Indeed, Noureddin's songs speak of the poet's love for an unavailable woman and draw heavily on the beauty of the natural world, in particular, flowers and birds, themes which French writers considered emblematic of Persian lyric poetry.[57] Noureddin's association with Persian poetry is further bolstered in the opera by the choice of an overtly Islamic name for him, literally: 'the light of religion', *din* being the Arabic word for religion, which appears seventy-nine times in the Quran. As well as marking the protagonist as Muslim, the name Noureddin may also be intended as an homage to the medieval poet Nur ed-Din 'Abd al-Rahmān Jāmi, who had lived under the Timurid Empire and was the author of *Leyli o Majnun*, a narrative poem in Persian about a man who falls madly in love with a woman whom he is not able to marry.[58] It is my contention that the opera's association of its male protagonist with the world of Persian poetry serves to cast him in a positive light, since this literary Orient was highly prized and idealized by the French public. Indeed, although the character's actions are not particularly honourable (he is effectively manipulating a young woman into sleeping with him outside of wedlock), the opera portrays him as a romantic hero, both through his words, which suggest that he is madly in love with Lalla-Roukh, and musically, by having the character sung by a tenor, the register typically reserved for the hero of the opera.

Neither Noureddin's nor Lalla-Roukh's singing parts, nor the music that accompanies these, feature Oriental markers. This musical approach in combination with the fact that the libretto is in French, results in songs and duets that have nothing foreign or exotic about them, aside from the odd reference to the region's geography. Oriental markers do crop up, however, in the parts sung by Lalla-Roukh's Indian retinue, as well as the instrumental music that accompanies them.[59] The opera establishes that Lalla-Roukh's entourage is Hindu: she is escorted by a troupe of *bayadères* (the French term for *devadasi*s, Hindu temple dancers) and her protector Baskir prays to Brahma. By association, then, this creates the impression that Lalla-Roukh herself shares the same religion – which would be historically inaccurate given that the character is a Mughal princess. This adds a cross-faith dimension to the love story: she is a Hindu; he is a Muslim. The addition is entirely the work of the French librettists: in Moore's text, the character of Baskir is not Hindu but 'a good Mussulman' named 'Fadlaheen'. In renaming Feramorz *Noureddin* (pronounced Noor-ed-deen) and renaming Fadlaheen *Baskir*, Carré and Lucas have thus swapped which character has the most Islamic sounding name, thereby associating Islam not with the grotesque warden who offers comic relief, but with the opera's alluring male romantic lead. This in itself is an interesting decision, since it runs counter to the widespread Islamophobia of French Orientalism: typically, the ancient Asian faiths (namely, Zoroastrianism, Hinduism and Buddhism) were depicted in far more positive terms than Islam.[60] The opera's creation of a religious distinction between Noureddin and Lalla-Roukh's entourage, however, becomes even more interesting when we consider it in light of Locke's formula for Orientalist opera plots, summarized above. According to this model, Noureddin effectively fulfils the role typically reserved for the male European character: a romantic hero sung by a tenor who is an outsider to the woman's community, and is opposed by one of her elders (Baskir), who is religious and sung by a baritone. But in *Lalla-Roukh*, this sympathetic male hero is not European, but a Muslim descendent of the Timurids. This suggests that according to the librettists, at least, the Islamic Persianate world was more culturally sympathetic to French audiences than Hindu India. Indeed, the minor characters of the *bayadères* and Baskir function as exotic and comedic foils to Noureddin, making him all the more relatable, much in the same way as non-European characters in most Orientalist works typically work to cast the European heroes in a more positive light. The growing popularity of Persian poetry among French readers must have played an important part in Lucas and Carré's decision to make their hero Persian and Muslim, and to present him as culturally closer to the audience than the opera's Indian characters. Of course, Locke's analysis is formulated on the basis of grand operas, which have tragic endings. In *Lalla-Roukh*, all is well that ends well, and the cultural differences between the two lovers are never an issue. Not so with *Le Mage* and *Thamara*, two grand operas that centre on the conflict between following one's heart and remaining loyal to one's people.

Jules Massenet and Jean Richepin's *Le Mage* (1891) is a grand opera loosely based on the life of the prophet Zoroaster (Zarathustra),[61] a subject which had already inspired Rameau's eighteenth-century opera *Zoroastre* and Nietzsche's *Also sprach Zarathustra*.[62] Much like these two other treatments of the figure of Zoroaster, this is a work of fiction: the only historical element in the opera is the fact that the title character is the Iranian founder of a new religion. Richepin's inaccurate portrayal of Zoroastrianism is exemplified by his choice to name the woman that Zoroaster falls in love with 'Anahita', which is the name of an ancient Iranian goddess, effectively confusing the names of humans and of deities in an opera ... about religion. The historical Zoroaster was a priest who reformed the ancient polytheistic religion of Iran (which shared many parallels with early Hinduism) by arguing that the God Ahura Mazda ('the Wise Lord') had created all other deities, ruled over them and was alone worthy of worship. Zoroaster also viewed the world as a conflict between a good principle (embodied by Ahura Mazda) and an evil principle (embodied by the deity Angra Manyu or Ahriman). According to him, the world would end on a final day of judgement, when the earth would be swallowed in a sea of molten metal, which would destroy those who had followed 'the lie' (i.e. the evil principle) and spare those who had followed the truth. Zoroaster's eschatology and single supreme God thus share important parallels with the Abrahamic faiths. In Richepin's libretto, Zoroaster is an Iranian military general who, after being rejected by his king and the woman whom he loves, goes into exile. During his time in exile, he becomes the prophet of a new religion which bears a striking resemblance to Christianity. As I will demonstrate, *Le Mage* greatly exaggerates the commonalities between Zoroastrianism and Christianity, with the ultimate aim of presenting the character of Zoroaster as a proto-Christian proselytizer. As such, it presents a powerful illustration of the dangers of the paradigm of similarity. Richepin is not balancing a set of commonalities and differences, he is erasing the differences between Zoroastrianism and Christianity.[63] This serves to align the protagonist's perspective with that of the audience, thereby appropriating Zoroaster as a proto-Western civilizer of backward Orientals. The opera's other two Iranian male characters are, in turn, portrayed according to the most tried and tested clichés of Orientalism, the better to set them up as foils to Zoroaster.

The plot of *Le Mage* hinges on two conflicts: the external military conflict between Iran and Touran (a central Asian kingdom situated north of Iran) and the internal religious conflict between Iran's old polytheistic religion and the new religion promulgated by Zoroaster. The first conflict takes the form of the improbable love story between Zoroaster, the general who defeated the Touranian forces, and Anahita, the captive queen of Touran. Anahita tells Zoroaster that a proud and savage woman such as her cannot love in servitude.[64] Anahita's conflict between patriotism and love is resolved in the final act when her soldiers storm her (forced) wedding to the king of Iran and massacre all the Iranians in the temple. Re-enthroned and with the agency to choose whom to love, Anahita is finally ready to requite Zoroaster's feelings. It is now her turn to seduce Zoroaster by telling him to forget that she has just vanquished his people. This love story between two former military enemies is interwoven with the story of the conflict between Zoroaster and the leader of the old religion: the magus Amrou, who is set on punishing Zoroaster for falling in love with Anahita instead of marrying his daughter. Amrou is a corrupt figure who does not hesitate to call on the *daevas* (the ancient deities rejected by the Zoroastrian faith) to harm Zoroaster. The opera's representation of Amrou's religion is crafted to be both morally abhorrent and deeply titillating to a modern French audience: it includes sex rituals, the consumption of *haoma* and forced marriage.[65] The conflict between the two magi is also resolved in the final act when a miracle proves that Zoroaster's God is the one true God. Zoroaster is the sole protagonist of this opera and is presented in an incontrovertibly heroic light: successful in battle, vulnerable in love, retaining his pride and dignity even after a calumnious accusation turns the king against him and taking a stand against an immoral and evil religion. He is sung, naturally, by a tenor. He represents the future, and this future sounds very Christian.

After leaving the Iranian court at the end of Act II, Zoroaster retires to the mountains, where we find him in Act III preaching to his followers. He informs them that Ahura Mazda Himself has spoken to him on the mountain top: 'Le Dieu terrible a répondu. / Sur mon front éperdu / Je sens encore le souffle de son Verbe' [The terrible God answered. / On my confounded brow / I still feel the breath of his Word].[66] This sentence is clearly intended to echo John 1:1 ('In the beginning was the Word'), which in the French Sacy Bible reads 'Au commencement était le Verbe, et le Verbe était avec Dieu; et le Verbe était Dieu.'. Zoroaster's language in fact becomes even more biblical in the sermon that follows, which combines the Christian ideology of eternal reward after death with a turn of phrase borrowed from the famous Sermon on the Mount of Matthew 5: 'Blessed are the poor in spirit: for theirs is the kingdom of heaven.' Zoroaster's sermon reads as follows:

> Heureux celui dont la vie
>   Pour le bien aura lutté toujours!
>   Car son âme est ravie
>   Au bonheur éternel des célestes séjours.
>   Les douleurs qu'il eut sur la terre
>   Lui deviendront là-haut des voluptés sans fin.[67]
> [Blessed is he who devoted his life / to fighting for good! For his soul is taken to the eternal beatitude of the heavenly abode / The sorrow he had on this earth / There will become eternal joy.]

And in case this stylistic parallel was not sufficient, the set for Act III depicts the base of a mountain, thereby establishing a clear visual reference to Christ's Sermon on the Mount. By Christianizing Zoroaster, Richepin makes him stand for a positive ancient Iran that is religiously close to the West. This Christianized/Westernized Iran has as its foil the negative ancient Iran embodied by the opera's two other Iranian male characters: the king and the old magus Amrou. This opposition between the old powers and the new religion, which is already strong in the libretto, is further emphasized by the allocation of the male singing parts: whereas Zoroaster is a tenor, these two characters are sung by a bass and a baritone.

The character of the king, whose costume is evocative of Assyrian and Achaemenid images of kingship,[68] corresponds to a timeless trope: the enamoured (or sex-crazed) Oriental despot. Upon discovering how beautiful Zoroaster's beloved Anahita is, the king decides he must have her for himself. This escalates to a prurient forced marriage scene, during which Anahita protests: 'Non, non je ne veux pas. Non, jamais!' [No, no, I do not want to. No, never!] To which the king responds: 'Va, tu seras à moi quand même! [...] Tu méprisas mes pleurs; connais donc mon pouvoir. / Je suis le Maître et je t'aime! / Prêtre, fais ton devoir!'[69] [No matter, you will be mine anyway! [...] You despised my tears; now you shall know my power. / I am the Master and I love you! / Priest, perform your duty.] As the king's sordid enabler, the magus Amrou, in turn, falls under another Orientalist stereotype: the evil vizier, who also happens to be the leader of a corrupt religion. Amrou himself openly admits that his religion is pure evil, calling the deities whom he worships: 'Dévas terribles et sombres, Dieux de la ruse et des ombres' [Terrible, dark Daevas, Gods of cunning and of the shadows].[70] The set for Amrou's temple functions as a powerful visual manifestation of this religion: 'L'endroit est ténébreux et sinistre, moitié salle, moitié caverne, avec ses piliers énormes et informes taillés à même le roc.'[71] [The place is dark and sinister, half hall, half cave, with its enormous and formless pillars cut out of the live rock.] Not only is this religion dark and sinister, but it is so primitive that it is being practised in a cave. We are worlds apart from the architectural sophistication of ancient Iran, plunged instead in an Orientalist fantasy where everything about the East, be it religion, morality or architecture, is by definition inferior to the West. The tall svelte pillars of Persepolis have been swapped for crude monoliths.[72]

The climax of this Orientalist fantasy of a primitive and barbaric Iran is the scene of the forced marriage between Anahita and the king, quoted above. The ceremony includes a ballet entitled 'Les mystères de la Djahi' [The mysteries of Jahi], which combines whirling (an Islamic mystical practice), the consumption of *haoma* and a sexual initiation in which a woman is brought to orgasm by another woman.[73] The music introducing this ballet is extremely menacing: it has neither a clear pulse, nor tonality, and thus deprives the audience of any sense of structure or context. This has the effect of placing the listener in a precarious position, the better to assail them with the loud sounds of crashing cymbals and ominous long unison notes played on low register brass, as well as a strident chorus cry of 'Djahi! Djahi!'[74] To further disorientate his audience, Massenet deploys these instruments spatially, so that the sound veers from the orchestra pit (from which the opening unison notes are played), to the brass and cymbal complement, which move location during the performance of the piece: the stage direction first places them on stage behind a curtain, and then off stage, in the wings. The chorus is equally hidden from sight, the stage direction describing it as 'invisible'.[75] The spatial movement of the sound, comparable to the use of stereophonic effects in contemporary music yet far more overwhelming by virtue of being performed by a live orchestra, in combination with the unstable pulse and tonality of the music, would have been terrifying to a nineteenth-century audience unaccustomed to such effects. The orgiastic character of this 'ballet' was further exaggerated by the costumes that Charles Bianchini designed for the female dancers who performed it, which fully expose the breasts.[76] The most surprising among these designs, which otherwise resemble fin de siècle depictions of Bacchantes in the style of Mucha (floor-length dresses, wreathes of flowers in the hair, no veil), is an outfit copied from an illustration in Jane Dieulafoy's *La Perse, la Chaldée et la Susiane*, a travelogue analysed in Chapter 3 (see Figures 4.5a and 4.5b).[77]

The drawing shows a woman wearing an Islamic veil, a jacket and a knee-length skirt typical of Qajar fashion, except for the detail that she wears no shirt, leaving her breasts partially exposed. Bianchini clearly intended for this design to be legible as a visual 'citation': the woman not only wears the exact same clothes, down to the flowers over her two ears and decorative sleeves, but strikes the exact same pose as the woman in the Dieulafoy illustration, left breast exposed, left hip jutting out, right knee bent and right hand nonchalantly carrying a bouquet of flowers. Did Bianchini believe this reference to Dieulafoy's travel-writing lent his designs an aura of 'authenticity'? The suggestion is laughable given that the opera is set two and a half millennia prior to Dieulafoy's travels in Iran – and that is even without going into the fact that there exist serious doubts with regard to the authenticity of the illustration itself.[78] Moreover, Bianchini did not dress any of the opera's male characters in Qajar styles, but chose instead a combination of Persepolitan-inspired designs for the king and ancient Greek-inspired designs for the Iranian soldiers. This was an opera clearly intended – however inaccurately – to be set in antiquity. I venture that it was the illustration's combination of an Islamic veil with exposed breasts that drew Bianchini to it. The inclusion of this veiled woman, much like the choreography's inclusion of whirling, serves to create a visual analogy between the opera's barbaric ancient religion and the Islamic faith. In other words, just as Zoroastrianism in this opera is a proxy for Christianity, so is Amrou's evil (and entirely imaginary) religion a proxy for Islam. For all its use of an Iranian protagonist, then, *Le Mage* works to cast both ancient pre-Islamic Iran and, through its visual language, modern Islamic Iran as a dangerous and primitive Other. Zoroaster may be the hero of the story, but he is also the exception that confirms the rule. The opera even ends with him renouncing Iran, for as he tells Anahita, in order to love her, he would have to forget: 'Ces ruines!... Ces morts!... Ma patrie abolie!' [These ruins!... these dead!... My homeland abolished!].[79] The word *abolie* is rather an overstatement: Anahita's army has killed the king of Iran and his retinue, but this does not exactly amount to wiping Iran off the map. And yet, that is precisely how Zoroaster interprets Anahita's rebellion. The fact that the opera ends with the two of them walking away, arm in arm, leaving the corpses of the other Iranians to burn along with the old temple could not be more clear: Zoroaster has chosen Anahita over his country. More implicitly, this ending also suggests that those who will be most receptive to his teachings are not to be found in Iran, but abroad. How great a leap would it have been for the audience to understand from this that Zoroaster's true descendants were not Iranian Muslims, but European Christians, whose religion is the ultimate monotheism and therefore the true realization of Zoroaster's teachings?

In profound contrast to *Le Mage*, which provides us with a rather dualist vision of a 'good' proto-Western Iran and a 'bad' Orientalized Iran, *Thamara*'s originality lies in its combination of positive and negative traits within one single character: King

198 Iran and French Orientalism

Figure 4.5a Charles Bianchini's costume design for a female 'slave' (*Le Mage*, 1891).

Source: 'Le Mage: soixante-sept maquettes de costume' (1891), BNF, département Bibliothèque-musée de l'opéra, D216-46 [ark:/12148/btv1b8455869r], folio 56.

Figure 4.5b 'Ziba Khanoum', illustration from Jane Dieulafoy's travelogue.
Source: Jane Dieulafoy, *La Perse, la Chaldée, et la Susiane* (Paris: Hachette, 1887), 271.

Noureddin, who is not to be confused with the male protagonist of the same name in *Lalla-Roukh*. Louis Gallet, who was one of the most prolific librettists of the fin de siècle, first published 'Thamara' as a short story in *La Nouvelle Revue*, before adapting it for the stage in 1891.[80] The short story's detailed references to architecture, specifically the Fire Temple of Baku (famous for having its flames fed directly by the oil reserves beneath it) and the 'palais des Khans' [palace of the Khans] situates the events in the second half of the eighteenth century, when following the collapse of the Safavid Empire, Baku became a vassal of Iran ruled by local feudal lords (Khans), until increasing Russian incursions led to its annexation by the Russian Empire in the early nineteenth century.[81] In Gallet's narrative, Baku has rebelled against its Iranian overlords, and so the king of Iran himself is leading a siege on the city, determined that Baku shall either submit to his rule or be wiped off the face of the earth. Thamara, a young virgin who serves as a priestess in the fire temple of Baku, becomes the city's hero when she accepts a perilous mission to stop the invader. The events of the story are entirely fictional: the Khans of Baku were allowed to rule semi-independently and therefore had no need to rebel against Iran; moreover, there was no Safavid ruler of the name of 'Noureddin'. By choosing this name, Gallet is therefore signalling from the outset that he is combining a historical setting with fictional characters and events. That said, Noureddin's characterization as a merciless conqueror does place him in the lineage of one real Iranian king: Nader Shah (ruled 1736–47), the fierce leader who united Iran after the fall of the Safavids and reconquered lost territory. As Junko Thérèse Takeda has shown, Nader Shah's French contemporaries deeply admired him for having 'reconciled domestic revolution with imperial expansion', an achievement that made him a role model for Napoleon Bonaparte.[82]

When the opera opens, Baku has been under siege from Noureddin's army for months; its people are dying of hunger and its soldiers are out of ammunition. Desperate times call for desperate measures, and so the city's elders decide to send Thamara, the most beautiful maid in the city, to seduce and then murder the fierce conqueror. If Thamara's fierce patriotism would have reminded French audiences of their own female national hero Joan of Arc, the method adopted to save the city points to an Old Testament source: the apocryphal story of Judith and Holofernes. Thamara accepts her mission in a dialogue that reads like a pastiche of a wedding ceremony. The priest asks: 'Noble fille, / Veux-tu venger ton peuple, ta famille, / Délivrer ton pays / Le veux-tu?' [Noble girl, / Will you avenge your people, your family, / And deliver your country, / Do you want to?]. Thamara responds: 'Je le veux!' [I do!].[83] This after all is a wedding of sorts, since she will be losing her virginity. The audience has yet to lay eyes on the character of Noureddin, but the words sung by the chorus of the people of Baku paint a damning picture. They warn Thamara:

> Sur le sultan au repoussant visage
>   Immonde et noir
>   Sur l'être brutal et sauvage
>   Quel sera ton pouvoir?
>   Que pourront ta beauté, ta grâce,
>   Sur ce monstre un seul moment?

[Over this sultan whose repulsive face / is disgusting and dark / Over this brutal savage / What will your power be? / What will your beauty and grace be capable of / Against this monster, for even a moment?].[84]

Heroic and inspired, Thamara responds that she will slay Noureddin no matter what: 'Il tombera le colosse puissant / Il nous paiera de tout son sang' [The powerful giant will fall / And will pay with all his blood].[85] Thamara's language paints her mission as an act of both personal and public revenge: this man has sowed destruction on her people and must therefore pay for it with his life. It is with this promise that Act I ends, and the action moves to the oblivious Noureddin's camp.

We meet Noureddin before Thamara does, in the classic pose of the Oriental despot: reclined on Persian carpets and cushions, surrounded by dancing women.[86] Much like the character of Achmet in Gautier's *La Péri* (see above), Noureddin is not satisfied with the pleasures of the harem and has begun to long for a truer love. In fact, he has just woken from a dream in which he saw a beautiful woman walking towards him. Noureddin's song, as he describes this dream vision, is heavily tainted by the lexical field of death: the woman is 'd'une beauté fatale' [of a fatal beauty], her eyes are 'profonds comme la nuit' [deep as the night], night being a common metaphor for death, her skin is 'd'une pâleur mortelle' [of a deathly pallor] and her lips are red like blood, the latter simile, of course, echoing Thamara's promise to spill Noureddin's blood.[87] Noureddin's vision ends with the woman – whom the audience knows to be Thamara – kissing him and, in the same moment, his soul departing from his body.[88] And so, before Thamara even enters Noureddin's tent, we know what is to come: she has promised to kill him and she will most likely succeed, since her victim has already had a premonition of his impending death. But lest we should feel too sorry for Noureddin, the libretto is prompt to remind us of his violent nature. Thamara's entrance is preceded by that of a messenger who informs Noureddin that Baku is not surrendering, despite being deprived of food and water. Noureddin first responds with 'nonchalance',[89] that if they will not surrender, then they will have to die. This nonchalance however soon gives way to a 'joie féroce' [ferocious joy], as Noureddin becomes increasingly riled up:

> Tes soldats tous! tes enfants et tes femmes
>   Je les exterminerai!
>   Leurs cadavres sanglants combleront nos tranchées [...]
>   À la place où demain, brouteront les troupeaux
>   Rien ne dira sinon un souffle d'épouvante
>   Qu'une cité fut là vivante.[90]
>   [All your soldiers! All your children and women, I shall exterminate them! / Their bloody corpses will fill our trenches. [...] / Tomorrow in the same place cattle will graze, / And nothing but a gust of fear / Will tell that there once was a living city there.]

Noureddin may have had a premonition of his death, but he is still a bloodthirsty killer. By the time Thamara enters his tent, we have thus been shown two sides to him: Noureddin as a victim of his love for Thamara and Noureddin as a cruel tyrant.

This double identity will become a key theme in the scenes that follow, leaving the audience unsure as to who between the sacrificial virgin and the assassination target is the real victim.

Upon meeting Thamara, it is Noureddin's soft side that prevails. The musical directions accompanying his song to Thamara indicate that his tone is '*très doux*' [very sweet],[91] and '*amoureux*' [loving],[92] which is in marked contrast to the 'imperious' tone employed towards his soldiers and his concubines.[93] It is as though love makes him a different man. Specifically, it robs him of his power as a terrible conqueror: 'Contre elle je voudrais vainement me défendre / Un mot m'a désarmé' [Against her I am defenceless, / She has disarmed me with one word].[94] And with an even more playful use of military language, he later declares: 'Thamara je subis ton empire' [Thamara I am under your empire].[95] In the French language, being under someone or something's 'empire' is a set phrase for being under its control, as with 'to be under someone's spell' in English. But in the context of the story, Noureddin's declaration also functions as an inversion of the political relationship between Iran (the imperial power) and Baku (the vassal state). Thamara too forms a favourable impression of Noureddin: 'Ma haine le voyait monstrueux et farouche' [My hatred made him monstrous and fierce], she sings, but instead she finds that he is 'jeune et clément' [young and clement].[96] Not only that, but Noureddin is handsome and sung by a tenor, which signals his status as the story's romantic hero.[97] The scene thus reveals the true conflict of the opera: that waged in Thamara's heart between patriotism and her personal attraction to the enemy – a theme that was also present in *Le Mage*. This conflict is only heightened when Noureddin declares his feelings to her: 'je t'aime / Le reste est vain! / Oui n'aurais-je à vivre qu'une heure dans tes bras / Oui, je dirais toujours: que je meure! […] je t'aime' [I love you, / the rest is vain! / Yes, if I only had one hour to live in your arms, / Yes I would still say: may I die! […] I love you].[98] By telling Thamara that he would willingly die for her love, Noureddin makes her even more averse to killing him. And so she forms an alternative plan: if she can convince Noureddin to spare her people, then she will not have to go through the pain of murdering the man with whom she has just fallen in love.

The plan is short-lived. At the first mention of mercy, Noureddin's entire demeanour changes: he becomes '[s]ubitement farouche' [suddenly fierce] – the very adjective that had been used by the people of Baku to warn Thamara against him – and 'cruel'.[99]

> J'ai dit que je t'aimais
>   Mais la vengeance encor plus que l'amour m'est chère
>   J'en ai fait le serment Bakou ne sera plus qu'un sépulcre fumant
>   C'est juré par Allah![100]
>   [I said that I loved you / But revenge is more dear to me than love / I swore that Baku would be nothing more than a smouldering sepulchre / It was sworn by Allah!]

Noureddin's dark side never vanished: it was merely dormant. It is also in this same moment that the religious difference between the two characters is reasserted: whereas Thamara is Zoroastrian, Noureddin is Muslim, and he will not break a promise made before his God, just as Thamara cannot abandon the mission with which she was invested by the priest of Baku. In *Lalla-Roukh* and *Le Mage*, the cultural differences between the lovers were ultimately either negligible or surmountable, but in *Thamara*, they are fatal. Upon learning that Noureddin will not change his mind, Thamara returns to her original plan to seduce him and then murder him, but not without some reticence. Ultimately, Act II ends not with Thamara seducing Noureddin, but Noureddin seducing her. What adds even greater tension to this seduction scene is that Thamara's resistance to Noureddin's sexual advances is born not from horror but from desire. She loves him and wants him, and this makes her fear intercourse all the more because she knows that it is the first stage in a plan that ends with his death. This is indeed what happens in Act III where Thamara chooses to follow her patriotic duty and murders Noureddin in his sleep.

Whereas in *Le Mage* there had been a clear distinction between the hero (the prophet Zoroaster) and the villains (the king of Iran and the magus Amrou), there is a certain level of ambiguity in *Thamara*. For if Noureddin is monstrous for wanting to destroy Baku, what of Thamara, who murders her lover in his sleep? Her actions are explicitly motivated by patriotism, which in the French fin de siècle context makes them heroic and selfless. But the manner of Noureddin's death also invites sympathy for him, since he does not die as a tyrant, but as a man made vulnerable by love. This ambivalence comes all the more to the fore if we return to Locke's paradigm for Orientalist opera. On the one hand, Thamara corresponds to the figure of the (proto-)Western protagonist who intrudes in an Oriental world and is seduced by a local, though of course in Gallet's libretto this premise is gender-flipped. On the other hand, Thamara is an Asian woman who instrumentalizes her sex appeal to murder an unarmed man. As well as the patriotic Judith, Thamara also resembles the rather less heroic biblical characters of Delilah and Salome, who in the fin de siècle were popular symbols of woman as a hyper-sexual, savage and destructive being. So is Thamara a freedom fighter or a *femme fatale*? And who is the real victim in this story: her or Noureddin?

Ultimately, both characters are victims of their love for one another. Unable to live with the fact that she killed the man whom she loved, Thamara commits suicide in the opera's final act, using the very same dagger with which she struck Noureddin. Her final words are: 'Je viens à toi!' [I'm coming to you], gesturing towards an afterlife in which their two souls might be reunited, irrespective of their different religious faiths.[101] Thus, although Gallet presents Thamara as a hero who will stop at nothing to save her city, he also highlights the waste and vanity of war: these two young people could have been happy together had they met in a different time and place; instead, ancestral enmities lead to their tragic deaths. Approached in this way, the opera becomes not a celebration of patriotism, but an Asian Romeo and Juliet. These two possible interpretations are contained within the single character of Noureddin: a tyrant worth slaying and a sensitive lover. Noureddin's ambivalence as a character is symptomatic of nineteenth-century French culture's wider ambivalence towards Iran. Just as Iran was viewed as both part of the Islamic Orient and also distinct from it, so does Noureddin both conform to and challenge Orientalist stereotypes. Gallet shows such stereotypes to be false by following the people of Baku's description of Noureddin as a 'dark monster' with Thamara's altogether different impression of him: 'son front charmant et pâle / A la pureté d'un beau jour / Son souffle parfumé s'exhale / Doux comme une plainte d'amour' [his charming and pale forehead / Has the purity of a bright day, / His perfumed breath is exhaled / As sweetly as a love lament].[102] This overt contrast between Thamara's expectations, which are based on prejudice, and her real-life encounter with Noureddin is a bold statement on Gallet's behalf, since it illustrates the limits of stereotypes. But while Noureddin is not a 'dark monster', he does nonetheless conform to the cliché of the Oriental despot: merciless in war and sensual in the harem, making Thamara tremble with fear and delight with declarations such as: 'Nour Eddin va t'aimer comme il n'aima jamais' [Noureddin is going to love you like he has never loved before].[103]

Noureddin's faith in Islam is the greatest source of difference between him and Thamara and, by extension, the audience: it is what makes him both polygynous and inflexibly committed to destroying Baku. Indeed, from the outset of the opera, the audience is encouraged to identify with the people of Baku: we learn of their suffering at the hands of their Persian aggressors and view them as the underdogs of the story. Moreover, as was shown with *Le Mage*, Zoroastrianism had positive associations in nineteenth-century French culture and was viewed as a precursor of Christianity. The reasons for this were mainly racial: Zoroastrianism was considered an Aryan religion, in contrast to Islam which scholars such as Ernest Renan had presented as a Semitic religion (see Chapter 2). This racialist ideology is not foregrounded in Gallet's libretto; however, it did inform Bourgault-Ducoudray's composition. As Peter Asimov has shown, the musical score of *Thamara* associates Zoroastrianism with Aryanism by drawing upon the Greek modes that Bourgault-Ducoudray was famous for transcribing and introducing to the wider French fin de siècle music community, modes which Bourgault-Ducoudray believed were the shared heritage of the world's various Aryan peoples, which included the French. Indeed, Asimov even identifies Thamara's final song in the opera as a rearrangement of a 'Greek melody' that Bourgault-Ducoudray had published fifteen years earlier.[104] Yet, although Noureddin follows Islam, which is considered a 'Semitic' faith, he is also ethnically Persian. This means that, in nineteenth-century racialist terms, he is just as Aryan as Thamara and the opera's modern French audience are. The Aryan myth thus only adds to the ambivalence of Noureddin and, by extension, Iran. Indeed, I believe that Noureddin embodies an image of Iran that is amenable and even lovable – as experienced by Thamara who goes from being fearful to pleasantly surprised, to madly in love – yet whose faith in Islam is also profoundly alienating. This is something that we previously encountered in travel-writing, where Islam tends to be viewed as the greatest source of cultural difference between France and Iran.[105] Yet, in *Thamara*, Islam is also a powerful aphrodisiac. If Noureddin is irresistible to Thamara, it is in great part because he is vastly more sexually experienced than her and therefore knows exactly how to make her experience 'l'extase inconnue' [unknown ecstasy].[106] Noureddin therefore speaks to a French idea of Iran as a profoundly seductive Other: an Orient that one cannot live with and yet cannot live without.

I opened this section by observing that the three operas studied do not conform to Locke's paradigm for Orientalist opera, since none of them centre on a male European protagonist. A closer examination, however, revealed that rather than dispensing entirely with this model, the use of Iranian characters allowed librettists to innovate within it. Indeed, both *Lalla-Roukh* and *Le Mage* follow Locke's formula with the difference that the role traditionally reserved for a European character (the brave romantic outsider with whom the audience identifies) is given to an Iranian character.[107] In *Lalla-Roukh* it is the Indian characters who become exotic foils to the Iranian protagonist; in *Le Mage* it is an Orientalized Iran, embodied by the characters of the king and the magus Amrou, that acts as a foil to the Christianized (and thus Westernized) Iran embodied by Zoroaster. What emerges here is that even when all characters in an opera are cultural others to France, there are still hierarchies in place. The presentation of Iran as a sympathetic Orient in French opera is thus mainly achieved through the emulation of the systemic binaries of Orientalism, as was the case in historiography with its reliance on the Aryan/Semite binary, and travel-writing with its frequent comparisons between the Persians and the Arabs or Turks. The opera that complicates these binaries the most is *Thamara*, since it combines both positive and negative traits within one single Iranian character, who does not function as a surrogate for the West, but as an Islamic Other. Although Gallet relies on two archetypal figures (the Oriental despot and the sacrificial virgin), he reinvigorates these tropes through ambiguity, inner conflict and shifting power dynamics. By portraying King Noureddin as dangerous, vulnerable and seductive, Gallet manages to both conform to Orientalist stereotype and leave some room for doubt, something that may well have resonated with French audiences who were enthusiastic about Iranian culture, while also remaining deeply suspicious of Islam.

A puppet play about Omar Khayyām (Maurice Bouchor)

The nineteenth century may have been the apogee of French opera, but Parisian audiences were not always after such pomp and grandeur. A tiny Iran could prove just as intriguing as the spectacular sets of *Lalla-Roukh*, *Thamara* and *Le Mage*. In this section I will be considering what is, from a contemporary perspective, the oddest work in my corpus: a highbrow puppet play about Omar Khayyām, which – going by the reviews – was considered one of the highlights of the Parisian cultural scene. But how was it that puppetry became regarded as high art? And why should the eleventh-century Persian poet, mathematician and astronomer Omar Khayyām have been selected for this avant-garde medium? These are the questions that I shall be addressing before taking a closer look at the treatment of Khayyām's quatrains in Maurice Bouchor's *Le Songe de Khèyam* (premièred 1892).

Founded in 1888 by marionette-maker Henri Signoret and a company of poets, the Petit-Théâtre de la Galerie Vivienne had one simple mission: to use the medium of puppetry to stage 'des ouvrages dramatiques de très haute valeur, que l'on ne connaît que par la lecture' [dramatic works of very high value, which we only know through reading].[108] These were classical and medieval works that were not staged at the grand institutional venues, either due to technical challenges or for fear that they would not appeal to a broad enough audience. The Petit-Théâtre's productions may have been diminutive in scale, but much artistry was employed in preparing them. The rods holding up Signoret's marionettes were concealed behind the stage and the strings operating their limbs were covered by their costumes, so that the 'petits acteurs' [little actors], as founding company member Maurice Bouchor fondly calls them, appeared to move independently.[109] (See Figure 4.6.) The marionette operators would also invest much time in rehearsing the blocking of each production, so that the marionettes could move as smoothly as possible. To compensate for the stiffness of their movements and their expressionless faces, the company's costume and set designers strove for detail and realism. Indeed, one reviewer noted that the miniature sets of the Petit-Théâtre were as beautiful as the ones being created for grand operas.[110] The marionettes' lines were spoken not by professional actors but by poets, often the authors of the plays themselves, who delivered them concealed from view.[111] The dialogue was typically in verse and accompanied by music composed by Paul Vidal, which was performed by musicians hidden behind the theatre set. Bouchor notes that the combined effect of the poetic language and live music was so powerful that it transformed the marionettes from rigid and clumsy objects into noble and graceful beings.[112] What soon emerged from these productions, which debuted with Aristophanes's *The Birds* and Shakespeare's *The Tempest*, was that far from being a fallback, the marionettes brought their own aesthetic language and creative advantages to the process. And so the company began to stage its own original productions: plays written especially for Signoret's marionettes, making the most of the opportunities that they offered. But what exactly were the advantages of replacing live actors with these Lilliputian figures made of cardboard and wood?

Both Bouchor, as the author of several of the company's original plays, and Anatole France, as a loyal spectator of the Petit-Théâtre, argued that marionettes aided the audience's suspension of disbelief because they were far less distracting than actors, who tended – either due to their fame or talent – to draw attention to their own person, and thus away from the dramatic work being performed.[113] The Petit-Théâtre's marionettes, by nature of their simplicity, could therefore showcase a text in a manner that was not possible with human performers.[114] Adrien Remacle, who reviewed *Le Songe de Khèyam* for the *Mercure de France*, made a similar remark, but in more direct terms: the marionettes of the Petit-Théâtre could give untrammelled expression to the author's vision because they were, quite literally, voiced by the author himself.[115] This, however, was not true of all productions: Bouchor proved not to have the most effective declamatory style, and so by the time that *Le Songe de Khèyam* was staged, the title role was performed by another member of the company, the poet Raoul Ponchon. A second important advantage of removing the actor from the picture, according to Bouchor, was that human performers typically struggled 'lorsqu'il s'agit d'interpréter les œuvres de génies qui n'appartiennent ni à notre époque ni à notre race' [when it is a case of performing works by geniuses from different times and different races].[116] According to Bouchor, portraying characters whose life had nothing in common with that of the actor required 'une abnégation entière de sa propre personne' [a complete abnegation of one's own self], which presented a great challenge.[117] The puppets solved this by being blank slates, free from the baggage of any particular custom or world view. The third and final advantage of puppetry lay in its unique tone, which the original creations of the Petit-Théâtre learned to exploit. Plays written for puppets

Figure 4.6 The marionettes of the Petit-Théâtre de la Galerie Vivienne.

Source: Recueil. Petit théâtre des marionnettes de Maurice Bouchor (1888–1926). Bibliothèque nationale de France, département Arts du spectacle, 8-RO-13530 (3).

could never be realistic, but in being liberated from a 'photographic' definition of realism (Bouchor's own term), they were free to explore a different kind of truth:

> Le sujet de toute œuvre littéraire, c'est l'âme humaine; il n'y en a point d'autre; et on peut dire sur ce sujet-là des choses vraies, d'une vérité profonde ou délicate, en négligeant certaines conditions habituelles de la réalité.[118]

> [The subject of each and every work of literature is the human soul; there is no other; but one can say true things on this subject, things of a profound or delicate truth, by eliding certain of the usual conditions of reality.]

These creatures who spoke only in verse, and resembled humans in form but not movement, could meditate on the human condition from a certain remove. The original creations of the Petit-Théâtre therefore privileged religious and philosophical themes. But this did not mean that their tone was uninterruptedly serious. Puppets are by nature funny and clumsy things, Bouchor writes, and so even in the most serious puppet play, earnest reflection should be contrasted with moments of comic relief. Citing Aristophanes and Shakespeare as his models, Bouchor describes the inherent challenge that this presents as follows: 'mêler le lyrisme le plus éperdu au comique le plus abandonné […] sans rompre l'unité de l'œuvre' [to combine the most passionate lyricism with the wildest comedy [...] without breaking the unity of the work].[119] Based on the reaction of theatre critics, Bouchor seems to have succeeded in doing so. One reviewer praised 'ce côtoiement étrange du mysticisme et de la gouaillerie, ce mélange, si plein de tact et de mesure, du sérieux et du bouffon' [this strange combination of mysticism and cheek, this tactful and measured mix of seriousness and farce] and qualified this as being emblematic of the 'Gallic' spirit.[120] In contrast to the ceremony and formality that an evening at the opera entailed, the marionettists and writers of the Petit-Théâtre de la Gallerie Vivienne had created a uniquely playful and audience-friendly venue for staging Iran.

As a subject for a play, the medieval Persian mathematician and poet Omar Khayyām offered Maurice Bouchor an opportunity to showcase the peculiar advantages of his chosen medium. Khayyām was indeed a 'genius' from another time and culture, which meant he was precisely the type of character that human actors struggled to portray. Puppets, by contrast, would be able to let the audience relish the wit and beauty of Khayyām's quatrains. Moreover, the fact that Khayyām was known first and foremost in France as a poet provided an added layer of charm to the script, as well as a justification for the fact that the character only spoke in verse, alexandrines to be precise, a conceit which in French classical theatre and grand opera requires a hefty suspension of disbelief. Indeed, the play even acknowledges this rather literal characterization of the poet as someone who speaks only in verse by having another character address him with the tongue-in-cheek epithet 'Ennemi de la prose' [Enemy of prose].[121] Last but not least, Khayyām's quatrains are wry and knowing, and their subject matter alternates between joyous enjoinders to seize the day, drink wine and find what pleasure we can in this life, and rather more sobering *memento mori*. Khayyām's quatrains, which Bouchor would have read in Jean-Baptiste Nicolas's prose translation, thus presented Bouchor with the very combination of seriousness and humour on which the Petit-Théâtre's productions so thrived.[122]

Le Songe de Khèyam is for the most part a monologue spoken by the character of Khayyām and is set during one single night on a town square 'au onzième siècle de l'ère chrétienne, dans une ville de Perse' [in the eleventh century AD, in a Persian town].[123] The play opens with Khayyām being kicked out from a tavern for pinching a waitress while drunk, making its tone low and farcical from the outset. With nothing left to do with the rest of the evening, Khayyām turns to the audience and proposes: 'Philosophons. Sur quoi? Sur le vin, chers amis.'[124] [Let us philosophize. About what? Wine, my dear friends.] The line breaks the fourth wall, turning the audience members into the marionette's confidants and accomplices, as it proceeds to inform them of its disdain for the Islamic ban on alcohol. Khayyām is then distracted by the entrance of two new characters: a jug (in French *cruche*, a translation of the Persian *kuzeh*, an earthen jar with a long narrow neck, which is a recurring image in Khayyām's quatrains) and a rose. Both the jug and the rose are 'almost as tall' as the Khayyām puppet and move of their own accord, which suggests that they are either products of his imagination or an alcohol-induced hallucination. The description of these supernatural objects in the stage directions is symptomatic of the fin de siècle vogue for decorative objects from Iran, which had been fuelled in particular by the exhibitions and sales held in the Persian Pavilions of the Paris World Fairs of 1878 and 1889.¹²⁵ The jug is 'd'une forme élégante et toute émaillée de bleu' [of an elegant shape and coated in blue enamel] and the rose is presented in 'un long vase de cuivre aux arabesques délicates' [a narrow copper vase decorated with delicate arabesques].¹²⁶ The marionette reacts to their entrance with lines that are overtly derivative of Khayyām's *kuzeh* quatrains, in which the clay worked by the potter serves as an allegory for the transience of human life: 'Les vivants deviendront la poussière des villes. / Chaque jour le potier pétrit dans ses mains viles / Des pieds de mendiants et des têtes de rois' [The living will become the dust of cities. / Every day the potter works with his lowly hands / The feet of beggars and the heads of kings].¹²⁷ Khayyām concludes that now that he can drink the wine contained within the magical jug and admire the beauty and perfume of the rose, he will want for nothing in this life. But this perfect picture is soon interrupted by the entrance of a third new character: a mischievous female figure, referred to in the script as 'L'Apparition'.

The introduction of the 'Apparition' takes us from the poetic to the trite. Khayyām now draws on the flowery language of Persian poetry not to reflect on his mortal condition, but to attempt a seduction. He is immediately rebuffed and reduced to ineloquent protestation. The dialogue between Khayyām and the Apparition is made all the more dynamic by the fact that some of her interruptions prevent the poet from completing the alexandrines that have hitherto structured his speech:

> L'APPARITION
> Je sais que rien n'est plus léger que tes serments.
> KHÈYAM
> Céleste fée aux yeux de narcisse…
> L'APPARITION
> > Tu mens.
> KHÈYAM
> Hélas! Je n'ai rien dit.¹²⁸
> [THE APPARITION
> I know that nothing is more fickle than your promises.
> KHAYYAM
> Beautiful narcissus-eyed fairy…
> THE APPARITION
> > You're lying.
> KHAYYAM
> But I haven't said anything.]

The Apparition proceeds to toy with Khayyām, with the assistance of an identical twin, who now also enters the scene. The two women taunt him from opposite ends of the stage, making him run back and forth in confusion. When Khayyām finally realizes that there are two of them, he declares that the double apparition is a symbol of female duplicity. This would be a neat, if misogynistic, exegesis, were it not immediately undercut by the Apparition herself, who has a more pedestrian explanation: 'Nous sommes deux, Khèyam, parce que tu vois double' [There are two of us, Khayyām, because you are seeing double].¹²⁹ By going from symbolism to alcoholism, the puppets revel in their ability to seamlessly shift from meditation to farce, and back again. Indeed, *Le Songe de Khèyam* ends on a both happy and highly mystical note.

Khayyām, having seen the error of his ways, begs God to forgive him for searching for happiness in the wrong place and professes his loyalty to Him. His words also redeem his love of wine, on which the play had opened and which had been mocked by the Apparition, which is now shown to lubricate his mysticism:

> Nul ne pénètrera, pas plus moi que les autres,
> Derrière le rideau qui voile tes secrets;
> Mais je suis avec toi quand je hume à longs traits
> Le breuvage pourpré dont la force m'enivre.
> Je ne te cherche plus, alors: je te sens vivre.
> Mon Dieu, toi seul es vrai; tout le reste est vapeur.
> Pourtant, sans se livrer à ce monde trompeur
> Que par ta rêverie en souriant tu crées,
> Le sage en peut bénir les merveilles sacrées.¹³⁰
> [No one, not I nor others, shall penetrate
> Behind the curtain that veils your secrets;
> But I am with you when I inhale in deep breaths
> The crimson drink whose power inebriates me.
> Then, I no longer seek you: for I feel you are alive.
> My God, you alone are true; all the rest is mist.
> Yet, without giving oneself up to this false world
> Which in your smiling reveries you create,
> The sage can nonetheless bless its sacred marvels.]

The secret to a life well lived is to enjoy what the physical world has to offer without becoming a slave to its illusions. On the basis of this monologue, we come to see the symbolic meaning of inhaling the perfume of the rose: unlike the female temptress, who inspires an all-consuming lust, the rose can be appreciated in a calm and self-contained manner. Rather than detracting from the poet's love of God, the rose supports it, for in admiring the flower, Khayyām is ultimately admiring its creator. This, Bouchor claims, is Khayyām's philosophy in a nutshell.¹³¹ But is it really?

Le Songe de Khèyam was written at a time when Khayyām's quatrains had gained immense popularity in both the English- and French-speaking world. Their elliptic brevity was both intriguing and exciting to readers accustomed to longer poetic forms. Khayyām's celebration of wine and the philosophical detachment he brought to such serious matters as death and religion also challenged Western stereotypes about Muslims being serious, rigid and close-minded, or, in Ernest Renan's terms, averse to science and philosophy (see Chapter 2). One journalist expressed his surprise at discovering this different side to Islamic literature by dubbing Khayyām 'un épicurien musulman [a Muslim Epicurean].¹³² But there was also some debate as to whether Khayyām should be viewed as a nihilist or as a mystic, or perhaps even as something in between, in other words: someone who believed in God, but without following the rigid rules and fixed interpretations of orthodox Islam. The French translator of Khayyām's quatrains, Jean-Baptiste Nicolas, claimed that Khayyām was a Sufi and that inebriation for him was a form of mystical initiation, akin to whirling or self-flagellation, as well as being a metaphor for God.[133] Bouchor repeats this information in the preface to *Le Songe de Khèyam*, though it contains at its heart a contradiction. Indeed, as was remarked by Nicolas's rival translator Edward Fitzgerald, it made no sense to state that wine for Khayyām was both an instrument of worship and a metaphor for the divine: either the wine was literal, or it wasn't. Fitzgerald also argued that many of Khayyām's quatrains were only intelligible if the wine was interpreted literally.[134] Moreover, he completely disagreed with Nicolas's claim that Khayyām was a Sufi, noting that 'in two Rubàiyàt of Mons. Nicolas' own Edition Sùf and Sùfi are both disparagingly named'.[135] That being said, Fitzgerald does admit that a small number of Khayyām's quatrains can be considered mystical. His interpretation is therefore closest to the middle ground perspective, according to which Khayyām was 'a Muslim Epicurean'. At the other end of the spectrum was Ernest Renan, who considered Khayyām to be neither a Sufi, nor an Epicurean Muslim, but 'le plus étonnant poëte nihiliste qui jamais ait écrit' [the most surprising nihilist poet who ever wrote].[136]

Bouchor's puppet play presents us with both extremes: Khayyām the nihilist and Khayyām the mystic. Rather than placing these interpretations in competition or seeking to find a compromise, he places them in sequence in order to create a narrative of conversion. This was by no means a unique approach: it was equally adopted by Bouchor's contemporaries Henri Cazalis and Armand Renaud in their Persian-inspired collections of poems (see Chapter 1). In Bouchor's narrative, Khayyām starts out as a caricature of Fitzgerald's impious sceptic, but after a spiritual ordeal, he finally becomes the mystic that Nicolas had made him out to be.[137] Bouchor associates the impious Khayyām with sexual desire for women (the waitress whom he pinches, the Apparition whom he chases), while the Sufi Khayyām is portrayed as rejecting the pleasures of the flesh. There is, however, no such condemnation of the senses in Khayyām's quatrains, which on the contrary celebrate sensual pleasure. For if Khayyām's poetry regularly meditates on the transience of life, this is not cause for misery or detachment, but for celebration, since it is on this very same basis that the lyric I enjoins his readers to seize the day by making merry. Bouchor is basing his ascetic Khayyām on Nicolas's preface and notes, which state that the study of Sufism taught Khayyām 'le mépris absolu des choses d'ici-bas' [absolute contempt for the things of this world].[138] But Bouchor, like Fitzgerald, cannot have missed the disjunct between Nicolas's paratext and the translated poems, which in their celebration of wine and earthly pleasures do not suggest an 'absolute contempt for the things of this world'. The internal contradiction in Nicolas's work explains why Bouchor sought a compromise in the figure of the rose, whose perfume offers a form of pleasure that is both sensual and chaste. This sublimation of sexual desire is matched by a sublimation of drunkenness: at the beginning of the play, Khayyām was a disorderly drunk; at the end of the play, it is wine that brings him closest to God. Bouchor thus created a Khayyām who appreciates earthly pleasures, as long as they do not distract him from his primary devotion to the divine, in keeping with Nicolas's wider assessment of the poet as a mystic, while also including at the beginning of his play the nihilistic and pleasure-seeking aspects of Khayyām's poetry that had been emphasized by other critics.

Where the play remains uncompromising, however, is in its association of women with sin. This was in fact a recurring theme in Bouchor's work. *Le Songe de Khèyam* premièred in conjunction with another puppet play by the same author entitled *La dévotion à Saint André*, which tells the story of Andrew the Apostle's temptation by Lucifer, who to corrupt him takes the form of a beautiful woman. *La dévotion à Saint André* ends with Andrew resisting this beautiful apparition and thus remaining true to his faith. The fact that the audience was viewing *Le Songe de Khèyam* right after a puppet show in which the female character was none other than the Devil himself, would have made it all the more clear that the character of the Apparition stood for the sinfulness of desiring women. Yet, such notions are entirely absent from Khayyām's quatrains, as well as from Nicolas's preface to his translation. That is because the play's central theme of vanquishing female temptation is neither Sufi nor nihilistic, but Catholic. This is the result of Bouchor's personal moral and religious beliefs, which had informed his writing from 1880 onwards.[139] Yet, by expressing this Catholic ideology in the style and vocabulary of Omar Khayyām (as translated by Nicolas), Bouchor was able to camouflage his personal brand of misogyny as having originated in the work of the medieval Persian poet. It is worth noting that, in this respect, *Le Songe de Khèyam* operates in a manner similar to that of two contemporary works from different genres: Jean Richepin's libretto for *Le Mage* (1891), which as we saw assimilates Zoroastrianism with Christianity by overstating the parallels between the two religions, and Henri Cazalis's *Les quatrains d'Al-Ghazali* (1896), which uses Khayyām's quatrains and the theologian Al-Ghazali's spiritual autobiography as a mouthpiece for the author's own religious syncretism (see Chapter 1). In all three cases, the author's personal religious views are dressed up in historic Persian garb. This creates an illusion of similarity and cross-cultural dialogue, when in fact, the Persian characters are reflecting the author's own beliefs back at them and by, extension, to their intended audience. Bouchor's writing process is the most ingenious of the three: he incorporates lines from Khayyām's quatrains into his script, but in a manner that alters their meaning. Rather than writing a new Khayyām from scratch, as Jean Richepin and Cazalis arguably did for the historic figures of Zoroaster and Al-Ghazali, Bouchor strategically edits Khayyām's poems to make them better serve the purposes of his play. Let us take a closer look at how he achieves this.

In the play's opening monologue, Khayyām declares:

Je suis ivre? Eh bien! soit; je le suis.
    Hérétique, idolâtre ou guèbre, je poursuis
    Un sublime dessin: que Dieu me délivre
    De ce malencontreux prophète et de son livre.[140]
    [I am drunk? So what if I am. / Heretic, idolater or Zoroastrian, I follow / One sublime goal: that God might free me / From that unfortunate prophet and his book.]

The anti-Islamic sentiment on which the sentence ends is an invention of Bouchor's: Khayyām's quatrains often express disdain towards those who follow a narrow definition of Islam, but never towards the religion or its prophet. Indeed, what emerges from Khayyām's quatrains is a firm belief that God is far more forgiving and flexible than religious clerics make Him out to be. The character's self-definition as a 'heretic' follows a similar editorial process: it takes its terminology from Khayyām, but employs it to formulate a much harder statement than what was written in the source poem, which I believe to be the following quatrain, as translated by Nicolas:

> Si je suis ivre de vin vieux; eh bien! je le suis. Si je suis infidèle guèbre ou idolâtre; eh bien! je le suis. Chaque groupe d'individus s'est formé une idée sur mon compte. Mais qu'importe, je m'appartiens et je suis ce que je suis.[141]

> [If I am drunk on old wine; so be it! If I am an infidel, a Zoroastrian or an idolater; so be it! Every group of individuals has formed its own view of me. But what does it matter: I belong to myself and I am what I am.]

By eliding the second half of the quatrain, Bouchor turns what had been a condemnation of gossip into a statement of fact. Bouchor selects and exaggerates in order to write a strongly atheistic Khayyām at the beginning of the play, which in narrative terms serves to make the puppet's final conversion to Sufism all the more dramatic. What is lost in the process is the knowing ambiguity of Khayyām's quatrains, which, both in the original Persian and in Nicolas's French translation, leave his relationship to Islam open to interpretation.

Where Bouchor's play does leave room for ambiguity is in its conclusion. Khayyām having finally reconciled his love of wine, of the rose and of God, turns to the audience and asks: 'Dis, n'est-il pas meilleur de trop boire avec Dieu / Que de prier sans lui dans l'ombre des mosquées?'[142] [Tell me, is it not better to have too much to drink with God / Than to pray without him in the shade of the mosques?] The idea of worshipping God outside of the mosque is a common theme in Sufi literature. Here, however, the trope is infused with a light and playful tone, since the character is not just talking about drinking wine, but about having *too much* to drink: an activity that tends to bring out humanity's grotesque side. The rhetorical question is also facetious in so far as it presents the audience with a false alternative: Khayyām proposes the lesser of two evils, without ever entertaining the possibility that one could also be in the presence of God while in the mosque. The play's final lines are therefore ambiguous and seem to point to the wider critical debate surrounding the interpretation of Khayyām's quatrains: was he a Sufi or was he a drunk?[143] Yet, although the line is loaded with subtext, alluding as it does to conflicting interpretations of Khayyām's poetry and to different schools of Islam, we must also remember that the words were coming from a marionette breaking the fourth wall. The tone was far from scholarly. In doing so, Bouchor's production was revelling in the irresistible mix of 'cheek and mysticism' that the Petit-Théâtre had pioneered. And although Bouchor had significantly altered Khayyām's quatrains in order to craft a conversion narrative with misogynist undertones, the play's conclusion did succeed in capturing their religious ambiguity and the lyric I's often humorous tone. The medium of puppetry proved ideally suited to heightening the script's irreverent spirit, making the voice of Khayyām cheekier than ever. With *Le Songe de Khèyam*, Parisian audiences were introduced to a side of Iranian culture that conformed neither to the Orientalist clichés surrounding the inflexibility of Muslims, nor to the prevailing idealization of Persian poetry as a world of delicate refinement. Khayyām the marionette may have been devoted to beauty and to God, but he was also funny and self-deprecating. He was the kind of Persian poet you wanted to have a glass of wine with.

Rebuilding Susa: Jane Dieulafoy and Camille Saint-Saëns's *Parysatis* (1902)

Fernand Castelbon des Beauxhostes, a wealthy wine merchant from the South of France, had one dream: to turn his hometown of Béziers into a cultural hub that would offer a national alternative to the Bayreuth Festival and at the same time decentralize the French performing arts, which were concentrated in Paris. This vision came to fruition in 1898, with the première of Camille Saint-Saëns and Louis Gallet's 'tragédie lyrique' *Déjanire* at the Arènes de Béziers, a recently constructed bullring which Castelbon des Beauxhostes had helped finance.[144] Setting to music the story of Hercules's death appealed greatly to Saint-Saëns. He was a classics enthusiast and believed that ancient Greek aesthetics could provide a viable alternative to both Wagnerism and French naturalism.[145] Castelbon des Beauxhostes's venue lacked the historical pedigree of the ancient Roman theatre of Orange, where Saint-Saëns had previously performed, but it did nonetheless benefit from a large amphitheatre structure and was situated in a Mediterranean landscape and climate. Jane Dieulafoy, who attended the production, noted with emotion: 'il semblait que l'on fut revenu au temps des jeux olympiques ou à ces jours lointains qui virent les magnifiques tragédies des Eschyle et des Sophocle.'[146] [It seemed that one had returned to the times of the Olympic Games or those distant days that witnessed the magnificent tragedies of Æschylus and Sophocles.] As an archaeologist who had sought to resurrect the past through museum displays and historical fiction, Dieulafoy would have been particularly receptive to the experience of stepping into an ancient world not only through the play's subject matter, but also through the context of its production. In contrast to the Parisian operas, which maintained a physical separation between the world of the characters on stage and that of the audience, in Béziers the set was intentionally constructed to blend into the surrounding landscape and was lit not by artificial lights, but by the same sun that shone upon the audience. *Déjanire*, like many of the Béziers productions that would follow, also pioneered a new relationship between music and drama. The production was a crossover between opera and theatre in which actors alternated between song and spoken dialogue, and the orchestral music would perform a range of roles, from the overtures, choruses, arias and ballets traditionally associated with opera, to the use of incidental music to underscore spoken dialogue, a feature traditionally associated with *mélodrame*. This genre innovation was conceptualized as an attempt to reconstruct ancient Greek dramatic art. It was also symptomatic of the greater artistic freedom offered by Béziers, in contrast to Parisian cultural institutions such as the Opéra and

Comédie-Française or the more established festival held at Orange.[147] This creative independence also made Béziers an ideal venue for a newcomer such as Dieulafoy, who had no prior experience of working in the performing arts. When in 1900, Saint-Saëns mentioned in conversation that he was interested in working on 'a Persian subject', the enterprising Dieulafoy seized the opportunity with both hands and, one month later, sent him a draft libretto.[148] It was a stage adaptation of their debut novel *Parysatis* (see Chapter 2).[149] Saint-Saëns accepted Dieulafoy's proposal and the pair set to work.

Following Saint-Saëns's feedback, Dieulafoy completed a new version of the libretto in May 1901 and in September of that year began corresponding with Castelbon des Beauxhostes on the practical aspects of the production. The letters, which run until the première of *Parysatis* in August 1902, cover everything from budget to casting and rehearsals, to set and costume design, and transportation from Paris to Béziers. Dieulafoy was therefore playing several roles in this production: they wrote the script, but they also co-produced, contributed to set and costume design, and were involved in directing rehearsals. This is in marked contrast to Saint-Saëns, who did not want to be involved in any aspect of the preparations beyond the initial redrafting of the libretto and the composition of the musical accompaniment.[150] Dieulafoy's correspondence and production notes reveal a meticulous attention to detail and a level of creative control that would have been impossible in any traditional venue for a production of this scale, especially for a beginner. Capitalizing on the prestige of Saint-Saëns's name and the creative freedom afforded by Béziers's decentralized location, Dieulafoy made their stage début with a production that included a five thousand square metre backdrop, four hundred and fifty musicians, two hundred and fifty choral singers, sixty dancers and even live horses. Clearly, the performing arts offered exciting new opportunities for Dieulafoy. But, as everyone knows, adapting a lengthy novel for a temporally limited medium such as film or theatre necessarily involves elisions and simplifications. So how did Dieulafoy rise to this challenge? What was gained and what was sacrificed in the transition from novel to 'drame lyrique'?

While fiction required the space and visuals of ancient Susa to be portrayed through lengthy descriptions, the performing arts gave Dieulafoy an opportunity to communicate the impressive scale, bright colours and elegant lines of this lost world in a far more direct manner: by physically reconstructing it. The visuals of the stage production of *Parysatis* were awe-inspiring both in their scale and in their pursuit of authenticity (see Figures 4.7a and 4.7b).

The set's backdrop was the Palace of Susa as reconstructed by the Dieulafoys,[151] complete with tall slender pillars capped with double-headed bulls, in imitation of the capital on display at the Louvre (see Figure 3.4). Two grand double staircases, adorned with a cuneiform inscription, led to the main stage area. The main stage was in turn connected to several elevated platforms via crenelated staircases in the style of the decorative glazed brickwork that once adorned the staircases of the historic palace, a section of which was equally on display at the Louvre. The costume designs, drawn by Dieulafoy's husband Marcel, exhibit a high level of detail, specifying patterns, colours and fabrics, and they closely imitate Achaemenid art. The costume design for the king shows him wearing a long robe with fanning sleeves and holding a flower in one hand and a sceptre in the other, which corresponds to the depictions

Figure 4.7a Photograph of Dieulafoy's production of *Parysatis* (1902), with orchestra.

Source: Historic postcard, author's own collection.

Figure 4.7b Photograph of Dieulafoy's production of *Parysatis* (1902), with audience members.

Source: Historic postcard, author's own collection.

of royalty in the bas-reliefs of Persepolis. The design also includes the application of *cabochons* [polished gems] in shades of green and red, which together form a pattern not dissimilar to that on the coats worn by the archers in the Susa frieze which had been excavated by the Dieulafoy mission (see Figure 3.4). Much to Dieulafoy's chagrin, for cost-saving purposes the final costumes did not execute the designs in all their details.[152] The king's costume was thus made out of a plain fabric without any applied gems. That said, the robe with its dramatic fanned sleeves remains structurally faithful to Dieulafoy's design. This, combined with the fact that the actor wearing it is standing under a parasol, in a horse-drawn chariot and holding what were presumably a flower and a sceptre (it is hard to tell from the old photograph), creates a rich ensemble of allusions to depictions of kingship in Achaemenid Persian art. The king's entrance, moreover, was welcomed by about a hundred extras portraying the members of the royal court and escorted by an equally large army, which gave the audience a very concrete sense of the pomp and power that surrounded these ancient monarchs.[153] The Béziers production thus offered an unprecedented – and to this day, unrivalled – reconstruction of the Achaemenid royal court both in terms of its physical scale and in its assiduous commitment to basing all of its set and costumes on historical sources. This was an incredible, and at the time undervalued, achievement. The set of *Parysatis* offers a formidable counter-narrative to that presented only a decade earlier by *Le Mage*, where ancient Persian architecture had been reduced to a primitive cave. By building Susa, rather than describing it as they had done in their novel, Dieulafoy communicated their knowledge in a far more immediate manner, manifesting the splendour of the Achaemenids for all to see. This reconstruction was disseminated far beyond Béziers through the production's official photographs, which were printed in magazines and as postcards for audience members to send to family and friends all over France. Figures 4.7a and 4.7b are two such postcards.

In contrast to the visual aesthetic of the production, Saint-Saëns's music for *Parysatis* bears no relationship to Iranian culture, ancient or modern. Erin Brooks has argued that it is a continuation of the musical style that Saint-Saëns had used to evoke antiquity in *Déjanire* (choirs singing in unison, modal melodies, pedal points), but with the further addition of Oriental markers.[154] Saint-Saëns had first been introduced to the Grecian modes adopted in *Déjanire* through the transcriptions of Bourgault-Ducoudray, the composer of *Thamara*, whose research Saint-Saëns had publicly declared his enthusiasm for as early as 1879, forecasting:

C'en est fait de l'excluvisme des deux modes majeur et mineur: les modes antiques rentrent en scène et, à leur suite, feront irruption dans l'art les modes de l'Orient dont la variété est immense.[155]

[The exclusivity of the major and minor mode is over: the ancient modes now enter the scene, and in their wake, the Oriental modes, whose variety is immense, will also surge.]

This progression from ancient Greek inspiration to Oriental inspiration is reflected in the evolution of Saint-Saëns's musical style from *Déjanire* to *Parysatis*. In order to evoke Persian antiquity, Saint-Saëns complemented the sobriety of the Grecian modes with a wide array of new sources which were according to him evocative of the Orient. These included synagogue music, medieval Spanish song and the vocalizes of an Egyptian cafe singer.[156] This eclecticism epitomizes the interchangeability of musical exoticism: it matters little whether the source originates in Europe or the Middle East, or whether it dates from antiquity, the Middle Ages or the present day, as long as it sounds *different*. It may seem surprising that Dieulafoy should have supported Saint-Saëns in this approach, given their own personal commitment to historical authenticity.[157] The apparent disjunct between the production's visual and musical language is, however, easily explained. Dieulafoy understood that it would have been difficult for the French general public to find enjoyment in hearing Iranian music for the first time, given that it differed so widely from their horizon of expectation.[158] Moreover, *Parysatis* is set over two millennia earlier in 401 BC, a period for which there are no musical records.[159] Thus, not only would have Iranian music sounded jarring to the audience, but it would not have lent the work any authenticity, since there was no evidence that the music enjoyed at the ancient Achaemenid court would have sounded anything like the music being performed in medieval or modern Iran. Saint-Saëns was therefore in a completely different situation to Dieulafoy in their capacity as set and costume designer: there was no model for him to refer to. Rather than comparing their enterprises, it is therefore more productive to judge Saint-Saëns's score on its own terms, and in particular in light of its role within the wider production. The composer needed to communicate the cultural distance and the grandeur of the Achaemenid court, while remaining captivating and enjoyable to an audience accustomed to Western music. Eight years earlier, when composing the incidental music for Sophocles's *Antigone*, which was his first foray into Grecian modes, Saint-Saëns had noted that he was not prepared to sign off on a piece of music that crossed the threshold of the audience's aural tolerance for difference.[160] If Saint-Saëns raised this concern when composing the incidental music for a well-known tragedy set in the familiar antiquity that was ancient Greece, one can imagine how much greater the challenge was with *Parysatis*, a work about unfamiliar characters set in a period that was both temporally and geographically removed from its modern French audience. The music had to simultaneously speak to this distance, while also emotionally connecting the audience to the events. It was a balancing act if there ever was one.

In nineteenth-century French opera, the highest concentration of musical exoticism is typically to be found in the ballet section, since it is the portion of the work that deliberately prioritizes spectacle over plot. We saw examples of this with David's *Lalla-Roukh*, where the entrance of the *bayadères* was marked by a score packed with Orientalist markers, and with Massenet's *Le Mage*, in which the ballet depicting the temple initiation was accompanied by deeply disconcerting and disorientating music. With this in mind, Saint-Saëns's instrumental music for the entrance of the ballet midway through Act II of *Parysatis* is particularly revealing of his wider compositional approach.[161] Saint-Saëns's ballet opens with a gentle and quiet introduction ('quasi adagio'), which consists of harp arpeggios overlaid with two drawn out and repeated notes on flute and clarinet. The sparseness of the melody and the instrumental texture of the harp and delicate wind instruments were not so much evocative of the Orient as they were of antiquity, and in particular ancient Greece. Rather than the geographic shift to the East, Saint-Saëns's introduction thus focuses on a journey back in time, signposting the Achaemenids as the contemporaries of the ancient Greeks. This, however, all changes with the sudden entrance of an energetic string section ('allegro ma non troppo'), which plays descending scales using the augmented second interval, the most notorious of all Oriental markers. The violins performing these scales are unaccompanied, as though to let the audience better appreciate that what they are hearing is indeed an 'Oriental' mode. To further drive the point home, the same scales are then repeated by the wind section. But just as the audience is starting to grow accustomed to this both repetitive and overt Orientalist signposting, things take a different turn. The wind and string instruments enter into dialogue and eventually converge into a sweeping and magisterial theme, underpinned by harp arpeggios. The theme thus manages to incorporate two musical styles that had at first appeared to be in conflict: the quiet, lulling classicism of the introductory harp music and the loud and flamboyant Orientalism of the violins. Yet, by working together to serve Saint-Saëns's captivating theme, these elements are no longer foregrounded as they were earlier. The listener notices first and foremost the beauty of the melody and the instrumental texture of the piece, not the classical and Orientalist markers that went into the construction of the theme. The remainder of the ballet features several exoticizing sequences, including variations on the augmented second scales first introduced by the strings and rapid clarinet ornamentation, thereby providing the audience with the exotic spectacle expected of such a ballet. Yet, every time the magisterial theme is reintroduced, this exoticism is layered with something beyond it, drawing the audience in and instilling within them a sense of awe at the grandeur of the Achaemenids.

Equally evocative of the Orient and of a distant past, Saint-Saëns's composition was surprising and exotic enough to excite its French audience members, yet accessible and beautiful enough to provide them with a profound sense of enjoyment. The ballet music of *Parysatis* did not possess the eeriness of Dukas's *La Péri* or the shock-factor of Massenet's *Le Mage*. As such, it never threatened to take the audience beyond what it was 'capable de supporter' [capable of tolerating].[162] This consideration was all the more important given that Béziers was a particularly mixed audience, made up of Parisian tourists and provincial working-class people who had rarely – if ever – witnessed operatic music, let alone 'Oriental' music. The grandeur of the orchestral texturing and sweeping themes of *Parysatis* thus acted as guide for the audience, making the pomp of the setting and tragic nature of the events all the more intelligible. The success of Saint-Saëns's approach is demonstrated by one particularly telling review by the critic René Lara, who travelled from Paris to review the production. Lara opens the review by describing the audience's warm reception of the production: 'dix mille spectateurs consacraient par leurs acclamations le succès de cette nouvelle manifestation d'art et saluaient d'une ovation indescriptible et inoubliable, le glorieux musicien et sa vaillante collaboratrice.'[163] [Ten thousand spectators consecrated through their cheers the success of this new artistic manifestation and saluted with an indescribable and unforgettable ovation the glorious musician and his valiant collaborator.] But as well as eliciting the enthusiasm of the wider public, Saint-Saëns's music was also just exotic enough to allow Lara to show off his erudition by claiming that the score used original ancient Persian melodies ('les anciennes mélodies persanes').[164]

So far I have focused on the visuals and the music of the stage version of *Parysatis*, given that its storyline had already been covered in Chapter 2. However, it is worth noting that as well as layering Dieulafoy's novel with a new visual and aural dimension, the stage version of *Parysatis* also radically altered both the plot and major theme of the work. Just as Maurice Bouchor reworked Khayyām's verses to give them a different meaning, so too did Dieulafoy use revision and elision to take their own work in a completely new direction. The novel *Parysatis* is named after its title character, the powerful mother of King Artaxerxes II and his rival brother Cyrus the Younger. It tells the story of how the Machiavellian Parysatis strove to maintain control of the government following the death of her husband, the king, instigating a war between her two sons. The climax of the novel comes when Parysatis assassinates her daughter-in-law and political rival Queen Stateira for having had too strong an influence on the king, who is Stateira's husband. The novel ends with Artaxerxes II as a figurehead and Parysatis ruling the Persian Empire better than any man has done before her. The stage version focuses on two minor events from the novel, which are paired together into a coherent narrative: first, Parysatis receiving the news that her younger son Cyrus is dead and, secondly, Artaxerxes II and his son Darius fighting over the deceased Cyrus's Greek concubine Aspasia. Stateira has been entirely removed as a character and Parysatis never seizes control of the throne. Moreover, Dieulafoy writes an entirely new series of the events to end the play on: Aspasia commits suicide in order to protect Darius from his father's wrath, and just as Artaxerxes is about to have Darius executed anyway, Parysatis intercedes to save her grandson's life. The play ends with Artaxerxes banishing his mother from court for being insubordinate. And so Parysatis leaves Susa forever, but not before setting a curse on her son. In brief, then, the stage version of *Parysatis* transforms its female characters from ruthless politicians into hapless victims, who act out of love, but are ultimately powerless before the cruelty of men. Nowhere is this pivot more explicit than in the character of Parysatis, who has gone from ordering murders to interceding to prevent them, and who has shrunk from protagonist to supporting actress. She has been replaced by the meek Aspasia, who has been promoted from minor character to romantic heroine. The absence of Stateira, who had been Parysatis's main antagonist in the novel, also radically alters the plot. The central conflict between mother-in-law and daughter-in-law is replaced by the far more predictable conflict between two men (the king and the prince) fighting over the same woman. As has been argued by René Girard and Eve Kosofsky Sedgwick, love triangles as a narrative device tend to foreground the relationship between the male characters as having greater importance than their relationship to the desired female character.[165] This is certainly the case in Dieulafoy's script, where Artaxerxes II perceives Darius's desire for Aspasia as a threat to his authority as king. The real cause of the conflict is therefore not that the son should love the same woman as his father, but that in doing so he goes against his father's will, which in turn makes the king fear for the stability of his rule. The erasure of the Parysatis–Stateira conflict also means that the story no longer has its compelling relationship between two women, which in the novel was predicated on a political rivalry. Instead, the stage version presents us with a heteronormative configuration of relationships in which women only exist in relation to men: Aspasia as an object of sexual desire and Parysatis as mother of the king and grandmother of the prince. As well as robbing the work of its bold and original focus on the political role of women, this rewriting also leaves us with only one overt theme: the decadence and despotism of Oriental rulers. The attentive reader will indeed have noticed that the character of Artaxerxes in the stage version of *Parysatis* is but another avatar of a character we had previously encountered in *Le Mage*: the ancient Iranian king motivated only by his lust and need to assert his authority over his romantic rivals. But whereas in *Le Mage*, at least, the lead female character of Anahita eventually triumphed and walked over the spoils of the dead king and his entourage, reclaiming her authority as queen of Touran, in *Parysatis* all that the female characters can do is either kill themselves or condemn the king's actions as they exit the stage. Why did Dieulafoy produce a libretto that went so far against the feminist vision that had animated their novel? How was it possible that even Jean Richepin's libretto, packed as it was with Orientalist tropes and female objectification, should have a stronger female lead than a work named after Parysatis, the most fearsome queen in ancient Persian history?

There are two explanations for this radical change in direction. The first comes from the collaboration with Camille Saint-Saëns, who gave Dieulafoy notes on the first version of the libretto. As noted above, Saint-Saëns was a great lover of classical culture for whom Béziers was an occasion to recreate ancient Greek theatre. The dramatic suicide of the romantic heroine and the mother's curse upon her descendants both conform to the tropes of ancient Greek tragedy. These elements could therefore have been the composer's suggestions. The second consideration is of a more commercial nature. The character of Parysatis, a middle-aged woman who kills and tortures her enemies and will stop at nothing to seize control of government, was not a very sympathetic protagonist. Dieulafoy's anti-heroine as depicted in her novel conformed neither to ideals of feminine virtue, nor to the negative stereotype of the *femme fatale* as a bestial irrational being, since all of her actions are meticulously premeditated. The problem of making such a character relatable to a modern French audience was only heightened by the story's setting in ancient Iran. Indeed, at the same time that Dieulafoy was developing their libretto in 1901, the open-air productions at Béziers were beginning to come under fire for their ancient Greek settings, which local journalists claimed were deeply alienating to audiences.[166] One of these critics specifically took aim at Castelbon des Beauxhostes for having chosen *Parysatis* as his next production, writing that audiences deserved to see works about 'des noms connus ou au moins facilement adéquats aux idées de nos populations' [names that are known to us or at least fit easily with the ideas of our people].[167] If the press was already saying that ancient Iran was an inappropriate subject for the French stage, what would they have to say about an Iranian woman who seized control of the world's first empire by killing anyone who stood in her way? By removing the character of Stateira from the story, Dieulafoy was able to avoid referring to the fact that the historical Parysatis had assassinated her son's wife, depicting her instead as a concerned mother: she first enters the stage to grieve the death of her son Cyrus and subsequently tries to diffuse the conflict between her grandson and remaining son. In order to make Parysatis even more relatable to the audience, Dieulafoy also takes away her political power. Indeed, although the stage Parysatis refers to her desire to influence political events, this desire never comes to fruition. This, then, is a muzzled Parysatis, a woman who 'stays in her place'– that is, far from the throne. In turn, Aspasia's elevation to a lead role is explained by the fact that the character is young and beautiful, but also humble and self-sacrificing and, perhaps most importantly, *Greek*. These were all qualities that would presumably have made her the most attractive female character in the novel. Ironically, Dieulafoy's efforts to make the libretto more agreeable to the public only made it less exciting. The characters became predictable and the story lost its narrative spine, which had been Parysatis's quest for power and her triumph over the multiple obstacles set on her path. Dieulafoy must have believed that they could only fight one battle at a time: the novel's feminist message had to give way to a new priority, that of disseminating the material culture of the Achaemenids. To attempt to do both things would surely have gone beyond what the audience was 'capable of tolerating'. The result of this creative approach, however, was a sumptuous shell built around an empty core: the excitement of the music and the historical reconstruction could not make up for the new Parysatis's lack of substance. In the words of Colette: 'Et Parysatis, dans tout ça, qu'est-ce qu'elle fabrique? / Parysatis, hé bien! elle donne son nom à la pièce.'[168] [And what on earth does Parysatis do in all of this? / Parysatis, well! She gives her name to the play.]

Conclusion

The works that we have just considered vary widely in terms of première date, venue, artistic medium, setting and internal cohesion; and yet they are also linked by noticeable trends and recurring themes. Persian literature is a key point of reference across these works: in some cases it provides the subject and inspiration for the entire script (*Le Songe de Khèyam*, Dukas's *La Péri*); in others it features indirectly through stylistic allusion, for example in the verbal seductions operated by the two Noureddins (*Lalla-Roukh* and *Thamara*). Ancient Iran is a privileged setting, in particular, in the context of war (*Le Mage*, *Parysatis*), though Dukas's *La Péri* escapes this categorization by removing the character of Eskandar from the context of his military conquest of Iran and approaching him instead through the same combination of myth and romance that Judith Gautier had used in her own adaptation of the *Shāhnāmeh*. Stage directions, as well as costume and set designs, also reveal a growing familiarity with Iran's artistic and architectural heritage, especially at the turn of the century. But, for all its interest in Iranian sources, the stage is also the context in which Iran was the most Orientalized. As I argued in this chapter's introduction, the performing arts consolidate the binary opposition of Self and Other both materially through the fourth wall and thematically due to the commercial imperative to play to the audience. Crowd-pleasing tropes included, for instance, the interconnected conceits of the harem of rival beauties (Gautier's *La Péri*, *Thamara*) and the cruel and lustful Oriental despot (*Le Mage*, *Thamara*, *Parysatis*). The Orientalization of Iran could, however, hold very different implications. In some productions, such as *Lalla-Roukh* and Dukas's *La Péri*,

Iran embodied an ideal of beauty and sentimentality, which was informed by Persian literature's elevated status in nineteenth-century French culture. This was a welcoming and desirable Orient, whose embrace provided the audience with a moment of respite from the disappointments of their own society. In other productions, however, the opposite was true: Iran was a dangerous Other, associated with war and destruction. To complicate matters further, some productions, such as *Le Mage* and *Thamara*, even managed to include both forms of Orientalism within one same production, by both idealizing and demonizing Iranian men.

Jane Dieulafoy's stage adaptation of *Parysatis* is a particularly interesting case study of the Orientalizing tendencies of the performing arts. Out of all the productions studied here, it is the most rigorously researched, since it was authored and co-produced by one of the period's foremost experts on ancient Iran. Indeed, in terms of historical reconstruction, it is worlds apart from *Le Mage*, whose Persian soldiers wore ancient Greek-style short skirts and worshipped an imaginary religion in a primitive temple.[169] And yet, the original novel's story of a woman's fight for political power, which as we saw in Chapter 2 was a very current theme at the time that Dieulafoy was writing, is discarded in favour of the tragedy of a European woman being preyed on by a lecherous Oriental despot. While in the original novel it was the Persian queen Parysatis with whom the reader was encouraged to identify, in the stage version, the heroine is the Greek Aspasia, who has the misfortune of falling into the hands of debauched Orientals.[170] Thus, while in material terms the production introduced the audience to the cultural peculiarities of the Achaemenid court, its plot reproduced the tired clichés of Orientalism. In this respect, *Parysatis* meets *Le Mage*, which relied on the very same trope of the predatory Oriental despot and his victim from the West. The production's dissemination of Achaemenid visual culture was therefore accompanied by a dehumanization of the Achaemenids themselves. As well as demonstrating the ways in which the performing arts are more likely to resort to negative stereotypes than poetry or fiction, the stage version of *Parysatis* also reminds us of the layered nature of the performing arts. Libretto, music and visuals can work of one accord or they can offer differing visions of Iran. This fact comes most dramatically to the fore when we compare the diverging approaches taken by Dieulafoy in *Parysatis* and Paul Dukas in *La Péri*. Dukas's libretto and score work hand in hand to mutually reinforce each other: the libretto (which was available to audiences) explained the narrative development of the music and choreography, and the music illustrated the different natures and personalities of the two characters whose actions were described in the libretto. René Piot too was highly cohesive in his creation of a set and costume design that worked together to look like a page out of a Persian book. As well as being internally consistent, Piot's visual language was also coherent with Dukas's vision, since it was inspired by the lavish miniature illustrations featured in Persian manuscripts of the *Shāhnāmeh*, the work that had inspired Dukas's libretto.

Ballet, theatre, opera and puppetry's combination of different artistic media makes them not only the most challenging, but also the most exciting of genres to analyse. A nineteenth-century audience member would have had their senses bombarded by a rich palette of music, speech, set and costume, while all the while their mind raced to correlate these disparate elements to a sense of story, character and setting.

This presented them with an overwhelming amount of material to parse through as they sought to determine what kind of place Iran was meant to be. Was it an ancestor or an ancient enemy? A land of roses and poetry or a threatening Muslim Other? A nation with its own history or an Orient just like all the others? The stage allowed what seemed to be irreconcilable alternatives to coexist, each of them foregrounded by different facets of the production. The performing arts revelled in Iran's plurality in the French imagination: all sources, be they historical, literary, material or just mere cliché, were valid as long as they provided dramatic plots, spectacular costumes and grandiose music, in one word: spectacle. This is all the more true of expensive large-scale productions such as those of the Paris operas and Béziers, where the priority was to fill seats. Indeed, while the combination of culturally specific elements with Orientalist stereotypes might seem contradictory to us, it did serve a practical function: that of providing the audience with a sense of structure and familiarity, which made the production's distant setting and foreign characters intelligible and thus accessible. The two productions that do away with this strategy are Bouchor's *Le Songe de Khèyam* and Dukas's *La Péri*, since these works are both predicated on the assumption that the audience had some pre-existing knowledge of Persian literature. In these two experimental productions of the turn of the century, the audience was to be guided not by Orientalist stereotypes, but by literary references to the quatrains of Khayyām and the Alexander of Ferdowsi's *Shāhnāmeh*. They represent the heyday of France's love of Iranian culture, one that was never to return.

Conclusion

Iran in nineteenth-century France was known as a civilization whose history and culture spanned two and a half millennia, encompassing two world religions (Zoroastrianism and Islam), three empires (Achaemenid, Sassanian and Safavid), centuries of artistic and architectural sophistication, and one of literature's greatest poetic traditions. For this reason, we cannot call the Iran of nineteenth-century French literature a Western creation, since this would ignore the wealth of cultural material that French authors were responding to, among which new translations of Persian literature play a particularly prominent role. Iran also cannot be reduced to a mere exotic Other or political foil to French culture, since to do so would ignore the numerous examples of admiration, identification and imitation studied over the course of this book. What this study demonstrates is that although Iran was part of the Islamic Orient, it also held a unique place within it, with 'the Persians' often being described as culturally closer to the French than any other Muslim people – Flandin even refers to them as 'the French of the Orient'. This perceived sympathy between France and Iran was also expressed through favourable comparisons between the Persians and other Orientals: the poetry of the Persians is more refined than that of the Arabs (Barbier de Meynard), the art of Persepolis demonstrates that the ancient Persians were more intelligent than the Egyptians and the Assyrians (Dieulafoy), the Shah Mosque of Esfahan speaks to an aesthetic sensitivity that is not present on the other side of the Tigris (Flandin). This distinction, however, often served to bolster racial and religious discrimination, elevating Iran as the exception that confirmed the rule. The exceptional status of Iran was used in particular to discredit Islam as a religion: the Persians were the most civilized in the region because they were 'not really Muslim', a notion that was propounded either by suggesting that they had remained loyal to Zoroastrianism (see Renan, and to a lesser degree Michelet), or by pointing out the parallels between Sufism and Hinduism or Buddhism (Cazalis) or by stressing that by virtue of being Shi'i, Iranians were altogether different to Sunni Muslims (Flandin and Dieulafoy). The Aryan myth was also used to cast the ancient Persians as ancestors, making them in effect proto-Europeans (Gobineau, Renan and Michelet). The aim of this was not so much to glorify Iranian history as to appropriate Iran's past glory to reflect positively on the West. In some instances, the appropriation was literal, as is the case with the archaeological mission at Susa, which would come to justify the appropriation of ancient Iranian artefacts as research into Europe's Aryan origins (Morgan).

Nineteenth-century France's particular relationship with Iran among all other Oriental nations is suggestive of a tipping point between an admiration for a cultural other, which inspires a desire for closeness and as such elicits identification, and the moment where a line is crossed from identifying with this cultural other to projecting oneself onto it and erasing its distinctness, the better to assimilate it into one's own culture. Richepin and Massenet's Christianization of the prophet Zoroaster in the opera *Le Mage* exemplifies the latter tendency. Yet, sometimes it is not so clear where the tipping point lies. Michelet, for instance, bases his admiration for the Zoroastrian religion on its scripture and as such is highly mindful of its cultural specificity. Yet, while his starting point is philological, his end goal is ideological: he argues that Zoroastrianism embodies the values of the 1789 Revolution. As such, it is hard to say when or where exactly the author goes from admiring Zoroastrianism as an alternative to the Abrahamic faiths to turning it into a screen onto which to project his own wants. It is perhaps fairer to say that in some cases, there is a bit of both. Overall, however, nineteenth-century French writers do share a common blind spot: they all find it easier to identify with Iranian figures from the past, specifically medieval poets and heroes from ancient Iranian history, than with contemporary Iranians. There are two explanations for this. First, Iran's history was easier to glorify than its present: the great empires of Iran were all in the past, as was the golden age of Persian poetry. More broadly, it is easier to idealize a time that is distant from our own. All this made Iranian history a fertile terrain for fantasy. Secondly, French writers' encounters with Persian poetry and Iranian history were primarily textual. As such they were doubly mediated, first by the work of the French translators and academics who made Persian literature available to the French reading public, and secondly by the act of reading, which is in itself interpretative, requiring us as it does to draw on our imagination to complete the picture. This double mediation has familiarizing implications, since readers are already putting a lot of themselves and of their culture into the text. Interacting with people 'in real life', by contrast, confronts us with our difference – this is true even of two people who speak the same language and share the same cultural background. In light of this, we should consider how dramatic the contrast would have been between reading Persian poems in translation in the comfort of one's Parisian drawing room and being the only two French people in a crowded caravanserai.

Cultural difference can take many different forms, some of which are easier to negotiate than others. Islam was viewed as the greatest marker of difference between French and Iranian culture, especially in terms of how it affected gender relations. This is most true of travel-writers, who could not minimize the importance of Islam in Iranian society as easily as scholars and historians did. That being said, travel-writers' reactions to Islamic customs are equally varied and in some cases shift over the course of their time in Iran. The horror of Loti's account of the self-flagellation rituals of the month of Muharram is matched by Bibesco's enthusiasm for ritualized mourning, as well as for the Islamic veil. Her panegyric to the veil, moreover, is the product of a slow evolution from incomprehension to over-identification, demonstrating that one same author's perspective can change over time. Cultural difference is at its most negotiable in the context of literature and the arts. French writers had a great admiration for Iranian cultural products and what made them different only added to their interest, as well as to their potential to inspire and stimulate artistic renewal in France. Cultural comparisons were often instrumental in helping French individuals familiarize themselves, as well as their readers, with works that they were encountering for the first time. Comparisons also enabled them to better discern what made Iranian art, architecture and literature unique. In comparing Hāfez to Lucretius, or Esfahan's Naqsh-e Jahān Square to Versailles or Saint Mark's Square, French authors did not seek to elevate the latter over the former. They were searching for better parameters to explain and appreciate what were for them new aesthetic experiences.

Anil Bhatti and Dorothee Kimmich's paradigm of similarity offers a productive framework for approaching French writers' negotiations of cultural difference, precisely because it argues for a more porous understanding of cultural boundaries in which differences and commonalities can coexist. Understood in this way, similarity differs from assimilation in that it does not seek to reduce or erase what makes the other *other*. This more balanced and ambivalent perspective has its predecessor in the work of Tzvetan Todorov, who described the respective limitations of universalism and cultural relativism and suggested that the only truly ethical position was to allow for a mix of both perspectives. The writers studied here may not have articulated the matter as clearly as these literary theorists, but many of their cultural comparisons and intertextual experiments show us that they were searching for precisely this type of balance. In some rare cases, these writers were even able to vocalize their cultural bias and acknowledge their limitations. There is a striking candour to Bibesco's words, 'Européenne, j'ai cru d'abord' [As a European woman, I thought at first] and an understated complexity to the episodes in which Jane Dieulafoy either overhears or imagines Iranians reacting to their presence among them. Nineteenth-century writers' views on cultural diversity were layered and multifaceted and should not be reduced to a single-minded focus on difference. The oppositional paradigm that we have inherited from Edward Said can at times rob us of opportunities to gain a richer understanding of this literary period. I do not wish to suggest by this that French writing on Iran did not include Orientalist clichés, racist grand narratives or imperialist associations of Europe with civilizational superiority. These politically charged tropes have come up time and again over the course of my analyses. But what I hope to have demonstrated is that such discourses existed alongside, and on some occasions were even intertwined with, far more tolerant and inclusive perspectives on cultural diversity than we tend to credit the period for. In particular, what never ceases to amaze me is just how much more educated nineteenth-century French intellectuals were about Persian literature and Iranian history than most of us Europeans are today.

One of the things that gave Iran such a unique status in nineteenth-century France was its association with a body of literature that had only recently become available in translation. Ferdowsi's *Shāhnāmeh*, Saʻdi's *Golestān*, Khayyām's *Robāiyāt* and Hāfez's *Ghazaliyāt* have been recurring reference points throughout this book because they were familiar names in Paris' literary and artistic circles. The more erudite among our authors go even further by also citing ʻAttār, Jāmi, Nezāmi and Rumi. What is most notable about this selection of authors is that it reflects native Persian speakers' understanding of their own literary canon. In this sense, French readers were not consuming a version of Iranian culture that had been created by the

West or crafted in Iran for Western export: when it came to classical literature, they were discovering Iranian culture on its own terms. The caveat to this, of course, is that they were reading these works in translation and, as such, their understanding was heavily mediated. Nineteenth-century readers would have had a completely different understanding of Khayyām based on whether they discovered him through Nicolas's French prose translation, which claimed that he was a mystic, or through Fitzgerald's English verse translation, which argued vehemently to the contrary. When read in the original, Persian poetry is extremely open to interpretation. This is due, first of all, to linguistic parameters such as grammar and spelling: whereas in most modern European languages the distinction between a noun and an adjective is obvious and the logical relation between words is made explicit by prepositions, these things are not necessarily spelt out in Persian. The reader is therefore often required to call on their own judgement when making sense of the grammar, let alone the symbolic meaning, of a sentence. Further grammatical challenges to interpretation include the fact that Persian has neither gender, nor articles, nor capitalization. In the case of lyric poetry, things are further complicated by Persian poets' adherence to strict rules of prosody and form, which encourage succinctness. Moreover, the ghazal's privileged theme of desire, which often walks the line between the mystical and the overtly erotic, requires a certain degree of ambiguity of the author. (The latter two points are less of an issue for narrative texts: the prose tales collected in Sa'di's *Golestān* and epic poems such as the *Shāhnāmeh* tend to be rather more straightforward to interpret.) The offshoot of these interpretative challenges is that French translators had to step into the breach and fill the gaps left by the author with their own understanding of the text. In doing so, they were producing a version of the work that was closer to their own sensitivities and therefore to those of their contemporary French readers. This is not to say that these translations did not preserve much of the original work, especially when it comes to narrative texts, which as I noted present fewer interpretative challenges. Jules Mohl's complete translation of the *Shāhnāmeh*, which was produced in tandem with a philological edition of the Persian text, was the work of a lifetime and its quality remains undisputed. Not all was lost in translation. This is most clear when we consider the fascinating examples of intertextuality that were engendered by such translations.

Intertextuality is premised, at a very basic level, on an assumption of commonality between French and Persian literature; otherwise, its very exercise would be impossible. When a French author takes a Persian author as their model, they are challenging the notion that the literature of Europe is superior to all others. Imitation belies admiration. It is an acknowledgement that the new writer has something to learn from their predecessor. Texts that successfully blend together elements of French and Persian literature are also fascinating because they blur the lines of cultural demarcation. As such, they are resistant to the categorizations and binary oppositions of Orientalism. As we have seen, intertextual references to Persian literature come in many forms, from brief citations and passing allusions, such as those we find in the epigraphs of Victor Hugo's *Les Orientales* and the poems of Théophile Gautier and Noailles, as well as the travel-writing of Loti, Dieulafoy and Bibesco, to works that draw their very structure and/or fabric from a Persian precedent. Examples of the latter would include Desbordes-Valmore's poem 'Les Roses de Saadi', premised as it is on an image from the preface of the *Golestān*, and Armand Renaud's *Les Nuits persanes*, a collection entirely predicated on a close engagement with the Persian lyric, as well as Judith Gautier's novel *Iskender*, of which the characterization, plot, structure and even literary style are derived from the precedent set by Ferdowsi. Although my focus in this book has been textual rather than visual, it is also worth noting that these types of allusions and imitations exist in other media, such as René Piot's set and costume designs for *La Péri*, which adopt the visual language of Persian miniature art. Turbaned and wearing a long flowery robe, the ballet's protagonist would only have been legible as the hyper-masculine conqueror Alexander the Great to those already familiar with the literary and visual culture of Iran.

Gender is known to hold an important function in Western representations of the Orient, and French writing on Iran is no exception. We recognize the double charge of the exoticization and eroticization of gender roles in travel-writers' voyeuristic fascination with the female space of the *andaruni* and the performing arts' concomitant obsession with the figure of the sexually debauched Oriental despot, who titillates French audience members by having unlimited access to the very thing that is forbidden to them: the bodies of Oriental women. But many of the texts studied here also question rigid gender roles, as well as the othering of the Orient. In the ghazals of Armand Renaud, the female beloved breaks her silence and proves herself more eloquent than the poet who pursues her affections. In doing this, Renaud questions not only the gendered dimension of Persian lyric poetry, but also that of French lyric poetry. No one was more familiar with the perception of lyric poetry as a male domain than Marceline Desbordes-Valmore, whose poems were repeatedly reduced by her male contemporaries to 'pure' expressions of 'femininity'. In 'Les Roses de Saadi', she writes a lyric 'I' who is both male and female, Persian and French, Saʿdi's and her own, thereby demonstrating the unreliability of such categorizations. Desbordes-Valmore may not have been aware of this, but in doing so she was paying homage to the malleability and ambiguity of the Persian language, which is itself genderless. Persian literature proves a rich source of counter-narratives about gender not only linguistically, but also thematically. Michelet praises Ferdowsi's headstrong female characters, who take charge of their destinies and, in some cases, their men. Under Dieulafoy's pen, the historical characters of Queen Parysatis and Artemisia of Caria demonstrate that the gendered division of labour is anything but natural or just. Ideals of masculinity are equally brought under question by French authors' engagement with Iranian sources. Michelet's reading of the *Avesta* allows him to rewrite the ancient Persians not as fierce warriors, but as peaceful farmers. In Judith Gautier's *Iskender*, Eskandar and Rostam's love for each other triumphs over their cultural differences and eclipses both their desire for women and the politics of empire-building. These men may be the world's most muscular and fierce warriors, but that does not prevent them from shedding tears and sharing kisses.

Gender plays an important role not only in how these authors position themselves in relation to Iran, but also how they position themselves – and are perceived – within the literary culture of nineteenth-century France. In contrast to Desbordes-Valmore's 'Les Roses de Saadi', which deliberately avoids any exotic markers, Judith Gautier, Anna de Noailles and Marthe Bibesco all capitalized on their personal association with

Persian literature to self-exoticize as (pseudo-)Oriental women. But this strategy was a double-edged sword, for although it garnered greater publicity for their writing, it also encouraged readers to reduce these authors to their gender identity. Dieulafoy not only refused such categorizations, but shifted between different gender positions depending on the genre and subject matter at hand. They are at their most masculine in their travel-writing, where they repeatedly other and sexualize Iranian women, and at their most feminine in their fiction and political activism, when they align themself with the great women of Iranian history and share these characters' frustrations in dealing with incompetent men. Yet, while Dieulafoy could challenge gender norms through their physical appearance and their writing, they would always be beholden to them by society. Their writing could not hold the same level of authority as that of institutionally recognized experts such as their husband Marcel and the Collège de France's Jules Michelet and Ernest Renan. The role played by gender difference in the literary culture of nineteenth-century France is perhaps at its most manifest in the politics of genre.

Every literary genre comes with its own set of conventions and horizon of expectation, which makes it an important consideration when analysing a text's representational practices. It is only natural that poets should be most interested in Persian poetry, that historians and historical novelists should be drawn to the rise and fall of the Achaemenid Empire, that travel-writers should mainly describe the everyday lives of their Iranian contemporaries, and that playwrights and composers should take the greatest liberties with the line between cultural specificity and unbridled exoticism. Yet, there are also many crossover interests spanning these genres, and these crossovers have a lot to reveal about the different requirements and practices associated with each one. Let us consider for instance the variety of functions played by the *Shāhnāmeh*, as translated by Jules Mohl. Gobineau and Michelet treat Ferdowsi's epic poem as a historical source. Beneath the legend, they search for details that reveal not only historical events, but also the psychology of Iran as a nation. When writing their historical novella *Rose d'Hatra*, Dieulafoy consulted different tellings of the story of Shapour and the besieged princess who fell in love with him. Ultimately, they went for Mirkhond's version of events rather than Ferdowsi's because its plot line better served their thematic exploration of women's role in society. Dieulafoy's interest is, therefore, in equal part historical and narrative. Judith Gautier's close intertextual engagement with the *Shāhnāmeh*, by contrast, foregrounds the poem's literary qualities, be it through its hyperbolic descriptions of women and battles, its merging of legend and history or its oral style of address to the reader. Dukas's ballet *La Péri*, finally, extracts a sense of character and local colour from the *Shāhnāmeh* and uses this intertextual reference to elevate the status of the libretto to that of a 'poème dansé'.

Genre can also be a very elastic category. Travel-writing, as we saw, encompasses many forms of writing: alongside its ethnographic observations of everyday life, it also includes geopolitical analysis, disquisitions on Iranian history, detailed descriptions of architecture and reflections on Persian literature. The performing arts, in turn, are an extremely varied and multifaceted genre category. Six performance genres were studied in this book (Romantic ballet, Russian ballet, grand opera, *opéra comique*, puppetry and open air theatre) and each of these comes with its own set of aesthetic conventions, tone, audience, technical considerations and financial requirements. Moreover, every one of these performances was multilayered, encompassing as it did the textual, the aural and the visual. These layers could work either in unison or in conversation, offering competing visions of Iran. Covering so many different forms of writing has been an extremely challenging, but also rewarding aspect of this research. The conclusions drawn at the end of each of the four chapters are self-standing and independently valid, but by comparing these different genres, we are also able to gain a better understanding of the particularities of each one. Moreover, it is only by taking a broad lens and thinking across genres that we can appreciate how widespread and far-reaching French interest in Iran was in the nineteenth century. If we consider the sheer breadth and variety of the writing studied here, as well as the collective longevity of these writers' interest in Iranian culture, which remains an evergreen subject of inspiration from Victor Hugo's polemically Romantic *Les Orientales* (1829), to the eventual première of Paul Dukas's *La Péri* on the eve of the First World War, then it is clear that we are not dealing with flukes or exceptions. The history, literature and culture of Iran were deemed substantial and significant enough to constantly warrant new interventions across different forms of writing.

There are five main veins to nineteenth-century French writing on Iran, namely, Iran as land of poetry, Iran as ancient enemy, Iran as ancestor, Iran as modern nation and Iran as imaginary Orient. Yet, each individual writer brought their own literary style, personal interests and political agendas to bear upon this material, resulting in a wide variety of interpretations. As I showed above with the example of Ferdowsi's *Shāhnāmeh*, the same work of Persian literature could be engaged with in a number of different ways. The same goes for Iran's ancient history, which, depending on the author, could serve to prove the existence of the Aryan race, the need for women's emancipation or the greatness of the Zoroastrian faith. As Chapter 3 demonstrated, even the realities of contemporary Iran could be described in widely diverging ways depending on travellers' experiences and their understanding of them. Iran's rich cultural heritage in combination with the multiplicity of views embodied by these different authors results in a pluralized set of representations and representational practices. As such, French writing on Iran cannot be reduced to one single narrative or *modus operandi*. Moreover, the texts studied here, for all their flights of fancy, all take inspiration from a cultural reality. Therefore, they demonstrate that the distinction between the 'real' Orient and the 'imaginary' Orient is far from being clear-cut. Finally, the layered, multifaceted and at times contradictory processes by which nineteenth-century French writers identified with Iranians and Iranian culture reveal the complex negotiations of cultural difference that existed alongside – and sometimes even within – the imperialist and racialist narratives that were emerging during this same period. The case of Iran thus gives us an altogether different lens from which to understand nineteenth-century French literature and its conceptualization of France's cultural place in the world and in history.

Notes

A Note on Terminology

1. William Jones, 'The Sixth Anniversary Discourse, Delivered 19 February 1789 by the President (on the Persians)', *Asiatick Researches* 2 (1790): 43–66 (43).

Introduction

1. Victor Hugo, *Les Orientales* (Paris: Bossange, 1829), 414.
2. Eugène Flandin, *Voyage en Perse*, 2 vols (Paris: Baudry, 1851), II: 414.
3. The reference study is Olivier Bonnerot's *La Perse dans la littérature et la pensée françaises au XVIIIe siècle: de l'image au mythe* (Paris: Champion-Slatkine, 1988), but for more recent contributions, see also Susan Mokhberi, *The Persian Mirror: Reflections of the Safavid Empire in Early Modern France* (Oxford: Oxford UP, 2019) and Junko Thérèse Takeda, *Iran and a French Empire of Trade, 1700–1808: The Other Persian Letters* (Liverpool: Liverpool UP, 2020).
4. Hāfez, but also ʿAttār, Jāmi, Ferdowsi all became available in French for the first time. See Javad Hadidi, *Az Saʿdi be Aragon: ta'sir-e adābi't-e fārsi dar adabi'āt-e farānseh* (Tehran: Markāz-e Nashr-e Dāneshgāhi, 1994), 214–47. Saʿdi had a longer history of being translated into European languages, though during the nineteenth century there was an effort to produce translations that were less heavily domesticating. On the history of Saʿdi's reception in Europe, see Elio Brancaforte, 'Persian Words of Wisdom Travel to the West: Seventeenth-Century European Translations of Saʿdi's Gulistan', *Daphnis* 45 (2017): 450–72, and 'Saʿdi at Large', special section of Iranian Studies 52 (2019): 5–6.
5. Edward Said, *Orientalism* (1978; London: Penguin, 2003), 21 and 56–7.
6. The Oriental Renaissance, which is discussed in the introduction to Chapter 2, is the subject of a landmark intellectual history by Raymond Schwab, which takes its title from the analogy frequently made by the period's intellectuals between the rediscovery of ancient Greek in the Renaissance and the development of the study of ancient Asian languages in the nineteenth century. Raymond Schwab, *La Renaissance orientale* (Paris: Payot, 1950).
7. 'Hommage d'une amitié fidèle'. Judith Gautier, *Iskender: Histoire persane* (Paris: Frinzine, 1886), frontispiece.
8. René Lara, 'Une Première à Béziers', *Le Gaulois* (18 August 1902): 2–3 (3).
9. The three notable exceptions to this are Javad Hadidi's *Az Saʿdi be Aragon* cited above, Zahra Shams-Yadolahi's *Le retentissement de la poésie de Hâfez en France: réception et traduction* (Uppsala: Uppsala Universitet, 2002), and Karim Hayati Ashtiani's unpublished doctoral thesis 'Les relations littéraires entre la France et la Perse de 1829 à 1897' (Université Lumière Lyon II, 2004). These reception studies however fail to

account for the wider implications of the case of Persian poetry regarding debates on Orientalism and cross-cultural representation.
10. France did however pursue financial and cultural imperialism in Iran. See Chapter 3, the section 'Plagued by the West'.
11. Said wrote (not uncontroversially) that his definition of Orientalism 'can accommodate Aeschylus, say, and Victor Hugo, Dante, and Karl Marx'. Said, *Orientalism*, 3.
12. On this, see Charles Forsdick and Jennifer Yee (eds), 'Towards a Postcolonial Nineteenth-Century', special issue of *French Studies* 72, no. 2 (2018), and in particular the editors' introduction, pp. 167–75.
13. The fact that different art forms and genres tend to favour different approaches to cross-cultural representation has also been noted by John M. MacKenzie. See his *Orientalism: History, Theory and the Arts* (Manchester: Manchester UP, 1995).
14. Victor Hugo, 'Préface', in *Les Orientales*, i–xi (ix). See also the poems 'Rêverie' (351–4) and 'Novembre' (383–90).
15. Said, *Orientalism*, 108.
16. This point is also made by Forsdick and Yee in 'Towards a Postcolonial Nineteenth-Century'.
17. Said, *Orientalism*, 2.
18. Ibid.
19. Ibid., 3.
20. This blurring of distinctions has been criticized in particular by Bernard Lewis in 'The Question of Orientalism', *New York Review of Books* (24 June 1982): 49–56, and Robert Irwin in 'An Enquiry into the Nature of a Certain Twentieth-Century Polemic', in *For Lust of Knowing: The Orientalists and Their Enemies* (London: Penguin, 2006), 277–309.
21. James Clifford, 'Orientalism by Edward Said', *History and Theory* 19, no. 2 (1980): 204–23 (208–9). Clifford is quoting directly from *Orientalism*.
22. Said, *Orientalism*, 96 and 201–4. John MacKenzie and Jennifer Yee's historically grounded contributions to this debate are of particular note. MacKenzie argues that many nineteenth-century expressions of 'sympathy and respect' have often gone unnoticed or ignored because they do not align with contemporary values (MacKenzie, *Orientalism*, xviii). Yee has shown how nineteenth-century French novels critiqued imperialism and exoticism through 'literary devices such as pastiche, parody, and narrative framing'. Jennifer Yee, *The Colonial Comedy: Imperialism in the French Nineteenth-Century Novel* (Oxford: Oxford UP, 2016), 114.
23. See, for instance, Jane Dieulafoy's reaction to the polychromy of Achaemenid art, completely at odds with the bland neoclassicism favoured by French official buildings. Jane Dieulafoy, *À Suse: journal de fouilles* (Paris: Hachette, 1888), 160.
24. René Thorel, 'Mme Dieulafoy', *La Revue illustrée* (1 September 1903): 15–36 (16).
25. Jean Lahor (Henri Cazalis), *En Orient* (Paris: Alphonse Lemerre, 1907), 7.
26. Marthe Bibesco, *Les Huit paradis* (Paris: Hachette, 1908), 166.
27. Charles Forsdick, 'Travelling Concepts: Postcolonial Approaches to Exoticism', *Paragraph* 24, no. 3 (2001): 12–29 (14). See also Forsdick, *Victor Segalen and the Aesthetics of Diversity: Journeys between Cultures* (Oxford: Oxford UP, 2000), in particular, pp. 47–57.

28. Said does on one occasion acknowledge the role played by familiarization in the 'othering' of the Orient: the representation of the Prophet Muhammad as an 'impostor', who is similar to Christ but irreducibly different. See Said, *Orientalism*, 72.
29. Anil Bhatti and Dorothee Kimmich, 'Introduction', in *Similarity: A Paradigm for Culture Theory*, ed. Anil Bhatti and Dorothee Kimmich (New Delhi: Tulika Books, 2018), 1–22.
30. Ibid., 14–15.
31. Jane Dieulafoy, 'À propos du roman historique', *Rose d'Hatra, L'Oracle* (Paris: Armand Colin, 1893), 1–10.
32. See, in particular, Henry Louis Gates Jr., 'Critical Response VII: Talkin "That Talk"', *Critical Inquiry* 13, no. 1 (1986): 203–10.
33. Tzvetan Todorov, *Nous et les autres: La réflexion française sur la diversité humaine* (Paris: Seuil, 1989).
34. Tzvetan Todorov, trans. Richard M. Berrong, 'The Origin of Genres', *New Literary History* 8, no. 1 (1976): 159–70 (163). For the French version, see Todorov, 'L'origine des genres', in *Les genres du discours* (Paris: Seuil, 1978), 44–60.
35. Thomas Pavel, 'Literary Genres as Norms and Good Habits', *New Literary History* 34, no. 2 (2003): 201–10.
36. Ibid., 205.
37. Todorov, 'Origin of Genres', 160.
38. I include Dieulafoy under the category of woman writer in this section because this is how they were identified by their publishers and readers at the time that they wrote. Dieulafoy, however, had a complex relationship with their gender identity and their writing often pushes against their categorization as a 'woman'. (On this, see Chapter 2, the section 'Ancient History? Iran as a Mirror to French Feminism (Jane Dieulafoy)' and Chapter 3, the section 'Among Women: Scenes from the Harem'.)
39. Marcel Dieulafoy's publication was the massive illustrated survey *L'art antique de la Perse*, 5 vols (Paris: Librairie centrale d'architecture, 1884–9). It was instantly the authoritative work on the subject and remains a reference.
40. Said, *Orientalism*, 19.
41. Ibid., 20. Emphases in the original.
42. Anwar Abdel Malek, 'Orientalism in Crisis', *Diogenes* 44 (1964): 107–8. Cited by Said, *Orientalism*, 97.
43. Said, *Orientalism*, 104.
44. See Chapter 3, the section 'Understanding Shi'ism'.
45. Said's two central case studies are Gustave Flaubert's private diaries and letters recounting his journey to Egypt and the Levant (1849–51) and William Lane's ethnographic survey *Manners and Customs of the Modern Egyptians* (1836). For a more concentrated example of Said's perceptive analysis of how style communicates authority, see his close reading of Sylvestre de Sacy's poetic anthology *Chrestomathie arabe* (Said, *Orientalism*, 126–9).
46. The intersection of gender and imperialism has been studied in the context of women's travel-writing. See, in particular, Billie Melman, *Women's Orients: English Women and the Middle East, 1718–1918: Sexuality, Religion, and Work* (London: Macmillan, 1992) and Bénédicte Monicat, *Itinéraires de l'écriture au féminin: voyageuses du 19ème siècle* (Amsterdam: Rodopi, 1996). The intersection of imperialism and the genre of the novel has been studied by Yee in *The Colonial Comedy*, see, in particular, pp. 9–13.

1 Poetry

1. William Jones, 'Traité sur la poesie Orientale', in *Histoire de Nader Chah* (London: Elmsly, 1770), 527–85 (246).
2. Ibid., 233.
3. As noted in the front matter, the adjective Oriental is used in this book when paraphrasing primary sources.
4. See Introduction, the section 'Beyond the Paradigm of Difference'.
5. Armand Renaud, *Les Nuits persanes* (Paris: Lemerre, 1870), 7.
6. Bibliothèque nationale de France. Département des Manuscrits. NAF 13359. Fonds Victor Hugo. II *Les Orientales*, 101 r–v. More on Fouinet below.
7. Maxime Du Camp, *Le Nil (Égypte et Nubie)* (Paris: Librairie nouvelle, 1854), 4.
8. Charles Baudelaire, 'Victor Hugo', in *Sur quelques uns de mes contemporains*, in *Œuvres complètes*, ed. Claude Pichois, 2 vols (Paris: Gallimard, 1975–6), vol. 2, 129–41 (131).
9. Victor Hugo, 'Préface', in *Les Orientales* (Paris: Hector Bossange, 1829), i–xi (iv).
10. Ibid., vii.
11. Ibid., viii.
12. Ibid., ix.
13. See Pierre Larcher, 'Autour des *Orientales*: Victor Hugo, Ernest Fouinet et la Poésie arabe archaïque', in *Orientalisme savant, Orientalisme littéraire: sept essais sur leur connexion* (Arles: Actes Sud, 2017), 51–89.
14. On the collections' innovations, see Franck Laurent, 'Présentation', in Victor Hugo, *Les Orientales, Les Feuilles d'automne*, ed. Franck Laurent (Paris: Librairie Générale Française, 2000), 5–23. On its reception, see Sandrine Raffin, 'Les Orientales. La Réception critique en 1829', in *Victor Hugo 5. Autour des 'Orientales', La Revue des Lettres modernes*, ed. Claude Millet (Paris-Caen: Minard, 2002), 107–38.
15. Du Camp, *Le Nil*, 4.
16. Emmanuel J. Chételat (ed.), *Les Occidentales ou Lettres critiques sur les Orientales de M. Victor Hugo* (Paris: Haute-cœur-Martinet, 1829), 6.
17. See, for instance, the analysis of the poem 'Adieux de l'hôtesse arabe', ibid., 79.
18. On these two types of sources, see Vincent Gille's 'L'air du temps. Sources et contexte des Orientales' and Christine Peltre's '… il dirait que c'est la mosquée' in *Les Orientales. Maison de Victor Hugo. 26.03–04.07 2010* (Saint Ouen: Paris Musées Éditions, 2010), 43–59 and 69–77.
19. BnF Fonds Hugo. II *Les Orientales*.
20. See Larcher, 'Autour des *Orientales*'.
21. Hugo, 'Notes', in *Les Orientales*, 391–422.
22. Hugo would revisit this form of pastiche in *La Légende des siècles* with the poem 'Le roi de Perse', a dialogue between a king and a shepherd. Victor Hugo, *La Légende des siècles: Nouvelle série, Tome I* (Paris: Calmann Lévy, 1877), 159–60.
23. Fouinet's translation reads: 'Je donnerais, ma foi mon esprit'. BnF Fonds Hugo II. *Les Orientales*. 99r.
24. Hugo, *Orientales*, 273.
25. On English translations of Ḥāfez, including the Shīrāzī Turk, see Alexander Bubb, 'The Race for Ḥāfez: Scholarly and Popular Translations at the Fin de Siècle', *Comparative Critical Studies* 17, no. 2 (2020): 225–44.
26. This is the passage (quoted in its entirety) on the manuscript (Figure 1.1).
27. Hugo, *Orientales*, 386.

28. Ibid., 390.
29. Published in 1819, Goethe's late collection of poems the *West-Östlicher Divan* (in English *West-Eastern Divan*) sought to weld together Goethe's own voice as a German poet with the forms and themes of medieval Persian poetry.
30. Théophile Gautier, *Émaux et Camées* (Paris: Didier, 1852), 1–2.
31. As has been shown by Raymond Schwab, the leading figures of the Romantic movement and of Oriental Studies frequented the same social circles. Raymond Schwab, *La Renaissance orientale* (Paris: Payot, 1950), 89–92 and 334–8.
32. See Hugo's preface to *Cromwell* (Paris: Tastu, 1828).
33. Ross Chambers for instance writes that choosing Nezāmi over Shakespeare 'exemplifies the choice of purely conventional expression […] over the drama of life'. Ross Chambers, 'Baudelaire's Street Poetry', *NCFS* 13, no. 4 (1985): 244–59 (254).
34. Patrick McGuinness has also argued that the relationship between inside and outside, or poetry and politics, in this poem is more complex than we might at first believe. See Patrick McGuinness, *Poetry and Radical Politics in* fin de siècle *France: From Anarchism to* Action française (Oxford: Oxford UP, 2015), 10.
35. Marcel Proust, 'Les Éblouissements', in *Le Figaro* (15 June 1907), 1.
36. Anna de Noailles, *Les Éblouissements* (Paris: Calmann-Lévy, 1907), 69–72 (69).
37. Ibid., 70.
38. Ibid., 71–2.
39. Ibid., 69 and 71.
40. Ibid., 70 and 72.
41. Ibid., 72.
42. Ibid.
43. Edward Said, *Orientalism* (1978; London: Penguin, 2003), 101.
44. Some illustrative examples are Henri de Régnier's description of Noailles as a 'princesse des *Mille et Une Nuits*', her friends' nickname for the sofa from which she hosted her salon: 'le Bain turc' [the Turkish bath], and Jacques Émile Blanche's portrait of Noailles 'en "Orientale de Delacroix"', both cited in Christine Peltre, 'Du Bain turc au *Gûlistan*: Anna de Noailles et le Voyage à Constantinople (1887)', in *Le voyage au féminin: perspectives historiques et littéraires, XVIIIe-XXe siècles*, ed. Nicolas Bourguignat (Amsterdam: Rodopi, 2008), 59–71 (61 and 64).
45. Noailles, *Les Éblouissements*, 71.
46. Edward Fitzgerald's *Rubaiyat of Omar Khayyam* was first published in 1859, with a second edition in 1861, third in 1872 and then multiple reissues throughout the 1880s, 1890s and 1900s. The reference French translation was Jean-Baptiste Nicolas's *Les Quatrains de Khéyam* (Paris: 1867).
47. Noailles, *Les Éblouissements*, 11–15 and 46–7.
48. Ibid., 11.
49. Ibid., 122–4 and 137–9.
50. Ibid., 122.
51. Ibid., 123.
52. Ibid., 137.
53. Moya Carey and Mercedes Volait, 'Framing "Islamic Art" for Aesthetic Interiors: Revisiting the 1878 Paris Exhibition', *International Journal of Islamic Architecture* 9, no. 1 (2020): 31–59.
54. Noailles, *Les Éblouissements*, 138.
55. Ibid.
56. Ibid., 139.

57. Ibid., 138.
58. Finn Thiesen, *A Manual of Classical Persian Prosody* (Wiesbaden: Harrassowitz, 1982), 3.
59. Théodore de Banville, *Petit traité de Poésie française* (Paris: Bibliothèque de l'écho de la Sorbonne, 1872), 9.
60. Renaud, *Les Nuits persanes*, 5.
61. Casimir Barbier de Meynard, *La Poésie en Perse* (Paris: Leroux, 1877).
62. Armand Renaud, *Les Nuits persanes, Idylles japonaises, Orient* (Paris: Lemerre, 1895).
63. For an illustrative example, see the close reading of Hāfez's Ghazal n°1 in Michael C. Hillmann, *Unity in the Ghazals of Hāfez* (Minneapolis: Bibliotheca Islamica, 1976), 8–27.
64. These introductions are known in Persian as *hamd*. For two canonical examples of *hamd*, see the openings of Sa'di's *Golestān* and of 'Attār's *The Conference of the Birds*. Renaud himself cites the latter in the notes to the second edition. See Renaud, *Les Nuits persanes, Idylles japonaises, Orient*, 291.
65. It is worth considering, by way of contrast, how the words 'par Allah' [by Allah] are used to other the Iranian character in the opera *Thamara* (1891). See Chapter 4, the section 'Of Poets, Prophets, and Kings'.
66. Renaud, *Les Nuits persanes*, 36.
67. L. P. Elwell-Sutton, "ARŪŻ", *Encyclopaedia Iranica*, II/6–7, 670–9, http://www.iranicaonline.org/articles/aruz-the-metrical-system [accessed 11 April 2022].
68. See, for example, Dick Davies, *Faces of Love: Hafiz and the Poets of Shiraz*, bilingual edition (Washington, DC: Mage, 2012).
69. Banville, *Petit traité*, 9. My translation and my emphasis. Though I am quoting the 1872 edition, it should be noted Banville's treaty was first published in 1871.
70. Lawrence Venuti, *The Translator's Invisibility: A History of Translation*, 2nd edn (London: Routledge, 2008).
71. See Ruth-Ellen St Onge, 'A Banquet for Alphonse Lemerre, the Poets' Publisher', *Mémoires du livre/Studies in Book Culture* 3, no. 1 (2011). https://www.erudit.org/fr/revues/memoires/2011-v3-n1-memoires1830163/1007580ar/ [accessed 10 July 2019].
72. Renaud, *Les Nuits persanes*, 50.
73. Ibid., 90.
74. On the masculine character of nineteenth-century French lyric, see Michael Danahy, 'Marceline Desbordes-Valmore et la fraternité des poètes', *NCFS* 19, no. 3 (1991): 386–93.
75. Renaud, *Les Nuits persanes*, 77–8.
76. In Sa'di's pithy words in the *Golestān*'s Book 'on Love and Youth', 'A slap from a lover is a raisin'. Sa'di, *Gulistan*, trans. Edward B. Eastwick (1880; London: Routledge, 2000), 515.
77. Renaud, *Les Nuits persanes*, 66.
78. Ibid., 91.
79. On Hāfez's use of religious allusion in his love poetry, see Dominic Parviz Brookshaw, *Hafiz and His Contemporaries: Poetry, Performance, and Patronage in Fourteenth-Century Iran* (London: I.B. Tauris, 2019), 233–67. For further context on the relationship between earthly and divine love, see Leonard Lewisohn, 'The Mystical Milieu: Hāfiz's Erotic Spirituality', in *Hafiz and the Religion of Love in Classical Persian Poetry*, ed. Leonard Lewisohn (London: I.B. Tauris, 2010), 31–73.

Renaud also cites the poet 'Wali' (most likely Shāh Neʻmatollāh Valī) as a source for this analogy. Renaud, *Les Nuits persanes, Idylles japonaises, Orient*, 295.
80. See Brookshaw, *Hafiz and His Contemporaries*, 126–9, and Domenico Ingenito, *Beholding Beauty: Saʻdi of Shiraz and the Aesthetics of Desire in Medieval Persian Poetry* (Leiden: Brill, 2021), 56–85.
81. See Davies, *Faces of Love*, and Brookshaw, *Hafiz and His Contemporaries*.
82. Jean Lahor (Henri Cazalis), *Les Quatrains d'Al-Ghazali* (Paris: Lemerre, 1896).
83. Jean Lahor (Henri Cazalis), *En Orient* (Paris: Alphonse Lemerre, 1907). These were in fact versified adaptations of existing translations.
84. Renaud, *Les Nuits persanes, Idylles japonaises, Orient*.
85. Lahor (Cazalis), *En Orient*, 6–7.
86. Ibid., 5.
87. See Nicolas, *Les Quatrains de Khéyam*, Auguste Schmölders, 'Ce qui sauve des égarement et éclaircit les ravissements', *Essai sur les écoles philosophiques chez les Arabes et notamment sur la doctrine d'Algazzali* (Paris: 1842): 16–87, and Casimir Barbier de Meynard, *Traduction nouvelle du Traité de Ghazali intitulé Al-Munqid min adâlal: le Préservatif de l'Erreur, Journal asiatique* 7: 10 (Paris: Imprimerie Nationale, 1877).
88. Lahor (Cazalis), *En Orient*, 6.
89. See, for instance, pp. 26–7, where Cazalis repeats the refrain 'Oh! qu'il est doux, près de l'aimée' [Oh how sweet it is, close to the beloved] in the first and fourth quatrain, and pp. 67–83, where the section title '*Le dialogue d'Allah et du poète*' introduces the quatrains as one single piece. Lahor (Cazalis), *En Orient*.
90. Ibid., 35.
91. Ibid., 100.
92. On the competing interpretations of Khayyām's religious and philosophical views, see Chapter 4, the section 'A Puppet Play about Omar Khayyām'.
93. Lahor (Cazalis), *En Orient*, 87.
94. Ibid., 91.
95. Ibid., 143.
96. Ibid., 144.
97. René Petitbon, *Les Sources orientales de Jean Lahor* (Paris: Nizet, 1962), 97.
98. Petitbon argues that Lahor was also inspired by the tolerance towards other religions expressed in Persian poetry. (Ibid., 108.)
99. Said, *Orientalism*, 71.
100. Lahor (Cazalis), *En Orient*, 6.
101. 'Le musulman […] et l'Européen […] n'ayant rien de commun dans la manière de penser et de sentir'. Ernest Renan, *De la part des peuples sémitiques dans l'histoire de la civilisation* (Paris: Lévy, 1862), 13. The passage is discussed in Chapter 2.
102. At the time that Jones made his case for the importance of translation in 1770, multiple translations of the *Golestān* were already in circulation. See Elio Brancaforte, 'Persian Words of Wisdom Travel to the West Seventeenth-Century European Translations of Saʻdi's Gulistan', *Daphnis* 45 (2017): 450–72.
103. Barbier de Meynard, *La Poésie en Perse*, 47.
104. See, for example, Saadi, 'Gulistan ou le jardin des roses', in 'Contes Orientaux II', in 'Littérature Orientale', in *Panthéon Littéraire* 135 vols (Paris: 1835–45), 58: 553–61.
105. Marceline Desbordes-Valmore, *Les Œuvres poétiques*, ed. Marc Bertrand, 2 vols (Grenoble: Presses Universitaires de Grenoble, 1973), vol. 2, 509. First published in *Poésies inédites* (1860).

106. For a philological analysis of Desbordes-Valmore's use of sources, see Julia Caterina Hartley, 'Beyond Orientalism: When Desbordes-Valmore Carried Sa'di's Roses to France', *Iranian Studies* 52, nos. 5–6 (2019): 785–808.
107. Yves Bonnefoy, 'Préface', in Marceline Desbordes-Valmore, *Poésies*, ed. Yves Bonnefoy (Paris: Gallimard, 1983), 7–34 (20).
108. This is where I disagree with Bonnefoy, according to whom the poem only records a failure of language.
109. Sa'di, *Golestān*, ed. Mohammad Javād Mashkur (Tehran: Eqbāl, 1963), 8–9.
110. Charles Augustin de Sainte-Beuve, 'Qu'est-ce qu'un classique?' (*Le Constitutionnel* (21 October 1850): 3–4.
111. This is the psychological interpretation of literary influence famously advanced by Harold Bloom in *The Anxiety of Influence: A Theory of Poetry* (New York: Oxford UP, 1973).
112. Said, *Orientalism*, 104.

2 History and historical fiction

1. Abraham Hyacinthe Anquetil-Duperron, *Zend-Avesta, ouvrage de Zoroastre*, 2 vols (Paris: Tilliard, 1771).
2. Sanskrit is the language of Buddhist and Hindu texts. It also offered a gateway into the Avestan language, with which it shared similarities. See William Jones, 'The Sixth Anniversary Discourse', *Asiatick Researches* 2 (1790): 43–66 (53–4).
3. Raymond Schwab, *La Renaissance orientale* (Paris: Payot, 1950), 13.
4. Jules Michelet, *La Bible de l'Humanité* (Paris: Chamerot, 1864), 484.
5. Ibid., 38.
6. On the ethnocentric limits of comparative religious studies, see Angus Nicholls's current work (forthcoming) on 'Literature and the Science of Comparison in Nineteenth-Century Germany and Britain: Four Case Studies'.
7. Michelet, *La Bible de l'Humanité*, 484.
8. Ibid., 485.
9. Anil Bhatti and Dorothee Kimmich, 'Introduction', in *Similarity: A Paradigm for Culture Theory*, ed. Anil Bhatti and Dorothee Kimmich (New Delhi: Tulika Books, 2018), 1–22. See Introduction.
10. William Jones, 'The Third Anniversary Discourse', *Asiatick Researches* 1 (1788): 415–31. Franz Bopp, *Über das Conjugationssystem Der Sanskritsprache in Vergleinchung mit jenem der grieschischen, Latenischen, persischen end germanischen Sprache* (Frankfurt: Andräischen, 1816).
11. David Motadel, 'Iran and the Aryan Myth', in Ali Ansari (ed.), *Perceptions of Iran: History, Myths, and Nationalism from Medieval Persia to the Islamic Republic* (London: I.B. Tauris, 2013), 119–45.
12. The term was first proposed by Anquetil-Duperron and was later deciphered on the tomb of Darius the Great in an inscription (known as 'the DNa inscription') which reads: 'I am Darius the great king, king of kings, king of countries containing all kinds of men, king in this great earth far and wide, son of Hystaspes, an Achaemenid, a Persian, son of a Persian, an Aryan, having Aryan lineage.'

13. For greater readability, I have only used scare quotes when first introducing the terms Aryan and Semite in this chapter. It should remain clear to the reader, however, that these categories are dubious constructions.
14. The ancient Greeks referred to the ancient Persians as *barbarians*, a term reserved for all those who did not speak their language.
15. On the problems with constructing Iran as a nation on the basis of language and ethnicity, see Mostafa Vaziri, *Iran as Imagined Nation: The Construction of a National Identity*, 2nd edn (Piscataway, NJ: Gorgias Press, 2013).
16. Ferdowsi (trans. Jules Mohl), *Livre des Rois*, 2nd edn, 7 vols (Paris: Imprimerie Nationale, 1876-8).
17. See Hayden White, *Metahistory: The Historical Imagination in 19th-Century Europe (Fortieth-Anniversary Edition)* (Baltimore: Johns Hopkins UP, 2014), and Lionel Gossman, *Between History and Literature* (Cambridge, MA: Harvard UP, 1990).
18. Michelet first used the term in the volume of the *Histoire de France* devoted to the sixteenth century (1855). The term was later popularized by Jacob Burkhardt in *Die Cultur der Renaissance in Italien* (1860).
19. Gossman, *Between History and Literature*, 166. A concrete example of this was the public sensation caused by Renan's opening lecture at the Collège de France: it attracted such a large crowd of admirers that the Minister of Education sought out strategies to minimize publicity. Ernest Renan, *Œuvres complètes*, ed. Henriette Pischari, 10 vols (Paris: Calmann-Lévy, 1947-61), vol. 10, 345 and 351.
20. Gossman, *Between History and Literature*, 166-7.
21. Pankaj Mishra, *From the Ruins of Empire: The Revolt against the West and the Remaking of Asia* (London: Allen Lane, 2012), 100.
22. These are the short stories 'L'Illustre magicien', 'Histoire de Gambèr-Aly', and 'La Guerre des Turcomans', which are all found in Gobineau's *Nouvelles asiatiques* (1876). A further text that I have chosen to exclude is Ernest Fouinet's *La Caravane des morts* (1836), a novel set in the Safavid period. While this piece of historical fiction no doubt merits further investigation, it predates both the translation of the *Shāhnāmeh* and the development of modern French historiography. As such, it does not engage with the reevaluation of Iran's ancient heritage and consequent reframing of Iran's relationship to Europe which is the subject of this chapter.
23. White, *Metahistory*, 135-62, especially 152.
24. 'Our parents the Aryans,' quoted from Michelet, *La Bible de l'Humanité*, iv.
25. See, in particular, Todorov, *Nous et les autres: La réflexion française sur la diversité humaine* (Paris: Seuil, 1989), Léon Poliakov, *Le Mythe aryen: Essai sur les sources du racisme et des nationalismes* (Paris: Calmann-Lévy, 1971); Maurice Olender, *Les langues du paradis: aryens et sémites, in couple providentiel* (Paris: Seuil, 1989) and Robert Young, *Colonial Desire: Hybridity in Theory, Culture, and Race* (London: Routledge, 1995).
26. Arthur de Gobineau, *Œuvres*, 3 vols (Paris: Gallimard, 1983), vol. 1, 603.
27. Young, *Colonial Desire*, 100.
28. Gobineau, *Œuvres*, vol. 1, 479 and 484.
29. Ibid., 353 and 480.
30. Ibid., 633-4.
31. Young, *Colonial Desire*, 32.
32. Gobineau was neither the first nor the last to support the theory of a westward Aryan migration. See Motadel, 'Iran and the Aryan Myth'.
33. Jones, 'The Sixth Anniversary Discourse', 65.

34. Gobineau, *Œuvres*, vol. 1, 493.
35. As noted by Young, blood (both literal and figurative) plays a central function in the *Essai* allowing Gobineau to bind together 'race as physical difference and race as cultural difference'. Young, *Colonial Desire*, 105.
36. Gobineau, *Œuvres*, vol. 1, 488–9.
37. Ibid., 485. It should go without saying that Gobineau had no way of verifying the skin tones of a people who had lived two thousand years before him.
38. Ibid., 635.
39. Ibid., 652.
40. Ibid., 636.
41. Ibid., 652–3.
42. Persian military losses to Greece in the West were in fact only minor concerns in relation to the overall size of the empire and the solidity of Persian rule over its eastern provinces.
43. Arthur de Gobineau, *Histoire des Perses*, 2 vols (Paris: Plon, 1869). The work is largely a summary of Ferdowsi's *Shāhnāmeh* and Mirkhond's *Rowzat os-safā*.
44. Ibid., vol. 2, 360. This had also been the subject of an abandoned play by Gobineau, published posthumously in Germany: *Alexandre le Macédonien: Tragédie en cinq actes*, 2nd edn (Strassburg: Trübner, 1902). The Persianization of Alexander will be at the heart of the following chapter section.
45. Ibid., vol. 2, 637.
46. Ibid.
47. Ibid.
48. The line drawn in the concluding pages of the *Histoire des Perses* will be maintained in Gobineau's *Nouvelles asiatiques* (1876). In contrast to the spirit of kinship with which the Achaemenids had been described, modern Iranian characters exemplify how 'l'esprit asiatique […] s'éloigne du nôtre' [the Asiatick mind […] differs from our own]. Arthur de Gobineau, *Nouvelles asiatiques*, ed. Jean Gaulmier (Paris: Garnier, 1965), 7.
49. Letter to Gobineau dated 26 June 1856, in Renan, *Œuvres complètes*, vol. 10, 203–5 (4).
50. Ibid., vol. 8, 576–7.
51. Ernest Renan, *De la part des peuples sémitiques dans l'histoire de la civilisation* (Paris: Lévy, 1862), 25–6.
52. A group of Catholic students had in fact planned to protest his inaugural lecture because they believed his views to be contrary to Christian values. Renan, *Œuvres complètes*, vol. 10, 340–3. The controversy would go national the following year when Renan published his *Vie de Jésus*, in which he argued that rather than *being* divine, Jesus Christ was exceptional for bringing humanity closer to the divine. Renan, *Vie de Jésus* (Paris: Lévy, 1863), 457.
53. Casimir Barbier de Meynard, *La Poésie en Perse* (Paris: Leroux, 1877), 31. The influence of racialist theories on this work is also clear in its reference to 'les pays de sang Iranien' [Iranian-blooded countries] (25).
54. Renan, *De la part des peuples sémitiques*, 13.
55. Robert Young argues that even Gobineau did not go as far as to endorse polygenesis, since the central role played by miscegenation in his writing presupposes that all races are part of the human species. Young, *Colonial Desire*, 103.

56. Todorov writes of Renan: 'La façade relativiste cache une construction simplement ethnocentriste.' [The relativist façade hides a purely ethnocentric construction.] Todorov, *Nous et les autres*, 158.
57. Robert Priest, 'Ernest Renan's Race Problem', *Historical Journal* 58, no. 1 (2015), 309–30.
58. Renan, *De la part des peuples sémitiques*, 14–17.
59. Ernest Renan, 'L'Islam et la Science', *Journal des Débats* (30 March 1883): 2–3 (2).
60. Ibid.
61. Ibid.
62. In his early and lesser-known essay 'Averroès et l'Averroïsme' (1852), Renan had not yet framed his rejection of Islamic philosophy around the racial opposition between Arabs and Persians. The essay does suggest that the teachings of the Quran are inimical to scientific enquiry; however, Renan also clearly assumes that there was such a thing as 'la philosophie arabe' and that Averroes was its last great champion. See Renan, *Œuvres completes*, vol. 3, 9–365 (15).
63. Renan, 'L'Islam et la Science', 3.
64. Ibid.
65. Ibid.
66. Ibid.
67. See the entries for Al-Afghani by Nikki Keddie in Ibrahim Kalin (ed.), *The Oxford Encyclopedia of Philosophy, Science, and Technology in Islam* (Oxford: Oxford UP, 2014) and by Oliver Leaman in Oliver Leaman (ed.), *The Biographical Encyclopaedia of Islamic Philosophy* (London: Bloomsbury, 2015).
68. On financial imperialism, see the section 'Plagued by the West' in Chapter 3.
69. Jamal al-Din Al-Afghani, open letter to the *Journal des Débats* (18 May 1883): 3.
70. Young, *Colonial Desire*, 32. It is worth noting that while Young identifies, like I do, a break between temporal and racialist views of civilization, Johannes Fabian instead sees a continuity between the two, arguing that the 'temporalization' of cultural difference plays an essential role in justifying imperialism. Johannes Fabian, *Time and the Other: How Anthropology makes its object* (New York: Columbia UP, 1983).
71. Al-Afghani, open letter, *Journal des Débats*.
72. Renan quotes these words back at the Minister of Education in a letter dated 27 February 1862. Renan, *Œuvres complètes*, vol. 10, 344. Following the dismissal, Renan thanked Jules Mohl (then Chair of Persian at the Collège de France) for interceding on his behalf (ibid., 416).
73. Al-Afghani, open letter, *Journal des Débats*.
74. Renan, *De la part des peuples sémitiques*, 13. Cited above.
75. Al-Afghani, open letter, *Journal des Débats*.
76. Ibid.
77. Ibid.
78. Ernest Renan, open letter, *Journal des Débats* (19 May 1883): 3.
79. Ibid.
80. Ibid.
81. Ibid.
82. I take the phrase 'denial of coevalness' from Fabian, *Time and the Other*, cited above.
83. We have the letters that the young Renan wrote to Michelet in June 1848 to express his profound admiration for his teaching and in January 1862 upon joining his ranks as a lecturer at the Collège de France. Renan, *Œuvres complètes*, vol. 10, 50 and 340–1. It is also clear from Michelet's diary that the two of them met regularly outside of work.

84. Renan, letter to Madame Michelet dated 19 décembre 1881, *Œuvres complètes*, vol. 10, 853.
85. Jules Michelet, *Journal*, 4 vols (Paris: Gallimard, 1959-76). Quoted from vol. 3, 167, but see also pp. 142 and 168.
86. White, *Metahistory*, 150-5.
87. Gossman, *Between History and Literature*, 189, and White, *Metahistory*, 162.
88. Michelet, *La Bible de l'Humanité*, iv.
89. White, *Metahistory*, 149.
90. Michelet, *La Bible de l'Humanité*, 78-9. The ancient Persians did in fact have temples. Michelet inherits the notion that they did not from Greek authors.
91. Ibid., 79.
92. Michelet quotes from Eugène Burnouf's revised edition of Anquetil-Duperron's *Zend-Avesta*, published in *Études sur la langue et sur les textes zends*, vol. 1 (Paris: Imprimerie nationale, 1850).
93. Michelet, *La Bible de l'Humanité*, 81.
94. Ibid., 84-5.
95. Ibid., 94-5.
96. Ibid., 97.
97. Ibid.
98. Ibid., 96-8.
99. White, *Metahistory*, 150.
100. Ibid., 162.
101. Michelet, *La Bible de l'Humanité*, 485.
102. Ibid., iv.
103. Ibid., i.
104. Ibid., ii.
105. Ibid., v-vi.
106. Ibid., vi.
107. In his diary, Michelet would describe the process of writing these two chapters as 'une des plus grandes fêtes de ma vie' [one of the greatest joys of my life]. Michelet, *Journal*, vol. 3, 168.
108. Michelet, *La Bible de l'Humanité*, 112.
109. Ibid., 112-14 (113-14).
110. Ibid., 113.
111. Ibid., 115. Gobineau's exact term is 'englober' (*Œuvres*, vol. 1, 653, quoted above.)
112. Ibid.
113. Renan, 'L'Islam et la Science', 2.
114. On this subject, see two recent doctoral theses: Sahba Shayani, 'The Representation of Women in Premodern Persian Epic Romance Poetry' (UCLA, 2020) and Nina Soleymani Majd, 'Lionnes et colombes: les personnages féminins dans le Cycle de Guillaume d'Orange, la Digénide, et le Châhnâmeh de Ferdowsi' (Grenoble, 2019).
115. Michelet, *La Bible de l'Humanité*, 121, note 1. Michelet spares Christianity from such criticisms on the basis that female figures, such as the Virgin Mary, play a central role in it.
116. Ibid., 122-3.
117. Ibid., 128-9.
118. Ibid., 486.
119. Ibid., 2.
120. Michelet, *Journal*, vol. 3, 168.

121. Napoleon compared his men to the ancient Romans upon departure for Egypt and himself to Alexander upon arrival in Alexandria. See Antoine-Clair Thibaudeau, *Histoire de la campagne d'Egypte sous le règne de Napoléon le grand*, 2 vols (Paris: Huzard, 1839), vol. 2, 55, and Napoléon Bonaparte, *Discours de guerre*, ed. Jacques-Olivier Bourdon (Paris: Édition Pierre de Taillac, 2011), 57. On Napoleon's emulation of Alexander, see Jacques-Olivier Bourdon, 'Napoléon et l'hellénisme', *Historiographie et identités culturelles* 20 (2014): 33–48, and Agnieszka Fulińska, 'Alexander and Napoleon', *Brill's Companion to the Reception of Alexander the Great* (Leiden: Brill, 2018), 545–75.
122. As well as being interested in Persian literature, Gautier also published translations of Chinese poems and works set in India and Japan.
123. Judith Gautier, *Iskender: Histoire persane* (Paris: Frinzine, 1886), 13–16.
124. Ibid., 80.
125. Théodore de Banville wrote a particularly enthusiastic review. See 'Iskender', *Gil Blas* (4 June 1886): 1.
126. The first public iteration of this notion was in a parliamentary speech by French prime minister Jules Ferry, which was delivered on 28 July 1885 and published in the *Journal Officiel*.
127. One reviewer indeed went so far as to caution that *Iskender* was not recommended reading for schoolchildren. See anonymous review in *Le Voltaire* (24 July 1894): 1.
128. See Gautier, *Iskender*, 48–53 for the battle and 21–2 and 127–8 for women.
129. Ibid., 163.
130. Ibid., 53. The lack of detail in *Iskender*'s scenes of violence should not be mistaken for squeamishness: we know from other novels that Gautier excelled at graphic violence. See Juliana Starr, 'Less Is Gore: Graphic Violence in the Fiction of Judith Gautier', *Women in French Studies* 21 (2013): 27–40.
131. Gautier, *Iskender*, vii.
132. At the time of the proposal, Mohsen allegedly had a temporary wife whom he planned to repudiate in favour of Judith, a notion unthinkable in France where marriage was for life and divorce was illegal. Suzanne Meyer-Zundel, *Quinze ans auprès de Judith Gautier* (Porto: Tipografia Nunes, 1969).
133. Eve Kosofsky Sedgwick, *Between Men: English Literature and Male Homosocial Desire* (New York: Columbia UP, 1985).
134. Gautier, *Iskender*, 73.
135. Ibid., 74.
136. Ibid., 94.
137. Ibid., 114.
138. Ibid.
139. Ibid., 115.
140. Ibid., 117.
141. Ibid., 118–19.
142. See the discussion of Aristotle's 'Nicomachean Ethics' in Ivy Schweitzer, *Perfecting Friendship: Politics and Affiliation in Early American Literature* (Chapel Hill: University of North Carolina Press, 2006), 35.
143. Gautier, *Iskender*, 120.
144. Ibid., 121.
145. Ibid., 157–8.
146. Ibid., 123.

147. Michel Foucault, 'De l'amitié comme mode de vie', *Dits et écrits: 1954–1988*, 4 vols, ed. Daniel Defert and François Ewalt (Paris: Gallimard, 1994), vol. 4, 163–7 (164).
148. Sedgwick, *Between Men*, 21.
149. Gautier, *Iskender*, 133–6.
150. Ibid., 137.
151. Ibid., 163.
152. Ibid., 165.
153. Ibid., 166.
154. Michael Lucey, *The Misfit of the Family* (Durham, NC: Duke UP, 2003).
155. Gautier, *Iskender*, 204–5.
156. Sedgwick, *Between Men*, 25–6.
157. Amanda Chapman, 'Queer Elasticity: Imperial Boyhood in Late Nineteenth-Century Boys' Adventure Fiction', *Children's Literature* 46 (2008): 56–77 (57).
158. Anne Vincent-Buffault, *L'exercice de l'amitié: pour une histoire des pratiques amicales aux XVIIIe et XIXe siècles* (Paris: Seuil, 1995), 10.
159. Gautier, *Iskender*, 166 and 181.
160. Ibid., 189.
161. Ibid., 190.
162. Ibid.
163. Ibid., 84 and 283.
164. By 'performative speech act', I refer to J. L. Austin's term for utterances that enact a change in status, for example, the words spoken in a marriage service or the naming of a ship. John Langshaw Austin, *How to Do Things with Words* (Oxford: Clarendon Press, 1975).
165. Jane Dieulafoy, *Rose d'Hatra* (Paris: Armand Colin, 1893), 1.
166. The two novellas were published in one same volume, Jane Dieulafoy, *Rose d'Hatra* (Paris: Armand Colin, 1893). *Rose d'Hatra* is pp. 13–164 and *L'Oracle* is pp. 165–274.
167. These contributions are recounted in the travelogue *La Perse, la Chaldée et la Susiane* (1887) and the dig diary *À Suse: Journal de fouilles* (1888), which are discussed in Chapter 3.
168. Rachel Mesch, *Before Trans: Three Gender Stories from Nineteenth-Century France* (Stanford, CA: Stanford UP, 2020).
169. Loliée, cited in ibid., 120.
170. Mesch started using the pronoun 'they' instead of 'she' for Dieulafoy in 2021. Citing the precedent set by Jen Manion and Kirstin Ringelberg, Mesch notes that although the gender neutral pronouns 'they/them/themself' did not exist at the time that Dieulafoy lived, adopting them in contemporary scholarship serves to acknowledge Dieulafoy's gender non-conformity and reach a richer understanding of them. Rachel Mesch, 'The Legs of the Orientalist: Jane Dieulafoy's Self-Portraits in Persia', *Yale French Studies* 139 (2021): 171–89.
171. Ibid., 172, note 6.
172. The two novels analysed by Mesch are *Volontaire* (1892) and *Frère Pelage* (1894). Dieulafoy refers to herself as 'audacieuse' at the beginning of the preface to *Parysatis*. Dieulafoy, *Parysatis* (Paris: Armand Colin, 1892), i.
173. Fonds Dieulafoy, Bibliothèque de l'Institut de France, MS 2683 (1).
174. Dieulafoy, *Parysatis*, 46.
175. Ibid., 367.
176. Ibid., 367–9.
177. Ibid., 370.

178. Ibid., 388.
179. See Annelise Maugue, *L'Identité masculine en crise au tournant du siècle 1871–1914* (1987; Paris: Payot & Rivages, 2001) and Edward Berenson, *The Trial of Madame Caillaux* (Berkeley, CA: Berkeley UP, 1992).
180. Edward Porter, 'Decadence and the Fin-de-Siècle Novel', in *The Cambridge Companion to the French Novel: From 1800 to the Present*, ed. Tim Unwin (Cambridge: Cambridge UP), 93–110 (98).
181. Berenson, *The Trial of Madame Caillaux*.
182. Dieulafoy, *Parysatis*, 388.
183. See Mirkhond (trans. Silvestre de Sacy), 'Histoire des rois de Perse, de la dynastie des Sassanides', in *Mémoires sur les antiquités de la Perse* (Paris: Imprimerie nationale exécutive du Louvre, 1793), 271–417 (287–9). Dieulafoy would also have been able to consult the original Persian text in the following edition: Mirkhond, *Histoire des Sassanides* (Paris: Firmin Didot, 1843), 183–4. See also Ferdowsi, *Livre des Rois*, vol. 5, 342–8. In Ferdowsi's version, Nadirah's father is called Tayer and Nadirah is called Malekeh.
184. In the *Shāhnāmeh*, the abducted Persian noblewoman is the protagonist's mother and the abductor is Tayer. This makes Nadirah/Malekeh a child of rape, giving her a motive for betraying her father.
185. Dieulafoy, *Rose d'Hatra*, 160.
186. Ibid., 23.
187. Ibid., 19.
188. Ibid., 195.
189. Ibid., 202–5.
190. Ibid., 245–6.
191. Ibid., 249.
192. Ibid., 253–4.
193. Ibid., 254.
194. Ibid., 255–6.
195. Ibid., 258–9.
196. On this, see Chapter 3, the section 'Among Women: Scenes from the Harem'.
197. See Margot Irvine, 'Imagining Women at War: Dieulafoy's 1913 Campaign', *Women in French Studies* 27 (2019): 119–30.
198. Dieulafoy, *Rose d'Hatra*, 203.
199. I refer to the concept of gender performativity first put forward by Judith Butler in 'Performative Acts and Gender Constitution: An Essay in Phenomenology and Feminist Theory', *Theatre Journal* 40, no. 4 (1988): 519–31.
200. Dieulafoy, *Rose d'Hatra*, 205.
201. Ibid.
202. Ibid., 207.
203. Ibid., 269.
204. Ibid.
205. Ibid., 271
206. Ibid., 273.
207. Ibid., 195.
208. Ibid., 273.
209. Ibid., 274.
210. Ibid., 25
211. Ibid., 25–6.

212. On this, see Rachel Mesch, *Having It All in the Belle Époque: How French Women's Magazines Invented the Modern Woman* (Stanford, CA: Stanford UP, 2013).
213. *Femina*, 15 August 1902. The photograph in fact shows Jane in a position of authority, towering over her seated husband. See figure 28 in Mesch, *Before Trans*, 101.
214. Dieulafoy, *Parysatis*, 223–5.
215. Ibid., 65. The excavation is recounted in detail in her *Journal de fouilles* and the frieze of archers remains to this day a centrepiece of the Louvre's collection of Iranian antiquities.
216. See, for example, René Thorel, 'Mme Dieulafoy', *Revue illustrée* (1 September 1903): 15–36.
217. Dieulafoy, *Rose d'Hatra*, 55.
218. Ibid., 246.
219. Ibid., 245.
220. See, for example, the accession scene in *Parysatis* (155–61), as well as Shapour not daring to break a vow taken in Mithra's name, and Xerxes praying for Artremisia during the Battle of Salamis (*Rose d'Hatra*, 136 and 218–19, respectively).
221. See, for example, the description of how the citizens of Susa deal with the summer heat. Dieulafoy, *Parysatis*, 231.
222. Ibid., i.
223. Ibid., 388, quoted above.
224. Fonds Dieulafoy, Bibliothèque de l'Institut de France, MS 2683 (1), quoted above.
225. Ibid.
226. MS 2685. Quoted in translation by Mesch, *Before Trans*, 99.
227. Irvine, 'Imagining Women at War'.
228. Gautier, *Iskender*, frontispiece.
229. Dieulafoy uses the term 'Aryan' both in *Parysatis* when describing the royal guards (391) and in *Rose d'Hatra* when referring to Shapour's soldiers (98).
230. Fabian, *Time and the Other*.
231. Jacques de Morgan, cited in Nader Nasiri-Moghaddam, *L'archéologie française en Perse et les antiquités nationales (1884–1914)* (Paris: Connaissances et Savoirs, 2004), 76.

3 Travel-writing

1. 'Not all roads lead to Persia.' Quoted from Jane Dieulafoy, *La Perse, la Chaldée et la Susiane* (Paris: Hachette, 1887), 2.
2. René de Chateaubriand, *Itinéraire de Paris à Jérusalem* (1811), Alphonse de Lamartine, *Voyage en Orient* (1835), Gustave Flaubert, *Voyage en Orient* (took place between 1849 and 1851, but was only published posthumously in 1910), Gérard de Nerval, *Voyage en Orient* (1851), Théophile Gautier, *Voyage pittoresque en Algérie* (1845, unfinished), *Constantinople* (1853), *Voyage en Égypte* (1869).
3. Already in 1801, Napoleon Bonaparte had realized that an alliance between France and Iran was essential to containing Russian and British ambitions in the region. The British, in turn, viewed Iran as a 'buffer state' that could be used to shield their Indian territories from Russia.
4. Dieulafoy, *La Perse*, 2.

5. Mary-Louise Pratt, *Imperial Eyes: Travel Writing and Transculturation*, 2nd edn (London: Routledge, 2008), 3.
6. The phrase 'genre composed of other genres' is taken from Mary Campbell, *The Witness and the Other World: Exotic European Travel Writing (400–1600)* (Ithaca, NY: Cornell UP, 1988), 6. The terms 'genre sans lois' and 'genre fuyant' are employed by Roland Le Huenen in 'Le récit de voyage: l'entrée en littérature', *Études littéraires* 20, no. 1 (1987): 45–57 (45). On travel-writing as a frontier genre, see Adrien Pasquali, *Le Tour des horizons: Critique et récits de voyage* (Paris: Klincksieck, 1994), 107, and Alain Guyot, *Analogie et récit de voyage: Voir, mesurer, interpréter le monde* (Paris: Garnier, 2012), 34.
7. Guyot, *Analogie et récit de voyage*, 34.
8. The travelogues that I am not including, for reasons of space, are Jules-Charles Teule, *Pensées et notes critiques extraites du journal de mes voyages*, 2 vols (Paris: Bertrand, 1842); Xavier Hommaire de Hell, *Voyage en Turquie et en Perse 1846–8*, ed. Adèle Hommaire de Hell, 4 vols (Paris: Bertrand, 1854–60); Ferdinand Méchin, *Lettres d'un voyageur en Perse* (Bourges: Jollet, 1867); Julien de Rochechouart, *Souvenirs d'un voyage en Perse* (Paris: Challamel, 1867) and Auguste Lacoin de Vilmorin, *De Paris à Bombay par la Perse* (Paris: Firmin-Didot, 1895).
9. As summarized in the section on Dieulafoy in Chapter 2, Rachel Mesch has argued that Dieulafoy is best understood as a transgender person at a time when there was no word for this. See Rachel Mesch, *Before Trans: Three Gender Stories from Nineteenth-Century France* (Stanford, CA: Stanford UP, 2020) and 'The Legs of the Orientalist: Jane Dieulafoy's Self-Portraits in Persia', *Yale French Studies* 139 (2021): 171–89.
10. Marcel Proust, letter to Marthe Bibesco, 29 March 1908. The letter is quoted in its entirety in Marthe Bibesco, *Au bal avec Marcel Proust* (Paris: Gallimard, 1928), 41–4 (42).
11. On this, see Peter Hulme and Russell McDougall, 'Introduction: In the Margins of Anthropology', in *Writing, Travel, and Empire in the Margins of Anthropology* (London: I.B. Tauris, 2007), 1–16.
12. In this section I use the term Persian rather than Iranian because 'Persan' is the most commonly adopted term in the primary texts, though 'Iranien' is also occasionally used.
13. Eugène Flandin, *Voyage en Perse*, 2 vols (Paris: Baudry, 1851), vol. 2, 413.
14. See ibid., vol. 1, 429; Arthur de Gobineau, *Trois ans en Asie* (Paris: Hachette, 1859), 232; and Dieulafoy, *La Perse*, 46.
15. Claude Anet, *Les Roses d'Ispahan: La Perse en automobile* (Paris: Juven, 1906), 162.
16. Flandin, *Voyage*, vol. 1, 170, and vol. 2, 46.
17. Flandin, *Voyage*, vol. 2, 413; Dieulafoy, *La Perse*, 158.
18. Flandin, *Voyage*, vol. 2, 404.
19. See Olivier Bonnerot, *La Perse dans la littérature et la pensée françaises au XVIIIe siècle: de l'image au mythe* (Paris: Champion-Slatkine, 1988), 72–5.
20. Flandin, *Voyage*, vol. 2, 415.
21. Dieulafoy, *La Perse*, 585.
22. Ibid., 586.
23. Ibid., 46 and 324.
24. Ibid., 453.
25. Dieulafoy, *La Perse*, 153.
26. Flandin, *Voyage*, vol. 2, 414.

27. Flandin, *Voyage*, vol. 1, 157.
28. The analogy is explicit in Dieulafoy's dig diary where penetrating the ruins of Susa is likened to the unveiling and sexual conquest of a woman. See Dieulafoy, *À Suse. Journal de fouilles* (Paris: Hachette, 1888), 285.
29. Flandin, *Voyage*, vol. 1, 158–65.
30. Ibid., 160.
31. Ibid., 160–1.
32. Ibid., 162–4.
33. Ibid., 165.
34. See, for example, Anet, *Roses*, 164 or Pierre Loti, *Vers Ispahan* (Paris: Calmann-Lévy, 1904), 242.
35. See Billie Melman, *Women's Orients: English Women and the Middle East, 1718–1918: Sexuality, Religion, and Work* (London: Macmillan, 1992), and Bénédicte Monicat, *Itinéraires de l'écriture au féminin: voyageuses du 19e siècle* (Amsterdam: Rodopi, 1996).
36. Dieulafoy, *La Perse*, 2.
37. On Dieulafoy's identity as transgender, see Mesch, *Before Trans*, cited above.
38. Dieulafoy, *La Perse*, 64 and 110.
39. Ibid., 37–8.
40. See Linda Nochlin, 'The Imaginary Orient', *The Politics of Vision: Essays on Nineteenth-Century Art and Society* (New York: Harper & Row, 1989), 33–59.
41. On the discrepancies between text and photographs, see Caroline Ferraris-Besso, 'La Subversion par l'image: *La Perse, la Chaldée et la Susiane* de Jane Dieulafoy', *Women in French Studies* 7 (2018): 241–58.
42. Guyot, *Analogie et récit de voyage*, 34, cited above.
43. Dieulafoy, *La Perse*, 87.
44. Jane Dieulafoy, *L'Orient sous le voile: de Chiraz à Bagdad* (Paris: Phébus, 2011).
45. Dieulafoy, *La Perse*, 68.
46. Ibid., 114.
47. Ibid., 78, 129.
48. Ibid., 200.
49. Inge Boer, 'Uncertain Territories: Travel as Exchange', in *Uncertain Territories: Boundaries in Cultural Analysis* ed. Mieke Bal, Bregje Van Eekelen and Patricia Spyer (Amsterdam: Rodopi, 2006), 97–101.
50. On Todorov's *Nous et les autres*, see book introduction.
51. Dieulafoy, *La Perse*, 209.
52. Ibid., 209–10.
53. Ibid., 210.
54. Melman makes this argument in relation to Lady Anne Blunt's writing. Melman, *Women's Orients*, 298. Emphasis in the original.
55. See Bhatti and Kimmich, as discussed in Introduction.
56. The same observation is made by Halia Koo in '(Wo)men Travellers: Physical and Narrative Boundaries', *Mosaic* 39, no. 2 (2006): 19–36.
57. Dieulafoy, *La Perse*, 158, 123–9 and 306–9.
58. Marthe Bibesco, *Les Huit paradis* (Paris: Hachette, 1908), 17–20.
59. Ibid., 21.
60. Ibid., 150–6.
61. Ibid., 150.
62. Ibid., 152–3.

63. Ibid., 155.
64. Ibid., 156.
65. Ibid., 154.
66. Ibid., 155.
67. Ibid., 212.
68. Ibid., 213–14.
69. Ibid., 154.
70. It should be noted that Qajar Iran was religiously diverse: Dieulafoy in particular devotes a lot of attention to minority communities, such as Zoroastrians, Bahai's, Jews and Christian Armenians. For reasons of space, I am focusing on travel-writers' treatment of Shi'ism, the official religion of Iran since the Safavid dynasty.
71. Flandin, *Voyage*, vol. 1, 254–5.
72. Ibid., 253.
73. Ibid., 348.
74. Ibid., 252.
75. Ibid., 254.
76. Ibid., 253.
77. Ibid., 251.
78. Dieulafoy, *La Perse*, 109.
79. Ibid.
80. Loti, *Vers Ispahan*, 175.
81. Ibid., 175–6.
82. Ibid.
83. Ibid., 176.
84. Ibid., 177.
85. Ibid.
86. Ibid., 175–7.
87. Ibid., 177–8.
88. Bibesco, *Les Huit paradis*, 161.
89. Ibid., 162.
90. Ibid., 163.
91. Bibesco did not speak Persian, so it is unclear who acted as her interpreter.
92. Bibesco, *Les Huit paradis*, 166.
93. Ibid., 161.
94. Loti, *Vers Ispahan*, 221.
95. Ibid., 222.
96. Ibid., 225.
97. Flandin, *Voyage*, vol. 1, 353.
98. Ibid., 354.
99. Gobineau, *Trois ans en Asie*, 208.
100. Ibid., 209.
101. Dieulafoy, *La Perse*, 256.
102. Ibid.
103. Ibid., 259.
104. Flandin, *Voyage*, vol. 2, 415.
105. Dieulafoy, *La Perse*, 309.
106. Flandin, *Voyage*, vol. 1, 343–4.
107. Dieulafoy, *La Perse*, 290.
108. Ibid.

109. Guyot, *Analogie et récit de voyage*, 33.
110. Loti, *Vers Ispahan*, 187.
111. Gobineau, *Trois ans en Asie*, 228.
112. Loti, *Vers Ispahan*, 208.
113. Flandin, *Voyage*, vol. 1, 344–5.
114. Loti, *Vers Ispahan*, 209.
115. Ibid.
116. Ibid.
117. Ibid., 209–10.
118. Gobineau, *Trois ans en Asie*, 228.
119. Dieulafoy, *La Perse*, 290; Loti, *Vers Ispahan*, 208.
120. The essay is preserved in the same manuscript group as the drafts for *La Perse*. Bibliothèque de l'Institut de France, Fonds Dieulafoy MS 2673 (3), Folio 80.
121. Flandin, *Voyage*, vol. 1, 339.
122. Ibid.
123. Ibid., 338.
124. Dieulafoy, *La Perse*, 290; Loti, *Vers Ispahan*, 227–8.
125. Flandin, *Voyage*, vol. 1, 342; Loti, *Vers Ispahan*, 206.
126. Gobineau, *Trois ans en Asie*, 212.
127. Loti, *Vers Ispahan*, 207.
128. Ibid.
129. Ibid.
130. Ibid., 225.
131. Ibid., 207.
132. Ibid., 208.
133. Ali Behdad has argued that the trope of claiming to have arrived 'too late' to experience the unspoilt Orient, while also simultaneously claiming to be its last witness, is a recurring one in Oriental travelogues from the second half of the nineteenth century. Ali Behdad, *Belated Travelers: Orientalism in the Age of Colonial Dissolution* (Durham, NC: Duke UP, 1994).
134. Anet, *Roses*, 241.
135. On Persepolis in early-modern travel-writing, see Bonnerot, *La Perse dans la littérature*, 243–4.
136. On the evolving display of the Louvre's Susa artefacts, see Marianne Cotty, 'Between Orientalism and Persomania: The Presentation of the Iranian Collections at the Louvre', in *The Elamite World* (London: Routledge, 2018), 63–79.
137. Flandin, *Voyage*, vol. 2, 149.
138. Ibid., 209.
139. Ibid., 211.
140. Loti, *Vers Ispahan*, 129.
141. Ibid., 133.
142. Ibid., 134.
143. Ibid.
144. Ibid., 129.
145. Dieulafoy, *À Suse*, 157. On this passage's biblical intertext and Dieulafoy's other meditations on decadence, see my chapter 'Gender, Orientalism, and Decadence in Jane Dieulafoy's *Journal de fouilles* and *Parysatis*', in *French Decadence in a Global Context: Exoticism and Colonialism* (Liverpool: Liverpool UP), 73–95.
146. Dieulafoy, *À Suse*, 157.

147. Loti, *Vers Ispahan*, 130–1.
148. Ibid., 136.
149. Flandin, *Voyage*, vol. 2, 165.
150. Ibid., 210.
151. Anet, *Roses*, 168.
152. Ibid., 16. On Gobineau's views on race, see Chapter 2, the section 'Nos parents les Aryas'.
153. Dieulafoy, *À Suse*, 160.
154. That Dieulafoy believes in the notion of an Aryan race is made clear by the fact that they actually employ the term when describing the ethnicities of the local men hired to undertake the work of excavation. Dieulafoy, *À Suse*, 120.
155. Loti, *Vers Ispahan*, 132.
156. Ibid., 132–3.
157. Dieulafoy, *À Suse*, 157.
158. René Thorel, 'Mme Dieulafoy', in *Revue illustrée* (1/9/1903), 15–36 (16).
159. While it is highly unlikely that Loti would have found such a fragment, Pierre Briant reminds us that there was a protracted scientific debate over the course of the long nineteenth century as to whether or not there existed any physical evidence to confirm historical accounts of the Persepolis fire. Viewed in this context, Loti's anecdote seems to have been an attempt to make his own contribution to this discussion. See Pierre Briant, 'Arthur de Gobineau (1816–1882) entre Darius et Alexandre', *Diwan* (2016): 737–57 (750–1).
160. Loti, *Vers Ispahan*, 142.
161. Ibid., 143.
162. Ibid., 142.
163. Ibid., 143.
164. Dieulafoy, *La Perse*, 407.
165. Flandin, *Voyage*, vol. 2, 211.
166. Ibid., 212.
167. Ibid.
168. Anet, *Roses*, 177.
169. See Gobineau, *Trois ans en Asie*, 215; Loti, *Vers Ispahan*, 298–9 and Bibesco, *Les Huit paradis*, 69.
170. Flandin, *Voyage*, vol. 1, 1–4. On attempts to establish trade between France and Iran from Louis XIV to Napoleon, see Junko Thérèse Takeda, *Iran and French Empire of Trade: The Other Persian Letters* (Liverpool: Liverpool UP, 2020).
171. Flandin, *Voyage*, vol. 1, 267–8.
172. Flandin makes this dichotomy explicit in a later passage, where having described British and Russian efforts to bribe local officials, he observes: 'la France persuade ou fait la guerre; elle n'achète ni les peuples, ni leurs gouvernements' [France either persuades or wages war; she does not buy peoples, nor their governments] (*Voyage*, vol. 1, 364).
173. Loti, *Vers Ispahan*, 117 and 301–2.
174. Flandin, *Voyage*, vol. 1, 269.
175. Dieulafoy, *La Perse,* 282.
176. Jalal Al-e Ahmad, *Gharbzadegi (Weststruckness)*, trans. John Green and Ahmad Alizadeh (Lexington, KY: Mazda, 1982), 12, 64 and 78–9.
177. Dieulafoy, *La Perse*, 282–5.
178. Ibid., 583–4.

179. Of course, any call to find a true Islamic or Middle Eastern cultural identity in opposition to Western cultural identity is problematic in so far as it is predicated on the same essentializing oppositions (East versus West), and pursues the same goals (nationalism) as those it defines itself against, as has been argued by Boroujerdi. The same problems are present in Dieulafoy's own conclusion, which assumes that 'the Orient' should have 'nations' and pursue 'progress'. Mehrzad Boroujerdi, *Iranian Intellectuals and the West: The Tormented Triumph of Nativism* (Syracuse, NY: Syracuse UP, 1996).
180. Dieulafoy, *À Suse*, 176, 328.
181. Ibid., 176.
182. Ibid., 328.
183. Nader Nasiri-Moghaddam, *L'archéologie française en Perse et les antiquités nationales (1884–1914)* (Paris: Connaissances et Savoirs, 2004), 69–70.
184. Dieulafoy, *À Suse*, 323.
185. Ibid., 262–3.
186. See Gaston Jollivat, 'Autour du Monde: Un Palais Retrouvé', *Le Figaro* (23 October 1886): 3.
187. Edward Said, *Orientalism* (1978; London: Penguin, 2003), 92–4. See also 96, where he states that: 'Orientalism overrode the Orient'.
188. Ibid., 101.
189. Ibid., 93.
190. Dieulafoy, *La Perse*, 35.
191. Anet, *Roses*, 16, 123.
192. Gobineau, *Trois ans en Asie*, 170.
193. Said, *Orientalism*, 100–2.
194. See Évanghélia Stead, 'Les Mille et Une Nuits', https://heritage.bnf.fr/bibliothequesorient/fr/les-mille-et-une-nuits (accessed 1 April 2023).
195. Marcel Proust, *À la recherche du temps perdu*, 4 vols, ed. Jean-Yves Tadié (Paris: Gallimard, 1987–9), vol. 1, 56 and vol. 2, 257–8.
196. On Dyiab's transmission of the tales to Galland, see Paulo Lemos Horta, *Marvellous Thieves: Secret Authors of the Arabian Nights* (Cambridge, MA: Harvard UP, 2019).
197. Ibid., 32.
198. Flandin, *Voyage*, vol. 2, 43; Loti, *Vers Ispahan*, 196.
199. Loti, *Vers Ispahan*, 187.
200. Ibid., 188.
201. Ibid., 208.
202. Ibid., 222.
203. Ibid., 226.
204. Flandin, *Voyage*, vol. 2, 43.
205. Loti, *Vers Ispahan*, 278.
206. Ibid., 275–6.
207. Anet, *Roses*, 169.
208. Loti, *Vers Ispahan*, 105.
209. Ibid., 278.
210. Bibesco, *Les Huit paradis*, 56–7.
211. Ibid., 101.
212. Anet, *Roses*, 234.
213. Ibid., 198.

214. On this, see my chapter '"Les noms magiques": Names, Places, and Persian-ness in Noailles, Bibesco, and Proust', in *Labours of Attention: Essays for Edward J. Hughes*, ed. Adam Watt (Oxford: Legenda, 2022), 243–55.
215. Bibesco, *Les Huit paradis*, i.
216. Ibid.
217. Ibid., 112, 127–36 and 207–8, 181, 199, 204 and 207, respectively.
218. Ibid., 181 and 200, respectively. Other travel-writers adopt the third person when discussing Persian poets; see, for example, Dieulafoy, *La Perse*, 432, and Loti, *Vers Ispahan*, 106–7.
219. Bibesco, *Les Huit paradis*, 98, 103.
220. Ibid., 181.
221. Ibid., 199–200.
222. Ibid., 179.
223. Gobineau, *Trois ans en Asie*, 178.
224. Bibesco, *Les Huit paradis*, 131.
225. Loti, *Vers Ispahan*, 105–6.
226. Bibesco, *Les Huit paradis*, 131–2.
227. Ibid., 191. The Simorgh also makes an appearance in Gautier's *Iskender*, a novel studied in Chapter 2.
228. Ibid., 192.
229. Ibid., 171.
230. Bibesco, *Les Huit paradis*, 193.
231. Ibid., 181, 152–3, 69 and 176–7, respectively.
232. Jonathan Culler, *Theory of the Lyric* (Cambridge, MA: Harvard UP, 2015), 187.
233. Bibesco received the Académie's Marcelin Guérin prize in 1909, which rewarded works on history, religion and philosophy.
234. Dieulafoy, *La Perse*, 431–2.
235. Ibid., 432.
236. Loti, *Vers Ispahan*, 106–7.
237. Dieulafoy, *La Perse*, 431, and Flandin, *Voyage*, vol. 1, 342.
238. Loti, *Vers Ispahan*, 106.
239. Dieulafoy, *La Perse*, 431.
240. Ibid., 376.
241. Lucretius translation from Lucretius, *On the Nature of Things*, trans. W. H. D. Rouse, revised by Martin F. Smith, Loeb Classical Library 181 (Cambridge, MA: Harvard UP, 1924). Hâfez translation my own.
242. Johannes Fabian, *Time and the Other: How Anthropology Makes Its object* (New York: Columbia UP, 1983).

4 Performing arts

1. Derek Scott uses as point of contrast Rameau's eighteenth-century ballet 'Les Indes galantes', in which people of all nations and ethnicities, be they Persian or Peruvian, are accompanied by the same style of music. Derek Scott, 'Orientalism and Musical Style', *Musical Quarterly* 82, no. 2 (1998): 309–35.
2. Hector Berlioz, 'Théâtre de l'Opéra-comique', *Journal des débats* (23 May 1862): 1–2 (2).

3. Gilles de Van, trans. William Ashbrook, 'Fin de Siècle Exoticism and the Meaning of the Far Away', *Opera Quarterly* 11, no. 3 (1995): 77–94.
4. Charles Beaugenêt, 'Lalla-Roukh de David', *La France musicale* (18 May 1862): 153–7.
5. De Van notes that the primitivism associated with depictions of exotic locales was motivated by France's desire to escape its own decadence. De Van, 'Fin de Siècle Exoticism', 83.
6. On the domesticating implications of song, see David Gramit, 'Orientalism and the Lied: Schubert's "Du liebst mich nicht"', *19th-Century Music* 27, no. 2 (2003): 97–115. There is an analogy here with the malleable lyric 'I' of poetry: just as the voices of Sa'di's sage and Desbordes-Valmore become one in 'Les Roses de Saadi' (Chapter 1), so does the song's lyric I become identified with the subjectivity of the performer, who sings in their own home and in their own clothes, thereby collapsing the distinction between self and other (or in this case performer and character).
7. Amanda Lee, 'Péris and Devadasis in Paris: Orientalist Ballet as Poetic Translation', *Nineteenth-Century Contexts* 41, no. 2 (2019): 117–40 (119).
8. Edward Said, *Orientalism* (1978; London: Penguin, 2003), 71.
9. Scott, 'Orientalism and Musical Style', 326.
10. René Lara, 'Review of "Parysatis" at the Arènes de Béziers', *Le Gaulois* (18 August 1902): 2–3 (3).
11. Ralph Locke, *Musical Exoticism: Images and Reflections* (Cambridge: Cambridge UP, 2009), 180–4.
12. The composer Friedrich Burgmüller was originally from Germany, but lived and worked in Paris from the age of twenty-six until his death. The choreographer Jean (or Giovanni) Coralli was born in Paris to Italian parents and was 'premier maître de ballet' at the Paris Opera from 1831.
13. Théophile Gautier, 'Notes et variantes', in *Œuvres complètes* III: *Théâtre et ballets*, ed. Claudine Lacoste-Veysseyre and Hélène Laplace-Claverie, with Sarah Mombert (Paris: Champion, 2003), 868.
14. The nature of these disagreements is detailed in Helen Julia Minors, 'La Péri, poème dansé (1911–12): A Problematic Creative-Collaborative Journey', *Dance Research* 27, no. 9 (2009): 227–52.
15. In ancient Zoroastrian sacred texts, *pairikā* are demonic beings that lead men into temptation, akin to the succubus of the West. In such a context, the word has been translated as 'witch' or 'sorceress'. From the medieval period onwards, however, these mythical creatures lost their negative associations and became the equivalent of Western fairies or nymphs. (Though as we shall see, Dukas may be seen as retaining some of the older negative associations.) In modern Persian, the adjective *parisā* (*pari*-like) is used to refer to a beautiful woman and is in fact a common first name. Siamak Adhami, '*pairikā*', *Encyclopedia Iranica Online* (last updated 1 September 2010) https://www.iranicaonline.org/articles/pairika (accessed 24 August 2021).
16. See Chapter 2, the section 'The Persian Alexander'.
17. Sarah Davis Cordova, 'Romantic Ballet in France: 1830–1850', in *The Cambridge Companion to Ballet*, ed. Marion Kant (Cambridge: Cambridge UP, 2007), 113–25 (117).
18. *La Péri* presents particularly strong parallels with Gautier's short stories about supernatural encounters with Oriental women from the past: 'Le Pied de momie' (1840), in which the narrator falls in love with an Egyptian princess, and 'La Mille et deuxième nuit' (1842), in which Schéhérazade comes to the narrator and asks *him* to

tell her a story. Théophile Gautier, *Romans et Contes* (Paris: Lemerre, 1897), 433–52 and 347–84, respectively.
19. Dukas believed that a ballet audience should ideally have some pre-existing knowledge of both its libretto and its musical score. See Minors, 'La Péri, poème dansé', 228.
20. Paul Dukas, *La Péri: poème dansé* (Paris: Durand, 1911).
21. Alexandre-Gabriel Decamps, 'Le supplice des crochets' (1837), first exhibited at the 1839 Salon.
22. Gautier, 'Notes et Variantes', 866.
23. The name Achmet is also likely a reference to Antoine Galland's orphan tale 'Histoire du Prince Ahmed et de la Fée Pari-Banou'. See Antoine Galland, *Les Mille et Une Nuits*, 12 vols (Paris: Barbin, 1704–17), vol. 12, 1–194.
24. Lee, 'Péris and Devadasis in Paris', 120–1.
25. Gérard de Nerval, 'La Péri', in *Œuvres complètes*, 3 vols (Paris: Gallimard, 1989), vol. 1, 974–5.
26. 'La Péri, Ballet de Coralli, Gautier et Burgmüller: Costume de Mlle Carlotta Grisi (rôle de La Péri)' (1843). BNF, département Bibliothèque-musée de l'opéra, C-261 (16-1617).
27. Nerval, 'La Péri', 974.
28. Dukas, *La Péri: poème dansé*, i.
29. Plutarch, trans. Bernadotte Perrin, *Lives, Volume VII: Demosthenes and Cicero. Alexander and Caesar* (Cambridge, MA: Harvard UP, 1919), 427–9.
30. Eskandar's transition from outside conqueror to legitimate king is enacted by the chapter transition from Chapter 19 'Dara' to Chapter 20 'Eskandar'. For more on this, see Chapter 2, the section 'The Persian Alexander'.
31. Judith Gautier, *Iskender: Histoire persane* (Paris: Frinzine, 1886).
32. Adhami, '*pairikā*'.
33. James Darmesteter, *The Zend-Avesta Part I: The Vendidad* (Oxford: Oxford UP, 1880), lxvi.
34. James Darmesteter, *Le Zend-Avesta: traduction nouvelle avec commentaire historique et philologique*, 2 vols (Paris: Leroux, 1891), vol. 1 91.
35. Dukas's friend Robert Brussel describes the former's personal library as including: 'le Japon, la Chine, la Perse et leur poésie raffinée, plus loin les Indes et leurs livres sacrés' [Japan, China, Persia and their refined poetry, further along the Indies and their sacred texts]. Robert Brussel, 'Paul Dukas', *La Revue Musicale* 166 (May–June 1936): 18–51 (27).
36. Minors, 'La Péri, poème dansé', 227.
37. Jean Bernier, '"La Péri", poème dansé de M. Paul Dukas, "Daphnis et Chloë", Ballet en trois tableaux de M. Michel Fokine. Musique de M. Maurice Ravel', *Comœdia* (1 July 1921): 494–5 (495).
38. Linda Nochlin has incisively described the voyeurism sanctioned by Oriental settings (as opposed to French settings) as 'simultaneous lip-licking and tongue-clicking'. See Linda Nochlin, 'The Imaginary Orient', in *The Politics of Vision: Essays on Nineteenth-Century Art and Society* (New York: Harper Row, 1989), 33–59 (44).
39. Léon Bakst, Trouhanova as 'La Péri', in 'Programme officiel des Ballets russes, Théâtre du Châtelet, juin 1911' [deuxième spectacle 13 et 15–17 juin 1911], BNF, département Bibliothèque-musée de l'opéra, RES-2248 (14-7) [ark:/12148/btv1b8415108j], 181. Proving more demure than the designer, the costumier's final product revealed

the gap between the breasts, but not the breasts themselves. See photograph of Trouhanova wearing Bakst's costume, cover of *Comœdia illustré* (15 June 1911).
40. Léon Bakst, Nijinsky as 'Iskender', in 'Programme officiel des Ballets russes', 145, and Léon Bakst, Eunuch costume for 'Schéhérazade' (1910), Metropolitan Museum of Art, catalogue reference: 2015.787.6.
41. See photograph of Nijinsky in costume for 'Schéhérazade', in 'Programme officiel des Ballets russes, Théâtre du Châtelet, juin 1911', folio 150r.
42. 'Aquarelles Originales des Costumes de "Shéhérazade"', colour insert in special supplement 'Les Ballets Russes' in *Comœdia illustré* (15 June 1910). Consulted in Maurice de Brunoff and Jacques de Brunoff (eds), *Collection des plus beaux numéros de 'Comoedia illustré' et des programmes consacrés aux ballets et galas russes depuis le début à Paris, 1909–1921* (Paris: 1922). BNF, département Bibliothèque-musée de l'opéra, B-144 [ark:/12148/btv1b8415200k].
43. Both images of Piot's designs are taken from issues of the art magazine *Comœdia*. Figure 4.3 illustrates a cover article about Trouhanova's production (24 May 1912): 1). Figure 4.4 illustrates an article about the first performance of *La Péri* at the Paris Opera in 1921, an occasion that marked its formal entrance into the canon of French ballet (1 July 1921): 494.
44. A colour reproduction of Piot's original set design was included in the ballet programme 'Concerts de Danse Natalia Trouhanowa' (Paris: Maquet, 1912), which has been partially digitized on diktat.com's auction catalogue: [https://www.diktats.com/en-gb/products/concerts-de-danse-natalia-trouhanowa-1912 (accessed 10 September 22).
45. A digitized version of René Piot's original costume design can be found on artnet.com's auction catalogue [http://www.artnet.com/artists/rené-piot/iskender-1AmYwqSxJmBBLZG4SQsbwA2 (accessed 10 September 22).
46. These two other ballets were d'Indy's *Istar* and Florent Schmitt's *La Tragédie de Salomé*, thus clearly creating a running theme of 'Oriental seductresses'. Minors, 'La Péri, poème dansé', 237.
47. Locke, *Musical Exoticism*, 180–4.
48. See 'Table 2.2. Exotic Operas at the *Opéra-Comique* and *Opéra* (1890–1898)' in Valeria Wenderoth, 'The Making of Exoticism in French Operas of the 1890s' (doctoral thesis, University of Hawaii, 2004), 117.
49. Thomas Moore, *Lalla Rookh* (London: Longman, Hurst, Rees, Orme, and Brown, 1817).
50. Michel Carré, Hippolyte Lucas and Félicien David, *Lalla-Roukh: Opéra-Comique en 2 actes. Partition réduite pour Piano et Chant par M. Charlot* (Paris: Girod, 1862), 50.
51. Ibid., 135.
52. Ibid., 216.
53. Ibid., 95.
54. Berlioz, 'Théâtre de l'Opéra-comique', 2.
55. Ibid.
56. Beaugenêt, 'Lalla-Roukh de David', 153.
57. See, for instance, Noureddin's references to Lalla-Roukh as 'Cette céleste fleur[,] cette perle divine!' [This celestial flower[,] this divine pearl!]' (Lucas et al., *Lalla-Roukh*, 32–3), and the association of the beloved's breath with the perfume of flowers in Noureddin's 'Romance' (ibid., 84–8).
58. Jāmī's poem had been available in French translation as early as 1807. See Jāmī, trans. Antoine-Léonard de Chézy, *Medjnoun et Leïlâ* (Paris: Valade, 1807).

59. See, in particular, the *bayadères* dance sequence in 'N°4. Chœur et airs de danse' (Lucas et al., *Lalla-Roukh*, 63–9).
60. See, for instance, Jules Michelet, *La Bible de l'Humanité* (Paris: Chamerot, 1864), which is analysed in Chapter 2.
61. Jean Richepin, *Le Mage: Opéra en cinq actes et six tableau* [libretto] (Paris: Dreyfous, 1891).
62. The book would not be translated into French until 1893, though there was already a growing interest in Nietzsche at the time *Le Mage* was written. Laure Verbaere, 'Les traductions françaises de Nietzsche – en Europe', *Études Germaniques* 251, no. 3 (2008): 601–21. Louis Pinto, *Les neveux de Zarathoustra* (Paris: Le Seuil, 1995).
63. As noted in the Introduction, Bhatti and Kimmich propose that the paradigm of similarity be used to explore and acknowledge the overlapping existence of both commonalities and differences between cultures. Anil Bhatti and Dorothee Kimmich, 'Introduction', in *Similarity: a Paradigm for Culture Theory*, ed. Anil Bhatti and Dorothee Kimmich (New Delhi: Tulika Books, 2018), 1–22.
64. Richepin, *Le Mage*, 38.
65. *Haoma*, referred to in Sanskrit as *soma*, is the juice of a sacred plant. European representations of its consumption typically present it as a hallucinogenic.
66. Richepin, *Le Mage*, 26–7.
67. Ibid., 27.
68. Charles Bianchini, 'Le roi', in 'Le Mage: soixante-sept maquettes de costume' (1891), BNF, département Bibliothèque-musée de l'opéra, D216-46 [ark:/12148/btv1b8455869r], folio 66.
69. Richepin, *Le Mage*, 37.
70. Ibid., 7.
71. Ibid., 12.
72. On Persepolis, see Chapter 3, the section 'Remembering "the Great of the Earth"'.
73. Richepin, *Le Mage*, 34–5.
74. Jahi or Jeh is the name of a female demon in a small number of Zoroastrian Middle Persian texts, most famous for being depicted as the consort of Ahriman. There is no evidence of her having been worshipped and the scene's sexual dimension is most likely inspired by ancient Greek reports of ritual prostitution in the temples of the Babylonian goddess Ishtar. See Albert de Jong 'Jeh', in *Encyclopedia Iranica Online* (last updated 13 April 2012), https://www.iranicaonline.org/articles/jeh (accessed 24 August 2022).
75. The changing location of the chorus and the complement are referred to in both Massenet's manuscript and the reduced piano score, further suggesting that it was one of the most innovative and memorable aspects of this opera. See Jules Massenet, *Le Mage* (manuscrit autographe), BNF, Département Bibliothèque-musée de l'opéra, A-655 (A 4), 553r and 561r, and Jules Massenet, *Le Mage: Opéra en cinq actes et six tableaux, partition pour chant et piano* (Bruxelles: Hartmann, 1891), 186 and 212.
76. Bianchini, 'Le Mage', folios 54–5, and also 57.
77. Bianchini, 'Le Mage', folio 56, and Jane Dieulafoy, *La Perse, la Chaldée, et la Susiane* (Paris: Hachette, 1887), 271.
78. There is no extant photograph for this portrait and there is therefore no way of verifying how many creative liberties were taken by the artist who produced the etchings illustrating Dieulafoy's text.
79. Richepin, *Le Mage*, 45.
80. Louis Gallet, 'Thamara: Légende persane', *La Nouvelle Revue* 13 (1881): 598–610.

81. Wenderoth's claim that the setting 'might be between the 12th and 13th century' is therefore invalid. Wenderoth, 'The Making of Exoticism in French Opera', 128.
82. Junko Thérèse Takeda, *Iran and a French Empire of Trade, 1700–1808: The Other Persian Letters* (Liverpool: Liverpool UP, 2020), 159.
83. Louis Gallet and Louis-Albert Bourgault-Ducoudray, *Thamara: Opéra en quatre tableaux. Partition réduite pour Chant et piano par Van den Heuvel* (Paris: Léon Grus, 1891), 44–5.
84. Ibid., 52–3.
85. Ibid., 56.
86. Ibid., 75.
87. Ibid., 86–8.
88. Ibid., 89.
89. Ibid., 96.
90. Ibid., 99–101.
91. Ibid., 105 and 111.
92. Ibid., 108.
93. Ibid., 107.
94. Ibid., 108–9.
95. Ibid., 120.
96. Ibid., 109–10.
97. In Gallet's short story, the narrator establishes that Noureddin is handsome. In the libretto, the king's good looks are verbalized by Thamara in her opening song in Act III (ibid., 156–7).
98. Ibid., 117–18.
99. Ibid., 127.
100. Ibid., 126–8.
101. Ibid., 203–4.
102. Ibid., 156–7.
103. Ibid., 119.
104. Peter Asimov, 'Transcribing Greece, Arranging France: Bourgault-Ducoudray's Performances of Authenticity and Innovation', *19th-Century Music* 44, no. 3 (2021): 133–69 (164–6). Asimov refers to the first melody from Bourgault-Ducoudray's *Trente mélodies populaires de Grèce et d'Orient* (Paris: Henry Lemoine, 1876).
105. See Chapter 3, the sections 'Among Women: Scenes from the Harem' and 'Understanding Shī'ism'.
106. Gallet and Bourgault-Ducoudray, *Thamara*, 143.
107. There is a parallel here with the representation of Jews in operas with ancient settings such as Verdi's *Aida*: typically portrayed as Others, in these contexts they function instead as proto-Westerners, by virtue of being precursors to Christianity. See Locke, *Musical Exoticism*, 182.
108. Maurice Bouchor, 'Le Petit-Théâtre des Marionettes', *La revue politique et littéraire* (28 June 1890): 802–7 (803).
109. Ibid., 807.
110. Arthur Pougin, 'Petit-Théâtre', *Le Ménestrel* (28 February 1892): 67.
111. The one exception was for parts requiring female voices, since the entire troupe was made up of men.
112. Bouchor, 'Le Petit-Théâtre des Marionettes', 806.

113. Bouchor, 'Le Petit-Théâtre des Marionettes', 804. See also Anatole France, 'Les marionnettes de M. Signoret', *La Vie littéraire*, 5 vols (Paris: Calmann-Lévy, 1921), vol. 2, 145–50.
114. Bouchor compares this to the use of masks in ancient Greek theatre. Maurice Bouchor, 'Le Petit-Théâtre des Marionettes', 807.
115. Adrien Remacle, 'Petit Théâtre', *Mercure de France* (1 April 1892): 355–6 (355).
116. Bouchor, 'Le Petit-Théâtre des Marionettes', 804.
117. Ibid.
118. Ibid., 807.
119. Ibid., 806.
120. Pougin, 'Petit-Théâtre', 67.
121. Maurice Bouchor, *Le Songe de Khèyam* (Paris: Flammarion, 1892), 17.
122. Jean-Baptiste Nicolas, *Les Quatrains de Khèyam* (Paris: Imprimerie impériale, 1867). In the absence of an extant manuscript in Khayyām's hand, there exists some debate as to which quatrains should be attributed to Khayyām. Some of the quatrains included by Nicolas are thus likely to be by imitators.
123. Bouchor, *Le Songe de Khèyam*, 10.
124. Ibid., 12.
125. On the French vogue for Persian decorative objects, see Moya Carey and Mercedes Volait, 'Framing "Islamic Art" for Aesthetic Interiors: Revisiting the 1878 Paris Exhibition', *International Journal of Islamic Architecture* 9, no. 1 (2020): 31–59.
126. Bouchor, *Le Songe de Khèyam*, 13 and 15.
127. Ibid., 14.
128. Ibid., 18.
129. Ibid., 28.
130. Ibid., 30.
131. Ibid., 8.
132. Léon Cahun, 'Un épicurien musulman du XIe siècle', *La Revue politique et littéraire* (3 April 1875): 946–9.
133. Nicolas, *Les Quatrains de Khèyam*, i–xv (iii and xiii).
134. Fitzgerald cites the quatrain in which Khayyām requests to have his corpse washed not with the Islamic ritual treatments but with wine, which is one of the first in Nicolas's anthology. (See Nicolas, *Les Quatrains de Khèyam*, 4.)
135. These observations are found in the preface to the second edition of Fitzgerald's *Rubàyiàt of Omar Khayyàm*, which was published in 1868 (i.e. six years after Nicolas's translation). Edward Fitzgerald, 'Omar Khayyām: The Astronomer-Poet of Persia', *The Rubàiyàt of Omar Khayyàm Rendered into English Verse: The Four Editions with the Original Prefaces and Notes* (London: Macmillan, 1899), 57–85 (75–85).
136. Ernest Renan, *Mélanges d'histoire et de voyages* (Paris: Calmann-Lévy, 1878), 144.
137. This progression is made explicit by the author in his preface. Bouchor, *Le Songe de Khèyam*, 8.
138. Nicolas, *Les Quatrains de Khèyam*, i.
139. On the Catholicism of Bouchor's wider oeuvre, see Jennifer Walker, *Sacred Music, Secular Spaces: Transforming Catholicism through the Music of Third-Republic Paris* (Oxford: Oxford UP, 2021), 75–98.
140. Bouchor, *Le Songe de Khèyam*, 12.
141. Nicolas, *Les Quatrains de Khèyam*, 148.

142. Bouchor, *Le Songe de Khèyam*, 31. The use of the second-person address ('tell me') is also a stylistic feature present in Khayyām's quatrains.
143. One reviewer argued that Bouchor's Khayyām was a far more religious person than the real Khayyām who was 'un ivrogne prolixe et déplaisant'. Marcel Fouquier, 'Premières', *Le XIXe siècle* (26 February 1892): 2.
144. Christopher Moore, 'Regionalist Frictions in the Bullring: Lyric Theater in Béziers at the Fin de Siècle', *19th-Century Music* 37, no. 3 (2014): 211–41.
145. Erin Brooks, '"Une culture classique supérieure": Saint-Saëns et l'esthétique antique', in F*igures de l'Antiquité dans l'opéra français: des* Troyens *de Berlioz à* Œdipe *d'Enesco*, ed. Jean-Christophe Branger and Vincent Giroud (Saint-Étienne, France: Université de Saint-Étienne, 2008), 235–58.
146. Fonds Dieulafoy, Bibliothèque de l'Institut de France, MS 2684, folio 142.
147. Moore, 'Lyric Theater in Bézier', 214–17.
148. Fonds Saint-Saëns, Château-musée de Dieppe, letter from Jane Dieulafoy dated 9 October 1900.
149. I adopt the pronoun 'they' for Dieulafoy in this section due to my focus on them as a historical individual. On my use of pronouns, see the section on Dieulafoy in Chapter 2.
150. Castelbon des Beauxhostes expressly instructed Dieulafoy not to bother Saint-Saëns with any of the practical aspects of the production, including casting. Fonds Dieulafoy, MS 2684, folio 10.
151. The opening stage direction states that the palace should be 'tel qu'il est reconstitué au Louvre' [as reconstructed at the Louvre]. Fonds Dieulafoy, MS 2683, folio 2.
152. Fonds Saint-Saëns, letter from Jane Dieulafoy dated 29 April 1902, 4.
153. The extras were local people (most of them workers from the wine industry) sourced by Castelbon des Beauxhostes. Jacqueline Gachet, *L'Opéra dans l'arène ou l'aventure de Fernand Castelbon mécène à Béziers* (Office Départemental d'action culturelle, 1989), 5–14. The choristers and instrumentalists were similarly sourced from local musical groups. Moore, 'Lyric Theatre in Béziers', 217.
154. Brooks, 'Une culture classique supérieure', 254.
155. Camille Saint-Saëns, 'Causerie musicale', *La Nouvelle Revue Française* 1 (1 January 1879): 643.
156. For musical analysis, see Brooks, 'Une culture classique supérieure'. Dieulafoy reports back to Saint-Saëns on her efforts to procure him the scores for a song heard in a synagogue and another song composed to mark the death of Isabella of Castile's son in a letter dated 7 October 1901. (Fonds Saint-Saëns.)
157. Ibid. See also letter dated 25 August 1902 in which Dieulafoy calls the music 'perfect'.
158. The travel-writer Eugène Flandin went so far as to define Persian music as 'barbaric'. Eugène Flandin, *Voyage en Perse*, 2 vols (Paris: Baudry, 1851–2), vol. 2, 59–60.
159. This had not deterred musicologist François-Joseph Fétis to proceed 'by induction' and determine what the music of ancient Iran sounded like on the basis of Sanskrit accounts of ancient Indian music, eighteenth-century Turkish music and medieval Persian and Arabic music treaties. See his *Histoire générale de la musique depuis les temps les plus anciens jusqu'à nos jours*, 5 vols (Paris: Didot, 1869), vol. 2, 350–9.
160. Camille Saint-Saëns, 'Les chœurs d'Antigone', *Le Figaro* (28 November 1893): 1.
161. Camille Saint-Saëns, *Parysatis. Partition pour chant et piano réduite par l'auteur* (Paris: Durand, 1902), 72–5.
162. Saint-Saëns, 'Les chœurs d'Antigone'.
163. René Lara, 'Une Première à Béziers', *Le Gaulois* (18 August 1902): 2–3 (2).

164. Ibid. More than an analysis of Saint-Saëns's composition, this section of the review reads like a paraphrase of Fétis's *Histoire générale de la musique*, cited above.
165. Eve Kosofsky Sedgwick, *Between Men: English Literature and Male Homosocial Desire* (New York: Columbia UP, 1985), 21. On this, see also Chapter 2, the section on Judith Gautier.
166. Moore, 'Lyric Theatre in Béziers', 231–3.
167. Marc Varenne writing for the 25 August 1901 special issue of *Le Titan* on Fauré's *Prométhée*. Quoted in Moore, 'Lyric Theatre in Béziers', 232.
168. Colette and Henry Gauthier-Villars, *Claudine s'en va* (Paris: Société d'éditions littéraires et artistiques, 1903), 287.
169. See Bianchini, 'Le Mage', folios 37, 38 and 41.
170. I should note that the Aspasia storyline and its attendant Orientalism is already present in the novel, but it was subordinated to the central plot of Parysatis's ascension to power.

Bibliography

Archival sources

Bibliothèque de l'Institut de France. Fonds Dieulafoy.
Bibliothèque nationale de France. Département Bibliothèque-musée de l'opéra, C-261. 'La Péri, Ballet de Coralli, Gautier et Burgmüller: Costume de Mlle Carlotta Grisi (rôle de La Péri)' (1843).
Bibliothèque nationale de France. Département Bibliothèque-musée de l'opéra, A-655 (A 4). Jules Massenet, *Le Mage* (manuscrit autographe, 1891).
Bibliothèque nationale de France. Département Bibliothèque-musée de l'opéra, D216-46. 'Le Mage: soixante-sept maquettes de costume' (1891).
Bibliothèque nationale de France. Département Bibliothèque-musée de l'opéra, RES-2248. 'Programme officiel des Ballets russes, Théâtre du Châtelet, juin 1911' (1911).
Bibliothèque nationale de France. Département Bibliothèque-musée de l'opéra, B-144. Maurice de Brunoff and Jacques de Brunoff (eds), *Collection des plus beaux numéros de 'Comœdia illustré' et des programmes consacrés aux ballets et galas russes depuis le début à Paris, 1909–1921* (Paris: 1922).
Bibliothèque nationale de France. Département des Manuscrits. NAF 13359. Fonds Victor Hugo.
Château-musée de Dieppe. Fonds Saint Saëns.

Primary sources

Al-Afghani, Jamal al-Din, open letter, *Journal des Débats* (18 May 1883): 3.
Al-Ghazali, trans. Casimir Barbier de Meynard, *Traduction nouvelle du Traité de Ghazali intitulé Al-Munqid min adâlal: le Préservatif de l'Erreur, Journal asiatique*, 7: 10 (Paris: Imprimerie Nationale, 1877).
Al-Ghazali, trans. Auguste Schmölders, 'Ce qui sauve des égarement et éclaircit les ravissements', Auguste Schmölders, *Essai sur les écoles philosophiques chez les Arabes et notamment sur la doctrine d'Algazzali* (Paris: 1842): 16–87.
Anet, Claude, *Les Roses d'Ispahan: La Perse en automobile* (Paris: Juven, 1906).
Anonymous, 'Iskender', *Le Voltaire* (24 July 1894): 1.
Anquetil-Duperron, Abraham Hyacinthe, *Zend-Avesta, ouvrage de Zoroastre*, 2 vols (Paris: Tilliard, 1771).
Banville, Théodore de, 'Iskender', *Gil Blas* (4 June 1886): 1.
Banville, Théodore de, *Petit traité de Poésie française* (Paris: Bibliothèque de l'écho de la Sorbonne, 1872).
Barbier de Meynard, Casimir, *La Poésie en Perse* (Paris: Leroux, 1877).
Baudelaire, Charles, *Œuvres complètes*, edited by Claude Pichois, 2 vols (Paris: Gallimard, 1975–6).
Beaugenêt, Charles, 'Lalla-Roukh de David', *La France musicale* (18 May 1862): 153–7.

Berlioz, Hector, 'Théâtre de l'Opéra-comique', *Journal des débats* (23 May 1862): 1–2.
Bernier, Jean, '"La Péri", poème dansé de M. Paul Dukas, "Daphnis et Chloë", Ballet en trois tableaux de M. Michel Fokine. Musique de M. Maurice Ravel', *Comœdia* (1 July 1921): 494–5.
Bibesco, Marthe, *Au bal avec Marcel Proust* (Paris: Gallimard, 1928).
Bibesco, Marthe, *Les Huit paradis* (Paris: Hachette, 1908).
Bonaparte, Napoléon, *Discours de guerre*, edited by Jacques-Olivier Bourdon (Paris: Édition Pierre de Taillac, 2011).
Bopp, Franz, *Über das Conjugationssystem Der Sanskritsprache in Vergleinchung mit jenem der grieschischen, Latenischen, persischen end germanischen Sprache* (Frankfurt: Andräischen, 1816).
Bouchor, Maurice, 'Le Petit-Théâtre des Marionettes', *La revue politique et littéraire* (28 June 1890): 802–7.
Bouchor, Maurice, *Le Songe de Khèyam: Caprice en un acte, en vers* (Paris: Flammarion, 1892).
Bourgault-Ducoudray, Louis-Albert, *Trente mélodies populaires de Grèce et d'Orient* (Paris: Henry Lemoine, 1876).
Brussel, Robert, 'Paul Dukas', *La Revue Musicale* 166 (May–June 1936): 18–51.
Burnouf, Eugène, *Études sur la langue et sur les textes zends*, vol. 1 (Paris: Imprimerie nationale, 1850).
Cahun, Léon, 'Un épicurien musulman du XIe siècle', *La Revue politique et littéraire* (3 April 1875): 946–9.
Carré, Michel, Hippolyte Lucas and Félicien David, *Lalla-Roukh: Opéra-Comique en 2 actes. Partition réduite pour Piano et Chant par M. Charlot* (Paris: Girod, 1862).
Chételat, Emmanuel J. (ed.), *Les Occidentales ou Lettres critiques sur les Orientales de M. Victor Hugo* (Paris: Haute-cœur-Martinet, 1829).
Darmesteter, James, *Le Zend-Avesta: traduction nouvelle avec commentaire historique et philologique*, 2 vols (Paris: Leroux, 1891).
Darmesteter, James, *The Zend-Avesta Part I: The Vendidad* (Oxford: Oxford UP, 1880).
Davies, Dick, *Faces of Love: Hafiz and the Poets of Shiraz*, bilingual edition (Washington, DC: Mage, 2012).
Desbordes-Valmore, Marceline, *Les Œuvres poétiques*, edited by Marc Bertrand, 2 vols (Grenoble: Presses Universitaires de Grenoble, 1973).
Dieulafoy, Jane, *À Suse: journal de fouilles* (Paris: Hachette, 1888).
Dieulafoy, Jane, *L'Orient sous le voile: de Chiraz à Bagdad* (Paris: Phébus, 2011).
Dieulafoy, Jane, *La Perse, la Chaldée et la Susiane* (Paris: Hachette, 1887).
Dieulafoy, Jane, *Parysatis* (Paris: Armand Colin, 1892).
Dieulafoy, Jane, *Rose d'Hatra* (Paris: Armand Colin, 1893).
Dieulafoy, Marcel, *L'art antique de la Perse*, 5 vols (Paris: Librairie centrale d'architecture, 1884–9).
Du Camp, Maxime, *Le Nil (Égypte et Nubie)* (Paris: Librairie nouvelle, 1854).
Dukas, Paul, *La Péri: poème dansé* (Paris: Durand, 1911).
Ferdowsi, trans. Jules Mohl, *Livre des Rois*, 2nd edn, 7 vols (Paris: Imprimerie Nationale, 1876–8).
Fétis, François-Joseph, *Histoire générale de la musique depuis les temps les plus anciens jusqu'à nos jours*, 5 vols (Paris: Didot, 1869).
Fitzgerald, Edward, 'Omar Khayyam: The Astronomer-Poet of Persia', *The Rubàiyàt of Omar Khayyàm Rendered into English Verse: The Four Editions with the Original Prefaces and Notes* (London: Macmillan, 1899), 57–85.

Flandin, Eugène, *Voyage en Perse*, 2 vols (Paris: Baudry, 1851).
Fouquier, Marcel, 'Premières', *Le XIXe siècle* (26 February 1892): 2.
France, Anatole, 'Les marionnettes de M. Signoret', *La Vie littéraire*, 5 vols (Paris: Calmann-Lévy, 1921), vol. 2, 145–50.
Galland, Antoine, *Les Mille et Une Nuits*, 12 vols (Paris: Barbin, 1704–17).
Gallet, Louis, 'Thamara: Légende persane', *La Nouvelle Revue* 13 (1881): 598–610.
Gallet, Louis, and Louis-Albert Bourgault-Ducoudray, *Thamara: Opéra en quatre tableaux. Partition réduite pour Chant et piano par Van den Heuvel* (Paris: Léon Grus, 1891).
Gauthier-Villars, Colette and Henry, *Claudine s'en va* (Paris: Société d'éditions littéraires et artistiques, 1903).
Gautier, Judith, *Iskender: Histoire persane* (Paris: Frinzine, 1886).
Gautier, Théophile, *Émaux et Camées* (Paris: Didier, 1852).
Gautier, Théophile, *Œuvres complètes* III: *Théâtre et ballets*, edited by Claudine Lacoste-Veysseyre and Hélène Laplace-Claverie, with Sarah Mombert (Paris: Champion, 2003).
Gautier, Théophile, *Romans et Contes* (Paris: Lemerre, 1897).
Gobineau, Arthur de, *Alexandre le Macédonien: Tragédie en cinq actes*, 2nd edn (Strassburg: Trübner, 1902).
Gobineau, Arthur de, *Histoire des Perses*, 2 vols (Paris: Plon, 1869).
Gobineau, Arthur de, *Nouvelles asiatiques*, edited by Jean Gaulmier (Paris: Garnier, 1965).
Gobineau, Arthur de, *Œuvres*, 3 vols (Paris: Gallimard, 1983).
Gobineau, Arthur de, *Trois ans en Asie* (Paris: Hachette, 1859).
Hugo, Victor, *La Légende des siècles: Nouvelle série, Tome I* (Paris: Calmann Lévy, 1877).
Hugo, Victor, *Les Orientales* (Paris: Hector Bossange, 1829).
Jāmi, trans. Antoine-Léonard de Chézy, *Medjnoun et Leïlâ* (Paris: Valade, 1807).
Jollivat, Gaston, 'Autour du Monde: Un Palais Retrouvé', *Le Figaro* (23 Ocotber 1886): 3.
Jones, William, 'The Sixth Anniversary Discourse', *Asiatick Researches* 2 (1790): 43–66.
Jones, William, 'The Third Anniversary Discourse', *Asiatick Researches* 1 (1788): 415–31.
Jones, William, 'Traité sur la poesie Orientale', *Histoire de Nader Chah* (London: Elmsly, 1770), 527–85.
Khayyām, trans. Jean-Baptiste Nicolas, *Les Quatrains de Khéyam* (Paris: 1867).
Lahor, Jean (Henri Cazalis), *En Orient* (Paris: Alphonse Lemerre, 1907).
Lara, René, 'Une Première à Béziers', *Le Gaulois* (18 August 1902): 2–3.
Loti, Pierre, *Vers Ispahan* (Paris: Calmann-Lévy, 1904).
Lucretius, *On the Nature of Things*, trans. W. H. D. Rouse, revised by Martin F. Smith, Loeb Classical Library 181 (Cambridge, MA: Harvard UP, 1924).
Massenet, Jules, *Le Mage: Opéra en cinq actes et six tableaux, partition pour chant et piano* (Bruxelles: Hartmann, 1891).
Meyer-Zundel, Suzanne, *Quinze ans auprès de Judith Gautier* (Porto: Tipografia Nunes, 1969).
Michelet, Jules, *La Bible de l'Humanité* (Paris: Chamerot, 1864).
Michelet, Jules, *Journal*, 4 vols (Paris: Gallimard, 1959–76).
Mirkhond, trans. Charles Defrémery, *Histoire des Samanides par Mirkhond* (Paris: Imprimerie Royale, 1845).
Mirkhond, *Histoire des Sassanides* [original Persian] (Paris: Firmin Didot, 1843).
Mirkhond, trans. Silvestre de Sacy, 'Histoire des rois de Perse, de la dynastie des Sassanides', *Mémoires sur les antiquités de la Perse* (Paris: Imprimerie nationale exécutive du Louvre, 1793), 271–417.
Moore, Thomas, *Lalla Rookh* (London: Longman, Hurst, Rees, Orme, and Brown, 1817).

Nerval, Gérard de, 'La Péri', Œuvres complètes, 3 vols (Paris: Gallimard, 1989), vol. 1, 974–5.
Noailles, Anna de, Les Éblouissements (Paris: Calmann-Lévy, 1907).
Plutarch, trans. Bernadotte Perrin, Lives, Volume VII: Demosthenes and Cicero. Alexander and Caesar (Cambridge, MA: Harvard UP, 1919).
Pougin, Arthur, 'Petit-Théâtre', Le Ménestrel (28 February 1892): 67.
Proust, Marcel, 'Les Éblouissements', Le Figaro (15 June 1907): 1.
Proust, Marcel, À la recherche du temps perdu, 4 vols, edited by Jean-Yves Tadié (Paris: Gallimard, 1987–9).
Remacle, Adrien, 'Petit Théâtre', Mercure de France (1 April 1892): 355–6.
Renan, Ernest, De la part des peuples sémitiques dans l'histoire de la civilisation (Paris: Lévy, 1862).
Renan, Ernest, 'L'Islam et la Science', Journal des Débats (30 March 1883): 2–3.
Renan, Ernest, Mélanges d'histoire et de voyages (Paris: Calmann-Lévy, 1878).
Renan, Ernest, in Œuvres complètes, 10 vols, edited by Henriette Pischari (Paris: Calmann-Lévy, 1947–61).
Renan, Ernest, open letter, Journal des Débats (19 May 1883): 3.
Renan, Ernest, Vie de Jésus (Paris: Lévy, 1863).
Renaud, Armand, Les Nuits persanes, Idylles japonaises, Orient (Paris: Lemerre, 1895).
Renaud, Armand, Nuits persanes (Paris: Lemerre, 1870).
Richepin, Jean, Le Mage: Opéra en cinq actes et six tableau [libretto] (Paris: Dreyfous, 1891).
Saʻdi, Golestān, edited by Mohammad Javād Mashkur (Tehran: Eqbāl, 1963).
Saʻdi, Gulistan, trans. Edward B. Eastwick (London: Routledge, 2000 [1880]).
Saʻdi, 'Gulistan ou le jardin des roses', in 'Contes Orientaux. II.', in 'Littérature Orientale', Panthéon Littéraire, 135 vols (Paris: 1835–45), vol. 58, 553–61.
Saint-Saëns, Camille, 'Les chœurs d'Antigone', Le Figaro (28 November 1893): 1.
Saint-Saëns, Camille, Parysatis. Partition pour chant et piano réduite par l'auteur (Paris: Durand, 1902).
Sainte-Beuve, Charles Augustin de, 'Qu'est-ce qu'un classique?' Le Constitutionnel (21 October 1850): 3–4.
Thibaudeau, Antoine-Clair, Histoire de la campagne d'Egypte sous le règne de Napoléon le grand, 2 vols (Paris: Huzard, 1839).
Thorel, René, 'Mme Dieulafoy', La Revue illustrée (1 September 1903): 15–36.
Trouhanova, Natalya, 'Concerts de Danse Natalia Trouhanowa' [ballet programme] (Paris: Maquet, 1912).

Secondary sources

Adhami, Siamak, 'pairikā', Encyclopedia Iranica Online (last updated 1 September 2010), https://www.iranicaonline.org/articles/pairika (accessed 24 August 2021).
Al-e Ahmad, Jalal, Gharbzadegi (Weststruckness) trans. John Green and Ahmad Alizadeh (Lexington, KY: Mazda, 1982).
Asimov, Peter, 'Transcribing Greece, Arranging France: Bourgault-Ducoudray's Performances of Authenticity and Innovation', 19th-Century Music 44, no. 3 (2021): 133–69.
Austin, John Langshaw, How to Do Things with Words (Oxford: Clarendon Press, 1975).

Behdad, Ali, *Belated Travelers: Orientalism in the Age of Colonial Dissolution* (Durham, NC: Duke UP, 1994).
Berenson, Edward, *The Trial of Madame Caillaux* (Berkeley, CA: Berkeley UP, 1992).
Bhatti, Anil, and Dorothee Kimmich, 'Introduction', in *Similarity: A Paradigm for Culture Theory*, edited by Anil Bhatti and Dorothee Kimmich (New Delhi: Tulika Books, 2018), 1–22.
Bloom, Harold, *The Anxiety of Influence: A Theory of Poetry* (New York: Oxford UP, 1973).
Boer, Inge, *Uncertain Territories: Boundaries in Cultural Analysis*, edited by Mieke Bal, Bregje Van Eekelen and Patricia Spyer (Amsterdam: Rodopi, 2006).
Bonnefoy, Yves, 'Préface', in Marceline Desbordes-Valmore, *Poésies*, edited by Yves Bonnefoy (Paris: Gallimard, 1983), 7–34.
Bonnerot, Olivier, *La Perse dans la littérature et la pensée françaises au XVIIIe siècle: de l'image au mythe* (Paris: Champion-Slatkine, 1988).
Boroujerdi, Mehrzad, *Iranian Intellectuals and the West: The Tormented Triumph of Nativism* (Syracuse, NY: Syracuse UP, 1996).
Bourdon, Jacques-Olivier, 'Napoléon et l'hellénisme', *Historiographie et identités culturelles* 20 (2014): 33–48.
Brancaforte, Elio, 'Persian Words of Wisdom Travel to the West: Seventeenth-Century European Translations of Saʿdi's Gulistan', *Daphnis* 45 (2017): 450–72.
Briant, Pierre, 'Arthur de Gobineau (1816–1882) entre Darius et Alexandre', *Diwan* (2016): 737–57.
Brooks, Erin, '"Une culture classique supérieure": Saint-Saëns et l'esthétique antique', in *Figures de l'Antiquité dans l'opéra français: des* Troyens *de Berlioz à* Œdipe *d'Enesco*, edited by Jean-Christophe Branger and Vincent Giroud (Saint-Étienne, France: Université de Saint-Étienne, 2008), 235–58.
Brookshaw, Dominic Parviz, *Hafiz and His Contemporaries: Poetry, Performance, and Patronage in Fourteenth-Century Iran* (London: I.B. Tauris, 2019).
Bubb, Alexander, 'The Race for Hāfez: Scholarly and Popular Translations at the Fin de Siècle', *Comparative Critical Studies* 17, no. 2 (2020): 225–44.
Butler, Judith, 'Performative Acts and Gender Constitution: An Essay in Phenomenology and Feminist Theory', *Theatre Journal* 40, no. 4 (1988): 519–31.
Carey, Moya, and Mercedes Volait, 'Framing "Islamic Art" for Aesthetic Interiors: Revisiting the 1878 Paris Exhibition', *International Journal of Islamic Architecture* 9, no. 1 (2020): 31–59.
Chambers, Ross, 'Baudelaire's Street Poetry', *NCFS* 13, no. 4 (1985): 244–59.
Chapman, Amanda, 'Queer Elasticity: Imperial Boyhood in Late Nineteenth-Century Boys' Adventure Fiction', *Children's Literature* 46 (2008): 56–77.
Clifford, James, 'Orientalism by Edward Said', *History and Theory* 19, no. 2 (1980): 204–23.
Cotty, Marianne, 'Between Orientalism and Persomania: The Presentation of the Iranian Collections at the Louvre', in *The Elamite World,* edited by Álvarez-Mon, Gian Pietro Basello and Yasmina Wicks (London: Routledge, 2018), 63–79.
Culler, Jonathan, *Theory of the Lyric* (Cambridge, MA: Harvard UP, 2015).
Danahy, Michael, 'Marceline Desbordes-Valmore et la fraternité des poètes', *NCFS* 19, no. 3 (1991): 386–93.
Davis Cordova, Sarah, 'Romantic Ballet in France: 1830–1850', in *The Cambridge Companion to Ballet*, edited by Marion Kant (Cambridge: Cambridge UP, 2007).
De Jong, Albert, 'Jeh', *Encyclopedia Iranica Online* (last updated 13 April 2012), https://www.iranicaonline.org/articles/jeh (accessed 24 August 2022).

De Van, Gilles, trans. William Ashbrook, 'Fin de Siècle Exoticism and the Meaning of the Far Away', *Opera Quarterly* 11, no. 3 (1995): 77–94.

Elwell-Sutton, L. P., "ARŪZ", *Encyclopaedia Iranica Online*, II/6–7, 670–9, http://www.iranicaonline.org/articles/aruz-the-metrical-system (accessed 11 April 2022).

Fabian, Johannes, *Time and the Other: How Anthropology Makes Its Object* (New York: Columbia UP, 1983).

Ferraris-Besso, Caroline, 'La Subversion par l'image: *La Perse, la Chaldée et la Susiane* de Jane Dieulafoy', *Women in French Studies* 7 (2018): 241–58.

Forsdick, Charles, 'Travelling Concepts: Postcolonial Approaches to Exoticism', *Paragraph* 24, no. 3 (2001): 12–29.

Forsdick, Charles, *Victor Segalen and the Aesthetics of Diversity: Journeys between Cultures* (Oxford: Oxford UP, 2000).

Forsdick, Charles, and Jennifer Yee, 'Towards a Postcolonial Nineteenth-Century', *French Studies* 72, no. 2 (2018): 167–75.

Foucault, Michel, 'De l'amitié comme mode de vie', in *Dits et écrits: 1954–1988*, 4 vols, edited by Daniel Defert and François Ewalt (Paris: Gallimard, 1994), vol. 4, 163–7.

Fulińska, Agnieszka, 'Alexander and Napoleon', *Brill's Companion to the Reception of Alexander the Great* (Leiden: Brill, 2018), 545–75.

Gachet, Jacqueline, *L'Opéra dans l'arène ou l'aventure de Fernand Castelbon mécène à Béziers* (Office Départemental d'action culturelle, 1989), 5–14.

Gates, Henry Louis Jr., 'Critical Response VII: Talkin "That Talk"', *Critical Inquiry* 13, no. 1 (1986): 203–10.

Gille, Vincent, 'L'air du temps. Sources et contexte des Orientales', in *Les Orientales. Maison de Victor Hugo. 26.03–04.07 2010* (Saint Ouen: Paris Musées Éditions, 2010), 43–59.

Gossman, Lionel, *Between History and Literature* (Cambridge, MA: Harvard UP, 1990).

Gramit, David, 'Orientalism and the Lied: Schubert's "Du liebst mich nicht"', *19th-Century Music* 27, no. 2 (2003): 97–115.

Hadidi, Javad, *Az Sa'di be Aragon: ta'sir-e adābi't-e fārsi dar adabiāt-e farānseh* (Tehran: Markāz-e Nashr-e Dāneshgāhi, 1994).

Hartley, Julia Caterina, 'Beyond Orientalism: When Desbordes-Valmore Carried Sa'di's Roses to France', *Iranian Studies* 52, nos. 5–6 (2019): 785–808.

Hartley, Julia Caterina, '"Les noms magiques": Names, Places, and Persian-ness in Noailles, Bibesco, and Proust', in *Labours of Attention: Essays for Edward J. Hughes*, edited by Adam Watt (Oxford: Legenda, 2022), 243–55.

Hayati Ashtiani, Karim, 'Les relations littéraires entre la France et la Perse de 1829 à 1897', doctoral thesis (Université Lumière Lyon II, 2004).

Hillmann, Michael C., *Unity in the Ghazals of Hāfez* (Minneapolis and Chicago: Bibliotheca Islamica, 1976).

Horta, Paulo Lemos, *Marvellous Thieves: Secret Authors of the Arabian Nights* (Cambridge, MA: Harvard UP, 2019).

Hulme, Peter, and Russell McDougall, 'Introduction: In the Margins of Anthropology', in *Writing, Travel, and Empire in the Margins of Anthropology*, edited by Peter Hulme and Russell McDougall (London: I.B. Tauris, 2007), 1–16.

Ingenito, Domenico, *Beholding Beauty: Sa'di of Shiraz and the Aesthetics of Desire in Medieval Persian Poetry* (Leiden: Brill, 2021).

Irvine, Margot, 'Imagining Women at War: Dieulafoy's 1913 Campaign', *Women in French Studies* 27 (2019): 119–30.

Irwin, Robert, 'An Enquiry into the Nature of a Certain Twentieth-Century Polemic', in *For Lust of Knowing: The Orientalists and Their Enemies* (London: Penguin, 2006), 277–309.
Kalin, Ibrahim (ed.), *The Oxford Encyclopedia of Philosophy, Science, and Technology in Islam* (Oxford: Oxford UP, 2014).
Koo, Halia, '(Wo)men Travellers: Physical and Narrative Boundaries', *Mosaic* 39, no. 2 (2006): 19–36.
Kosofsky Sedgwick, Eve, *Between Men: English Literature and Male Homosocial Desire* (New York: Columbia UP, 1985).
Larcher, Pierre, 'Autour des *Orientales*: Victor Hugo, Ernest Fouinet et la Poésie arabe archaïque', in *Orientalisme savant, Orientalisme littéraire: sept essais sur leur connexion* (Arles: Actes Sud, 2017), 51–89.
Laurent, Franck, 'Présentation', in Victor Hugo, *Les Orientales, Les Feuilles d'automne*, edited by Franck Laurent (Paris: Librairie Générale Française, 2000), 5–23.
Leaman, Oliver (ed.), *The Biographical Encyclopaedia of Islamic Philosophy* (London: Bloomsbury, 2015).
Lee, Amanda, 'Péris and Devadasis in Paris: Orientalist Ballet as Poetic Translation', *Nineteenth-Century Contexts* 41, no. 2 (2019): 117–40.
Lewis, Bernard, 'The Question of Orientalism', *New York Review of Books* (24 June 1982): 49–56.
Lewisohn, Leonard, 'The Mystical Milieu: Hāfiz's Erotic Spirituality', in *Hafiz and the Religion of Love in Classical Persian Poetry*, edited by Leonard Lewisohn (London: I.B. Tauris, 2010), 31–73.
Locke, Ralph, *Musical Exoticism: Images and Reflections* (Cambridge: Cambridge UP, 2009).
Lucey, Michael, *The Misfit of the Family* (Durham, NC: Duke UP, 2003).
MacKenzie, John M., *Orientalism: History, Theory and the Arts* (Manchester: Manchester UP, 1995).
Malek, Anwar Abdel, 'Orientalism in Crisis', *Diogenes* 44 (1964): 107–8.
Maugue, Annelise, *L'Identité masculine en crise au tournant du siècle 1871–1914* (Paris: Payot & Rivages, 2001 [1987]).
McGuinness, Patrick, *Poetry and Radical Politics in fin de siècle France: From Anarchism to Action française* (Oxford: Oxford UP, 2015).
Melman, Billie, *Women's Orients: English Women and the Middle East, 1718–1918: Sexuality, Religion, and Work* (London: Macmillan, 1992).
Mesch, Rachel, *Before Trans: Three Gender Stories from Nineteenth-Century France* (Stanford, CA: Stanford UP, 2020).
Mesch, Rachel, 'The Legs of the Orientalist: Jane Dieulafoy's Self-Portraits in Persia', *Yale French Studies* 139 (2021): 171–89.
Minors, Helen Julia, '*La Péri, poème dansé* (1911–12): A Problematic Creative-Collaborative Journey', *Dance Research* 27, no. 9 (2009): 227–52.
Mishra, Pankaj, *From the Ruins of Empire: The Revolt against the West and the Remaking of Asia* (London: Allen Lane, 2012).
Mokhberi, Susan, *The Persian Mirror: Reflections of the Safavid Empire in Early Modern France* (Oxford: Oxford UP, 2019).
Monicat, Bénédicte, *Itinéraires de l'écriture au féminin: voyageuses du 19ème siècle* (Amsterdam: Rodopi, 1996).
Moore, Christopher, 'Regionalist Frictions in the Bullring: Lyric Theater in Béziers at the Fin de Siècle', *19th-Century Music* 37, no. 3 (2014): 211–41.

Motadel, David, 'Iran and the Aryan Myth', in *Perceptions of Iran: History, Myths, and Nationalism from Medieval Persia to the Islamic Republic*, edited by Ali Ansari (London: I.B. Tauris, 2013).

Nasiri-Moghaddam, Nader, *L'archéologie française en Perse et les antiquités nationales (1884–1914)* (Paris: Connaissances et Savoirs, 2004).

Nochlin, Linda, *The Politics of Vision: Essays on Nineteenth-Century Art and Society* (New York: Harper & Row, 1989).

Olender, Maurice, *Les langues du paradis: aryens et sémites, in couple providentiel* (Paris: Seuil, 1989).

Pavel, Thomas, 'Literary Genres as Norms and Good Habits', *New Literary History* 34, no. 2 (2003): 201–10.

Peltre, Christine, 'Du *Bain turc* au *Gûlistan*: Anna de Noailles et le Voyage à Constantinople (1887)', in *Le voyage au féminin: perspectives historiques et littéraires, XVIIIe-XXe siècles*, edited by Nicolas Bourguignat (Amsterdam: Rodopi, 2008), 59–71.

Peltre, Christine, '…il dirait que c'est la mosquée', in *Les Orientales. Maison de Victor Hugo. 26.03–04.07 2010* (Saint Ouen: Paris Musées Éditions, 2010), 69–77.

Petitbon, René, *Les Sources orientales de Jean Lahor* (Paris: Nizet, 1962).

Pinto, Louis, *Les neveux de Zarathoustra* (Paris: Le Seuil, 1995).

Poliakov, Léon, *Le Mythe aryen: Essai sur les sources du racisme et des nationalismes* (Paris: Calmann-Lévy, 1971).

Porter, Edward, 'Decadence and the fin-de-siècle novel', in *The Cambridge Companion to the French Novel: From 1800 to the Present*, edited by Tim Unwin (Cambridge: Cambridge UP), 93–110.

Pratt, Mary-Louise, *Imperial Eyes: Travel Writing and Transculturation*, 2nd edn (London: Routledge, 2008).

Priest, Robert, 'Ernest Renan's Race Problem', *Historical Journal* 58, no. 1 (2015): 309–30.

Raffin, Sandrine, 'Les Orientales. La Réception critique en 1829', in *Victor Hugo 5. Autour des 'Orientales', La Revue des Lettres modernes*, edited by Claude Millet (Paris-Caen: Minard, 2002), 107–38.

Said, Edward, *Orientalism* (London: Penguin, 2003 [1978]).

Schwab, Raymond, *La Renaissance orientale* (Paris: Payot, 1950).

Schweitzer, Ivy, *Perfecting Friendship: Politics and Affiliation in Early American Literature* (Chapel Hill, NC: University of North Carolina Press, 2006).

Scott, Derek, 'Orientalism and Musical Style', *Musical Quarterly* 82, no. 2 (1998): 309–35.

Shams-Yadolahi, Zahra, *Le retentissement de la poésie de Hâfez en France: réception et traduction* (Uppsala: Uppsala Universitet, 2002).

Shayani, Sahba, 'The Representation of Women in Premodern Persian Epic Romance Poetry', doctoral thesis (UCLA, 2020).

Soleymani Majd, Nina, 'Lionnes et colombes: les personnages féminins dans le Cycle de Guillaume d'Orange, la Digénide, et le Châhnâmeh de Ferdowsi', doctoral thesis (Université Grenoble Alpes, 2019).

St Onge, Ruth Ellen, 'A banquet for Alphonse Lemerre, the poets' publisher', *Mémoires du livre/Studies in Book Culture* 3, no. 1 (2011), https://www.erudit.org/fr/revues/memoires/2011-v3-n1-memoires1830163/1007580ar/ (accessed 10 July 2019).

Starr, Juliana, 'Less Is Gore: Graphic Violence in the Fiction of Judith Gautier', *Women in French Studies* 21 (2013): 27–40.

Takeda, Junko Thérèse, *Iran and a French Empire of Trade, 1700–1808: The Other Persian Letters* (Liverpool: Liverpool UP, 2020).

Thiesen, Finn, *A Manual of Classical Persian Prosody* (Wiesbaden: Harrassowitz, 1982).
Todorov, Tzvetan, *Nous et les autres: La réflexion française sur la diversité humaine* (Paris: Seuil, 1989).
Todorov, Tzvetan, 'L'origine des genres', in *Les genres du discours* (Paris: Seuil, 1978), 44–60.
Todorov, Tzvetan, trans. Richard M. Berrong, 'The Origin of Genres', *New Literary History* 8, no. 1 (1976): 159–70.
Vaziri, Mostafa, *Iran as Imagined Nation: The Construction of a National Identity*, 2nd edn (Piscataway, NJ: Gorgias Press, 2013).
Venuti, Lawrence, *The Translator's Invisibility: A History of Translation*, 2nd edn (London: Routledge, 2008).
Verbaere, Laure, 'Les traductions françaises de Nietzsche – en Europe', *Études Germaniques* 251, no. 3 (2008): 601–21.
Vincent-Buffault, Anne, *L'exercice de l'amitié: pour une histoire des pratiques amicales aux XVIIIe et XIXe siècles* (Paris: Seuil, 1995).
Walker, Jennifer, *Sacred Music, Secular Spaces: Transforming Catholicism through the Music of Third-Republic Paris* (Oxford: Oxford UP, 2021).
Wenderoth, Valeria, 'The Making of Exoticism in French Operas of the 1890s', doctoral thesis (University of Hawaii, 2004).
White, Hayden, *Metahistory: The Historical Imagination in 19th-Century Europe (Fortieth-Anniversary Edition)* (Baltimore, MD: Johns Hopkins UP, 2014).
Yee, Jennifer, *The Colonial Comedy: Imperialism in the French Nineteenth-Century Novel* (Oxford: Oxford UP, 2016).
Young, Robert, *Colonial Desire: Hybridity in Theory, Culture, and Race* (London: Routledge, 1995).

Index

Achaemenid(s)
    as ancestors 1–3, 58–9, 61–4, 101–2, 146, 149, 169, 189, 225
    art and architecture 6, 60, 111, 142–9, 154–5, 168, 172, 175–6, 181, 196, 215–17, 223
    elegy to 145, 147–8
    Empire 1–3, 10, 13–14, 62–4, 69, 72, 76, 112, 143, 225, 230
    in fiction 10, 87–100
    on the stage 15, 214–23
    rulers 7, 79, 87–100, 144–7, 162, 169, 181, 196, 217
Alexander (of Macedon, the Great) 13, 27–8, 47, 54, 64, 78–9, 143, 148, 169, 177, 180, 188, 229
    as literary character see Eskandar
Al-Afghani, Jamal al-Din 60, 69–72, 101, 103
Al-e Ahmad, Jalal 149–55
Al-Ghazali 6–7, 45–49, 55, 69, 212
andaruni see under harem
Anet, Claude 2, 107, 109, 111, 142, 145, 149, 157, 159, 161
archaeology 109, 149, 154–5
Arab(s)
    conquest of Iran 3, 59, 68, 146
    versus Iranians 66–72, 77, 101–3, 111–14, 136, 205, 225
    world 2, 66, 78, 178
arabesque (musical term) 174, 182, 209, 219
Arabic (language and literature) 17–19, 46, 53, 66, 69, 71, 138, 157–9, 192
architecture *see under* Achaemenid *and* Safavid
arts and crafts 32, 150, 160–1, 208–9
Aryan race (myth of) 1–3, 10, 13, 48–9, 58–78, 101–3, 112, 146, 169, 190, 204–5, 225, 230

Assyrian(s) 63, 76, 111–12, 196, 225
'Attār 2, 21, 23, 27, 50, 227

Baku 200–4
ballet
    in opera 190, 193, 196–7, 214, 218–19
    Romantic 15, 174, 176–9
    Russian 15, 177, 183–9
Barbier de Meynard, Casimir 36, 50, 66, 225
Baudelaire, Charles 19, 37, 100, 177
Berlioz, Hector 171–2, 191
Bibesco, Marthe 2–3, 6–8, 14, 32, 107, 109–10, 116, 123–9, 132–4, 150, 160–8, 226–30
Bouchor, Maurice 15, 172, 176, 205–14
Bourgault-Ducoudray, Louis-Albert 15, 175, 204, 217
British Empire 3, 105–7, 149–52, 154–5
Buddhism 48, 193, 225

Cairo 137, 178–9
Carré, Michel *see Lalla-Roukh*
Carthage 20, 75
Castelbon des Beauxhostes, Fernand 15, 176, 214–15, 221
Cazalis, Henri 6–7, 13, 20, 35–6, 45–50, 53–5, 69, 211–12, 225
Chételat, Emmanuel J. 20–3, 35, 56
Christianity 23, 37, 57, 70–6, 78, 102, 120, 129–36, 194–7, 204–5, 212, 226
    see also *under* cultural comparison
civilization(s)
    decline and fall of 10, 62, 92, 103, 134, 141–2, 146, 169
    European 6, 57–8, 61–2, 75, 79, 85, 101–2, 148, 150–1, 227
    Greek versus Persian 3, 13, 57, 62–3, 69, 72, 79, 144
    progress of 62–3, 67, 70, 78, 102

see also mission civilisatrice *and* Orientalist stereotypes: barbarity *and* Westernization
coevalness 62–3, 72, 102, 169
Collège de France 50, 65–6, 70, 72, 76, 78, 230
Constantinople *see* Istanbul
conversion 23, 39, 47–8, 211–13
cultural comparison 6, 14, 58, 107, 113, 227
   Christianity and Islam 61, 65–8, 129, 133–6
   European and Iranian architecture 137–8, 140–1, 144, 146
   European and Persian literature 157, 165–7
cultural identity
   fluidity of 29–30, 71, 83–8, 89, 103
   Iranian 3, 59, 68–71, 76–8, 112, 110–14, 153, 175–7, 180
cultural hybridity 29–30, 39–45, 78–88, 182
cultural relativism 8, 50, 58, 67, 120–6, 153, 165–9, 227

David, Félicien *see* Lalla-Roukh
defamiliarization 29, 128, 182
Desbordes-Valmore, Marceline 8, 11, 13, 18, 20–1, 50–6, 172–3, 192, 228–9
Diaghilev *see* ballet: Ballets Russes
Dieulafoy, Jane 4, 6–8, 13–15, 60, 64, 102–10, 169, 225, 227–30
   La Perse, la Chaldée et la Susiane 108, 110–23, 125–36, 138, 140–1, 148–57, 165–8, 197–9
   À Suse. Journal de fouilles 108–9, 143–7
   L'Oracle 93–8, 100
   Parysatis (novel) 10–11, 88–93, 98–101
   Parysatis (stage version) 172, 175–6, 214–23
   Rose d'Hatra 93, 99
diplomacy 1–3, 60, 81–2, 84–6, 91, 106–8, 150
disappointment, disillusionment 28–31, 36, 41, 48, 54, 78, 130, 156, 161, 168, 179, 223

Egypt, Egyptian 24, 32, 59, 75–6, 111, 144, 218, 225
eroticism 5, 20, 30, 44, 55, 82–8, 116–20, 129, 228–9

see also harem *and* Orientalist stereotypes: sexualization *and* sexuality
Esfahan 6, 14, 32, 107, 109, 123, 127, 129, 136–42, 144, 152, 158–61, 163, 168–9, 225, 227
Eskandar
   in Dukas's *La Péri* 177, 179–89, 222
   in Ferdowsi's *Shāhnāmeh* 79–80, 224, 229
   in Gautier's *Iskender* 78–88, 102, 229
   in Nezāmi's *Eskandar Nāmeh* 27–8, 55
exceptionalism of Iran 4, 64, 68, 111–12, 197, 225
exoticism, exoticization 2, 7–8, 15, 21–4, 29–30, 34, 45–9, 54–6, 116–9, 122, 140, 150, 158–61, 172–9, 182–4, 193, 205, 218–19, 225, 229–30
   self-exoticization 21, 30, 49, 229–30

familiarization 7, 39, 49, 113, 125, 127, 138, 226
féerie 116, 158–60
femininity 7, 85, 96–8, 117–19, 229–30
   see also gender
feminism 88–101, 103, 119–20, 176, 221–2
Ferdowsi 2–3, 13, 21, 54, 59–60, 62, 77–81, 86, 88, 93, 102–3, 162–5, 167, 180–1, 224, 227, 229–31
Fitzgerald, Edward 30, 211, 228
Flandin, Eugène 1, 4, 14, 107–16, 120, 129–52, 158–61, 164–9, 225
Flaubert, Gustave 41, 81, 105
Fouinet, Ernest 18–19, 21, 23
French Empire 2, 78, 80, 88, 152–3, 179

Gallet, Louis 15, 175, 200–5, 214
Gautier, Judith 2, 11, 13, 60, 78–88, 101–3, 172, 180–1, 222, 229–30
Gautier, Théophile 5, 105
   Émaux et camées 13, 18, 20–1, 25–8, 30, 34–5, 41, 54, 164, 179, 192, 228
   La Péri 15, 87, 174–80, 187, 189, 201, 222
gender
   in ancient Iran 76–8, 88–101
   authority 11–12, 60–1, 89, 98–101, 103, 229–30
   in Qajar Iran 114–29

challenging gender roles 42–5, 76, 85–6, 88–101, 116–17, 229–30
reinforcing gender roles 97–9, 118–20, 220–1
genre 9–15, 55–6, 60–1, 106–9, 124, 168–9, 171–6, 177–8, 206–8, 214–15, 223–4, 230–1
ghazal 1–2, 23, 36–7, 39–45, 55–6, 165, 167, 192, 212, 227–9
Gobineau, Arthur de 5, 13, 60, 103, 110, 142, 225, 230
  Essai sur l'inégalité des races humaines 10–11, 61–5, 69–70, 72, 75–8, 88, 101–2
  Histoire des Perses 69, 72
  Trois ans en Asie 106–8, 134–6, 138–42, 157, 162, 168–9
Goethe 12, 25–8, 41, 54, 179, 192
gol o bolbol 41, 171–2, 191
good versus evil 73–6, 194–7
Greece, Greek
  ancient 3, 10, 13, 57–8, 61–3, 66–7, 69–72, 75–6, 96, 100–2, 218–19, 144, 146, 165, 182, 197, 214, 217, 219–21, 223
  modern 21–3, 29
  modes 204, 217–18
Greco-Persian Wars 76, 79, 87–8, 91, 94

Hāfez 2, 17–19, 21, 23, 25–8, 30–2, 35, 39–45, 54, 56, 160, 162–3, 165–8, 192, 227
harem
  ancient 85, 88–93, 98
  andaruni 14, 107, 110, 114–29, 131, 169, 229
  Western fantasies of 114, 119, 178, 184, 189, 201, 204, 222, 229
Hinduism 48, 73, 75–6, 193–4, 225
historical fiction 9, 11, 13–14, 60, 78–102, 214–15, 230
historiography 10–11, 13, 58–80, 102–3, 205
Hugo, Victor 1, 3–6, 13, 18–29, 32, 34–6, 39, 45, 48–9, 51, 53–4, 56, 105, 178, 228, 231
humour 50, 95–6, 106, 110, 120–3, 174, 190–3, 205–14

identification
  with characters on stage 173–6, 189, 204–5, 223

with Iranian women 6–7, 99, 108, 116, 119–23
with Iranian historical figures 6–7, 45–6, 49, 73, 100–2, 147, 223, 226
with Persian poets 31–4, 56, 162–5, 173
imitation
  in literature 1–3, 10–11, 17, 21, 23, 35–50, 54–6, 228–9
  in visual arts 172, 179, 184, 187–8, 197–9, 215–17
imperialism 5, 7, 69, 78–88, 114, 128, 149–55, 168, 229
  see also archaeology
  see also British Empire, French Empire *and* Ottoman Empire *and* Empire *under* Achaemenid *and* Russia
India, Indian 4, 24, 32, 48–9, 61–3, 72–5, 78, 85–6, 109, 111, 144, 150, 172, 179, 189–93, 205
Indo-European languages 58–9, 65–7, 102
  see also Aryan
intertextuality 10, 13–14, 21, 41, 50–6, 156–68, 227–8, 230
Islam 7, 37–9, 47–50, 59–72, 77–8, 103, 125–36, 141, 161–2, 192–3, 208, 210–13, 225–6
  eroticization of 196–7, 204 (*see also* harem, Western fantasies of)
  exoticism of 15, 19, 23, 49, 114, 173–5
  Iran's lack of faith in 3, 68, 72, 101–2, 225
  Shi'i versus Sunni 14, 68–9, 112, 130, 132, 225
  Sufi 23, 36, 41, 48, 211–13, 225
  suspicion towards 5, 65–9, 72, 101, 120, 131–2, 196–7, 204–5, 226
  see also under cultural comparison: Christianity and Islam *and* Orientalist stereotypes: fanaticism
Islamic veil 114–20, 122, 125–8, 169
Istanbul 28–9, 137

Jāmi 162, 192, 227
Jones, William xiii, 17–20, 23, 50, 54, 57–8, 62

Khayyām 2, 15, 30–2, 45–8, 56, 162, 165, 167, 172, 176, 205–14, 220, 224, 227–8
Kosofsky Sedgwick, Eve 82, 85, 220

Lahor, Jean *see* Cazalis, Henri
Lallah-Roukh (opera) 15, 171–2, 175, 189–94, 200, 203, 205, 218, 222
Leconte de Lisle 21, 101
Locke, Ralph 175, 189, 193, 203–5
Loti, Pierre 12, 14, 109, 130–4, 136, 138–42, 144–51, 158–61, 163–9, 226, 228
Louis XIV 19, 140
Louvre 2, 99, 108, 143, 149, 154–5, 175, 215
Lucas, Hippolyte *see* Lalla-Roukh
Le Mage (opera) 15, 189–97, 202–5, 212, 217–19, 221–3, 226

marionette theatre 2, 15, 176, 205–14, 230–1
masculinity 82, 84–5, 90–2, 94–7, 108, 118–9, 182–3, 229–30
  see also gender
Massenet, Jules *see Le Mage*
Michelet, Jules 3, 11, 13, 57–63, 72–8, 101, 103, 146, 225–6, 229–30
Mille et Une Nuits 4, 15, 51, 138–40, 142, 157–61, 164, 168, 182–4, 191
Mirkhond 93, 102, 230
mission civilisatrice 6, 8, 61, 80, 85, 102–3, 151–3, 194
Mohl, Jules 1, 19, 48, 80, 228, 230
Montesquieu 1, 9
Moore, Thomas 190, 192–3
Muharram 14, 129–34, 169, 226
music 27, 41, 115, 141, 171–96, 204, 206, 214–24

Napoleon (Bonaparte) 54, 79, 107, 150, 200
Napoleon III 25–7
Nerval, Gérard de 105, 179
Nezāmi 2, 26–8, 35, 55
Nicolas, Jean-Baptiste 46, 208, 211–13, 228
Nijinsky 177, 183–4, 186
Noailles, Anna de 11, 13, 18, 20–1, 25, 28–35, 47, 51, 54–6, 128, 161, 164, 228
noble savage (myth of) 74–6, 78
nostalgia 24, 134, 142, 145–6

open-air theatre 214–22
opera 2–4, 15, 171–7, 189–206, 208, 214, 218–19, 223–4, 226, 230
Orient as Western fantasy
  in ballet 174–5, 177–9, 184–7
  in music 171, 174, 217–19
  in opera 171–6
  in painting 114, 118
  in poetry 21–5, 29–30, 48, 54
  in travel-writing 157, 159–61
  see also harem, *Mille et Une Nuits* and Orientalist stereotypes
Oriental Studies (academic discipline) 5, 17–9, 36, 48–51, 57–8, 66, 81, 103, 157, 181, 226
Orientalist stereotypes
  barbarity 12, 20–1, 56–9, 72, 113, 130–1, 144, 148, 151, 183, 194, 196–7, 217, 223
  decadence 3, 59, 68, 102, 141, 221
  despotism 102, 201, 204–5, 221–3
  fanaticism 112, 129–36, 141, 153, 189, 196, 210
  questioning stereotypes 35–6, 122, 144–6, 148, 203–5, 210, 214
  sexualization 4, 21, 114, 118–9, 175–6, 182–3, 193, 196–7, 203–4, 223, 229–30
  see also harem, Western fantasies of *and* Islam, fear of
Ottoman Empire 23, 32, 54
  see also Turkey

pari 4, 15, 158–60, 177, 181–9
Parnasse, Parnassian (literary movement) 1, 18, 35, 45–9
Persepolis 3, 14, 109, 142–9, 157, 169, 196, 217, 225
Persian
  character 110–14, 132, 134–6
  gardens 30–2, 124, 128, 134, 140, 159, 161–3
  Gulf 105, 108
  language 17–19, 35, 58–9, 66, 81, 100, 122–3, 166, 228–9
  literature *see* 'Attār, Ferdowsi, Hāfez, Khayyām, Nezāmi, Rumi, Sa'di
  miniature art 30, 32, 34, 160, 163, 172, 175, 182, 187–8, 223, 229
Persia as poetic ideal 3, 14, 21, 24–35, 41, 162–5, 179, 189, 192–3, 222–3, 226
Petit-Théâtre de la Galerie Vivienne 15, 205–14
philology 13, 17, 60, 65–7, 73, 190, 226, 228

photography 32, 98–9, 108, 117–18, 120–3, 126, 168, 207, 216–17
Plutarch 14, 79, 90, 93, 100, 148, 157, 180–1
poetry 1–3, 6, 10, 12–13, 15, 17–56, 66–7, 73, 80, 109–10, 114, 132, 134, 157, 162–9, 172, 174, 176, 178–9, 189–93, 205–214, 223–6, 228–31
progress *see under* civilization
Proust, Marcel 28, 109, 158, 161
puppetry *see* marionette theatre

Qom 32, 109, 159–60
quatrain
    French 30–4, 36, 39, 45–9, 55
    Persian 1, 2, 15, 30, 32, 36, 45–6, 176, 205–214, 224

race *see* Aryan
racism *see* Aryan
reading 14, 20, 25, 27–31, 107, 110, 148, 156–8
religion(s) *see* Buddhism, Christianity, Islam, Zoroastrianism
    history of 48, 57–61, 65–78
Renan, Ernest 4, 6, 48–9, 60–2, 64–78, 101, 103, 110, 155, 161, 204, 210–11, 225, 230
Renaud, Armand 8, 13, 18, 20–1, 35–46, 49–50, 54–6, 191, 211, 229
Richepin, Jean *see Le Mage*
Rimsky-Korsakov, Nikolai 181, 183
robā'ē see quatrain
Romanticism 1, 3, 6, 18, 27–8, 35, 58, 105, 176–9, 183, 230–1
ruins 142–9, 157, 168, 197
Rumi 21, 28, 50, 162, 227
Russia, Russian 3, 121, 149, 181–3, 187
    Empire 105, 200
    see also under ballet

Sa'di 39, 227–8
    in Anna de Noailles 28–33, 56
    in Armand Renaud 39
    Jane Dieulafoy 165
    in Marceline Desbordes-Valmore 50–6, 192, 228–9
    in Marthe Bibesco 162–3
    in Pierre Loti 165

    in Théophile Gautier 27
    in Victor Hugo 18–25, 35, 54
Safavid(s) 68, 112, 152, 200, 225
    art and architecture 6, 134–42, 187–8
    rulers: Nader Shah 200, Shah Abbas 140, Shah Hossein 134
Said, Edward 1, 4–9, 12–4, 20, 25, 29–30, 34, 49, 54, 56, 59, 106–7, 123, 135, 156–7, 165, 172, 174, 227
    see also Orientalist stereotypes
Saint-Saëns, Camille 15, 176, 214–22
Sainte-Beuve, Charles Augustin de 54
Samarkand 172, 190–2
Sassanian(s) 64, 69, 72, 93–4, 183, 225
Schwab, Raymond 1, 57–8, 101
Semite *see under* Aryan
sexuality
    female 42–5, 191, 126, 191
    male heterosexual 44, 95–6, 211–12, 221
    male homosexual 165
    queer 82–8, 103, 114–19
Shāhnāmeh see Ferdowsi
Shakespeare 26–7, 54, 206–7
Shiraz 23, 31–2, 41, 43, 45, 160, 162, 165–6, 168, 192
similarity
    assimilation 46–9, 194–5, 212
    between the ancient Greeks and Persians 62–3, 102
    between France and Iran 110, 113–14, 129, 160–1
    between Persian literature and European literature 41–5, 62, 102
    as defined by Bhatti and Kimmich 6–7, 21, 45, 49–50, 55, 58, 75, 134, 167, 227
    in Gautier's *Iskender* 83–5
    see also Achaemenid(s), as ancestors
Sufism *see under* Islam
Susa 3, 14–15, 88–90, 99–102, 109, 142–7, 149, 153–5, 155, 214–22, 225

ta'zieh 129–31, 157, 168
Tehran 1, 105, 107–9, 122, 141
Thamara (opera) 4, 15, 175, 189–90, 194–205, 217, 222–3
Thousand and One Nights, see *Mille et Une Nuits*

Timurid 190-3
Todorov, Tzvetan
  on cultural difference 7-8, 18, 49-50, 57-8, 67, 120, 227
  on genre 9-12
translation 1, 5, 13, 17-21, 23-5, 27, 36-7, 39, 45-6, 50-1, 54-7, 59, 80, 93, 102, 157, 161, 208, 210-13, 225-8
travel 1-3, 6, 8-9, 11-2, 14, 62, 76, 100, 105-69, 172, 179, 190-2, 197
  imaginary versus physical 15, 28-34, 156-69
travel-writing 12-5, 25, 89, 96, 99-100, 105-69, 172, 174, 197, 204-5, 226, 228-31
Trouhanova, Natalya 177, 185, 187
Turkey, Turks 2, 4, 23-4, 94, 112, 114, 136, 153, 205

see also Istanbul *and* Ottoman Empire
Turkish language 17-18, 109

universalism 6-10, 13, 17-18, 21, 25, 50-5, 58, 65, 67, 70-1, 75, 113, 120-3, 127, 133-4, 153, 167, 173, 227

versification 20, 23, 36, 45-6, 55

Westernization 102, 149, 152-3, 168, 179, 195, 205
White, Hayden 59-60, 73-4

Zoroaster (as character) 173-4, 190, 194-7, 203, 205, 212, 225
Zoroastrianism 3, 57, 59, 68, 74-7, 100, 102-3, 141, 145-6, 180-1, 193-4, 197, 202, 204, 212-3, 225-6, 231

www.ingramcontent.com/pod-product-compliance
Lightning Source LLC
Chambersburg PA
CBHW071807300426
44116CB00009B/1231